# Social Justice and Advocacy in Counseling

*Social Justice and Advocacy in Counseling* provides a thorough and up to date grounding in social justice and advocacy for counseling students and faculty.

Chapters address issues of discrimination and oppression and their effect on individuals and cultural groups through a variety of activities and handouts related to each of the eight CACREP core standards. The book's final section focuses on activities and handouts related to counseling specialties, including school, career, and addictions counseling.

This book will help counselor educators increase student awareness, knowledge, and skills. For students, the practical activities bring the concept of social justice alive in important ways and will continue to be a handy reference as they develop their careers and promote access and equity.

**Mark Pope, EdD**, is Thomas Jefferson Professor and Curators' Distinguished Professor Emeritus at the University of Missouri—St. Louis. He is past President of the American Counseling Association and author of ten other books on improving teaching.

**Mariaimeé Gonzalez, PhD, LPC**, is a faculty member in the Clinical Mental Health Counseling Program and coordinator of the multicultural concentration at Antioch University Seattle. She is also on the board of the Washington Counseling Association.

**Erika R. N. Cameron, PhD, NCC**, is an associate professor and chair of the Department of Counseling and Marital and Family Therapy at the University of San Diego. She is a certified school counselor in California, Hawaii, and Missouri. She is past President of the Western Association of Counselor Education and Supervision.

**Joseph S. Pangelinan, PhD, LPC**, is an assistant professor of medicine and director of cultural awareness and diversity in the Department of Medicine at Washington University School of Medicine in St. Louis.

# Social Justice and Advocacy in Counseling

## Experiential Activities for Teaching

Edited by Mark Pope, EdD,
Mariaimeé Gonzalez, PhD,
Erika R. N. Cameron, PhD, and
Joseph S. Pangelinan, PhD

Routledge
Taylor & Francis Group

NEW YORK AND LONDON

First published 2020
by Routledge
52 Vanderbilt Avenue, New York, NY 10017

and by Routledge
2 Park Square, Milton Park, Abingdon, Oxon, OX14 4RN

*Routledge is an imprint of the Taylor & Francis Group, an informa business*

*Library of Congress Cataloging-in-Publication Data*
A catalog record for this title has been requested

ISBN: 978-1-138-28529-3 (hbk)
ISBN: 978-1-138-28530-9 (pbk)
ISBN: 978-1-315-18068-7 (ebk)

Typeset in Stone Serif
by Apex CoVantage, LLC

Visit the eResources page: www.routledge.com/9781138285293

# Contents

# Foreword

In 2001, when I was president of the American Counseling Association (ACA), I asked the founders of the Counselors for Social Justice (an ACA division) to develop a set of advocacy competencies that could be used by practitioners to make a difference in their worlds. Mary Arnold, Reese House, Judy Lewis, and Rebecca Toporek answered that call and developed a three dimensional model that is still actively used. These ACA Advocacy Competencies can be found on the ACA website, counseling.org, under "Knowledge Center." They provide a road map for intervention at the client/student, school/community, and societal arenas. The development and publication of these competencies were followed by a special issue of the *Journal of Counseling & Development* and a book, *ACA Advocacy Competencies: A Social Justice Framework for Counselors.*

The 2018 Board of Directors of the Counselors for Social Justice has officially endorsed *Social Justice and Advocacy in Counseling: Experiential Activities for Teaching.* This most recent addition to the social justice and advocacy in counseling literature takes us further on this important journey and provides simple and practical activities for infusing social justice principles into the coursework that all counseling students must complete. Some of the 80 activities that especially intrigued me include: Observing Our Community: Examining the Social and Cultural Constructs That Impact Power and Privilege; How We Got Here: Empathy in the Land of Immigrants; Songs Make Me Want to Fight or Just Do Something; Universal Language, Different Responses: Using Music to Teach Multiculturalism. Don't they make you want to keep on reading?

Having difficult conversations about race and other cultural issues has been a challenge for many, even those who are truly committed and want to make a difference in the lives of their students, their clients, and their students' students and clients. This book provides timely resources to meet that challenge. And each of these activities makes it fun. I see this book as an essential component for every counselor educator. Pope, Gonzalez, Cameron, and Pangelinan have done the profession an important service.

Jane Goodman, PhD*
Professor Emerita of Counseling
Oakland University
Rochester, Michigan

---

\* Dr. Jane Goodman is a former president of the American Counseling Association, Counselors for Social Justice, National Career Development Association, and American Counseling Association Foundation.

---

# About the Editors

**Mark Pope,** EdD, NCC, MCC, MAC, ACS, is Thomas Jefferson Professor and Curators' Distinguished Professor in the Counseling Programs at the University of Missouri—St. Louis. He served as chair of the Department of Counseling and Family Therapy there for a decade. He has been teaching and infusing social justice and advocacy counseling into his classes for over 30 years. He is the author/editor of ten books, 30+ book chapters, 40+ journal articles, and 100+ professional presentations at the international, national, and state levels. He has a passion for developing resources that enable counselor educators to teach interesting and effective classes in such areas as career counseling, multicultural counseling, multi-ethnic/multi-racial counseling, spirituality in counseling, and social justice/advocacy counseling. Dr. Pope is former president of the American Counseling Association, National Career Development Association, Association for LGBT Issues in Counseling, and Society for the Psychology of Sexual Orientation and Gender Diversity (APA Division 44) as well as editor of *The Career Development Quarterly*, the preeminent professional journal for career counseling and career development.

**Mariaimeé Gonzalez,** PhD, LPC, is a core faculty member of the Clinical Mental Health Counseling program at Antioch University Seattle. She currently teaches in the masters and the Counselor Education and Supervision PhD programs. She serves as the Coordinator of the Multicultural Concentration that is designed to provide advanced knowledge and skills related to the multicultural and social justice competencies applied in clinical and community settings. She has been an advocate for legislation and social policy for underserved communities and has instilled a social justice and advocacy framework in her teaching, research, clinical supervision, and clinical practice. Dr. Gonzalez is a former board member of the Puerto Rican Society in St. Louis, Missouri, and the American Counseling Association Human Rights Committee. Dr. Gonzalez has taught globally and promotes the importance of understanding mental health and human rights concerns as a member of the global community. She has been active in presenting on social justice issues at a variety of national and international conferences and engaging in ongoing community service. She is currently the secretary for the American Counseling Association of Washington.

**Erika R. N. Cameron,** PhD, is an associate professor and chair of the Department of Counseling and Marital and Family Therapy at the University of San Diego. She has worked as a school counselor and career counselor in a variety of diverse settings including primary, middle, and secondary schools, universities, residential facilities, and community agencies in Hawaii, Missouri, and California. Dr. Cameron has taught graduate counseling courses and presented programs at the local, regional, national, and international levels on social justice and advocacy counseling. She currently serves on the School of Leadership and Education Sciences' Multicultural and Social Justice Committee (MSJC) at the University of San Diego. The MSJC provides professional development activities for educators focused on multiculturalism, diversity, and social justice. Dr. Cameron has been teaching and counseling for social justice and advocacy for many years.

**Joseph S. Pangelinan,** PhD, LPC, is an assistant professor of medicine and director of Cultural Awareness and Diversity at Washington University in St. Louis. He has taught multicultural counseling, crisis counseling, group counseling, career counseling, and both practicum and field experience courses for many years at universities in the St. Louis metropolitan region. He served as a counselor and in various leadership roles at Logos School, an alternative school for emotionally disturbed adolescents, in St. Louis. Dr. Pangelinan is also co-editor with Dr. Mark Pope and Dr. Angela Coker of the book *Experiential Activities for Teaching Multicultural Competence in Counseling* (published by the American Counseling Association) and coauthor of a chapter titled "Using the ACA Advocacy Competencies in Career Counseling" in the book *ACA Advocacy Competencies: A Social Justice Framework for Counselors* (published by the American Counseling Association). He is from Micronesia.

# About the Contributors

**Roberto L. Abreu,** MS, EdS, NCC, is a doctoral candidate in Counseling Psychology at the University of Kentucky. Roberto received a bachelor's degree in Science Education and a master's degree in Clinical Mental Health Counseling from Florida International University (FIU). Roberto's research interests focus on LGBTQ and people of color. Roberto has over seven years of teaching experience. Some of the courses taught by Roberto include Cultural Competence in Health Care and Human Development and Learning.

**Dr. Hector Y. Adames** is an associate professor in the Counseling Psychology Department at The Chicago School of Professional Psychology. He is the editor of *Latina/o Psychology Today (LPT)* and the coauthor of a textbook titled *Cultural Foundations and Interventions in Latino/a Mental Health: History, Theory, and Within Group Differences* by Routledge. He has earned a number of awards including the 2014 Distinguished Professional Early Career Award from NLPA.

**Sinem Akay-Sullivan,** PhD, LPC, RPT, Certified Trauma-Focused Cognitive Behavioral Therapist, received her master's degree in Counseling and PhD in Counselor Education at the University of North Texas. She teaches graduate-level counseling courses in the Sam Houston State University Department of Counseling as an adjunct professor. She also has a private practice in Woodlands, Texas, working with children and teenagers who struggle with a wide range of emotional and behavioral issues.

**Brendon Alaniz** is working toward his Bachelor's degree at Maryville University. He plans to pursue a graduate degree. He has been an active member of the Relationships and Brain Sciences Research Laboratory since 2016.

**Dr. Kristine M. Augustyniak** is a professor of Counseling at Niagara University. Her research publications include evidence-based approaches in assessment and intervention planning for youth suffering from mental health concerns, trauma, and bullying. Her scholarship examines applied approaches to school-based violence and bullying prevention. She is involved in a number of advocacy efforts to foster community mental health services.

**Dani Baker,** MA, LMFT, ATR-BC, is teaching faculty within The School of Applied Psychology, Counseling, and Family Therapy at Antioch University Seattle. She is currently a second-year doctoral student in Counselor Education and Supervision PhD program, where she is studying relational shame, vulnerability, and resiliency in the context of social justice and advocacy. She has over 15 years of experience facilitating groups with children, teens, adults, and families. As a board-certified art therapist, she recognizes the value and power of using creative, non-verbal approaches in her work as a group facilitator, clinician, and teacher.

**Courtney Ballard** is currently studying Clinical Mental Health Counseling in the Counseling & Human Development Department at South Dakota State University. She has particular interest in researching children's response to grief and loss and in researching issues related to human sexuality. She also pursues topics relevant to social justice in order to promote best practices while working with underserved populations.

**Dannette Gomez Beane** is a fourth year PhD student in Counselor Education at Virginia Tech, where she also serves as the director for the Office of Recruitment and Diversity Initiatives in the Graduate School. She is currently co-teaching a course in Counseling Diverse Populations and conducts research about counselor engagement with social justice movements. Dannette holds a master's degree in Counseling from Virginia Tech and a bachelor's degree in Multicultural Communications from Hollins University.

**Jennifer E. Beebe** is an assistant professor at Niagara University. She has worked in multiple settings such as schools, agencies, and a college counseling center. Her line of research has been focused on bullying and counselor training and supervision. Jennifer has partnered with local schools to increase education and intervention efforts to reduce bullying among students. She has presented at national, regional, and state conferences on bullying, vicarious trauma, and supervision and training.

**Jenny Benson** graduated from Lock Haven University's Clinical Mental Health Counseling program in May 2015. She was hired as an outpatient therapist shortly after graduating and now is working toward attaining her supervised hours to be a Licensed Professional Counselor in Pennsylvania. Her interests are in creative counseling and working with diverse clients.

**Jennifer L. Murdock Bishop,** PhD, LPC, is associate professor of Counselor Education at University of Northern Colorado. Her research foci are community engaged scholarship, counselor identity, career transitions in college, and online and experiential learning. She is the career services faculty in residence, University 101 Faculty Evaluation Committee chair, and an NCC, Master Career Counselor, Master Career Development Professional, LPC (CO), and Special Services Provider-School Counselor (CO).

**Courtney R. Boddie,** PhD, LPC, NCC, is the director of Counseling Services, Southern Illinois University—Edwardsville. His scholarship explores minoritized college populations with a focus on African American men and students with disabilities. Courtney has an extensive background in post-secondary disability, including work as an executive function coach, learning specialist, and instructor in a program for college learners with neurodevelopmental disabilities.

**Jayna Bonfini** has significant research, teaching, and clinical experience with adolescents and adults struggling with various mental health issues, trauma histories, and substance abuse problems. She counsels adolescents, adults, and their families in private practice, consults and counsels for a local high school, and teaches counseling and psychology as a part-time faculty member at Robert Morris University.

**Monica Boyd-Layne,** LCPC, is a PhD candidate in Counseling Education and Supervision. Current research includes exploration of the phenomenon of belonging with African American female graduate students. During her current tenure as assistant clinical director she supervisors counselors to work with persons living with mental health, trauma, and substance use issues. Further research will consider the complexity of racial identity to broaden the usefulness of the Discrimination Model.

**Kesha Burch,** LCPC, is the founder of Burch Counseling & Consulting, a private practice and mental health consulting business in Chicago, Illinois. Kesha is a doctoral candidate in Counselor Education & Supervision at the Chicago School of Professional Psychology. She is a 2014 State of Illinois DFI Fellowship recipient and a 2015 Bouchet Graduate Honor Society inductee. Her clinical work, research, and teaching interests are concerned with the intersection of mental health and culture.

**Rebecca Byler** is a master's candidate at the University of San Diego in the Clinical Mental Health Counseling specialization. She serves as a parent support coach and group facilitator for parents facing homelessness in San Diego.

**Wendell J. Callahan** has extensive experience as a school psychologist, researcher, and program director. Since retiring from the San Diego County Juvenile Court and Community Schools, Dr. Callahan became a professor of practice at the University of San Diego. Dr. Callahan holds a PhD in Clinical Psychology from the University of California, San Diego and a master's degree in Counseling from San Diego State University. Dr. Callahan also holds California credentials in educational administration, school psychology, school counseling, and school social work.

**Sarah Campbell,** PhD, LAC, NCC, was a 2016 NARACES Emerging Leader recipient, and is a senior lecturer at Messiah College. Her relevant experience includes conducting research that looked at how counselors-in-training described their process of becoming a social justice advocate (SJA). She regularly presents on the topic of SJA and infuses SJA in her graduate courses. Sarah serves as an advocate in her role as a counselor and counselor educator and supervisor.

**Dasha Carver,** BA, is a first year master's student in Marriage and Family Therapy at St. Louis University, where she is also pursuing the programs concentration in Medical Family Therapy. Her current research interests include sexual minority advocacy and mental health outcomes, bi- and multiracial stereotypes, racial identity and mental health, competency in therapy when working with sexual minorities, and assessment of risk and resiliency in romantic relationships.

**James H. Castillo,** PhD, NCC, ACS is an Assistant Professor of Counseling at Alfred University. He has professional school and mental health experience and has a passion for engaging with and advocating for traditionally underserved and at-risk populations (i.e. individuals with disabilities, youth and families who have experienced trauma).

**Thomas A. Chavez** is an assistant professor in Counselor Education at the University of New Mexico. He currently teaches multiculturalism, child/adolescent counseling, and school counseling. Some of his interests include effective adolescent interventions, culturally responsive interventions, and integration of traditional healing in contemporary counseling. His social justice/advocacy work includes collaboration and education on traditional methods of health and well-being with local communities.

**Dr. Nayeli Y. Chavez-Dueñas** is an associate professor at The Chicago School of Professional Psychology, where she serves as the faculty coordinator for the concentration in Latina/o Mental Health in the Counseling Psychology Department. She is the associate editor of *Latina/o Psychology Today (LPT)* and the coauthor of a textbook titled *Cultural Foundations and Interventions in Latino/a Mental Health: History, Theory, and within Group Differences* by Routledge.

**Madeline Clark,** PhD, LPC, NCC, ACS, is an assistant professor of Counselor Education at the University of Toledo. Her research interests include multiculturalism and diversity, women's issues in counseling, intersectionality, and how poverty and social class impact client outcomes and the counseling process.

**Karlie Collins** is a Clinical Mental Health Counseling graduate student at Northeastern State University. She has had experience volunteering in multicultural settings and is interested in pursuing more diverse service opportunities. After receiving her degree, she will pursue her LPC in Oklahoma.

**Jennifer M. Cook** is a multiculturally focused counselor educator committed to advocacy and social justice. She identifies strongly with strength-based methods and culturally relevant practices, and she utilizes experiential teaching methods to instill these perspectives in her students. Her research interests focus on counselor preparation and counselor multicultural development, with emphasis on social class and socioeconomic status.

**Dr. Katrina Cook** is an associate professor at Texas A&M University—San Antonio and has done extensive writing in multicultural activities. As a counselor educator Dr. Cook has taught multicultural counseling/social justice and has presented at state, national, and international conferences in the topic of multicultural diversity, which has included experiential activities to develop awareness among counselor professionals and counselors-in-training.

**Deanna N. Cor,** PhD, LPC, NCC, is an assistant professor in the Counselor Education department at Portland State University. Dr. Cor's research focuses on developing and enhancing multicultural counseling competencies in counseling students and current practitioners, specifically for working with clients identifying as trans and gender nonconforming. Her clinical specialty areas include working with LGBTQ individuals, exploring life transitions, and relational concerns.

**Jenny L. Cureton,** PhD, is assistant professor of Counselor Education and Supervision at Kent State University. Her experience includes counseling people of color, LGBTQQIA people, people with disabilities, and international students and teaching master's counseling courses in career, multicultural, and trauma among other topics and undergraduate classes on career development and leadership. Her research focuses on crisis/trauma and related education and career resiliency among marginalized populations.

**Eric Dafoe,** Ph.D., Licensed School Counselor, NCC. His publications, presentations, and research agenda focuses on expressive arts, school counseling, multicultural advocacy in schools, school-based mental health services, and counselor supervision.

**Cort Dorn-Medeiros,** PhD, LPC, CADC III, is an assistant professor in the Counseling Psychology department at the Lewis & Clark College Graduate School of Education and Counseling in Portland, Oregon. Dr. Dorn-Medeiros' courses include Diversity and Social Justice and Introduction to Professional Mental Health and Addictions Counseling. Research interests include LGBTQ issues in counseling and counselor education and queer identity in Internet gaming and gaming subcultures.

**Acacia Douglas,** BA, is a first year master's student in Marriage and Family Therapy at St. Louis University, where she is also pursuing the programs concentration in Medical Family Therapy. Acacia's research interests include families with children, children of divorce, and research.

**Dr. Meredith Drew** is an assistant professor in the Graduate Counseling program at William Paterson University. She has extensive experience as a school counselor and has worked with the homeless, substance abuse, and adolescent population. She also is a certified school counselor in LPC in NJ, NCC, and ACS. Her areas of interests include examining the role of personal counseling, supervision of counselors, self-care, and online learning.

**Charles Edwards** is a Nationally Certified Counselor (NCC) and Nationally Certified School Counselor (NCSC). Dr. Edwards has over 15 years of experience working as a teacher and counselor. He is presently an assistant professor of School Counseling. His research focuses on the effectiveness of professional school counselors in supporting students' academic, personal-social, and career development within urban school systems and communities. Dr. Edwards actively integrates music in his practice.

**Ana Estrada,** PhD, LMFT, is an associate professor at the University of San Diego. She has over 25 years of experience in facilitating and coaching children, adolescents, adults, and their families in applying strength-based perspectives in seeking educational equity, strengthening parenting skills, and sustaining permanent housing.

**Minnah W. Farook,** MA, EdS, is a doctoral candidate in Counseling Psychology at the University of Kentucky. She graduated from Wayne State University with a bachelor of science in Psychology and attained a master of arts in Clinical Psychology, Counseling Specialization, from The Chicago School of Professional Psychology. Minnah's research interests focus on acculturation, sociopolitical factors that affect marginalized communities, multicultural competence, and psychotherapy outcomes.

**Andy Felton** is an assistant professor for the Clinical Mental Health Counseling program at the University of Wisconsin—Stout in Menomonie, Wisconsin. He regularly incorporates creative and experiential methods in an effort to enhance student development. Andy's research interests focus on how to strengthen pedagogy, clinical supervision, and clinical practice using integrative, creative, and experiential methods.

**Thomas Field,** PhD, LMHC-WA, LPC-VA, NCC, CCMHC, ACS, is an associate professor of Counseling at City University of Seattle. Thom has ten years of counseling experience with over 1,000 clients in a variety of settings. His research has received national recognition from the American Mental Health Counselors Association and Council for Accreditation of Counseling and Related Educational Programs. For more information, visit his website: www.thomfield.com/.

**Katherine Nordell Fort,** PhD, LMHC, is faculty and co-chair of the Clinical Mental Health Counseling program at Antioch University Seattle. She teaches clinical skills, counseling theories, human development, group counseling, career counseling, and supervision. She is dedicated to local and national social justice advocacy, access to education for at-risk populations, and the internationalization of counseling. She has a private practice and supervises counselors working toward state licensure.

**Michelle Ghoston** is an assistant professor at Gonzaga University, and is licensed in Washington and Virginia. Her experience spans a diverse array of clients from differing cultures and backgrounds. Her work as a counselor informs her work as an educator, training school counselors, M&F counselors, and clinical mental health counselors. In addition to the work done in the community and the classroom, Dr. Ghoston has delivered numerous presentations in the United States and Canada.

**Victoria Giegerich,** MA, LPC, is a PhD student in Counselor Education and Supervision at Kent State University. Her experience includes counseling individuals, groups, couples, and families in a hospital setting and providing training in Motivational Interviewing. Her teaching experience includes master's courses in group work, motivational interviewing, practicum, and counseling skills. Her research focuses on supervision, motivational interviewing, relational-cultural theory, and addictions.

**Jenifer Cortes Gray** is a Clinical Mental Health Counseling graduate student at Northeastern State University. Her clinical research interests include historical trauma with diverse populations. She currently works as a mental health tech in an inpatient hospital.

**Jennifer Greene-Rooks,** PhD, is an assistant professor in the Professional Counseling program at Texas State University. Her background is in School Counseling at an international school serving the needs of refugee students and American born students together. Dr. Greene-Rooks has done research in multicultural counseling competence, trauma, and dissociation. She teaches the counseling diversity class with a focus on privilege, oppression, and intersectionality.

**Sara Haas,** Ph.D., LPC, Licensed School Counselor, NCC. Her publications, presentations, and research agenda focuses on play therapy, expressive arts, school counseling, trauma, multicultural advocacy in schools, and counselor supervision.

**Maria Haiyasoso,** PhD, LPC, NCC, is an assistant professor at Texas State University. Dr. Haiyasoso provides counseling for child survivors of abuse and neglect, nonoffending caregivers, and adult survivors of domestic violence from rural areas and underprivileged backgrounds. Dr. Haiyasoso's research includes counseling survivors of child sexual abuse, play therapy, parent-child relationships, utilizing relational-cultural theory in counseling, and counselor wellness.

**Kristopher Hall** is a fourth-year tenure-track faculty member at the University of San Diego. He has been conducting groups since 2007 and has taught groups courses both domestically and internationally. He also writes and presents in areas of multicultural development including relational-cultural theory and multicultural microskills infusion.

**Dr. Timothy Hanna** is an assistant professor of Pastoral Clinical Mental Health Counseling at Neumann University. He earned his PhD in Counselor Education and Supervision from Loyola University Maryland's Pastoral Counseling program and also holds a master's degree in Theological Studies from Weston Jesuit School of Theology. He is a licensed clinician with counseling research experience in social justice and multiculturalism, religion and spirituality, and personality and ideology.

**John Harrichand,** MA, resident in counseling (VA), is a graduate teaching assistant and doctoral student in Counselor Education and Supervision at Liberty University. His teaching and research interests include professional advocacy, counselor identity development, emotional intelligence, and resilience. His clinical experience involves working with community and college student populations. He holds chapter and division leadership positions within the Virginia Counseling Association.

**Dr. DeAnna Henderson** is the Campus College Chair for the College of Social Sciences at the University of Phoenix, Central Valley Campus. She was a tenured associate professor at Alabama State University. She also served as the chief operations officer of The Neighborhood House, Inc. DeAnna is a Licensed Professional Counselor, National Certified Counselor, and Certified Rehabilitation Counselor. She holds a PhD in Counselor Education and Supervision from Ohio University.

**Heidi L. Henry** is a doctoral student in Counselor Education at Sam Houston State University. She is a Licensed Professional Counselor in the state of Texas and is interested in preparing counselors-in-training to be multiculturally competent and advocates for social justice, specifically in the areas of religious diversity, sizeism, and LGBT issues. She currently serves as a teaching assistant for the course Cross Cultural Issues in Counseling at Sam Houston State University.

**Jessica Henry** is currently an assistant professor at The Pennsylvania State University. She has expertise in rehabilitation counselor education, crisis counseling, multicultural counseling, disability identity, coping, and resilience with an emphasis on disability services for persons with acquired and congenital disabilities.

**Tamara J. Hinojosa** is an assistant professor in the Counseling program at Texas A&M University—San Antonio. She teaches Group Counseling, Human Growth & Development, Practicum, and electives centered on women's identity development over the lifespan. Her research centers on identity development of historically marginalized groups and innovative counselor training methods. Dr. Hinojosa focuses her advocacy efforts on the promotion of higher education opportunities for underrepresented groups.

**Reginald W. Holt,** Ph.D., LPC, NCC, MAC is a licensed mental health and substance abuse professional counselor with a broad range of behavioral healthcare and academic experiences. Educational background includes a Ph.D. in Counselor Education, M.A. in Clinical Psychology, and post-graduate training in an Advanced Psychodynamic Psychotherapy Program.

**Dr. Amber Hughes** is an assistant professor at Morehead State University. Dr. Hughes earned her PhD in Counselor Education and Supervision from the University of Tennessee and her MEd in School Counseling from Vanderbilt University. Dr. Hughes has worked as a school counselor, an academic advisor, and a career counselor. Her research interest is in career counseling, specifically in using creativity in career counseling and career development of at-risk and underserved populations.

**Megan Dooley Hussmann,** MSEd, is a counseling doctoral student at the University of Missouri—St. Louis and is the director of Congregational Care at The Gathering United Methodist Church. She has taught Building Community, Culture, and Learning in Education and designs intercultural learning opportunities for the congregation that she works with. Megan has conducted research focused on education in Nepal and Botswana and has worked with refugee clients in the St. Louis area.

**Brian Hutchison,** PhD, LPC, MCC, is an associate professor, international studies fellow, and coordinator of the School Counseling program at the University of Missouri St. Louis. Brian is the president-elect of the Asia Pacific Career Development Association (2017–2018; APCDA). He received the 2014–2015 Social Justice Advocacy Award from the Association of Humanistic Counseling. Brian is the founder of the St. Louis Cultural Competence Institute.

**Edward E. Jacobs** is an associate professor in the Counseling, Rehabilitation Counseling, and Counseling Psychology Department at West Virginia University. He serves as the program coordinator for the master's program in Counseling. Ed has taught at WVU for more than 40 years and has written books on both individual and group counseling where the topics of social justice and advocacy are addressed. As coordinator, he has been adamant about students being aware of the importance of advocacy.

**Michael Jones,** a 2013 NBCC Minority Fellow, is a Licensed Professional Counselor, Nationally Certified Counselor, and Distance Credentialed Counselor. He is a counseling faculty member at Messiah College in Mechanicsburg, Pennsylvania. His relevant experience includes teaching multicultural counseling and integrating social justice advocacy as a part of his classes. He is a member of AMCD and speaks frequently on advocacy in the area of multiculturalism and utilizing technology in counseling.

**Dr. Mary-Anne Joseph** has a master's degree in Rehabilitation Counseling from Winston Salem State University and a doctorate in Counselor Education and Supervision from Ohio University. Dr. Joseph is a Certified Rehabilitation Counselor and a Licensed Professional Counselor. She has previously worked as a Vocational Rehabilitation Counselor specializing in transition services. Currently Dr. Joseph works as an assistant professor of Rehabilitation Studies at Alabama State University.

**Dr. Judith Justice** has served as professor and director of Indiana Wesleyan University Graduate School Counseling since 2005, and recently retired after 19 years as a K–12 school counselor. She also counsels for churches, courts, and as a disaster mental health counselor with the American Red Cross. Judy holds a doctorate of Family and Youth Studies from Nova Southeastern University, with an MS in Counseling, BS in Elementary Education, and AS in Early Childhood, all from Indiana University.

**Dr. Elizabeth Keller-Dupree** is an associate professor of Psychology and Counseling at Northeastern State University. Her research interests include prosocial development, wellness and well-being practices, and experiential education. She is an LPC-S, a certified PK–12 school counselor, and a Nationally Certified Counselor, and she owns and operates Enrichment Counseling and Consultation in Tulsa, Oklahoma.

**Alexandria Kerwin,** PhD, LPC, is currently serving as an assistant professor at the University of Mississippi within the Department of Leadership and Counselor Education. She is a Licensed Professional Counselor and has experience working with children, adolescents, adults, and refugees. Dr. Kerwin's research interests include power dynamics, professional identity, and counselor education.

**Jeanna R. Knight** is a family therapist who provides clinical services in private practice and primary care settings. She is currently pursuing a Ph.D. in Medical Family Therapy at Saint Louis University.

**Dr. Margaret Lamar** is an assistant professor at Palo Alto University, where she is the Clinical Mental Health program coordinator. Her teaching focus includes professional identity, ethics, research, and career counseling. She researches issues in counselor education, researcher development, and women's issues. Dr. Lamar is a licensed counselor, specializing in university and clinical mental health counseling. She attended the University of North Texas and the University of Northern Colorado.

**Amber Letcher,** PhD, is an assistant professor of Human Development in the Department of Counseling and Human Development at South Dakota State University. Her research focuses on youth development and risk taking in the context of early peer relationships. Since 2006, Dr. Letcher has worked with at-risk populations including runaway and homeless youth, homeless mothers and their young children, substance-abusing mothers with children, and substance-using youth.

**Lauren Levy** is a master's candidate in the Clinical Mental Health Counseling specialization at the University of San Diego. She is a counseling trainee at a local sexual assault and domestic violence center whose mission is to end relationship and sexual violence, provide advocacy services, and promote social justice. She is also coaching parents in strengthening their parenting and sustaining permanent housing at a school for homeless children.

**Dr. Chi-Sing Li** is an associate professor in the Department of Counselor Education at Sam Houston State University. He is a Licensed Professional Counselor Supervisor and Licensed Marriage and Family Therapist Supervisor in the state of Texas. He is particularly interested in multicultural counseling and social justice issues and the supervision and training of counselor interns.

**Jennifer Austin Main,** LPC, RPT-S, is a doctoral candidate in Counselor Education and Supervision at the University of Mississippi, where she and her therapy dog Rook offer play therapy services to children and families in the community. Prior to coming to Ole Miss, Jennifer owned and operated a private practice and specialized in play therapy and canine assisted play therapy. Jennifer and Rook are involved in on-campus advocacy work and make frequent therapy dog visits in her local community.

**Dr. Mary G. Mayorga** is an associate professor at Texas A&M University—San Antonio. She has been a counselor educator since 2005. In that time she has written articles on multicultural competency among school counselors. Dr. Mayorga has taught multicultural counseling and social justice/advocacy during her time as a counselor educator and has presented at state, national, and international conferences on the issues of multicultural competencies among counselors-in-training.

**Carlos Medina V** is a doctoral candidate in Counselor Education and Supervision at Penn State University. He has worked with college students, children and adolescents, student-athletes, and the LGBTQA+ population. His current research focuses on identity development and expression, social justice and advocacy, and discrimination within communities. He uses his research and teaching to advocate for student success and diverse representation within the counseling profession.

**Shekila Melchior** is a doctoral candidate at Virginia Tech with a research focus on the social justice identity development of school counselors. Shekila has presented at the state and national level (VSCA, ASCA, ACES) on advocating for undocumented students and developing a social justice identity development. Shekila incorporates social justice into her coursework through experiential activities.

**Dr. Dixie Meyer,** associate professor, is faculty in the Department of Family and Community Medicine at St. Louis University. She is a Licensed Professional Counselor and a nationally certified counselor. She is an advocate for social justice and includes a social justice mission in her courses. Her research interests include couples counseling, drama therapy, and neurobiological applications in counseling.

**Tanya Middleton** is a doctoral student at the University of Akron.

**Rieko Miyakuni** is a doctoral candidate at Governors State University. Her passion for social justice advocacy led her to work for the host committee for Creating Change Chicago 2016, launch the Gender and Sexuality Studies Student Club, and currently serve on the Campus Inclusion Team. Her research interests include promoting mental health among LGBTQ populations, academic success among students of color, racial and economic justice, and postcolonial and black feminist theories.

**Dr. Suzanne D. Mudge,** NCC, NCSC, LPC is Professor, Department Chair for Counseling, Health & Kinesiology, and Interim Associate Dean for the College of Education & Human Development at Texas A&M University - San Antonio. She received her Ph.D. in Counselor Education and Supervision from St. Mary's University in San Antonio.

**Joy Mwendwa,** PhD, MA, NCC, is an assistant professor in the Department of Counselor Education and Family Studies at Liberty University. Her research interests include immigrant counseling, the development of the counseling profession, international counseling, qualitative and indigenous research methodologies, and multicultural issues in counseling. She is a counselor educator, counselor, and advocate. She has also served as a college and community-based counselor for ten years.

**Abigail Nedved,** MA, is a second year PhD student in the Medical Family Therapy program at St. Louis University. She received her master's degree in clinical psychology at Southern Illinois University— Edwardsville. Her current research interests include understanding how family attachment and neurological functions affect persons who suffer from an eating disorder.

**Melissa (Mel) Odegard-Koester,** PhD, LPC, NCC, CCH, holds a PhD in Counselor Education and Counseling from Idaho State University. She is currently an associate professor at Southeast Missouri State University and coordinates the overall Counseling programs as well as the Mental Health Counseling program. Her professional research and publications highlight the need for counselor educators, supervisors, and professional counselors to incorporate social justice paradigms into their work.

**Dr. Delila Owens** is an associate professor and coordinator of School Counseling. She earned her doctor of philosophy degree from Michigan State University in 2002. Her primary areas of research include school counseling, multicultural counseling, and urban education. She has authored or coauthored over 30 refereed journal articles and book chapters.

**Rebecca A. Palomo** is a doctoral student in Interdisciplinary Learning and Teaching at the University of Texas at San Antonio (UTSA). She is an adjunct faculty at UTSA in the College of Education and Human Development. Also, she is a certified teacher, PK through 6, who taught in an inner city elementary school for ten years. Her research is in the field of literacy and how literacy practices can empower and seek social justice for those whose voices have been marginalized or silenced.

**Mazna Patka,** PhD, is a community psychologist, working at Zayed University in Dubai. Her research focuses on critical consciousness and social movements, particularly involving individuals with intellectual disabilities.

**Tiffany J. Peets,** PhD, is an assistant professor of Counseling and Human Development at Walsh University. She practices as a licensed clinical counselor/supervisor. She teaches Research and Program Evaluation, Assessment, Ethics, Advanced Abnormal Psychology, Diagnosis, and Practicum in Counseling. Research interests include supervision, family systems, women's issues, mental health of older adults and caregivers, and social advocacy for diverse and marginalized populations.

**Kristine Ramsay-Seaner,** PhD, is an assistant professor of Counseling in the Department of Counseling and Human Development at South Dakota State University. Her research focuses on diversity, equality, and gerontology. A strong proponent for advocacy, Dr. Ramsay-Seaner is committed to meeting the needs of underserved populations in her community as well as incorporating advocacy in her student's professional identity.

**Jennifer E. Randall Reyes** teaches as an adjunct instructor at both West Virginia University and West Virginia Wesleyan College. Her classes focus on strengthening social advocacy in the field of counseling by supporting future professional counselors at both the undergraduate and graduate levels to better understand how the overlapping layers of their own identity shapes who they will become as mental health providers. She also lectures and trains in schools and community settings on diversity.

**Nicole Randick,** EdD, ATR-BC, LPC-S, NCC, is an associate faculty member at Adler Graduate School in Richfield, Minnesota. She served as a counselor and art therapist for at-risk students for 12 years before teaching. She also served for several years as a director of alternative schools for high-risk high school students. Areas of research and interest include wellness, clinical supervision, expressive arts in counseling, and social justice and advocacy for historically marginalized youth.

**Solange Ribeiro,** PhD (sciences), MA, LPC-S, has been a counselor and counselor educator for 17 years. She is a core faculty member at Adler Graduate School in Richfield, Minnesota. Her main areas of interest are multicultural and social justice counseling competence, ethics, and clinical supervision. Her efforts toward development of social justice include advocacy for clients and the profession, and the creation of a low-cost community-counseling clinic at the University of Alabama at Birmingham.

**Candice Robbins,** MA, currently works with adults with serious mental illnesses and helps them manage their symptoms, transition, and achieve qualify of life in their own community. She recently completed her thesis, which examined psychological empowerment among students participating in leadership programs to inform students' leadership programs practices at Governors State University. The goal of her project was also to transform and shape the community through research and social justice.

**Shamire Rothmiller** is currently a doctoral student in the Counselor Education and Supervision Program with emphasis in Rehabilitation Counseling at the University of Iowa. Her research interests include substance use among ethnic minority populations, developmental trauma, and interpersonal learning.

**Toni Saia** is currently a doctoral student at the University of Arizona studying rehabilitation counseling. She is also the community action coordinator at DIRECT Center for Independence. She facilitates advocacy trainings to empower others to take control of their lives. Advocating for herself and other people with disabilities is her number one priority. She will stop at nothing to make sure people with disabilities have equal access in all areas of our lives.

**Carrie Sanders** is a visiting assistant professor at Virginia Tech and currently teaches Counseling Diverse Populations for the master's-level counseling program. She enjoys offering students experiential educational opportunities to connect with the content and facilitate meaningful discussions about their growth and development as counselors-in-training.

**Christine J. Schimmel** is an associate professor in the Counseling, Rehabilitation Counseling, and Counseling Psychology Department at West Virginia University. She serves as assistant department chair as well as program coordinator for the School Counseling program. Chris has devoted more than 18 years to teaching and training. Her primary scholarship interests include work in group counseling and school counseling, where social justice and advocacy are ever present.

**Brandi Schmitt** is currently a second year graduate student in the Clinical Mental Health Counseling program at South Dakota State University. Her research interests include multiculturalism, such as privilege and bias, within the counseling relationship as well as the experiences of disenfranchised grief. Her advocacy interests include women's rights, diversity, and promoting the quality of life in older adults. She is professionally committed to serving the needs of adults across the lifespan.

**Angela Schubert,** PhD, LPC, CCMHC, is currently an assistant professor and program coordinator at Central Methodist University. She has seven years of teaching experience in counselor education and seven years of counseling supervision experience, and she is the co-chair of the ACA Sexual Wellness in Counseling Network. Her professional goals are to advocate through education and service. Dr. Schubert's professional interests include sexual wellness, intersectionality, and applications of relational-cultural theory.

**Camelia Shaheed** earned a BA in Psychology, an MA in Rehabilitation Counseling, and is currently working on a doctorate in Counseling Education and Supervision after 20+ years of practice as a mental health counselor and administrator.

**Alison Phillips Sheesley** is a PhD candidate in Counselor Education and Supervision at the University of Northern Colorado. She is a play therapist who is interested in researching a wide variety of topics, including the mental health benefits of improv comedy, counselors' participation in integrated care systems, and Medicaid policy related to mental health services.

**Matthew R. Shupp** is an assistant professor in Shippensburg University's Department of Counseling and College Student Personnel. He served as a student affairs professional for 12 years in a variety of institutional settings. He is both a National Certified Counselor (NCC) through the National Board for Certified Counselors (NBCC) as well as a Distance Credentialed Counselor (DCC).

**Azra Karajic Siwiec** is an associate professor of Counselor Education at Walsh University. She has been teaching for over a decade at Walsh University, particularly social and cultural diversity classes in school and mental health counseling. She is mental health counselor and has been active in career development in multiple roles within the Ohio Career Development Association. She has authored numerous presentations on teaching and social and cultural issues.

**Justyn Smith** is a doctoral student in the Counselor Education program at Sam Houston State University. His professional presentations and teaching experience include topics of social justice. His research interests include exploring factors such as school, family, and sociocultural aspects that affect the African American male. Justyn is also interested in multicultural training, ethical issues, and lesbian, gay, bisexual, and transgender issues related to various aspects of counseling.

**Kevin C. Snow**, PhD, MA, NCC, ACS, is an assistant professor of Counseling at Texas A&M University—Commerce. His research includes spirituality and spiritual inclusion, qualitative research methodology, and advocacy in social justice/multicultural issues in counseling and counselor education. He is a skilled educator on many topics, has extensive clinical and community-based experience counseling and advocating with diverse clients, and is active with several professional associations.

**Dionne Sterner** graduated from Lock Haven University's Clinical Mental Health Counseling program in December 2015. She was hired as an outpatient therapist shortly after graduating and now is working toward attaining her supervised hours to be a Licensed Professional Counselor in Pennsylvania. Her interests are in creative counseling and children and adolescents.

**Jeffrey Sullivan**, PhD, LPC-S, RPT, graduated from the University of North Texas with his master's degree in Counseling and doctorate in Counselor Education. He is an assistant professor of Counselor Education at Sam Houston State University in Huntsville, Texas. His research interests include play therapy, parenting interventions, and counselor development.

**Tabitha Tabbert** is a master's candidate in the Clinical Mental Health Counseling specialization at the University of San Diego. She is active in pre-practicum field experiences and serves as a support coach for parents impacted by homelessness in downtown San Diego.

**Jessica Z. Taylor**, PhD, LPC, NCC, is currently an assistant professor and program coordinator at Central Methodist University. She has six years of experience teaching in Counselor Education, and she is co-chair of the ACES Teaching Interest Network. Dr. Taylor's professional interests include teacher preparation and teaching mentoring in counselor education, counseling needs of young adult cancer survivors, applications of relational-cultural theory, and crisis intervention.

**Dr. Angelica M. Tello** is an assistant professor of Counseling at the University of Houston—Clear Lake. She earned a PhD in Counselor Education and Supervision from the University of Texas at San Antonio. She is also a LPC in the state of Texas and an NCC. She has taught multicultural and social justice counseling courses. Additionally, her research is focused on the counseling needs and experiences of marginalized communities, such as Latinx college students and unaccompanied refugees.

**Kassie Terrell** is a doctoral candidate in Counselor Education at the University of Mississippi. Kassie has a personal and professional commitment to building a multicultural and diverse learning environment that fosters social justice and advocacy. She has developed competencies in teaching graduate courses in counseling; providing supervision; presenting at conferences; conducting scholarly research; providing counseling for children, adults, and couples; and participating in advocacy and service.

**Christina Thaier,** MEd, PLPC, NCC, utilizes narrative theory to teach cultural consciousness at the University of Missouri—St. Louis, where she is currently pursuing a PhD in Counselor Education. She works with individuals and couples at Change, Inc., a private practice in St. Louis. Her advocacy work has been featured by the American Counseling Association and Chi Sigma Iota. She is currently researching the use of narrative pedagogy within her own teaching practices.

**Sumedha Therthani,** M.Phil., was a licensed clinical psychologist in India. Currently she is a doctoral student in the Counselor Education and Supervision program at the University of Mississippi. She has experience working with children and adults of varying ages and populations. Her research interests include substance use, multicultural issues in counseling, and professional identity in Counselor Education.

**Arianna Trott,** MA, LMHC, NCC, is currently a doctoral student at the University of New Mexico studying Counselor Education. Her focus is on promoting social justice by addressing health and behavioral health disparities. Arianna consults on behavioral health research and evaluation, including work in substance abuse prevention and early childhood development and education.

**Carrie VanMeter** is an associate professor of Counselor Education at Walsh University, where she has served as the coordinator of School Counseling Professional Practice for the past seven years. She is dual licensed as a Professional Clinical Counselor and a Licensed School Counselor. She has been active with advocating at the state level in her multiple roles on the Ohio Counselor Political Action Committee. She has authored numerous presentations on teaching and cultural diversity.

**Kristin Vincenzes** is the Clinical Mental Health Counseling program director at Lock Haven University. As an assistant professor, she has taught almost all of the courses in the counseling curriculum. Dr. Vincenzes is a Licensed Professional Counselor and has a private practice where she is a Give an Hour provider. Dr. Vincenzes' research and advocacy efforts focus on the military, self-care for helping professionals, clinical supervision, and addictions.

**Jordan Westcott** is a Clinical Mental Health Counseling graduate student at Northeastern State University. Her clinical and research interests include social justice, advocacy, and diversity. She assists in organizing community service events for her counseling graduate cohort and is interested in pursuing further opportunities for research. She plans to obtain an LPC and later pursue a PhD program.

**Dr. Marisa White** has a strong counselor identity with experiences related to counselor education, including teaching, counseling, supervision, research, and service to the profession. Her passion for social justice advocacy has been continuously demonstrated in her professional endeavors including her dissertation, legislative committee work, clinical experiences with clients who have an HIV+ status, addiction diagnoses, and/or a criminal background, and her research interests.

**Tyler Wilkinson,** assistant professor, has been teaching an assessment/testing for five years in which he has increasingly tried to find ways to use the subject to address how assessment/testing can be used in ways that are reductionistic and do not promote the complexities of clients. He tries to use this course to help students think more critically about using information from clients within the clients' cultural context to maximize understanding.

**Lauren Wilson** is a licensed clinical social worker in the state of Missouri and has over 10 years of field experience with various populations. Research interests include integrated behavioral health in primary care and suicide prevention.

**Zeynep Yilmaz** is a PhD student in Rehabilitation Counseling at the University of Arizona. She received her master's degree in Rehabilitation Psychology from the University of Wisconsin—Madison. In addition to teaching and research, she loves community involvement, direct client interaction, and supervising counselor students. A huge part of her community involvement includes advocacy and disability rights.

# Introduction

Social justice and advocacy may lead to more inclusive and equitable communities for all, especially those who have been marginalized. For many training participants, developing awareness, knowledge, and skills in social justice and advocacy thought and practice can be challenging and rewarding. Experiential activities are guided, safe, and structured for participants to explore all aspects of social justice and advocacy. Experiential activities are active forms of self-reflections and dialogues with other participants. Often, these activities involve sharing different or similar experiences, personal narratives, senses, memories, thoughts, beliefs, and emotions. In a well facilitated social justice and advocacy experiential program, participants' competence will approach, and maybe even move beyond, the edges of their understanding, learning, and relating. Our many collaborators are passionate about social justice and advocacy and have shared their finest experiential activities in this book.

Although the book editors have organized the social justice and advocacy experiential activities into chapters with primary topic areas, educators and supervisors will find many of the activities are also applicable to other Council for the Accreditation of Counseling and Related Programs (CACREP) core standard or counseling subspecialties. The chapters have been categorized into three sections.

In section one, the educator and supervisor will be introduced to activities that elucidate the principles of social justice and advocacy to the reader. In section two, the educator or supervisor will find many activities that address the CACREP core principles with a social justice and advocacy point of view. Finally, in section three, the educator or supervisor will find social justice and advocacy experiential activities for the different counseling specialty areas.

## HOW TO USE THIS BOOK

### Precautions

Before you implement an activity from this book, we encourage you to be intentional and thoughtful about how and when you implement each activity. As with good comics, timing and delivery are key essential tools. The facilitator of the activity should use best judgement to assess which activity to use and when to incorporate the activity with the students/group. Some chapters do offer a trigger warning and recommendations on how to create and foster a safe space to implement the activity. We encourage intentionality to create and foster a safe space

### Finding the Right Activity

On the first page of each chapter, you will find that the editors have provided a chart labeled *Course Recommendations* that suggests which social justice advocacies, CACREP courses, and counseling specializations the activity is suggested to be used for. The objectives from the chapter are aligned with subcategories under each of the three primary categories to help the educators and supervisors locate a chapter that will best meet their goal.

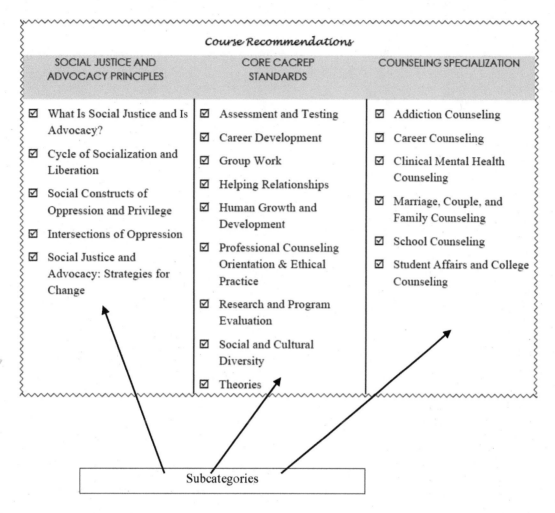

## Indexes

At the end of the book, you will find four indexes. The first will list the page number for each author's activity. The second index, *Social Justice and Advocacy Principles*, will list the page numbers associated with the editor's recommendations of activities that embody each of the five social justice and advocacy themes. The third index, *Core CACREP Course*, will list the page numbers associated with each of the editor's course recommendations. The fourth index, *Counseling Specialization*, will list the page numbers associated with each of the editor's counseling specialization recommendations.

# SECTION 1

# Social Justice and Advocacy Principles

In this section, educators and supervisors will find chapters with experiential activities that align with different social justice and advocacy principles. These social justice and advocacy principles were divided into subcategories exploring social justice and advocacy, the cycle of socialization and liberation, social constructs of oppression and privilege, intersections of oppression, and social justice and advocacy: strategies for change. The principles build upon each other in regard to one's progression as a social justice and advocacy counselor. The subcategories What Is Social Justice and Advocacy? and Cycle of Socialization and Liberation allow for educators and supervisors to implement principles that focus on educating and increasing the importance of understanding this paradigm as mental health professionals and providing a foundational context needed to understand the role of social justice and advocacy counseling. Subcategories Social Constructs of Oppression and Privilege and Intersections of Oppression focus on one's own relationship with oppression and liberation. Last, the subcategory Social Justice and Advocacy: Strategies for Change involves principles focused on practical applications to integrate social justice and advocacy into the community.

## WHAT IS SOCIAL JUSTICE AND ADVOCACY?

*These activities are designed to be used in introducing the definition of social justice and advocacy. Characterized as the fifth force in counseling, social justice and advocacy counseling illuminates the connection between human development and the oppressive system. "The social justice counseling paradigm —uses social advocacy and activism as a means to address inequitable social, political, and economic conditions that impede the academic, career, and personal/social development of individuals, families, and communities" (Ratts, 2009, p. 160). Activities will be focused on educating and increasing the importance of understanding this paradigm as mental health professionals and providing a foundational context needed to understand the role of social justice and advocacy counseling.*

## CYCLE OF SOCIALIZATION AND LIBERATION

*These activities are designed to be used in explaining and determining the cycles of socialization and liberation. Activities focused on the cycle of socialization and liberation will allow for further exploration on the intra- and interpersonal development of oppression within a system and provide opportunities to examine these tenets in order to achieve liberation.*

## SOCIAL CONSTRUCTS OF OPPRESSION AND PRIVILEGE

*These activities are designed to demonstrate how oppression and privilege are socially constructed. Activities will provide learning opportunities to explore the complexities as well as the influence of oppression and privilege on identity. These activities will highlight the influence of power and privilege within an oppressive society and the importance to become aware of one's own privilege and impact on others, and vice versa, and to understand one's own level of oppression and the lack of systemic power in others.*

# INTERSECTIONS OF OPPRESSION

*These activities are designed to demonstrate the intersection of oppression (e.g., racism and classism). Intersectionality is a framework that recognizes the multiple aspects of identity and complicated marginalizations and oppressions. Activities in this chapter will highlight how multiple oppressions are enacted intersectionally and how to provide opportunities to inspire change.*

# SOCIAL JUSTICE AND ADVOCACY: STRATEGIES FOR CHANGE

*These activities are designed to demonstrate how individuals go out and create change in the community. Social justice advocacy counseling is a counselor-advocate-scholar model (Ratts & Pederson, 2014) that provides a framework to promote mental health professionals, educators, and scholars to become competent change agents. Activities will include practical applications to integrate social justice and advocacy into the community.*

# CHAPTER 1

## The Journey
### Exploring Social Justice Identity Development Through Critical Incidents

*Shekila Melchior*

---

### Course Recommendations

| SOCIAL JUSTICE AND ADVOCACY PRINCIPLES | CORE CACREP STANDARDS | COUNSELING SPECIALIZATION |
|---|---|---|
| ☑ Cycle of Socialization and Liberation | ☑ Professional Counseling Orientation and Ethical Practice<br>☑ Social and Cultural Diversity | ☑ Clinical Mental Health Counseling<br>☑ School Counseling<br>☑ Student Affairs and College Counseling |

---

## TOPIC

The purpose of this activity is to provide students with the opportunity to explore their developing social justice identity.

## LEARNING OBJECTIVES

1. Definitions of social justice and advocacy
2. Bobbie Harro's Cycle of Liberation (Harro, 2000)
3. Identify or begin to identify a social justice issue for which one would like to advocate
4. Explore or begin exploring critical incidents in one's work as a counselor that motivate one to advocacy
5. Discover areas of shared interests with colleagues that could lead to collaboration

## TARGET POPULATION

Master's or doctoral level students

## GROUP SIZE

10–15 (recommendation would be for small groups if class is larger)

# TIME REQUIRED

45–60 minutes

# SETTING

This activity should be conducted after rapport has developed in the course. The activity should take place in a setting that is safe for students, and students should not be obligated to respond if the critical incident is a personal experience they do not wish to share. The hope is for a more diverse group that will allow students to gain knowledge about new areas of advocacy and issues that are significant to their colleagues.

# MATERIALS NEEDED

- Lined index cards
- Journey map handout
- Pens or pencils

# INSTRUCTIONS FOR CONDUCTING ACTIVITY

1. Defining social justice and advocacy.
2. Social justice: social justice can be defined as "an internal sense of conscience, a moral duty, and sense of righteousness to the world" (Hunsaker, 2011). Social justice envisions an equitable society that is physically and psychologically safe for all members (Bell, 1997).
3. Brief discussion on what social justice and advocacy looks like in the field of counseling:
   a. Discussing the American Counseling Association (ACA) Advocacy Framework (Ratts, DeKruyf, & Chen-Hayes, 2007)
   b. Discussing relevant American School Counselors Association (ASCA) position statements (ASCA, 2012)
   c. Our role as advocates
4. Instructor should provide a brief presentation on the Cycle of Liberation.
5. Provide one lined index card to each student:
   a. On the side without lines have the student write a social justice issue they currently or hope to advocate for.
   b. On the lined side have the students write meaningful experiences or major events in their life that led them to their social justice issue (this is a time to remind them of your Cycle of Liberation discussion focusing on the critical incident).
6. Have students reflect on their journey toward advocacy so far and what they hope to achieve as an advocate for their specific social justice issue, utilizing the journey map to track their process.

# DISCUSSION

In a larger class (20 or more), students in groups of three to four should discuss their personal journey (disclosing what they wish) to advocacy. Students should also discuss in small groups any similarities they may have and opportunities for collaboration. This small group discussion should be around 10 minutes. Then in the large group, students will discuss their group findings and how they plan to collaborate in the future. (Warning: students might have a personal experience that influenced their social justice identity development that could be triggering for them. Encourage students to share what they are most comfortable with.)

# REFERENCES

American School Counselor Association. (2012). *The school counselor and cultural diversity: Equity for all students.* Retrieved from www.schoolcounselor.org/school-counselors-members/about-asca-(1)/position-statements

Bell, L.A. (1997). Theoretical foundations for social justice education. In M. Adams, P. Griffin, & L.A. Bell (Eds.), *Teaching for Diversity and Social Justice-A sourcebook* (pp.1–14). New York, NY: Routledge.

Harro, B. (2000). Cycle of liberation. In M. Adams (Ed.), *Readings for diversity and social justice.* New York: Routledge.

Hunsaker, R. C. (2011). Counseling and Social Justice. *Academic Questions, 24,* 319–340. doi:10.1007/s12129-01109242

Ratts, M. J., DeKruyf, L., & Chen-Hayes, S. F. (2007). The ACA advocacy competencies: A social justice advocacy framework for professional school counselors. *Professional School Counseling, 11*(2), 90–97. doi:10.5330/PSC.n.2010-11.90

# SUGGESTED BACKGROUND READING

American School Counselor Association. (2012). *The school counselor and cultural diversity: Equity for all students.* Retrieved from www.schoolcounselor.org/school-counselors-members/about-asca-(1)/position-statements

Harro, B. (2000). Cycle of liberation. In M. Adams (Ed.), *Readings for diversity and social justice.* New York: Routledge.

Ratts, M. J., DeKruyf, L., & Chen-Hayes, S. F. (2007). The ACA advocacy competencies: A social justice advocacy framework for professional school counselors. *Professional School Counseling, 11*(2), 90–97. doi:10.5330/PSC.n.2010-11.90

## HANDOUT

# Handout 1.1: The Journey Map

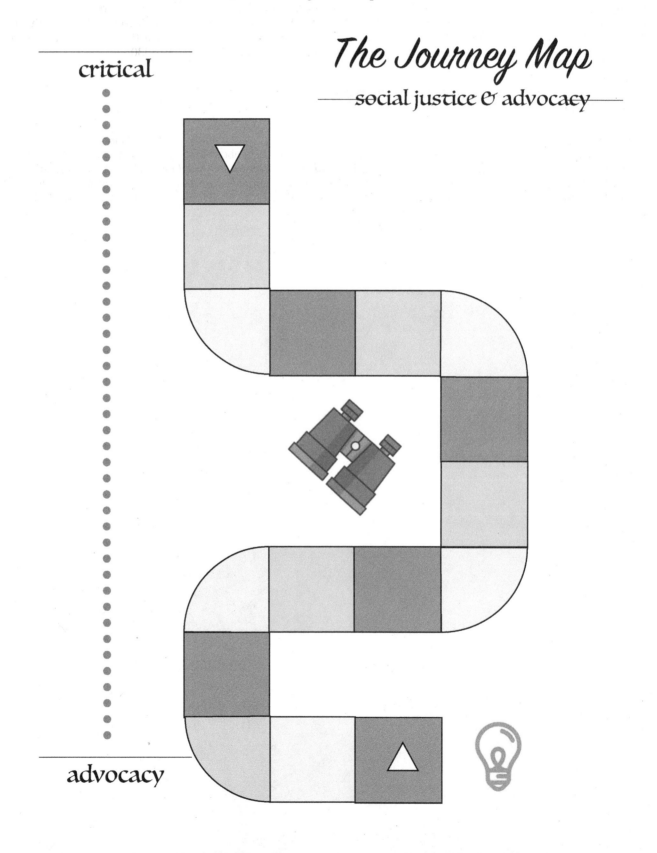

# Handout 1.2: Sample Image

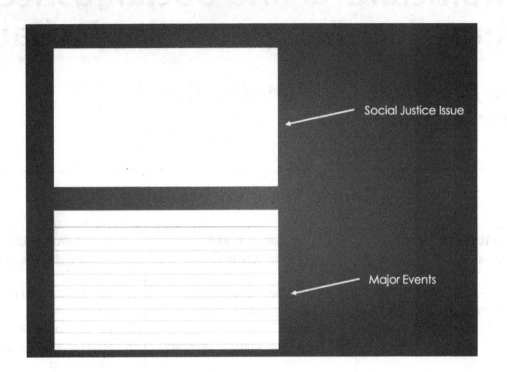

# CHAPTER 2

# A Multicultural and Social Justice Counseling Competencies Debate

*Tamara J. Hinojosa, Carlos Medina V, and Suzanne D. Mudge*

## Course Recommendations

| SOCIAL JUSTICE AND ADVOCACY PRINCIPLES | CORE CACREP STANDARDS | COUNSELING SPECIALIZATION |
|---|---|---|
| ☑ What Is Social Justice Counseling and Advocacy | ☑ Professional Counseling Orientation and Ethical Practice <br> ☑ Social and Cultural Diversity | ☑ Clinical Mental Health Counseling <br> ☑ School Counseling <br> ☑ Student Affairs and College Counseling |

## TOPIC

The focus of this activity is on the multicultural and social justice counseling competencies (MSJCC) and helping students reflect on the research and literature surrounding these competencies.

## LEARNING OBJECTIVES

- Students will be able to interpret and compare research findings and scholarly literature both supporting and critiquing the MSJCC.
- Students will demonstrate evaluative skills by using scholarly resources to defend a viewpoint about the MSJCC.

## TARGET POPULATION

The target population for this activity is counseling graduate students who are in a course in which they have had exposure to the MSJCC. We suggest that this activity be used as a culminating experience in which students identify and evaluate scholarly resources focused on the use of MSJCC. Therefore, this activity should be used at the end of a curriculum unit focused on MSJCC or at the end of the semester.

## GROUP SIZE

10–15 students

# TIME REQUIRED

Approximately 60 minutes will be needed for this activity. The first 5 minutes will be used to explain the activity to students and to divide the students into two groups. Then students will have 15 minutes to meet in their groups and research and prepare for the debate. The debate will contain two rounds. The first round will include team one having 5 minutes to present their argument. Then team two will have 5 minutes to present their argument. Both teams will then have 5–10 minutes to discuss and prepare their rebuttals. The second round will include team one having 5 minutes to present their rebuttal. Then team two will have 5 minutes to present their rebuttal, which will conclude the debate. Ten minutes will then be used to debrief the activity.

# SETTING

The best location to conduct the activity is a large classroom and/or computer lab in which students have space to meet in small groups, research their topic, and discuss and prepare their arguments. Both groups will then need space to present their arguments and rebuttals (e.g., a podium, space to face each other).

# MATERIALS NEEDED

- PowerPoint or handout providing instructions for students.
- Research materials: if the activity is conducted in a computer lab, students will be able to conduct research about their topic using the Internet on the computers. If instructors do not have access to a lab, they can, however, ask students to prepare before the activity and bring research materials (e.g., articles, textbooks) to class, or professors can bring hardcopies of articles and books for students to use. Please see suggested background reading for research materials that students can use.
- Timer to time each team's arguments and rebuttals (e.g., stopwatch, online timer).

# INSTRUCTIONS FOR CONDUCTING ACTIVITY

1. Explain to students that they will be participating in a debate and define debate including the terms argument and rebuttal.
2. Present the general topic they will be debating: do counselors need multicultural and social justice counseling competencies? Sub-topics for debate may include: (a) is self-awareness essential to a counselor's development as a multicultural and social justice competent counselor? (b) can the counselor's understanding of the client's worldview be deliberately developed/enriched by the counselor? and (c) is it appropriate for a counselor to address public policy issues that impede client development?
3. Explain that the class will be divided into two teams and the teams will have the following issue: team one: FOR MSJCC and team two: AGAINST MSJCC. Then divide the class into two teams. The teams do not get a choice about which viewpoint they will defend, which challenges the students to research and defend a perspective that they may not agree with. The suggested structure of the debate can be as follows or altered to fit the needs of the students.

## Round One

Team one—present argument FOR multicultural and social justice counseling competencies (5 minutes)

Team two—present argument AGAINST multicultural and social justice counseling competencies (5 minutes)

## Discussion Period

This period is used for teams to prepare their responses (5–10 minutes).

## Round Two

Team one rebuttal (5 minutes)
Team two rebuttal (5 minutes)

4. Allow each team to have approximately 15 minutes to research for the debate. Explain to students that they should use this time to learn about their issue, gather research findings to support their assertions, and develop a debate strategy (e.g., will there be one speaker for the team? Will all team members speak? How will they present their arguments?). If instructors are concerned that not all students will participate, instructors can require that all students speak during the debate and/or that all students demonstrate an active role on the debate team (e.g., facilitator, researcher, etc.).
5. After the research time is up, start the debate using a timer to keep track of each team's time limit and the format as provided in step 3.
6. After the debate is complete, instructors can facilitate a discussion about whom students think won the debate. Conversely, instructors may also choose to select a winner. If instructors choose this option, they may want to consider the following:
   - Were debate teams organized and persuasive?
   - Did debate team members use research and cite evidence to support their assertions?
   - Did debate team members respond to all of their opponents' arguments?
   - Did debate team members challenge flaws in the opposing team's arguments?

# DISCUSSION

Helpful debriefing questions include:

- How did it feel debating this topic?
- What are your thoughts after learning about both sides of this topic?
- Now that you are reaching the end of this course and have participated in this debate, do you think we, as a profession, need MSJCC?

# BIBLIOGRAPHY

Choque, K., & Mouraz, A. (2015). Debate as a practice in higher education curricula. In C. Leite, A. Mouraz, & P. Fernandes (Eds.), *Curriculum studies: Policies, perspectives, and practices* (pp. 191–199). Portugal: Euro ACS.

Fickling, M. J., & Gonzalez, L. M. (2016). Linking multicultural counseling and social justice through advocacy. *Journal of Counselor Leadership and Advocacy, 3*(2), 85–94.

Gervey, R., Drout, M. O. C., & Wang, C. C. (2009). Debate in the classroom: An evaluation of a critical thinking teaching technique within a rehabilitation counseling course. *Rehabilitation Education, 23*(1), 61–73.

Gess, J. (2016). Social justice in counselor education: Teaching advocacy across the core. *Journal of Counselor Leadership and Advocacy, 3*(2), 124–134.

Kennedy, R. (2007). In-class debates: Fertile ground for active learning and the cultivation of critical thinking and oral communication skills. *International Journal of Teaching and Learning in Higher Education, 19*(2), 183–190.

# SUGGESTED BACKGROUND READING

Bassey, S., & Melluish, S. (2013). Cultural competency for mental health practitioners: A selective narrative review. *Counselling Psychology Quarterly, 26*(2), 151–173.

Coleman, H. K., & Wampold, B. E.(2003). Challenges to the development of culturally relevant, empirically supported treatment. In D. B. Pope-Davis, H. L. K. Coleman, W. M. Liu, & R. L. Toporek (Eds.), *Handbook of multicultural competencies in counseling and psychology* (pp. 227–246). Thousand Oaks, CA: Sage Publications.

Collins, S., Arthur, N., Brown, C., & Kennedy, B. (2015). Student perspectives: Graduate education facilitation of multicultural counseling and social justice competency. *Training and Education in Professional Psychology, 9*(2), 153.

Constantine, M. G., Hage, S. M., Kindaichi, M. M., & Bryant, R. M. (2007). Social justice and multicultural issues: Implications for the practice and training of counselors and counseling psychologists. *Journal of Counseling & Development, 85*, 24–29.

Cook, A. L., Hayden, L. A., Gracia, R., & Tyrrell, R. (2015). Exploring outcomes of a targeted supervisory training curriculum on developing multicultural competency and social justice advocacy. *Counseling Outcome Research and Evaluation, 6*(2), 126–140.

Patterson, C. H. (2004). Do we need multicultural counseling competences? *Journal of Mental Health Counseling, 26*(1), 67–73.

Ratts, M. J., Singh, A. A., Nassar-McMillan, S., Butler, S. K., & McCullough, J. R. (2016). Multicultural and social justice counseling competencies: Guidelines for the counseling profession. *Journal of Multicultural Counseling and Development, 44*(1), 28–48.

Ratts, M. J., Singh, A. A., Nassar-McMillan, S., Butler, S. K., McCullough, J. R., & Hipolito-Delgado, C. (2015). *Multicultural and social justice counseling competencies*. Alexandria, VA: AMCD.

Smith, L. C. (2015). Queering multicultural competence in counseling. In R. D. Goodman & P. C. Gorski (Eds.), *Decolonizing "multicultural" counseling through social justice* (pp. 23–39). New York: Springer.

Sue, D. W., Arredondo, P., & McDavis, R. J. (1992). Multicultural counseling competencies and standards: A call to the profession. *Journal of Counseling & Development, 70*, 477–486.

Weinrich, S. G., & Thomas, K. R. (2004). The AMCD multicultural counseling competences: A critically flawed initiative. *Journal of Mental Health Counseling, 26*(1), 81–93.

# CHAPTER 3

# Social Justice Book Club

*Delila Owens and Judith Justice*

## Course Recommendations

| SOCIAL JUSTICE AND ADVOCACY PRINCIPLES | CORE CACREP STANDARDS | COUNSELING SPECIALIZATION |
|---|---|---|
| ☑ Social Constructs of Oppression and Privilege<br>☑ Intersections of Oppression | ☑ Human Growth and Development<br>☑ Professional Counseling Orientation and Ethical Practice<br>☑ Social and Cultural Diversity | ☑ Addiction Counseling<br>☑ Career Counseling<br>☑ Clinical Mental Health Counseling<br>☑ Marriage, Couple, and Family Counseling<br>☑ School Counseling<br>☑ Student Affairs and College Counseling |

## TOPIC

Semester Social Justice Book Club

## LEARNING OBJECTIVES

The primary objective is to promote diverse perspectives, multiculturalism, and social consciousness and to increase social justice advocacy. Another aim is to foster higher order thinking skills to better service underserved groups in counseling.

## TARGET POPULATION

Graduate students in Counselor Education Program

## GROUP SIZE

3–5 students per group

## TIME REQUIRED

7–10 weeks

## SETTING

Classroom

## MATERIALS NEEDED

Assigned book

## INSTRUCTIONS FOR CONDUCTING ACTIVITY

Instructor will give students a list of books that includes but is not limited to *Sisters of The Yam: Black Women and Self-Recovery* by bell hooks, *A Child Called It* by Dave Pelzer, and *Great Speeches by Native Americans* by Bob Blaisdell. Students are to read the book as a group and prepare a 50-minute presentation for the entire class toward the end of the semester. Special attention must be given to promoting social justice, counseling implications, and recommendations for the book's targeted audience.

## DISCUSSION

Students are to prepare a 50-minute presentation for their entire class and leave 10–15 minutes open for questions and answers.

## BIBLIOGRAPHY

Ratts, M. J., Singh, A. A., Nassar-McMillan, S., Butler, S. K., & McCullough, J. R. (2016). Multicultural and social justice counseling competencies: Guidelines for the counseling profession. *Journal of Multicultural Counseling and Development, 44*(1), 28–48.

Sue, D. W., & Sue, D. (2015). *Counseling the culturally diverse: Theory and practice* (6th ed.). Hoboken, NJ: John Wiley & Sons, Inc.

## HANDOUT

# Handout 3.1: Social Justice Book Club Presentation Rubric

Name_____                    Date_____

The following items will dictate your group grade, based on a Likert-type scale, 1–10 points, with 1 being the least effective and 10 being the most effective:

 1. Presentation gave thorough presentation of content:                           ____/10
 2. Presentation promoted social justice:                                         ____/10
 3. Presentation highlighted counseling implications using a social justice perspective:  ____/10
 4. Presentation gave recommendations for the book's targeted audience:           ____/10
 5. Presentation showed equal distribution of group member participation:         ____/10
 6. Presentation was sensibly organized with flow of content:                     ____/10
 7. Presentation remained within the 50-minute time constraints:                  ____/10
 8. Discussion remained within the 15-minute time constraints:                    ____/10
 9. Discussion encouraged respectful, informative question and answer responsiveness:  ____/10
10. Presenters gave resources at the end of their presentation:                   ____/10

# CHAPTER 4

# All Buttoned Up

*Jennifer E. Randall Reyes, Christine J. Schimmel, and Edward E. Jacobs*

## Course Recommendations

| SOCIAL JUSTICE AND ADVOCACY PRINCIPLES | CORE CACREP STANDARDS | COUNSELING SPECIALIZATION |
|---|---|---|
| ☑ Social Construct of Oppression and Privilege<br>☑ Intersection of Oppression | ☑ Group Work<br>☑ Human Growth and Development<br>☑ Professional Counseling Orientation and Ethical Practice<br>☑ Social and Cultural Diversity | ☑ Clinical Mental Health Counseling<br>☑ Marriage, Couple, and Family Counseling<br>☑ School Counseling<br>☑ Student Affairs and College Counseling |

## TOPIC

Identity is rarely as simple as checking a box on a demographic sheet. This activity explores the intersectionality (Jun, 2010) of identity by using a multi-sensory approach to examining how our hot button topics influence our behavior, beliefs, and work as professional counselors.

## LEARNING OBJECTIVES

1. Participants will increase their awareness of the various identities that are choices, and those that are not.
2. Participants will explore how their subscription to various identities impacts their perspective of whom they are in both their personal and professional life.
3. Participants will compare and contrast their various identities through group processing.

## TARGET POPULATION

Pre-professional counseling students at both the undergraduate and graduate levels

## GROUP SIZE

20–30

## TIME REQUIRED

At least 90 minutes, which could vary with class size, to increase participation on the part of all students. It should be noted that graduate students may be able to participate at a slightly deeper level than undergraduate students, and it is therefore recommended that more time be allotted.

## SETTING

A traditional classroom setting is sufficient. Leaders of this activity should also construct the room in such a way that it allows participants to freely move as needed.

## MATERIALS NEEDED

Activity leaders will need to collect or purchase buttons for all participants to have several buttons (three to five each). Buttons should be of various shapes, sizes, and colors.

## INSTRUCTIONS FOR CONDUCTING ACTIVITY

1. Setting up the activity (5–10 minutes):
   a. Place all buttons on a table toward the front of the room. The table should touch a wall so that there is a barrier from students accessing buttons placed at the back of the table by simply walking around the table. Place larger buttons toward the front of the table and smaller buttons toward the back, where it is more difficult for students to reach them.
   b. Activity leader explains that students will be thinking about their own demographic identities and selecting multiple buttons to represent the categories that make up their identities. Activity leader visually illustrates (this could be projected at the front of the classroom on a board, whiteboard, smart board, overhead projector, PowerPoint, etc.) the following demographic categories for participants to see as they are selecting their buttons: race, gender, age, ability level, sexual orientation, language, political views, religious views, socioeconomic status (SES), occupational identity (either former identities such as military background and/or the distinction between clinical mental health and school counselors).
2. Activity leader provides invitation to participate (2–3 minutes):
   a. Experiential education is about choice and electing to be a voluntary member of this group.
   b. Should you feel uncomfortable at any point, you may choose to return to your seat and sit quietly or come to the activity leader for help and support.
   c. Activity leader then has students who are participating number off from 1 to 4 throughout the room.
3. Introduction to the activity and instructions (2–3 minutes):
   a. Allowing enough space for one another to explore concepts with respect and a commitment from the classroom, use foundational rules that encourage dialogue rather than debate.
   b. Select as many buttons as you need to represent the identities you feel best represent you as a person.
4. Participants select buttons (5–7 minutes):
   a. The activity leader keeps time and states that there will only be 5 minutes total to pick buttons. Participants that numbered off as the "1s" get to go first, and the activity leader describes this group as white males. They are asked to stand first and come get their buttons. After a full minute, the "2s" are asked to stand and come get their buttons, while being identified as white women. (Activity leader can consider allowing extra time for the "1s" even though they were initially only

given 1 minute.) After another full minute, the "3s" are asked to do the same and are identified as men of color by the activity leader. Finally, the "4s" are asked to take their turn after another full minute. The activity leader identifies this final group as women of color.

5.  Participants return to their seat and take out a piece of paper or electronic device to reflect in writing about why they chose the buttons that they did to represent the categories that make up their identity. Participants should be given the verbal instruction that they will have at least 5–10 minutes to briefly summarize their initial reflections, knowing that they will need adequate time for the group processing. (5–10 minutes).

6.  Activity leader then asks participants to get up and move around the room to get into groups of three to four participants to discuss their initial reflections.

Activity leader: "Mill around the room and get with two to three other folks and share your thoughts about the buttons you have chosen, what they represent to you, and any interesting thoughts you had as you sit and reflect on your choices. What was the experience like of having to reach toward the back of the table or work around the other groups that were already at the table, or have less time when you couldn't simply walk around the table to make that task easier? How does that relate to what you know of currently of the concepts of privilege, social justice, and minority status? We will do this for about 15 minutes. Be sure that open dialogue is encouraged in your small group, and remember, this is not a time for debate, but rather sharing and listening."

Activity leader should circulate around the room at this time to encourage participants to all be sharing equally in their smaller group, while monitoring that there is dialogue rather than debate happening. Activity leader is constantly monitoring for safety throughout this activity, but especially while participants are in these smaller groups processing. Time allotted for this portion of the activity is dependent on developmental levels of participants and their level of comfort with one another in sharing (15–20 minutes).

7.  Activity leader then has participants move back into a whole class and requests volunteers (getting at least one-quarter of the total participants) to individually share their written reflections, or their experiences of sharing in their small group discussion aloud (5–10 minutes).

Activity leader: "Now that you have had a chance to share in small groups, I would love for some of you to share how that experience was for you."

8.  Activity leader ensures that there is time to wrap up this discussion by conducting a final, closing round. Give students the following prompt and let them know that everyone will have a chance to speak.

Activity leader: "Let's take a few final minutes to reflect with either a word or a short phrase of what stood out to you about this experience today. In other words, what are you taking away?"

# DISCUSSION

The activity leader should, after allowing for many of the participants to share in large group, begin to more deeply process the activity by asking the following prompts:

•   What were your initial reactions to the various stipulations on who got to choose buttons first? What were your reactions to the different time constraints placed on you to make your choices? What was your reaction to group 1 being given more time? Where might you place additional groups, such as LGBT populations, into this scenario? What about socioeconomic status?
•   How did it feel to share your buttons?
•   What does this experience have you thinking about or processing?
•   How is this exercise impacting you personally?

- How do you think this exercise is impacting you as a professional (i.e., how is the awareness that is being highlighted in this exercise likely to impact your work as a helper/counselor/social worker/ psychologist, etc.)?
- Which buttons that you may be uncovering in this exercise are likely to trip you up or cause you to get stuck as a helper? What work do you need to do to attempt to understand those buttons and address them appropriately?

## BIBLIOGRAPHY

Jacobs, E., & Schimmel, C. J. (2013). *Impact therapy: The courage to counsel*. Morgantown, WV: Impact Therapy Associates.
Jun, H. (2010). *Social justice, multicultural counseling and practice: Beyond a conventional approach*. Thousand Oaks, CA: Sage Publications.

## SUGGESTED BACKGROUND READING

Jun, H. (2010). The millennium and two essential ingredients for multicultural competencies. In *Social justice, multicultural counseling and practice: Beyond a conventional approach* (pp. 1–12). Thousand Oaks, CA: Sage Publications.

# CHAPTER 5

# Digital Storytelling

*Sarah Campbell and Michael Jones*

## Course Recommendations

| SOCIAL JUSTICE AND ADVOCACY PRINCIPLES | CORE CACREP STANDARDS | COUNSELING SPECIALIZATION |
|---|---|---|
| ☑ Cycle of Socialization and Liberation<br>☑ Social Constructs of Oppression and Privilege<br>☑ Intersection of Oppression<br>☑ Strategies for Change | ☑ Group Work<br>☑ Helping Relationships<br>☑ Human Growth and Development<br>☑ Social and Cultural Diversity | ☑ Addiction Counseling<br>☑ Clinical Mental Health Counseling<br>☑ Marriage, Couple, and Family Counseling<br>☑ School Counseling<br>☑ Student Affairs and College Counseling |

## TOPIC

This activity will help students develop a greater understanding of social justice advocacy and how they can empower individuals who are systematically disadvantaged.

## LEARNING OBJECTIVES

- Increases self-awareness through students engaging in reflective practices and dialogue of their internal and external experiences
- Promotes students to decode their reality and unveil myths about their reality
- Supports students in achieving critical consciousness
- Supports students in their transformational process of becoming a social justice advocate
- Promotes transformative action

## TARGET POPULATION

Graduate counselors and counselor educators in training

## GROUP SIZE

5–15 people

# TIME REQUIRED

- Preparation: 3–4 hours to create the digital story
- Processing: 1–3 hours to process in a group setting each student's digital story. The processing time will vary depending on the number of students who do the activity.
- Three hours would be the maximum amount of time needed to process.

# SETTING

This activity can be conducted in a traditional on-ground teaching environment or in an online teaching environment. The only difference for online students would be that the processing of the activity would need to be in a video-based, online environment to allow all students the opportunity to engage with the digital story.

# MATERIALS NEEDED

- Students would need to have access to the slideshow presentation software (PowerPoint, Prezi, Animoto, etc).
- Digital media (pictures, music, video clips, literary work, etc.).
- Computer.
- If the student is doing the digital story in an online class they would also need to use video software such as Adobe Connect, Zoom, etc. in order to share the video with the rest of the class

# INSTRUCTIONS FOR CONDUCTING ACTIVITY

1. Students will create a digital story, ranging from 3 minutes and 30 seconds up to 5 minutes.
   a. In this story, the student will reflect on a time in their life when they witnessed or personally experienced marginalization, oppression, or privilege. These would be examples of events where an individual or group was in need of social justice advocacy.
   b. They can respond in one of two ways:
      i. If the student intervened as a social justice advocate, they will describe in their story the motivation behind their effort to get involved, describe the emotional impact their actions had upon them, describe the process of how they got involved in the advocacy project, and report if they reached their desired goal of the advocacy project.
      ii. If the student did not intervene as a social justice advocate, they will describe what barriers kept them from getting involved, discuss the emotional impact of not getting involved, describe what they could have done to get involved, and reveal what their desired outcome of the project would have been.
2. Student will use the slideshow presentation software, digital media, and computer to put together their digital story that follows the preceding guidelines.
   a. Due to this being a digital story, the students are not allowed to use their voice in the digital story. The digital story will tell the story for the students.
   b. Once the assignment is complete, the students can share their digital story with their peers in class and process with each other about the experience they had in regard to the advocacy project.

# DISCUSSION

- The debriefing process includes processing within the group and a post-activity journal assignment. Dialogue and reflection are essential components of students achieving critical consciousness, which leads to transformation.
- The debriefing process will include opportunities for students to participate in both of these practices. Students will first debrief in the group, once all students have an opportunity to present their digital stories. Students will also be given a journal assignment to complete following the group debriefing.
- Some topics/questions for use in the group debriefing and/or the follow up journal assignment may include:
  1. Please take a few minutes to reflect on your experience creating your digital story and share anything you can about your experience.
  2. Please take a few minutes to reflect on your experience participating in the group processing and share anything you can about your experience.
  3. Please share in detail any feelings generated from your participation in this digital storytelling experience.
  4. What thoughts, if any, about your experience participating in this digital storytelling activity stand out to you and why?
  5. What new awareness, if any, was generated from your participation in this digital storytelling activity?
  6. Is there any other information or insight you feel was significant with reference to your participation in this digital storytelling experience and your personal and professional growth as a counselor-in-training?
  7. How do you foresee your participation in this digital storytelling activity affecting others in your life or those you may encounter as a counselor-in-training and professional counselor?
  8. Please reflect on your participation in this study and share how you understand the effect or potential effect of your experience on your future as a counselor-in-training and social justice advocate?

# BIBLIOGRAPHY

Briant, K. J., Halter, A., Marchello, N., Escareo, M., & Thompson, B. (2016). The power of digital storytelling as a culturally relevant health promotion tool. *Health Promotion Practice, 17*(6), 793–801. doi:10.1177/1524839916658023

Campbell, S. (2015). *Mental health counselor trainees' advocacy identity development: A qualitative study* (Doctoral dissertation). Retrieved from ProQuest database. (Order No. 10002502).

Freire, P. (1970). *Pedagogy of the oppressed* (M. B. Ramos, Trans.). New York: Seabury Press.

Grant, N. S., & Bolin, B. L. (2016). Digital storytelling: A method for engaging students and increasing cultural competency. *Journal of Effective Teaching, 16*(3), 44–61.

Ratts, M. J., & Wood, C. (2011). The fierce urgency of now: Diffusion of innovation as a mechanism to integrate social justice in counselor education. *Counselor Education & Supervision, 50*(3), 207–222.

Shelton, C., Warren, A., & Archambault, L. (2016). Exploring the use of interactive digital storytelling video: Promoting student engagement and learning in a university hybrid course. *Techtrends: Linking Research & Practice to Improve Learning, 60*(5), 465–474. doi:10.1007/s11528-016-0082-z

# SUGGESTED BACKGROUND READING

Brady-Amoon, P., Makhija, N., Dixon, V., & Dator, J. (2012). Social justice: Pushing past boundaries in graduate training. *Journal for Social Action in Counseling & Psychology, 4*(2), 85–99.

Ceja Alcal, J., Austin, M., Granroth, M., & Hewitt, B. (2016). Online inclusive pedagogy: A call-and-response dialogue on digital storytelling. *Education for Information, 32*(1), 71–85. doi:10.3233/EFI-150963

Chang, C. Y., Crethar, H. C., & Ratts, M. J. (2010). Social justice: A national imperative for counselor education and supervision. *Counselor Education & Supervision, 50*(2), 82–87.

De Vecchi, N., Kenny, A., Dickson-Swift, V., & Kidd, S. (2016). How digital storytelling is used in mental health: A scoping review. *International Journal of Mental Health Nursing, 25*(3), 183–193. doi:10.1111/inm.12206

Freire, P. (1992). *Pedagogy of the oppressed.* New York: Continuum.

Matias, C. E., & Grosland, T. J. (2016). Digital storytelling as racial justice. *Journal of Teacher Education, 67*(2), 152–164. doi:10.1177/0022487115624493

Odegard, M. A., & Vereen, L. G. (2010). A grounded theory of counselor educators integrating social justice into their pedagogy. *Counselor Education & Supervision, 50*(2), 130–149.

Ratts, M. (2009). Social justice counseling: Toward the development of a fifth force among counseling paradigms. *Journal of Humanistic Counseling, Education & Development, 48*(2), 160–172.

West-Olatunji, C. (2010). If not now, when? Advocacy, social justice, and counselor education. *Counseling & Human Development, 42*(8), 1–12.

# CHAPTER 6

# How We Got Here
## Empathy in the Land of Immigrants

*Sinem Akay-Sullivan and Jeffrey M. Sullivan*

## Course Recommendations

| SOCIAL JUSTICE AND ADVOCACY PRINCIPLES | CORE CACREP STANDARDS | COUNSELING SPECIALIZATION |
|---|---|---|
| ☑ Cycle of Socialization and Liberation<br>☑ Social Constructs of Oppression and Privilege | ☑ Group Work<br>☑ Helping Relationships<br>☑ Professional Counseling Orientation and Ethical Practice<br>☑ Social and Cultural Diversity | ☑ Clinical Mental Health Counseling<br>☑ Marriage, Couple, and Family Counseling<br>☑ School Counseling<br>☑ Student Affairs and College Counseling |

## TOPIC

Helping students to understand the nature of negative bias toward immigrants. Encouraging the students to help break the cycle of socialization to promote social justice for immigrants.

## LEARNING OBJECTIVES

1. Helping students to understand their own family origins from an immigration perspective
2. Increasing student knowledge related to societal attitudes toward immigrants and the cycle of socialization that contributes to discrimination
3. Encouraging empathy toward immigrants and immigrant communities
4. Facilitating discussions about the roles that counselors can play to break the cycle of socialization and promote social justice

## TARGET POPULATION

Counseling students in the first semester of their master's education

## GROUP SIZE

10–25 students. The class will be divided into small groups for this activity (three to five people in each group). A class discussion will be held after the activity is completed within the small groups.

# TIME REQUIRED

1.5–2 hours for a group of 10–15 students; 2–3 hours for a group of 15–25 students. More time may be needed for groups with more diverse backgrounds.

# SETTING

This activity will be best conducted in a classroom setting to allow for open discussion without any interruptions. Each small group will gather around a table. If tables are not available, small desks can be grouped together to create a larger work space. If neither option is feasible, the instructor can tape the papers on the walls of the classroom with enough space between papers to make the discussion within the groups easier.

# MATERIALS NEEDED

- The instructor will need to print out pictures of immigrants from the New York Public Library Digital Collections website. (Go to https://digitalcollections.nypl.org and search for "Ellis Island Photographs.")
- Direct link for the website: https://digitalcollections.nypl.org/collections/ellis-island-photographs-from-the-collection-of-william-williams-commissioner#/?tab=about&scroll=36
- Each small group should have one to two pictures. The number of the pictures given to each group will depend on the class size and time limitations.
- Each small group will need a large paper and two to three markers with different colors.
- Scotch tape will be provided for students to tape their finalized paper on the walls for class presentation.

# INSTRUCTIONS FOR CONDUCTING ACTIVITY

1. Two weeks before this activity, assign students homework to ask their family members about their family origins. Encourage students to gather immigration stories and pictures if available.
   a. Let the students know that this assignment of gathering information, pictures, and stories will not be graded but it is highly encouraged to make the upcoming activity more meaningful. This will prevent students from being marginalized and feeling excluded if they are unable to obtain information or prefer not to share it with the class.
2. In class, first have an introduction to the topic by discussing with students the cycle of socialization (Griffin, Bell & Adams, 2007). Facilitate a discussion about how the cycle of socialization works and how people contribute to continuation of oppression toward minorities.
3. Give picture(s) of immigrants who came to the U.S. in the early 1900s to the small groups and read the history of the pictures from the New York Public Library website: https://digitalcollections.nypl.org/collections/ellis-island-photographs-from-the-collection-of-william-williams-commissioner#/?tab=about
4. Ask students to come up with the history of the person/people in the picture(s) within their small groups. Tell them to make assumptions about the people looking at their physical appearances, postures, facial expressions, clothing, etc.
5. Ask small groups to take turns and share with the classroom the assumptions they made about the people in the pictures. Encourage them to explain their reasons for making these assumptions.
6. Encourage students to point out the ways that they are like and not like the people that are being described.

7. Tell the students which countries the people in the pictures were coming from and ask them if this information changed their presumptions.
8. Connect the discussion about the cycle of socialization to the stereotypes and presumptions students had about the people in the pictures.
9. After the discussions about the pictures are finalized, encourage the students to share their own family immigration/migration history with the class.
10. Help students to see the similarities between the people in the pictures and their own ancestors.
11. Facilitate a discussion about judgment of people by their looks and their status as immigrants, and connect the discussion to the cycle of socialization.
12. Open a discussion about promoting social justice through awareness and action as aspiring counselors.

## DISCUSSION

1. What feelings do you have when you look at the pictures of immigrants who came to the U.S. in the early 1900s?
2. Why do you think they came here?
3. What are the feelings that the people in the picture might have at the time of entering the U.S.?
4. Have you ever felt the way that you imagine the person in the picture might be feeling? (Encourage students to give details about their own experiences if possible.)
5. What do you think they needed most when they first got here? How do you think they were treated by the locals?
6. How do you think they overcame the obstacles they might have faced?
7. How do you think their experiences right after they entered the U.S. impacted following generations?
8. In what ways are the people in the pictures like you? In what ways were they similar to your own ancestors?
9. What are the reasons for the presumptions that you had about the person/the people in the picture? Looks, facial expressions, cleanliness, skin color, etc.
10. Where do you think these assumptions are coming from?
11. Did your assumptions change after figuring out their countries of origin? How? Why?
12. What are the obstacles that your own ancestors experienced, if any?
13. How do you think these experiences impacted your family culture over the long term?
14. How can counselors contribute to or help break the cycle of socialization?

## BIBLIOGRAPHY

Gerber, D. A. (2011). *American immigration: A very short introduction*. Oxford: Oxford University Press.
Griffin, P., Bell, L. A., & Adams, M. (2007). *Teaching for diversity and social justice*. New York: Routledge.

## SUGGESTED BACKGROUND READING

Gerber, D. A. (2011). *American immigration: A very short introduction*. Oxford: Oxford University Press.
University of South Carolina. (n.d.). *Understanding the cycle of socialization*. Retrieved from https://sc.edu/eop/trainings/Cycle_ofSocializationHandout.pdf

# CHAPTER 7

# Awareness of Social Injustices

*Michelle Ghoston*

## Course Recommendations

| SOCIAL JUSTICE AND ADVOCACY PRINCIPLES | CORE CACREP STANDARDS | COUNSELING SPECIALIZATION |
|---|---|---|
| ☑ What Is Social Justice and Advocacy?<br>☑ Social Construct of Oppression and Privilege<br>☑ Intersections of Oppression<br>☑ Strategies for Change | ☑ Helping Relationships<br>☑ Social and Cultural Diversity | ☑ Clinical Mental Health Counseling<br>☑ Marriage, Couple, and Family Counseling<br>☑ School Counseling<br>☑ Student Affairs and College Counseling |

## TOPIC

Challenging novice counselors to identify incidents of injustice that are observed in their day-to-day lives. Further challenging students to acknowledge their own areas of privilege and how they may advocate for marginalized groups.

## LEARNING OBJECTIVES

1. Learn to recognize social injustices and microaggressions.
2. Learn to acknowledge one's own privilege.
3. Learn to assess and acknowledge one's own reactions to injustices happening in one's day-to-day life.
4. Learn to view situations from the perspective of others.
5. Learn that social injustices happen all around us on a regular basis.

## TARGET POPULATION

This activity is suited for all levels of counseling students and professionals.

## GROUP SIZE

The number of participants can vary according to the size of the class (5–50).

# TIME REQUIRED

Students are allowed two to three weeks between identifying an observation and completing the assignment. The group size, number of participants, and participant demographics do not alter this activity.

# SETTING

The activity is designed for a classroom over the course of a semester. It is intended that once a student has personally observed a social injustice (cannot be something told to them by a third party or something seen on any form of media), they post/write about the event via Blackboard (or some medium that would allow their peers to read and comment on the event/observation). This activity can be done with any demographic.

# MATERIALS NEEDED

A source by which to post and read observations (computer or smartphone) and a medium such as Blackboard to set up posting options.

Two precautions are given to the students. First, you are not to put yourself in harms' way to intervene in any situation(s) you perceive to be a social injustice. Talking about these situations with a supervisor, advisor, or professor may be helpful to sort out your feelings, thoughts, and beliefs. Second, acknowledge that friends, family, or even you may engage in social injustices and that can be difficult to accept. Again, talking about these situations with a supervisor, advisor, or professor may be helpful to sort out your feelings, thoughts, and beliefs.

# INSTRUCTIONS FOR CONDUCTING ACTIVITY

1. Instructor explains/defines what is a social injustice. A video clip is shown to demonstrate an example.
2. Visit www.facebook.com/Upworthy/videos/1141203362587187/.
3. Instructor indicates that these are things that are observed going forward from the day the instructions are given and beyond (not something that occurred in the past).
4. Instructor indicates that the event should be observed occurring to someone else or themselves. It cannot be something told to them, read about, or viewed on any form of media (printed or electronic).
5. Once the event/situation has been observed, the student should post details about the event.
   a. What did they observe?
   b. What was their reaction?
   c. How would they address a similar situation if a client indicates the same event/situation happening to them?
6. Students are to respond to two social injustice posts made by their peers. The response can be that of:
   • Concern
   • Questions
   • Expression of one's own feelings
   • Thoughts, behaviors, or beliefs as they relate to what their peer(s) has posted
   Discussions in Blackboard are encouraged. If the author of the post wishes they may respond to their peers, thus allowing for deeper discussions about the event or situation.
7. Instructor will monitor all posts and select three or four posts to be discussed in class following the due date. If there is a topic believed to be too sensitive to discuss with the entire class the author of the post should be in contact with the instructor prior to the class meeting.

8. Students are asked to make three separate posts over the course of the semester (specific due dates are set and identified in the syllabus).

## DISCUSSION

The students can debrief in three separate ways. First, students are encouraged to seek out their academic advisors if needed to discuss an event/situation related to this activity that could create stress or discomfort for them. Second, students are encouraged to discuss the noted event(s)/situation(s) on Blackboard. This allows support and feedback directly from their peers and the instructor, when necessary and appropriate. Finally, students are provided time in the classroom to discuss postings, events, and situations about which they remain unclear, concerned, or in some way distressed.

## BIBLIOGRAPHY

Lee, A. Poch, R., Shaw, M. & Williams, R. (2012). Practicing a pedagogy that engages diversity. *ASHE Higher Education Report*, 38(2), 83–101.

Ratts, M. J., Singh, A. A., Nassar-McMillan, S., Butler, S. K., & McCullough, J. R. (2016). Multicultural and social justice counseling competencies: Guidelines for the counseling profession. *Journal of Multicultural Counseling and Development*, 44(1), 28–48.

## SUGGESTED BACKGROUND READING

Ratts, M. J., Singh, A. A., Nassar-McMillan, S., Butler, S. K., & McCullough, J. R. (2016). Multicultural and social justice counseling competencies: Guidelines for the counseling profession. *Journal of Multicultural Counseling and Development*, 44(1), 28–48.

# CHAPTER 8

## Observing Our Community
### Examining the Social and Cultural Constructs That Impact Power and Privilege

*Tamara J. Hinojosa and Rebecca A. Palomo*

### Course Recommendations

| SOCIAL JUSTICE AND ADVOCACY PRINCIPLES | CORE CACREP STANDARDS | COUNSELING SPECIALIZATION |
|---|---|---|
| ☑ Social Constructs of Oppression and Privilege | ☑ Social and Cultural Diversity | ☑ Clinical Mental Health Counseling<br>☑ Marriage, Couple, and Family Counseling<br>☑ School Counseling<br>☑ Student Affairs and College Counseling |

## TOPIC

The focus of this activity is on learning how social and cultural constructs contribute to oppression.

## LEARNING OBJECTIVES

1. Students will discover and dissect social and cultural constructs that impact a selected group of historically marginalized individuals.
2. Students will propose helpful counseling and advocacy methods for their selected group of historically marginalized individuals.

## TARGET POPULATION

The target population for this activity is counseling graduate students who are in a social and cultural diversity course and who are aware of the definition and role of counselors as advocates. We also recommend this activity for students who are gaining awareness of the social and cultural constructs that impact the power and privilege of individuals.

# GROUP SIZE

This activity is conducted by individual students and then presented to the entire class. Therefore, this would work with classes of all sizes.

# TIME REQUIRED

This activity is a project conducted by individual students that will require either the whole semester or several weeks.

# SETTING

This activity will occur partially in the classroom and partially in students' local communities.

# MATERIALS NEEDED

- PowerPoint or handout providing instructions for students
- Resources for students to present their final project (e.g., computer, projector, etc.)

# INSTRUCTIONS FOR CONDUCTING ACTIVITY

Instructors will first facilitate a lecture and discussion about societal and cultural constructs and how they can impact individuals (see list later in chapter for suggested readings on this topic).

Next, instructors can provide the following instructions to students:

1. Select a group of individuals that has experienced historical marginalization (e.g., women, older adults, people with disabilities).
2. Take a field trip to a community resource or location that is open to the public, to learn more about this group. Please note that the purpose of this field trip is to visit a public space in which you can observe the environment without violating anyone's privacy (for more clarification on this see Mulhall, 2003). During your field trip take observational notes documenting the following:
   - How this environment seems to impact the group you are learning about
   - Your own internal thoughts and reactions
   Examples of community resources or locations include:
   - Visiting a women's clothing store and observing the types of items being sold at this store, the store decorations, advertisements, etc.
   - Visiting a theme park and observing the resources available to people with disabilities
3. Using your field trip notes, write a five to seven page critical analysis addressing the following points:
   - Describe the group you selected and describe the community resource or location you visited.
   - Based on what you observed during your field trip, explain what you learned about the social and cultural constructs that seem to impact your selected group.
   - As a counselor, discuss how you could work effectively with this client population. Include relevant theories, counseling techniques, and counseling goals.
   - As an advocate, what are strategies you could implement to empower this group?
4. Students will present their findings and what they learned to the class with an emphasis on applicability to diversity, social justice, and advocacy. After each presentation, students will have time to take questions and comments from their peers as well.

# DISCUSSION

After all students have presented their paper to the class, instructors can facilitate a discussion about what students have learned. Helpful debriefing questions include:

- What was it like to learn about various groups and the way social and cultural constructs have impacted their lives?
- After hearing your classmates present, how have your perceptions of privilege and oppression changed?
- How do we promote awareness of these social and cultural constructs?
- How do we as counselors work to challenge some of these social and cultural constructs that can be strongly embedded in our everyday lives?

# BIBLIOGRAPHY

Fickling, M. J., & González, L. M. (2016). Linking multicultural counseling and social justice through advocacy. *Journal of Counselor Leadership and Advocacy, 3*(2), 85–94. doi:10.1080/2326716X.2015.1124814

Gess, J. (2016). Social justice in counselor education: Teaching advocacy across the core. *Journal of Counselor Leadership and Advocacy, 3*(2), 124–134. doi:10.1080/2326716X.2015.1133334

Hipolito-Delgado, C. P., Cook, J. M., Avrus, E. M., & Bonham, E. J. (2011). Developing counseling students' multicultural competence through the multicultural action project. *Counselor Education and Supervision, 50*(6), 402–421. doi:10.1002/j.1556-6978.2011.tb01924.x

Manis, A. A. (2012). A review of the literature on promoting cultural competence and social justice agency among students and counselor trainees: Piecing the evidence together to advance pedagogy and research. *Professional Counselor, 2*(1), 48–57.

Mulhall, A. (2003). In the field: Notes on observation in qualitative research. *Journal of Advanced Nursing, 41*(3), 306–313. doi:10.1046/j.1365-2648.2003.02514.x

# SUGGESTED BACKGROUND READING

Anderson, S. K., & Middleton, V. A. (2011). *Explorations in diversity: Examining privilege and oppression in a multicultural society*. Belmont, CA: Cengage Learning.

Lee, M. A., Smith, T. J., & Henry, R. G. (2013). Power politics: Advocacy to activism in social justice counseling. *Journal for Social Action in Counseling and Psychology, 5*(3), 70–94.

MacLeod, B. P. (2013). Social justice at the microlevel: Working with clients' prejudices. *Journal of Multicultural Counseling and Development, 41*(3), 169–184. doi:10.1002/j.2161-1912.2013.00035.x

Robinson-Wood, T. (2017). *The convergence of race, ethnicity, and gender: Multiple identities in counseling* (5th ed.). Los Angeles, CA: Sage Publications.

Singh, A., Urbano, A., Haston, M., & McMahan, E. (2010). School counselors' strategies for social justice change: A grounded theory of what works in the real world. *Professional School Counseling, 13*(3), 135–145. doi:10.5330/PSC.n.2010-13.13

# CHAPTER 9

## Who's Left Out Sticker Activity

*Katrina Cook and Mary G. Mayorga*

### Course Recommendations

| SOCIAL JUSTICE AND ADVOCACY PRINCIPLES | CORE CACREP STANDARDS | COUNSELING SPECIALIZATION |
|---|---|---|
| ☑ Cycle of Socialization and Liberation<br>☑ Social Constructs of Oppression and Privilege<br>☑ Strategies for Change | ☑ Group Work<br>☑ Helping Relationships<br>☑ Human Growth and Development<br>☑ Professional Counseling Orientation and Ethical Practice<br>☑ Social and Cultural Diversity | ☑ Addiction Counseling<br>☑ Clinical Mental Health Counseling<br>☑ Marriage, Couple, and Family Counseling<br>☑ School Counseling<br>☑ Student Affairs and College Counseling |

## TOPIC

The primary focus of the activity is for students to identify how people are left out of groups. Students may also use this activity when they provide group counseling.

## LEARNING OBJECTIVES

- Students will understand how cliques form and how some individuals are left out of groups.
- The instructor will model how to conduct this activity so students can use it when they provide group counseling.
- Students will identify ways they can advocate for their clients by challenging the institutionalized inequalities and status quo.

## TARGET POPULATION

This activity is appropriate for adults and children (third grade or older).

## GROUP SIZE

There needs to be enough participants for several subgroups to be formed. A minimum of 15 participants to a maximum of 50 would be suggested.

# TIME REQUIRED

This activity could be completed in 30 minutes most of the time. However, depending on the number of participants, and the depth of the discussion afterward, it could take more time.

# SETTING

The setting can be any classroom setting. Participants will be asked to stand up and move around the room, so there needs to be enough space for them to do that.

# MATERIALS NEEDED

The instructor will need stickers (dot shaped or star shaped) in five different colors. The activity calls on the sticker being placed on the participant's forehead, but some participants may not be comfortable with that. In that case, place the sticker on the shoulder where the participant still cannot see it. However, placing it on the forehead does provide opportunities for participants to see expressions of the faces of the other participants who are rejecting them. Encourage giving the participants a choice.

# INSTRUCTIONS FOR CONDUCTING ACTIVITY

1. Inform participants that they will be participating in an activity, but do not give much information about the nature of the activity.
2. Inform the students that they may not verbally communicate during the activity. All communication must be done by hand gestures or facial expressions.
3. Place a sticker on each participant's forehead (or shoulder if they are not comfortable with the forehead). Have three to four groups with the same color. However, reserve one colored sticker so that only one participant has that color.
4. Ask the participants to find the group they "belong to" by gathering with other people who have the same color sticker they have.
5. As participants look for their group, it will become evident that one participant does not match any of the other groups and is alone.
6. Discuss the activity using the following questions.

# DISCUSSION

Address all participants first, and then individually address the participant that was left out:

1. What was this activity like for you?
2. How did you find the group that you "belonged to"?
3. What was it like for you when other groups did not include you?
4. How could you (as a member of either the majority group or the minority group) challenge the status quo or systemic inequalities inherent in the process of the activity? What would be the benefits and risks of this approach?
5. From a social justice perspective, what would be the benefits and risks of providing counseling services for the individual who was isolated?
6. From a social justice perspective, what would be the benefits and risks of promoting self-advocacy for the individual who was isolated?

7.  As the individual who was isolated, what did you most want or need from the majority group?
8.  What did you learn from this activity?
9.  How could you use this activity in your own counseling practice?

## BIBLIOGRAPHY

Cook, K., & Mayorga, M. (2014, October). *Creative activities to help counseling students understand unearned privilege.* Paper presentation at the meeting of the Rocky Mountain Counseling Association for Counselor Education and Supervision, Jackson Lake, WY.

Jerome, B. (2017, January 24). *Stars for diversity: Teaching tolerance: A project of the Southern Poverty Law Center.* Perspectives (Online resource exchange page). Retrieved from www.tolerance.org/exchange/starts-diversity

Vera, M. E., & Speight, S. L. (2003). Multicultural competence, social justice, and counseling psychology: Expanding our roles. *The Counseling Psychologist, 31*(3), 253–272.

## SUGGESTED BACKGROUND READING

Brammer, R. (2012). *Diversity in counseling* (2nd ed.). Belmont, CA: Brooks/Cole.

# CHAPTER 10

## Building Awareness of Privilege and Oppression
### A Resource Access Activity

*Jennifer Greene-Rooks and Maria Haiyasoso*

### Course Recommendations

| SOCIAL JUSTICE AND ADVOCACY PRINCIPLES | CORE CACREP STANDARDS | COUNSELING SPECIALIZATION |
|---|---|---|
| ☑ What Is Social Justice and Advocacy?<br>☑ Social Constructs of Oppression and Privilege<br>☑ Intersections of Oppression | ☑ Professional Counseling Orientation and Ethical Practice<br>☑ Social and Cultural Diversity | ☑ Clinical Mental Health Counseling<br>☑ School Counseling<br>☑ Student Affairs and College Counseling |

## TOPIC

This experiential activity is a lead-in to learning about social justice by connecting the concept of privilege to having access to physical and social resources and oppression as a lack of access to needed resources.

## LEARNING OBJECTIVES

- Understanding privilege as having access to more resources (physical and through assistance)
- Understanding oppression as having less access and support
- Connecting social justice to concepts of privilege and oppression

## TARGET POPULATION

This activity is designed for master's-level counselor education students but could be adapted for children or adolescents in schools.

## GROUP SIZE

8–32 people broken up into four-person groups

## TIME REQUIRED

20–30 minutes

## SETTING

Designed to be conducted in a classroom setting

## MATERIALS NEEDED

- A variety of blocks (Lego-type and wooden); about five blocks per person in the room
- Wooden sticks (e.g., popsicle sticks or tongue depressors)
- String (skein of yarn works as well)
- Paper clips—about 100
- Cotton balls
- School glue—one per group
- Scissors—one per group
- Markers

## INSTRUCTIONS FOR CONDUCTING ACTIVITY

- Task for all groups: create a tall, free-standing building.
- Instructions for all groups before you begin: you will work as a group with the supplies given to you. You may only use the provided supplies.
  - This task is timed. At the end of the timed task, all groups will go around the room to see the other groups' structures.
- Each group will be given separate written instructions as described in the following. Instructor should hand out the supplies or have the group pick them up along with the individual group instructions.

## Group/Supplies/Instructions

- Group 1
  - Supplies:
    - LEGO-type blocks
    - Wooden blocks
    - Wooden sticks (like tongue depressors)
    - String
    - Paper clips
    - Paper
    - Cotton balls
    - Glue
    - Tape
    - Scissors
  - Instructions: stack blocks.
  - Suggestions: use other supplies such as the string, paper, scissors, etc. to create a door way, backdrops, or other creative pieces (example: a moat, draw bridge). You may ask the instructor for more information, tips, suggestions, or assistance.

- Group 2
  - Supplies:
    - Wooden blocks
    - Wooden sticks (like tongue depressors)
    - String
    - Paper
    - Cotton balls
    - Glue
    - Scissors
    - Markers
  - Instructions: stack blocks.
  - Suggestions: use other supplies to add creative pieces to the structure (example: a door). You may only ask the instructor one time for more information, tips, suggestions, or assistance.
- Group 3
  - Supplies:
    - Wooden sticks (like tongue depressors)
    - String
    - Paper
    - Cotton balls
    - Glue
    - Scissors
    - Markers
  - Instructions: use supplies however you wish and try to be creative. You may not ask the instructor for more information, tips, suggestions, or assistance.
- Group 4
  - Supplies:
    - String
    - Paper
    - Cotton balls
    - Glue
    - Markers
  - Instructions: use supplies provided. You may not ask the instructor for more information, tips, suggestions, or assistance.
- During the activity, circulate among the groups, noticing their reactions. Be available to help group 1 throughout the activity.

# DISCUSSION

After the activity, bring the groups together for processing. Allow them time to express their feelings and what they noticed throughout. Some possible processing questions include:

- How was it to work with your group? With your supplies? With your instructions?
  - How was it to see others have more resources to work with? Fewer resources? To have access to instructor help? Not have access?
  - In the beginning of the activity, what was it like to know others would see your work? What was it like when they actually did see your work?
  - How was it to see others' work?
  - Other observations/thoughts/feelings.
- After the processing, tie the discussion into the topic of privilege and oppression.
  - What was is it like to have access to more/fewer supplies and more/less help?
  - What was it like to notice the other groups having more/less than you did?

- What kind of awareness (or lack of awareness) did you notice in yourself and in others?
- How does that relate to historical or current situations outside this room?
- How would the concept of social justice relate to this activity?

# BIBLIOGRAPHY

Achenbach, K., & Arthur, N. (2002). Experiential learning: Bridging theory to practice in multicultural counseling. *Guidance and Counselling, 17*(2), 39–45.

Arredondo, P. (1999). Multicultural counseling competencies as tools to address oppression and racism. *Journal of Multicultural Counseling & Development, 77*, 102–108.

Arredondo, P., Toporek, R., & Brown, S. P. (1996). Operationalization of the multicultural counseling competencies. *Journal of Multicultural Counseling & Development, 24*, 42–78.

Arthur, N., & Achenbach, K. (2002). Developing multicultural counseling competencies through experiential learning. *Counselor Education & Supervision, 42*, 2–14.

Hays, D. G., Chang, C. Y., & Dean, J. K. (2004). White counselors' conceptualization of privilege and oppression: Implications for counselor training. *Counselor Education and Supervision, 43*, 242–257.

Hays, D. G., Chang, C. Y., & Decker, S. L. (2007). Initial development and psychometric data for the privilege and oppression inventory. *Measurement and Evaluation in Counseling and Development, 40*, 66–79.

Hays, D. G., Dean, J. K., & Chang, C. Y. (2007). Addressing privilege and oppression in counselor training and practice: A qualitative analysis. *Journal of Counseling & Development, 85*, 317–324.

Stadler, H. A., Suh, S., Cobia, D. C., Middleton, R. A., & Carney, J. S. (2006). Reimagining counselor education with diversity as a core. *Counselor Education & Supervision, 45*, 193–206.

# SUGGESTED BACKGROUND READING

Frye, M. (1983). Oppression and the use of definition. In *Politics of Reality: Essays in Feminist Theory*. Berkeley, CA: Crossing Press.

McIntosh, P. (1990). White privilege: Unpacking the invisible knapsack. *Independent School, 49*, 31.

# CHAPTER 11

## My Client's Value Box

### *Mary-Anne Joseph and DeAnna Henderson*

**Course Recommendations**

| SOCIAL JUSTICE AND ADVOCACY PRINCIPLES | CORE CACREP STANDARDS | COUNSELING SPECIALIZATION |
|---|---|---|
| ☑ What Is Social Justice and Advocacy?<br>☑ Cycle of Socialization and Liberation<br>☑ Intersections of Oppression | ☑ Human Growth and Development<br>☑ Professional Counseling Orientation and Ethical Practice<br>☑ Social and Cultural Diversity | ☑ Clinical Mental Health Counseling |

## TOPIC

This activity is intended to assist participants in exploring their personal values and how these values can impact the services they provide to clients from other cultural backgrounds different from their own cultural background. This activity will also assist participants in learning how their cultural values can lead to social injustices for their clients and how they can work to combat these potential issues.

## LEARNING OBJECTIVES

1. To assist participants in surveying their values
2. To assist participants in learning about the values of clients from varying types of cultures
3. To assist participants in assessing how their cultural values can have an impact on social justice issues that may be a challenge for their clients
4. To assist participants in learning how to manage their cultural biases to avoid imposing their values on their clients
5. To assist participants in developing strategies to minimize the social injustices faced by their clients

## TARGET POPULATION

This activity is suited for counseling students and/or counselor trainees.

## GROUP SIZE

This activity is well suited for groups of 8–12 participants.

# TIME REQUIRED

This activity takes approximately 45–60 minutes. The length of time needed to complete the activity may be impacted by the number of members in the group.

# SETTING

This activity can be conducted in a general classroom setting.

# MATERIALS NEEDED

- One or two packs of note cards
- One or two packs of construction paper (ensure that each pack has at least six different colors)
- 8–12 small boxes that are at least 6 inches by 6 inches by 6 inches in size, depending on the amount of participants
- 8–12 pencils with erasers, depending on the amount of participants
- 8–12 magazines, depending on the amount of participants
- 8–12 desks and chairs depending on the amount of participants
- 8–12 black sharpie markers depending on the amount of participants
- 8–12 glue sticks or rolls of clear scotch tape depending on the amount of participants

# INSTRUCTIONS FOR CONDUCTING ACTIVITY

Provide each participant with three note cards.

1. Ask participants to make a list of ten values that are essential to their life on the first note card.
2. Ask participants to rank their values from one to ten, one being the most essential value and ten being the least essential value, and write their values in rank order on the second note card.
3. Ask students to write a list of ten values that are the opposite of their top ten values in the same rank order on the third note card. These opposite values will represent the client's values.
4. Provide each participant with six sheets of construction paper (ensure that each sheet of construction paper is a different color).
5. Ask participants to select a sheet of construction paper to represent their top six values and write the value at the top left side of the appropriate piece of construction paper. The client's value should be written beside each of the participant's values in parentheses. (It may be best to instruct participants to write their value in pencil and then trace over the writing with the black sharpie marker to avoid mistakes.)
6. Provide each participant with one small box.
7. Ask participants to glue or tape one piece of their construction paper where they have written their values and the client's values to each side of their box.
8. Provide each participant with a magazine.
9. Ask participants to select pictures and/or terms from the magazine that represent the client's values and tape/glue these pictures/statements to the appropriate side of the box where the client's value appears.

# DISCUSSION

Once all participants have designed their client's values box ask them to present the box to the group and respond to the following questions:

- What are you top six values and what are your client's top six values?
- How can your values lead to social injustices for your client?
- What strategies can you employ to ensure that your cultural values do not lead to social injustices for your client?
- Ask students what tools they would put in their box to assist them in assisting their clients in overcoming the social injustices they may encounter?

# BIBLIOGRAPHY

Bishop, D. R. (1992). Religious values as cross-cultural issues in counseling. *Counseling and Values*, *36*(3), 179–191.

Comstock, D. L., Hammer, T. R., Strentzsch, J., Cannon, K., Parsons, J., & Salazar II, G. (2008). Relational-cultural theory: A framework for bridging relational, multicultural, and social justice competencies. *Journal of Counseling & Development*, *86*(3), 279–287.

Mifsud, D. (2013). Crossing cultures. *Therapy Today*, *24*(6), 50–51.

Tjeltveit, A. C. (1986). The ethics of value conversion in psychotherapy: Appropriate and inappropriate therapist influence on client values. *Clinical Psychology Review*, *6*(6), 515–537.

# SUGGESTED BACKGROUND READING

Chen-Hayes, S. F. (2001). Social justice advocacy readiness questionnaire. *Journal of Gay & Lesbian Social Services*, *13*(1/2), 191–204.

Comstock, D. L., Hammer, T. R., Strentzsch, J., Cannon, K., Parsons, J., & Salazar II, G. (2008). Relational-cultural theory: A framework for bridging relational, multicultural, and social justice competencies. *Journal of Counseling & Development*, *86*(3), 279–287.

Iwasaki, M. (2005). Mental health and counseling in Japan: A path toward societal transformation. *Journal of Mental Health Counseling*, *27*(2), 129–141.

Kim, B. S., Ng, G. F., & Ahn, A. J. (2005). Effects of client expectation for counseling success, client-counselor worldview match, and client adherence to Asian and European American cultural values on counseling process with Asian Americans. *Journal of Counseling Psychology*, *52*(1), 67. doi:10.1037/0022-0167.52.1.67

Li, L. C., & Kim, B. S. (2004). Effects of counseling style and client adherence to Asian cultural values on counseling process with Asian American college students. *Journal of Counseling Psychology*, *51*(2), 158. doi:10.1037/0022-0167.51.2.158

Mifsud, D. (2013). Crossing cultures. *Therapy Today*, *24*(6), 50–51.

Tjeltveit, A. C. (1986). The ethics of value conversion in psychotherapy: Appropriate and inappropriate therapist influence on client values. *Clinical Psychology Review*, *6*(6), 515–537.

Worthington, E. L. (1988). Understanding the values of religious clients: A model and its application to counseling. *Journal of Counseling Psychology*, *35*(2), 166.

# CHAPTER 12

## A Class Culture of Liberation
### Framing Course Content Through Self and Others

*Megan Dooley Hussmann, Brian Hutchison, and Christina Thaier*

### Course Recommendations

| SOCIAL JUSTICE AND ADVOCACY PRINCIPLES | CORE CACREP STANDARDS | COUNSELING SPECIALIZATION |
|---|---|---|
| ☑ Social Constructs of Oppression and Privilege | ☑ Career Development<br>☑ Helping Relationships<br>☑ Professional Counseling Orientation and Ethical Practice<br>☑ Social and Cultural Diversity<br>☑ Theories | ☑ Addiction Counseling<br>☑ Career Counseling<br>☑ Clinical Mental Health Counseling<br>☑ Marriage, Couple, and Family Counseling<br>☑ School Counseling<br>☑ Student Affairs and College Counseling |

## TOPIC

Based on Paulo Freire's *Pedagogy of the Oppressed*, the purpose of this activity is for students to connect the purpose of the course to the context of their own life on an individual, interpersonal, and political level. By allowing students to give voice to their own experiences, it is communicated to students that they have a knowledge base that is valid and important, and that they are also teachers in this course. In additional to affirming student experiences as a source of knowledge, students will be guided to identify whose voices and experiences they have not been exposed to or have been minimally exposed to in relation to the course content.

## LEARNING OBJECTIVES

- Students will contextualize their own experiences as they relate to the purpose of the course through personal reflection and class dialogue.
- Students will connect with one another by recognizing shared experiences.
- Student will learn from one another by recognizing differences between their own experiences and the experiences of their peers.
- Students will reflect on whose voices and experiences are not represented in the classroom and how those missing voices might impact their educational experience.

# TARGET POPULATION

Any students

# GROUP SIZE

Ideally 20 students

# TIME REQUIRED

2 hours

# SETTING

Classroom

# MATERIALS NEEDED

None

# INSTRUCTIONS FOR CONDUCTING ACTIVITY

This activity is intended to be completed during the first few classes and pairs well with reviewing the syllabus. It will be most effective if some level of trust has already started to form within the group before starting this activity. This activity is also a powerful way to build trust among a group through dialogue.

## Pre-Class Personal Prep Work

Before they come to class, ask students to reflect on their personal connections to the course content. They should journal a response to the follow questions:

- What personal experiences do I have related to the content of the course?
- What do I know about history that has helped shape my personal experiences related to the course?
- Who do I think has had different experiences than me?
- How much do I know about the history of people who have had different experiences than me?
- How can I become more informed about experiences that I have not had?

## In Class Work

1.  INTRODUCTION (20 minutes)
    a.  Explain the purpose of today's class is to engage in dialogue so that we can better understand what our experiences related to the purpose of this course have taught us. We will dialogue about how our experiences might impact what we see and what we might miss related to the content of the course. In order to do this, the class will need to commit to the values of dialogue outlined by Paulo Freire in Chapter 3 of *Pedagogy of the Oppressed*. In the world outside of the classroom it is difficult to ensure that individuals are invested in these values, but as a class community, we are capable of

prioritizing humanism and can use this space to practice what it can look like to pursue liberation pedagogy.
   b.   Review what Freire outlined and ask students for their thoughts. Which of these values are important to students and why? Are there aspects that students can't commit to? What does that mean for the class? It is important that the teacher models each of these elements while facilitating.
   c.   Seek consensus from the class that these are values that they will commit to practicing during this activity, and be prepared to discuss with the class what to do if people won't commit to these. How does that class want to respond if someone does not want to commit to practicing these values? Based on *Pedagogy of the Oppressed*, dialogue requires that we:
      •   Name the world—honor that every human has the right to name the world.
      •   Have a profound love for the world and for people.
      •   Embrace humility.
      •   Have an intense faith in humankind, faith in their power to make, and remake, to create and recreate, faith in their vocation to be more fully human.
      •   Have hope.
      •   Think critically.
2.   GUIDE TO FACILITATING (30 minutes)
   a.   Have the class sit in a circle where every person can see the whole group. The teacher will act as a facilitator through this process.
3.   PERSONAL EXPERIENCES (25 minutes)
   a.   Ask students to share their experiences related to the course content and the historical context that has shaped these experiences. Remind students that the goal of dialogue is to speak their truth and to seek greater understanding of others.
4.   MAKE CONNECTIONS (25 minutes)
   a.   What similarities did they hear in their experiences?
   b.   What does it feel like to have these similarities?
5.   DIFFERENCES AND WHO'S MISSING (20 minutes)
   a.   What differences did they hear in their experiences?
   b.   What does it feel like to have these differences?
   c.   Whose voices weren't included in this dialogue?

# DISCUSSION

## Debrief

•   What was this experience like?
•   What knowledge does this class have?
•   What knowledge is missing?
•   How can we commit to learning about others' experiences as they relate to this course both as a class and as individuals?
•   How does having or not having an awareness of the history that shapes your experience and the experience of others influence your perspective?

## Homework

Have students journal a reaction to the dialogue:

•   What was this activity like for you?
•   How are you connected to oppression and liberation?

## Note to Instructor

Suggested continuing skill reinforcement check-in: have an in-class dialogue or journal assignment prompt at week 5, week 10, and week 15. Have students reflect on:

1.  Are there new insights into how your personal experiences shape the way you relate to the course content covered so far?
2.  How are you connected to oppression and liberation in relation to the course content?
3.  Whose voices have you heard in this class so far and whose voices are missing?
4.  What can you do and what can we as a class do to include those voices?

## BIBLIOGRAPHY

Freire, P. (1970). *Pedagogy of the oppressed*. New York, NY: The Seabury Press.

Martin-Bara, I. (1994). *Writings for a liberation psychology*. Cambridge, MA and London, UK: Harvard University Press.

Moane, G. (2003). Bridging the personal and the political: Practices for a liberation psychology. *American Journal of Community Psychology, 31*(1), 91–101.

## SUGGESTED BACKGROUND READING

Freire, P. (1970). *Pedagogy of the oppressed*. New York, NY: The Seabury Press.

# CHAPTER 13

# Exploring Intersections of Privilege and Oppression

*Madeline Clark*

## Course Recommendations

| SOCIAL JUSTICE AND ADVOCACY PRINCIPLES | CORE CACREP STANDARDS | COUNSELING SPECIALIZATION |
|---|---|---|
| ☑ Intersection of Oppression | ☑ Human Growth and Development<br>☑ Social and Cultural Diversity | ☑ Clinical Mental Health Counseling |

## TOPIC

The focus of this activity is to help students explore their individual sociopolitical relationship to privilege and oppression on various identity factors.

## LEARNING OBJECTIVES

1. Understand and be able to clearly operationalize the definitions of privilege and oppression.
2. Identify the privileged group among various identity factors (i.e., age, ability status, race, etc.)
3. Identify students' own statuses across intersecting identity factors and determine if those statuses are privileged or oppressed.
4. Explore how personal intersections of privilege and oppression impact their lived experiences and their subsequent counseling work.

## TARGET POPULATION

Counseling students or supervisees

## GROUP SIZE

2+

# TIME REQUIRED

Approximately 1 hour. A larger group will likely increase activity length due to time of discussion and processing.

# SETTING

This activity can be utilized in a classroom, group supervision, or triadic supervision.

# MATERIALS NEEDED

Participants will need a writing utensil and writing surface. Facilitator will need to provide worksheets and have a large writing surface, such as a whiteboard.

# INSTRUCTIONS FOR CONDUCTING ACTIVITY

1. Begin the activity by explaining that it will require participants to identify components of their own identity that may make them uncomfortable. Remind students that they can opt out of identifying any personal status that they would not like to reveal on the second worksheet.
2. Review definitions of privilege and oppression with participants. Allow students to operationalize those definitions in pairs or small groups.
3. Hand out two copies of the RESPECTFUL-G worksheet to each participant.
4. As a group/class, operationalize each identity definition (i.e., age, race) and identify what subset of that group is privileged on the whiteboard. For example, when operationalizing gender, you may define that as an individual's particular gender identity and gender expression. The privileged subset of gender would be cisgender males. You will repeat this with each identity factor. Encourage participants to operationalize definitions and identify privileged groups to the best of their ability. Participants will fill these definitions/identities on their first worksheet.
5. At this time, allow participants to complete the second worksheet on their own; this time they will fill out their own identity statuses as they related to the overall group (i.e., a cisgender female will fill in cisgender female for gender).
6. As participants complete the second worksheet, ask them to identify on which identity factors they are privileged (i.e., matching the first worksheet) and identity factors where they experience oppression (not matching the first worksheet).
7. Conclude the activity with processing and discussion of the worksheets.

# DISCUSSION

The facilitator can choose, based on group size, if breaking up participants into a small group for discussion would be appropriate. For classroom sizes, groups of approximately three to six work well.

Discussion prompts include:

1. What was the process of completing this activity for you? What did it make you feel?
2. What did you learn about yourself in relation to others by completing this activity?
3. What was surprising about this activity?
4. How do you believe your intersecting privileges and oppression impact your development? How do they impact your counseling skills and relationships with clients?

5. How does your privileged and/or oppressed identity status(es) impact your work with clients?
6. What implications do the results of this activity have on your social justice identity?
7. What is your primary takeaway from this activity?

Finally, give participants space to give feedback on the activity, their likes, dislikes, and what the facilitator could do differently the next time the activity is conducted.

## BIBLIOGRAPHY

D'Andrea, M., & Daniels, J. (1997, December). RESPECTFUL counseling: A new ways of thinking about diversity counseling. *Counseling Today, 40*(6), 30, 31, 34.

D'Andrea, M., & Daniels, J. (2001). RESPECTFUL counseling: An integrative model for counselors. In D. Pope-Davis & H. Coleman (Eds.), *The interface of class, culture, & gender in counseling* (pp. 417–466). Thousand Oaks, CA: Sage Publications.

## SUGGESTED BACKGROUND READING

Crenshaw, K. (1991). Mapping the margins: Intersectionality, identity politics, and violence against women of color. *Stanford Law Review, 43*(6), 1241–1299. doi:10.2307/1229039

D'Andrea, M., & Daniels, J. (2001). RESPECTFUL counseling: An integrative model for counselors. In D. Pope-Davis & H. Coleman (Eds.), *The interface of class, culture, & gender in counseling* (pp. 417–466). Thousand Oaks, CA: Sage Publications.

**HANDOUT**

# Handout 13.1: RESPECTFUL G Worksheet

### RESPECTFUL G
Adapted by M. Clark from D'Andrea & Daniels, 2001.

**R**eligion/Spirituality:

**E**conomic Class Background:

**S**exual Identity:

**P**sychological Development:

**E**thnic/Racial Identity:

**C**hronological/Lifespan Challenges:

**T**rauma:

**F**amily Background:

**U**nique Physical Characteristics:

**L**ocation & Language:


**G**ender:

# CHAPTER 14

# Microaggression Exploration

*Mary-Anne Joseph and DeAnna Henderson*

## Course Recommendations

| SOCIAL JUSTICE AND ADVOCACY PRINCIPLES | CORE CACREP STANDARDS | COUNSELING SPECIALIZATION |
|---|---|---|
| ☑ What Is Social Justice and Advocacy? <br> ☑ Intersections of Oppression <br> ☑ Strategies for Change | ☑ Career Development <br> ☑ Professional Counseling Orientation and Ethical Practice <br> ☑ Research and Program Development | ☑ Career Counseling |

## TOPIC

This activity is intended to teach students how to actively advocate for the minimization and potential elimination of the use of microaggressions that compromise the integrity of clientele from minority populations.

## LEARNING OBJECTIVES

- To assist participants in learning about the origination of microaggressions
- To assist participants in learning about the negative impact of microaggressions
- To assist participants in learning how to correct microaggressions
- To assist participants in learning how to advocate for social change that has the potential to minimize and ultimately eliminate the use of microaggressions

## TARGET POPULATION

This activity is suited for counseling students and counselor trainees.

## GROUP SIZE

This activity is well suited for groups of 8–12 participants.

# TIME REQUIRED

This activity takes approximately 30–45 minutes. The length of time needed to complete the activity may be impacted by the number of members in the group.

# SETTING

This activity can be conducted in a general classroom setting. Participants should be arranged in a circle.

# MATERIALS NEEDED

- 8–12 note cards depending on the number of participants.
- 8–12 microaggression statements.
- Please note that some microaggression statements may be offensive to group participants.

# INSTRUCTIONS FOR CONDUCTING ACTIVITY

1. Arrange participants in a circle seated in chairs or at desks.
2. Inform group members that the purpose of this activity is to assist them in learning about microaggression and learning how to combat and correct microaggressions that may be used to demoralize clientele from minority populations.
3. Inform participants that some statements may be offensive and invite participants to share their concerns about the microaggression if they find the microaggression to be particularly offensive.
4. Give each student a note card that contains a microaggression.
5. One at a time ask each participant to read the assigned microaggression statement on their card to the group.
6. Once the participant has read the assigned microaggression to the group, ask the participant to discuss why the microaggression is offensive and how the microaggression statement can be corrected.
7. Repeat this process until all participants have completed steps 3 and 4.

# DISCUSSION

Describe the process by which the participants will debrief the activity. Include helpful questions or prompts for the participants.

# BIBLIOGRAPHY

Davis, D. E., DeBlaere, C., Hook, J. N., Rice, K. G., & Worthington, E. L., Jr. (2015). Intergroup forgiveness of race-related offenses. *Journal of Counseling Psychology*, *62*(3), 402–412. doi:10.1037/cou0000081

Osanloo, A. F., Boske, C., & Newcomb, W. S. (2016). Deconstructing macroaggressions, microaggressions, and structural racism in education: Developing a conceptual model for the intersection of social justice practice and intercultural education. *International Journal of Organizational Theory & Development*, *4*(1), 1–18.

# SUGGESTED BACKGROUND READING

Davis, D. E., DeBlaere, C., Hook, J. N., Rice, K. G., & Worthington, E. L., Jr. (2015). Intergroup forgiveness of race-related offenses. *Journal of Counseling Psychology*, *62*(3), 402–412. doi:10.1037/cou0000081

Osanloo, A. F., Boske, C., & Newcomb, W. S. (2016). Deconstructing macroaggressions, microaggressions, and structural racism in education: Developing a conceptual model for the intersection of social justice practice and intercultural education. *International Journal of Organizational Theory & Development*, *4*(1), 1–18.

Solorzano, D., Ceja, M., & Yosso, T. (2000). Critical race theory, racial microaggressions, and campus racial climate: The experiences of African American college students. *Journal of Negro Education*, *69*(1/2), 60–73.

Sue, D. W., Capodilupo, C. M., Torino, G. C., Bucceri, J. M., Holder, A., Nadal, K. L., & Esquilin, M. (2007). Racial microaggressions in everyday life: Implications for clinical practice. *American Psychologist*, *62*(4), 271–286. doi:10.103770003-066X.624.271

Sue, D. W., Lin, A. I., Torino, G. C., Capodilupo, C. M., & Rivera, D. P. (2009). Racial microaggressions and difficult dialogues on race in the classroom. *Cultural Diversity and Ethnic Minority Psychology*, *15*(2), 183–90. doi:10.1037/a0014191

Yosso, T. J., Smith, W. A., Ceja, M., & Solorzano, D. G. (2009). Critical race theory, racial microaggressions, and campus racial climate for latina/o undergraduates. *Harvard Educational Review*, *79*(4), 659–690.

# CHAPTER 15

## If Wishes Were Horses, Beggars Would Ride
### An Experiential Counseling Activity

*Camelia Shaheed*

### Course Recommendations

| SOCIAL JUSTICE AND ADVOCACY PRINCIPLES | CORE CACREP STANDARDS | COUNSELING SPECIALIZATION |
|---|---|---|
| ☑ Social Constructions of Oppression and Privilege<br>☑ Intersections of Oppression | ☑ Group Work<br>☑ Helping Relationships<br>☑ Professional Counseling Orientation and Ethical Practice<br>☑ Social and Cultural Diversity | ☑ Career Counseling<br>☑ Clinical Mental Health Counseling<br>☑ School Counseling<br>☑ Student Affairs and College Counseling |

## TOPIC

The activity will assist counseling students in learning about the social, political, and economic contradictions that persist in American culture. The activity will also raise awareness, via discussion, about the variety of ways students can take action to minimize oppressive elements as counselors and community leaders.

## LEARNING OBJECTIVES

1. Develop a greater awareness of socially constructed categories.
2. Identify the goal(s) of social justice from a counseling perspective.
3. Identify the process of social justice (what are the paradigms?) from a counseling perspective.
4. Identify a realistic vision of social justice from a counseling perspective.
5. Explore how counselors can counterbalance how social norms are appropriated, internalized, and normalized.

## TARGET POPULATION

Graduate counseling students during their study of social justice and advocacy

# GROUP SIZE

At least 15 participants for a full experience

# TIME REQUIRED

The activity needs a minimum of 60 minutes, but can take less or more time depending on instructor goals.

# SETTING

A room sufficiently large to accommodate break out groups. Tables and chairs must be moveable.

# MATERIALS NEEDED

Questionnaire, pencils, discussion questions, poster paper/blackboards/dry-erase boards (chalk, dry-erase markers), markers

# INSTRUCTIONS FOR CONDUCTING ACTIVITY

The facilitator will give a questionnaire and pencil to each participant/class member.
    The facilitator will provide the following directions, and solicit and field any questions: (5 minutes)

1. I've just passed out a questionnaire. There are 30 statements.
2. Read each statement in full before responding. Now, you may not fully agree with every statement. For those statements that you do not fully agree with, consider if the statement is "mostly true" or "mostly false." Then, select your response (yes or no) accordingly.
3. Try not to overthink this. This is not a scientific questionnaire. It is generic and is only meant to stimulate conversation.
4. Please do not leave any statements unanswered.
5. You should complete the questionnaire in approximately 10 minutes.
6. When you're finished, please turn your paper over and wait for further instructions.

When all participants/class members have completed the questionnaire, the facilitator will ask them to break into small groups of four to five participants, depending on the size of the group or class.
    When everyone is in a breakout group, the facilitator will provide the following directions (5 minutes):

1. Each of you will tally the questionnaire responses.
2. "Yes" response = 1 point.
3. "No" response = 0 points.
4. Add all your points together and circle the total at the top of the page.
5. **15–30 points** = *You're quite privileged.*
6. **10–14 points** = *You're moderately privileged. You've experienced both sides and, as a result, have a unique perspective to share.*
7. **9 points or less** = *You're not privileged.*

The facilitator will provide each breakout group with a copy of the discussion questions, a sheet of poster paper, and a marker (5 minutes).

The facilitator will provide the following instructions (5 minutes):

1. The breakout group has 10 minutes to discuss what the questionnaire totals mean to them.
2. Please do not engage in Anglo-Saxon-heterosexual-Judeo-Christian-male bashing for at least three reasons. One, this is not the venue for that. It would be unproductive, and it disrespects differences between individuals. Two, no one should feel or be made to feel embarrassed or guilty for being (un) privileged. Three, it doesn't get anyone *out and up*. As future leaders and advocates, explore ways *through* today's reality, and discuss methods to facilitate enduring change. Today, we are here to discuss how all of us can reasonably influence current social structures and paradigms.
3. You have 20 minutes to complete the discussion questions I passed out and make notes on the poster paper.
4. Elect a representative from your breakout group. When your 20 minutes are up, that representative will have 5 minutes to share your group's highlights with other breakout groups.
5. When we're done, we can take 5 more minutes to address final questions, express final thoughts, and wrap up.

# DISCUSSION

Based on what you know, witnessed, or experienced, consider and explore the social, political, and economic contradictions and privileges that persist in today's society or reality; and explore reasonable responses or actions that counselors (leaders and advocates) can take.

Write your conclusions on the poster paper provided.

1. Which of the 30 questions shocked you?
2. What are the obvious socially constructed categories in your small group? For example, in the U.S., social categories are marked by race, class, and gender, among many other factors. Are constructions "real"? What makes them "real" or feel real?
3. Define oppression. How is oppression manifested and perpetuated in the U.S.? Oppression is very flexible, which is at least one reason it has endured. Keeping that in mind, how can counselors expose and challenge the durability and flexibility of oppression?
4. From a counseling perspective, what are at least four social justice goals?
5. From a counseling perspective, what is the process of establishing social justice (the paradigms)? Consider the role of culture and diversity. For example, some countries offer free health care for all, but not in the U.S.
6. Every group has a "vision." What are some practical visions of social justice in your group?
7. How can counselors act as a counterbalance to how social norms are appropriated, internalized, and normalized?

# BIBLIOGRAPHY

Brown, K. (2004). Leadership for social justice and equity: Weaving a transformative framework and pedagogy. *Educational Administration Quarterly*, 40(1), 77–108.

Constantine, M., Hage, S., Kindaichi, M., & Bryant, R. (2007). Social justice and multicultural issues: Implications for the practice and training of counselors and counseling psychologists. *Journal of Counseling & Development*, 85, 24–29.

# SUGGESTED BACKGROUND READING

American Psychological Association. (2003). Guidelines on multicultural education, training, research, practice, and organizational change for psychologists. *American Psychologist*, 58, 377–402.

Dixon, A., Tucker, C., & Clark, M. (2010). Integrating social justice advocacy with national standards of practice: Implications for school counselor education. *Counselor Education & Supervision, 50*, 103–115.

Fondacaro, M., & Weinberg, D. (2002). Concepts of social justice in community psychology: Toward a social ecological epistemology. *American Journal of Community Psychology, 30*, 473–492.

Thompson, C., Murry, S., Harris, D., & Annan, J. (2003). Healing inside and out: Promoting social justice and peace in a racially divided U.S. community. *International Journal for the Advancement of Counseling, 25*, 215–223.

**HANDOUT**

# Handout 15.1: If Wishes Were Horses, Beggars Would Ride: Discussion Questions

## Discussion Questions

Based on what you know, witnessed, or experienced, consider and explore the social, political, and economic contradictions and privilege that persist in today's society or "reality"; and explore reasonable responses or actions that counselors (leaders and advocates) can take.

Write your conclusions on the poster paper provided.

1. What are the obvious socially constructed categories in your small group? For example, in the U.S., social categories are marked by race, class, and gender, among many other factors. Are constructions "real"? What makes them "real" or feel real?
2. Define oppression. How is oppression manifested and perpetuated in the U.S.? Oppression is very flexible, which is at least one reason it has endured. Keeping that in mind, how can counselors expose and challenge the durability and flexibility of oppression?
3. From a counseling perspective, what are at least four social justice goals?
4. From a counseling perspective, what is the process of establishing social justice (the paradigms)? Consider the role of diversity.
5. Every group has a "vision." From a counseling perspective, what are some realistic counseling visions of social justice?
6. How can counselors counterbalance how social norms are appropriated, internalized, and normalized?

# Handout 15.2: If Wishes Were Horses, Beggars Would Ride: Questionnaire

## If Wishes Were Horses: An Experiential Counseling Activity on Social Justice Questionnaire

|  |  |  |
|---|---|---|
| 1.  I have never hidden my sexuality. | Yes | No |
| 2.  I have never felt unsafe because of my gender. | Yes | No |
| 3.  I grew up in a neighborhood where the police were never called. | Yes | No |
| 4.  I don't take public transportation. | Yes | No |
| 5.  I inherited money or other valuables when family members died. | Yes | No |
| 6.  No one in my family has ever been arrested. | Yes | No |
| 7.  I'm never stopped by the police unless I'm at fault. | Yes | No |
| 8.  I've traveled internationally at least once. | Yes | No |
| 9.  No one has ever directed a racial slur at me. | Yes | No |
| 10.  I am a man. | Yes | No |
| 11.  I have never been denied a job because of my gender. | Yes | No |
| 12.  I don't or won't have student loans. | Yes | No |
| 13.  I have never gone to bed hungry or skipped a meal to save money. | Yes | No |
| 14.  I buy new clothes at least once every month. | Yes | No |
| 15.  I never worry about paying rent. | Yes | No |
| 16.  I went to a private school. | Yes | No |
| 17.  I went to college. | Yes | No |
| 18.  I had a reliable car in high school. | Yes | No |
| 19.  I had a reliable car in college. | Yes | No |
| 20.  I can go to the doctor when I need to. | Yes | No |
| 21.  I can go to a counselor, psychiatrist, or therapist when I need to. | Yes | No |
| 22.  I can afford all my medications. | Yes | No |
| 23.  I do not have a disability. | Yes | No |
| 24.  I am attractive. | Yes | No |
| 25.  I have been stopped at airport security several times. | Yes | No |
| 26.  I have never felt ashamed or felt I needed to hide my religious beliefs. | Yes | No |
| 27.  I have never worried about my weight. | Yes | No |
| 28.  I have always had cable. | Yes | No |
| 29.  I have a salaried job. | Yes | No |
| 30.  I generally travel for Spring Break. | Yes | No |

# CHAPTER 16

# Coming Face-to-Face With Oppression

*Thomas A. Chavez and Arianna Trott*

## Course Recommendations

| SOCIAL JUSTICE AND ADVOCACY PRINCIPLES | CORE CACREP STANDARDS | COUNSELING SPECIALIZATION |
|---|---|---|
| ☑ Intersections of Oppression | ☑ Group Work<br>☑ Helping Relationships<br>☑ Social and Cultural Diversity | ☑ Clinical Mental Health Counseling<br>☑ Marriage, Couple, and Family Counseling<br>☑ School Counseling |

## TOPIC

The primary focus of this activity is to provide participants with an opportunity to dialogue about oppression and discrimination through personal experiences and witnessing such occurrences. Based on the article "Five Faces of Oppression" by Iris Young (1990), this activity aims to promote discussion about exploitation, marginalization, cultural imperialism, violence, and powerlessness and emphasizes the importance of processing through open dialogue to support or encourage understanding and appreciation of both common as well as different experiences between sociocultural groups.

## LEARNING OBJECTIVES

Participants will identify and develop a deeper understanding of oppression and how its various forms operate in the context of diverse sociocultural groups. Participants will be able to clearly express and process personal experiences related to oppression and its five components.

## TARGET POPULATION

Students or counselor educators who want to promote dialogue regarding oppression

## GROUP SIZE

8–30 participants broken up into four to six groups with two to five participants per group

# TIME REQUIRED

A minimum of 90 minutes (more time could be beneficial with larger groups)

# SETTING

Classroom (with capacity to form dyads and large group discussion circles)

# MATERIALS NEEDED

Annotated reading on the "Five Faces of Oppression" (see reference later in chapter)

# INSTRUCTIONS FOR CONDUCTING ACTIVITY

Prior to starting the activity, the facilitator will prepare slips of papers with labels of various sociocultural groups (e.g., race, class, gender, sexual orientation, religion, spirituality, age, disabilities, etc.). The facilitator will break up the participants into four to six groups, each group containing no less than two participants. The facilitator will then have each group randomly choose a slip of paper to select one of the sociocultural groups. Each group will be instructed to read the "Five Faces of Oppression," having their randomly selected sociocultural group in mind. For the next 15–30 minutes each group will discuss among themselves what oppression means, how the five components apply to their selected sociocultural group, and how they have personally been affected (related to their selected sociocultural group). Each group will choose a representative to do about a 5-minute report to the remainder of the class regarding what was discussed including how historical injustices and inequities have impacted the selected sociocultural group.

# DISCUSSION

The facilitator will have the groups come back together and reform into a large discussion circle. Each group will have its representative report to the large discussion circle and then discuss the following questions:

1.  What are the common elements shared between groups? What experiences are specific to each group?
2.  How did your discussion group define your sociocultural group? Who was included and excluded from that definition? What are the criteria of belonging in your sociocultural group?
3.  What are your personal experiences with belonging to a particular sociocultural group? How have your personal experiences impacted how you view other sociocultural groups? How have your personal experiences and beliefs shaped your views on oppression?
4.  What other faces might oppression have?
5.  How might these faces show up in the counseling relationship? In a school or community agency? What role does the counselor have in reducing and ameliorating oppression? How can a counselor assist in the development and exercise of individual capacities and collective communication and cooperation of respective sociocultural groups explored?
6.  Based on this discussion, what action, policy, or step could you take to address oppression in your community?

# BIBLIOGRAPHY

Ozdogu, D. (2009, June 15). *Five faces of oppression* [assignment modules]. Retrieved from https://mrdevin.files.wordpress.com/2009/06/five-faces-of-oppression.pdf
Young, I. M. (1990). *Five faces of oppression, justice and the politics of difference*. Princeton, NJ: Princeton University Press.

# SUGGESTED BACKGROUND READING

Ozdogu, D. (2009, June 15). *Five faces of oppression* [assignment modules]. Retrieved from https://mrdevin.files.wordpress.com/2009/06/five-faces-of-oppression.pdf
Young, I. M. (1990). *Five faces of oppression, justice and the politics of difference*. Princeton, NJ: Princeton University Press.

# CHAPTER 17

# Sociodrama
## Exploring Oppression in Relation to Sociopolitical Issues

*Heidi L. Henry, Chi-Sing Li, and Justyn Smith*

## Course Recommendations

| SOCIAL JUSTICE AND ADVOCACY PRINCIPLES | CORE CACREP STANDARDS | COUNSELING SPECIALIZATION |
|---|---|---|
| ☑ Social Constructs of Oppression and Privilege | ☑ Social and Cultural Diversity | ☑ Clinical Mental Health Counseling<br>☑ Student Affairs and College Counseling |

## TOPIC

The focus of this activity is for counselors-in-training to engage in a sociodrama to increase awareness of how political actions contribute to the oppression of specific groups. While it can be adapted for any sociopolitical issue, this activity focuses specifically on Trump's Executive Order 13769, commonly referred to as the "Muslim ban."

## LEARNING OBJECTIVES

1. To gain awareness of how governmental actions, such as Executive Order 13769, contribute to the oppression of certain religious groups and refugees
2. To increase empathy for oppressed groups in America, such as Muslims and refugees from Muslim countries
3. To understand how oppression impacts the role of a counselor

## TARGET POPULATION

Master's- or doctoral-level class

## GROUP SIZE

10–20

# TIME REQUIRED

Overall time estimate to complete activity is 45 to 60 minutes. More time would be needed if the group is larger or more advanced in its counselor training.

# SETTING

The ideal location to conduct the activity is a classroom with enough open space for participants to move around freely. The greater the number of participants the larger the amount of open space is needed.

# MATERIALS NEEDED

- 10–15 sheets of colored paper with quotes or pictures of specific individuals representing their viewpoints. Quotes or pictures can be selected by the facilitator prior to activity.
- Laminate or place them in sheet protectors for future use.
- Use different color paper to represent the opposing viewpoints, e.g., green for those opposing the ban and blue for those supporting the ban.

# INSTRUCTIONS FOR CONDUCTING ACTIVITY

While this activity deals specifically with Trump's executive order banning Muslims from entering the U.S. from seven different countries, it can be adapted for any sociopolitical topic concerning issues of oppression and privilege.

Prior to activity, facilitator should search for quotes or pictures from different viewpoints. Quotes can be from community leaders, religious leaders, politicians, policy makers, media spokespersons, community members, etc. Laminate or place them in sheet protectors for future use.

Have participants stand in a circle in an open area of the classroom. Prepare participants for the activity by stating that this activity is not meant to prove that one side is right and the other is wrong, but rather to increase awareness of how actions such as presidential executive orders impact us as counselors and advocates for social justice.

1. Sharing information
   a. Facilitator will objectively share the facts concerning Executive Order 13769.
   b. Facilitator will ask participants to share any missing factual information concerning the topic.
2. Reading out name, statements, or pictures from different viewpoints
   a. Facilitator will distribute papers with statements or pictures describing a specific person and his/her/their viewpoint on Executive Order 13769.
   b. Participants will go around the circle reading or describing their viewpoint.
3. Demonstration
   a. Facilitator and another participant will roleplay acting as two individuals from viewpoints on the same side.
   b. Facilitator and another participant will roleplay acting as two individuals from opposing viewpoints.
4. Roleplaying
   a. Papers are placed on the ground face down. Participants pick up one paper.
   b. Participants pair up and engage in a discussion taking on the position or viewpoint of the person on the paper for 1 to 2 minutes.

- This is repeated for three or more rounds.

Differentiation:

- It is important that the facilitator is continually assessing participants' reactions to determine the appropriate level of intensity. The following are ways to increase the level of intensity and deepen the affective experience.
- During step 2, facilitator can go behind each participant as they read, and the facilitator can emphatically state an emotion the person from that viewpoint is having, such as "I am angry!"
- During step 4, facilitator can ask the participants to pair up or combine in groups of three or four. The following process questions 4 and 5 can be adjusted to discuss the experience whenever there are two people on the same side against two people on the opposing side or three against one.
- Facilitator can ask the participants in each pair to put him or herself into the other persons' shoes and tap into their emotion. Facilitator would then ask the participant to share that emotion with the group.

## DISCUSSION

Class instructor will facilitate discussion of the whole class by asking the following questions.

1. What thoughts and feelings did you have while participating in the activity?
2. What was your experience like whenever you had to roleplay the side of the issue with which you agreed?
3. What was your experience like whenever you had to roleplay the side of the issue with which you disagreed?
4. What was it like whenever you were roleplaying with others on the same side of the issue?
5. What was it like whenever you were roleplaying with others on the opposite side of the issue?
6. How is this experience related to oppression and privilege?
7. How would you use what you gained from this experience in your work as a counselor?
8. What are some ways you would use your role as an advocate in this issue?
9. Activity extension: write a letter to a state legislator or elected government official advocating for his/her/their support for or opposition to Executive Order 13769.

## BIBLIOGRAPHY

Crowe, A., & Villalba, J. A. (2012). Infusing multiculturalism into human service education using sociodrama. *Journal of Human Services, 32*(1), 41–55.
Exec. Order No. 13769, 3 C.F.R. 8977 (2017).

## SUGGESTED BACKGROUND READING

Blatner, A. (2006). Enacting the new academy: Sociodrama as a powerful tool in higher education. *ReVision, 28*(3), 30–35. doi:10.3200/REVN.28.3.30-35

# HANDOUT

# Handout 17.1: Sociodrama: Exploring Oppression in Relation to Sociopolitical Issues

## DONALD TRUMP

(President of the United States)

*Trump's executive order bars citizens of seven Muslim-majority countries from entering the United States for the next 90 days, suspends the admission of all refugees for 120 days and indefinitely suspends the Syrian refugee program.*

## SALLY YATES

(former US Deputy Attorney General)

*I am not convinced that the defense of the executive order is consistent with these responsibilities nor am I convinced that the executive order is lawful. Consequently, I will not present arguments in defense of the executive order, unless and until I become convinced that it is appropriate to do so.*

## CHUCK SCHUMER

(New York Senator)

*The executive order is mean-spirited and un-American. We are gonna introduce legislation to overturn this and move it as quickly as we can. I, as your senator from New York, will claw, scrap and fight with every fiber of my being until these orders are overturned.*

## ELIZABETH WARREN

(Massachusetts Senator)

*This is a constitutional crisis and a moral crisis. We are here to ask the rest of the United States Senate to overturn Donald Trump's unconstitutional, illegal, and immoral executive order. We have that power. All we need is the courage to stand up and do what is right. This is why we came to United States Senate to stand up and do what is right.*

## KELLYANNE CONWAY

(Counselor to President Trump)

*The executive order is meant to be preventing not detaining. I think the upside being greater protection of our borders of our people. It's a small price to pay to have 300 and some who have been detained. They are expected to be released in due course. This is what we do to keep the nation safe.*

# RUDY GIULIANI

(former New York City Mayor and current White House Cybersecurity Adviser)

*President Trump tasked me with coming up with a way to legally implement his executive order banning immigration from seven predominantly Muslim countries. The areas of the world that create danger for us, which is a factual basis, not a religious basis.*

# DANA BOENTE

(Deputy Attorney General)

*I am humbled and incredibly honored to serve as acting attorney general. Based upon the Office of Legal Counsel's analysis, which found the executive order both lawful on its face and properly drafted, I hereby direct the men and women of the Department of Justice to do our sworn duty and to defend the lawful orders of our president.*

# JAVAD ZARIF

(Iranian Foreign Minister)

*The US decision to restrict travel for Muslims to the US is an obvious insult to the Islamic world and in particular to the great nation of Iran. Iran will take reciprocal measures in order to safeguard the rights of its citizens until the time of the removal of the insulting restrictions of the government of the United States against Iranian nationals.*

# PAUL RYAN

(former Speaker of the House)

*Our number one responsibility is to protect the homeland. . . . It's time to reevaluate and strengthen the visa vetting process. President Trump is right to make sure we are doing everything possible to know exactly who is entering our country.*

# A TRUMP SUPPORTER

*Not taking in Syrian refugees and closing our borders isn't "mean" or "heartless." I lock the doors to my house every night. I don't lock them because I hate the people outside of my house. I lock them because I love the people inside.*

# AZADEH NAJAFIAN

(an immigrant from Iran)

*Shocking, really shocking. We all are victims of politics, and we haven't done anything wrong in our whole life. We're all humans and we all share the same world and deserve a place to be happy and healthy.*

# THERESA MAY

(Prime Minister of Britain)

*May initially failed to condemn Trump's executive order, but then backtracked, releasing a statement late on Saturday night saying that she "did not agree" with the policy.*

# CHAPTER 18

## Gender Messages
### A Timeline Activity

*Angelica M. Tello*

### Course Recommendations

| SOCIAL JUSTICE AND ADVOCACY PRINCIPLES | CORE CACREP STANDARDS | COUNSELING SPECIALIZATION |
|---|---|---|
| ☑ Cycle of Socialization and Liberation<br>☑ Social Constructs of Oppression and Privilege | ☑ Human Growth and Development<br>☑ Social and Cultural Diversity | ☑ Clinical Mental Health Counseling |

## TOPIC

The focus of the activity is to help students understand the impact of gender messages on their personal lives. In addition, students will identify how gender messages can lead to experiences of privilege, oppression, or marginalization.

## LEARNING OBJECTIVES

1. Students will identify the gender messages they have received from society, media, and their families.
2. Students will gain an understanding of how the gender messages provided moments of privilege, marginalization, or oppression in their lives.
3. Students will engage in discussion around the gender messages and intersections of their cultural identities.
4. Students will discuss strategies for countering gender messages that are sexist and lead to oppression.

## TARGET POPULATION

This activity is best suited for counseling graduate students and counseling interns.

## GROUP SIZE

This activity can accommodate any group size. The activity discussion can be modified for large classes and small group settings.

# TIME REQUIRED

This activity will take approximately 60 minutes to complete. However, the required time to complete the activity can be altered to accommodate the group size.

# SETTING

The activity is best suited in settings where group discussions can occur.

# MATERIALS NEEDED

Each participant will need paper and a writing utensil, such as a pencil or pen, to complete the activity.

# INSTRUCTIONS FOR CONDUCTING ACTIVITY

1. Participants will be asked to draw a horizontal line across a sheet of paper. The line should be centered on the sheet of paper, because it will serve as the base for a timeline.
2. Participants will then reflect on the messages they have received from society, media, and family members regarding their gender.
3. Next participants will document when they received the message on their timeline. Their timeline will start from birth until their current age. Above the timeline, participants will document positive messages they received about their gender identity. Below the timeline, participants will document the negative messages they received about their gender.
4. After about 15–20 minutes of documenting their gender messages, participants will gather around in a circle facing each other. If the group is larger than ten, participants can sit lecture style to accommodate the group size and space.
5. Participants will debrief the activity and answer process questions regarding their personal timeline. Students will engage in discussion around the gender messages and intersections of their cultural identities.
6. After the group debriefing, students will discuss strategies for countering gender messages that are sexist and lead to oppression/marginalization.

# DISCUSSION

Participants will first be asked to share their overall experiences of creating their timeline. Then participants can be asked:

1. What gender messages stood out to you?
2. How did these gender messages impact your life?
3. What privileges did you experience as a result of the gender message?
4. What gender messages led to marginalization or oppression?
5. How did the gender messages impact other cultural identities you hold?
6. How can these messages impact our work as counselors?

After the instructor facilities this discussion, participants will also be asked to share strategies for countering messages that are sexist and lead to oppression/marginalization.

# BIBLIOGRAPHY

Holtzman, L., & Sharpe, L. (2014). *Media messages: What film, television, and popular music tech us about race, class, gender, and sexual orientation.* New York, NY: Routledge.

Medved, C. E., Brogan, S. M., McClanahan, A. M., Morris, J. F., & Shepherd, G. J. (2006). Family and work socializing communication: Messages, gender, and ideological implications. *Journal of Family Communication, 6,* 161–180.

# SUGGESTED BACKGROUND READING

Gilbert, L. A., & Scher, M. (2009). *Gender and sex in counseling and psychotherapy.* Portland, OR: Wipf & Stock Publishers.

Goodman, L. A., Liang, B., Helms, J. E., Latta, R. E., Sparks, E., & Weintraub, S. R. (2004). Training counseling psychologists as social justice agents: Feminist and multicultural principles in action. *The Counseling Psychologist, 32,* 793–837.

# CHAPTER 19

## LGBTQ Fishbowl

*Deanna N. Cor*

### Course Recommendations

| SOCIAL JUSTICE AND ADVOCACY PRINCIPLES | CORE CACREP STANDARDS | COUNSELING SPECIALIZATION |
|---|---|---|
| ☑ Social Constructs of Oppression and Privilege<br>☑ Strategies for Change | ☑ Career Development<br>☑ Group Work<br>☑ Helping Relationships<br>☑ Social and Cultural Diversity | ☑ Addiction Counseling<br>☑ Career Counseling<br>☑ Clinical Mental Health Counseling<br>☑ Marriage, Couple, and Family Counseling<br>☑ School Counseling<br>☑ Student Affairs and College Counseling |

## TOPIC

The purpose of this activity is to expand the knowledge and awareness of students identifying as straight and cisgender by bearing witness to the disclosures and experiences of LGBTQ volunteers.

## LEARNING OBJECTIVES

1. To enhance knowledge and awareness surrounding experiences of oppression and discrimination of people in the LGBTQ community
2. To facilitate multicultural and social justice counseling competencies in counselors-in-training, specifically in regard to LGBTQ clients
3. To provide a safe environment for LGBTQ clients to share their experiences with future counselors-in-training

## TARGET POPULATION

Graduate students in Counselor Education Program

## GROUP SIZE

30–35 maximum including students and volunteers

# TIME REQUIRED

One class period or typically 2.5 hours including a 10-minute break

# SETTING

During one class session with a room big enough for two concentric circles. Instructors should work hard to include a number of LGBTQ participants equal to or greater than the number of straight and cisgender participants.

# MATERIALS NEEDED

Chairs, space big enough for the number of people involved in the activity, and a list of questions the facilitator will ask participants.

# INSTRUCTIONS FOR CONDUCTING ACTIVITY

## Pre-Activity Work

This activity is best experienced when there is a combination of participants with varying perspectives. As we know, intersectionality is a vital part of our work as counselors. As such, facilitators should work to include out, LGBTQ participants from various racial/ethnic, religious, socioeconomic, educational, documentation, and gender perspectives. Additionally, including participants from the community as well as students in the course who have identified with the LGBTQ community can increase the impact of the activity. I have asked students to participate in the past, if they are willing, in individual emails. Of course, LGBTQ students should always have the option to not participate if they do not wish to share their experiences with their classmates, professors, and community members. If possible, the number of LGBTQ participants should be equal to or greater than the number of straight and cis observers.

## Setup

Arrange the room to include two concentric circles: one inner and one outer. There should be the appropriate number of chairs for participants and observers. If the facilitator identifies within the LGBTQ+ community, they may consider sitting in the first circle and disclosing as they see fit. If the facilitator identifies outside of the LGBTQ+ community, they may consider facilitating from outside the second circle.

1. Introductions
   a. Ask each participant in the inner circle to introduce themselves including their name, pronouns (e.g., he/him/his, they/them/theirs, she/her/hers), and salient identities.
   b. Note: for individuals who do not use pronouns, it is useful to use the person's name instead. Also, if a person does not include pronouns, the facilitator may inquire, use the person's name, or utilize gender neutral pronouns (e.g., they/them/theirs).
2. Guidelines
   a. Provide all participants and observers with the following guidelines:
      i. Participants are asked to share as openly and honestly as they feel comfortable.
      ii. Participants are encouraged to talk directly with one another and respond to each other's disclosures.

     iii.  During the first portion of the activity, observers in the outer circle are asked to refrain from commenting on anything the participants are discussing. Rather, they are encouraged to simply be present with these disclosures.

3.  Questions for the participants in the inner circle:
    a.  What was it like when you first began exploring your LGBTQ+ identity?
    b.  What have your coming out experiences been like? What's been a positive aspect? What's been most difficult?
    c.  Can you share your experiences with discrimination and oppression on individual and systemic levels?
    d.  Have there been times/life circumstances/environments where one or more of your identities have become more salient to you?
    e.  What have your experiences with identifying within the LGBTQ+ community been in the context of the counseling field?
    f.  What do you love about your identity? What do you take pride in?

At the conclusion of the inner circle discussion, have the participants and the observers switch places. If the facilitator identifies within the LGBTQ+ community, they may consider facilitating from outside the second circle. If the facilitator identifies outside of the LGBTQ+ community, they may consider sitting in the second circle and disclosing as they see fit.

4.  Questions for the observers
    a.  When did you first know you were straight and cisgender?
    b.  What experiences of privilege have you had?
    c.  When in your life have you become aware of systems that oppress LGBTQ+ people?
    d.  What was it like for you to hear about each participant's experiences?
5.  Guidelines
    a.  Participants here are encouraged to ask each other questions. It can be helpful to provide group norms to frame ways of communicating respectfully and from a place of curiosity. This will vary depending on the facilitator's knowledge of group dynamics.

At the conclusion of the inner circle discussion, have the participants and the observers move into one larger circle.

6.  Questions for volunteers:
    a.  What do you need from your straight and cis counterparts?
    b.  How can they be allies to you?
7.  Questions for students:
    a.  Given what has been shared today, what do you want to communicate to our volunteers?
    b.  What are your biggest personal takeaways?
    c.  How will you commit to disrupting trans- and homophobia?
8.  Final thoughts and reflections

## DISCUSSION

Debriefing is largely conducted during the final portion of the activity when all participants are joined in one larger circle. Suggested questions could include:

1.  Questions for volunteers:
    a.  How can your straight and cis counterparts be allies to you?
    b.  How would you best feel supported through allyship?

2. Questions for students:
   a. Given what has been shared today, what do you want to communicate to our volunteers?
   b. What are your biggest personal takeaways?
   c. How will you commit to disrupting trans- and homophobia?

Facilitators should feel free to ask additional questions taking into consideration the needs of their particular students/audience. Facilitators can find helpful ideas for disrupting homophobia, transphobia, and heterosexism at https://everydayfeminism.com/2013/11/things-allies-need-to-know/.

# BIBLIOGRAPHY

Harper, A., Finnerty, P., Martinez, M., Brace, A., Crethar, H. C., Loos, B., . . . Hammer, T. R. (2013). Association for lesbian, gay, bisexual, and transgender issues in counseling competencies for counseling with lesbian, gay, bisexual, queer, questioning, intersex, and ally individuals. *Journal of LGBT Issues in Counseling, 7*(1), 2–43. doi:10.1080/1553860 5.2013.755444

Kim, B. S., & Lyons, H. Z. (2003). Experiential activities and multicultural counseling competence training. *Journal of Counseling & Development, 81*(4), 400–408. doi:10.1002/j.1556-6678.2003.tb00266.x

Utt, J. (2013). *10 things all 'allies' need to know: Everyday feminism.* Retrieved from https://everydayfeminism.com/2013/11/things-allies-need-to-know/

# SUGGESTED BACKGROUND READING

Arredondo, P., & Arcinega, G. M. (2001). Strategies and techniques for counselor training based on the multicultural counseling competencies. *Journal of Multicultural Counseling and Development, 29*, 263–273.

Cole, E. R., Case, K. A., Rios, D., & Curtin, N. (2011). Understanding what students bring to the classroom: Moderators of the effects of diversity courses on student attitudes. *Cultural Diversity and Ethnic Minority Psychology, 17*(4), 397–405.

Harper, A., Finnerty, P., Martinez, M., Brace, A., Crethar, H. C., Loos, B., . . . Hammer, T. R. (2013). Association for lesbian, gay, bisexual, and transgender issues in counseling competencies for counseling with lesbian, gay, bisexual, queer, questioning, intersex, and ally individuals. *Journal of LGBT Issues in Counseling, 7*(1), 2–43. doi:10.1080/1553860 5.2013.755444

Ratts, M. J., Singh, A. A., Nassar-McMillan, S., Butler, S. K., & McCullough, J. R. (2015). Multicultural and social justice counseling competencies: Guidelines for the counseling profession. *Journal of Multicultural Counseling and Development, 44*, 28–48.

# CHAPTER 20

# The Advocacy Action Plan

*Jennifer M. Cook*

## Course Recommendations

| SOCIAL JUSTICE AND ADVOCACY PRINCIPLES | CORE CACREP STANDARDS | COUNSELING SPECIALIZATION |
|---|---|---|
| ☑ Strategies for Change | ☑ Social and Cultural Diversity | ☑ Addiction Counseling<br>☑ Clinical Mental Health Counseling<br>☑ Marriage, Couple, and Family Counseling<br>☑ School Counseling<br>☑ Student Affairs and College Counseling |

## TOPIC

The goal of this activity is to guide individuals through advocacy action planning from pre-planning through post-advocacy action.

## LEARNING OBJECTIVES

1. Determine a specific population/topic on which to focus participants' advocacy.
2. Prepare for their Advocacy Action Plan by determining their strengths, needs, and goals.
3. Write a detailed, useable Advocacy Action Plan.

## TARGET POPULATION

Students and professional counselors

## GROUP SIZE

Varies; activity can be accomplished individually, in dyads, or in small groups.

# TIME REQUIRED

It is recommended learners take as much time as needed to be thoughtful and intentional about their Advocacy Action Plan. If working through the Advocacy Action Plan in a dyad or small group, additional time will be needed for individual reflection and group discussion. The estimated time for each portion of the Advocacy Action Plan is based on an individual completing the plan in a setting guided by an instructor. Instructors should include time for discussion.

1. Pre-advocacy action planning: 40 minutes.
2. Advocacy action planning: 60–120 minutes.
3. Putting your Advocacy Action Plan into action: 30 minutes to explain/discuss areas listed. Use times listed in the "Advocacy Action Planning" section to estimate how long your Advocacy Action Plan will take to complete.
4. Post-advocacy action: 30–60 minutes.

# SETTING

Where the activity originates will vary based on whether participants are engaging in this activity in a classroom setting or if they are completing their Advocacy Action Plan on their own. The action portion of the Advocacy Action Plan will most likely take place outside the classroom environment, and the possibilities for where Advocacy Action Plans can be enacted are endless.

# MATERIALS NEEDED

At minimum, students need the Advocacy Action Plan handout, extra paper, and a writing implement. Some students might prefer to fill in their Advocacy Action Plan on a computer or tablet instead of longhand, so send an electronic copy of the Advocacy Action Plan handout to students. Instructors may choose to brainstorm ideas with students and have discussion in each area, so a black-/whiteboard, a smart board, or large sheets of paper can be used to write out class ideas.

# INSTRUCTIONS FOR CONDUCTING ACTIVITY

The instructions for this activity are included in each step of the worksheet. How instructors use the worksheet will vary based on course goals and instructor style. For example, instructors may choose to use this activity during one class session, or they could use it to guide a semester long project. The following are recommendations for instructors in whatever capacity they choose to use this activity.

1. Encourage students throughout the process. Many students have a difficult time imagining what kind of action they would do or how they would actually do it. Your encouragement and stating there are no wrong answers can go a long way to build their confidence.
2. Allow students to "think big," be imaginative, and explore ideas; then help them get specific and be concrete as they determine how their ideas translate into actionable items.
3. Add in brainstorming, mind mapping, discussion, etc. where you believe it will be helpful and meaningful to your students and where they are developmentally.
4. Make consistent connections between advocacy action and students' work/future work with clients.

# DISCUSSION

This activity requires instructors to check in with students consistently, while providing students with the opportunity to reflect individually and with peers. The following are questions instructors can use to guide large and small group discussion or individual reflection.

## Process-Oriented Questions

- What was it like for you to explore X (e.g., your strengths, the population you care about most, etc.)?
- What came up for you when you thought about what issues related to inequality bother you most?
- What part of your Advocacy Action Plan felt easiest for you? Most challenging?
- During our discussion, who has provided you with further insight or made you think more about your process? In what way(s)?
- What do you believe is propelling your forward to complete your Advocacy Action Plan? What might be holding you back?

## Content-Oriented Questions

- What questions do you have or what clarifications do you need about the section you are about to complete?
- How can you make your goal a SMART goal?
- How realistic are the times you estimated you needed for each step and the completion deadlines?
- What is one way you can strengthen your Advocacy Action Plan?
- What feedback did you receive about your Advocacy Action Plan? How did you integrate the feedback you received?

# BIBLIOGRAPHY

Chung, R. C., & Bemak, F. P. (2012). *Social justice counseling*. Thousand Oaks, CA: Sage Publications.

Glosoff, H. L., & Durham, J. C. (2010). Using supervision to prepare social justice counseling advocates. *Counselor Education & Supervision, 50*(2), 116–129. doi:10.1002/j.1556-6978.2010.tb00113.x

Johnson, A. G. (2006). *Privilege, power, and difference* (2nd ed.). New York, NY: McGraw Hill.

Lee, C. C., & Rodgers, R. A. (2009). Counselor advocacy: Affecting systemic change in the public arena. *Journal of Counseling and Development, 87*(3), 284–287. doi:10.1002/j.1556-6678.2009.tb00108.x

Ratts, M. J. (2008). A pragmatic view of social justice advocacy: Infusing microlevel social justice advocacy strategies into counseling practices. *Counseling and Human Development, 41*(1), 1–8.

Ratts, M. J., Singh, A. A., Nassar-McMillian, S., Butler, S. K., & McCullough, J. R. (2015). *Multicultural and social justice counseling competencies*. Retrieved from www.multiculturalcounseling.org/index.php?option=com_content&view=article&id=205:amcd-endorses-multicultural-and-social-justice-counseling-competencies&catid=1:latest&Itemid=123

Roysircar, G. (2009). The big picture of advocacy: Counselor, heal society and thyself. *Journal of Counseling and Development, 87*(3), 288–294. doi:10.1002/j.15566678.2009.tb00109.x

# SUGGESTED BACKGROUND READING

Chung, R. C., & Bemak, F. P. (2012). *Social justice counseling*. Thousand Oaks, CA: Sage Publications.

Glosoff, H. L., & Durham, J. C. (2010). Using supervision to prepare social justice counseling advocates. *Counselor Education & Supervision, 50*(2), 116–129. doi:10.1002/j.1556-6978.2010.tb00113.x

Johnson, A. G. (2006). *Privilege, power, and difference* (2nd ed.). New York, NY: McGraw Hill.

Lee, C. C., & Rodgers, R. A. (2009). Counselor advocacy: Affecting systemic change in the public arena. *Journal of Counseling and Development, 87*(3), 284–287. doi:10.1002/j.1556-6678.2009.tb00108.x

Ratts, M. J. (2008). A pragmatic view of social justice advocacy: Infusing microlevel social justice advocacy strategies into counseling practices. *Counseling and Human Development, 41*(1), 1–8.

Ratts, M. J., Singh, A. A., Nassar-McMillian, S., Butler, S. K., & McCullough, J. R. (2015). *Multicultural and social justice counseling competencies.* Retrieved from www.multiculturalcounseling.org/index.php?option=com_content&view= article&id=205:amcd-endorses-multicultural-and-social-justice-counseling-competencies&catid=1:latest&Ite mid=123

Roysircar, G. (2009). The big picture of advocacy: Counselor, heal society and thyself. *Journal of Counseling and Development, 87*(3), 288–294. doi:10.1002/j.15566678.2009.tb00109.x

## HANDOUT

# Handout 20.1: Advocacy Action Plan

## PRE-ADVOCACY ACTION PLANNING

Many of us want to engage in advocacy, yet knowing where to start can be a challenge. Please answer the following questions to the best of your ability. Bullets or lists work great! Jot down as many ideas as possible.

1.  What population do you feel most passionate about?
2.  What do you perceive to be a "social problem" in your community?
3.  What types of inequality do you see frequently?
4.  What systemic inequalities/issues do you notice your clients encounter most frequently?
5.  Have you noticed something that "makes your blood boil" when you hear about it? What is it?
6.  What are your strengths? List professional and personal strengths.

After you have your answers, read through them and note the following:

*   What themes do you notice in your answers?
*   Which questions did you write the most about?
*   What group/issue do you feel as if you gravitate toward most?
*   How will your strengths influence the advocacy choices you make?

This will begin to give you an idea of where you might like to start. Evaluate your ideas combined with your strengths and choose one topic or population for your work. Remember, you can branch out to other topics or populations in the future. Right now, choose only one.

## ADVOCACY ACTION PLANNING

Now it's time to sketch your Advocacy Action Plan. The first time you work through these questions, write whatever comes to mind, no matter how broad or general your answers may sound. The second time you work through it, get more specific and add as many details as possible.

1.  Goal (*What do I want to see improved/changed?*)
2.  Who will my goal impact? (*What specific population are you aiming to impact?*)
3.  How will I know I met my goal? (*How will I evaluate the effectiveness of my advocacy plan?*)
4.  Is my advocacy action *on behalf* of a person or group, or is it *with* a person or group?
5.  Time frame (*How long will it take to reach my goal?*)
6.  What do I need in order to work toward my goal? (*What tangible and intangible resources do I need that I don't have now?*)
    *   Knowledge:
    *   Awareness:
    *   Skills:
    *   Human resources:
    *   Material resources:
    *   Other:

# Steps and Timing

In the first box, write out the steps you plan to take to work toward your goal. In the second box, indicate how long you believe it will take you. Be as specific as you can and use *verbs* to begin each step statement to make them actionable. Please add additional rows to the table as needed. Include all of the areas listed in the planning section. You can always adjust your plan later as circumstances change or issues arise.

| Steps | | Time Needed |
|---|---|---|
| 1 | *e.g., gather specific information about how many people are affected by the problem in my community.* | *60 minutes* |
| 2 | | |
| 3 | | |
| 4 | | |

The next step is to set your timeline. A timeline will allow you to set concrete deadlines so you continue to work toward your goals associated with your Advocacy Action Plan. After you have a good idea of the steps you need to take and how long they will take to accomplish, assign completion dates for each step. Again, it's okay to adjust your plan and timeline, yet you *always* want to set a new date in which to complete your steps, otherwise it is too easy to lose momentum and leave your plan incomplete.

| Plan Step | Time Needed | Complete By: |
|---|---|---|
| 1 | *e.g., 60 minutes* | *January 25* |
| 2 | | |
| 3 | | |
| 4 | | |

As you complete this section, ask another person to read it and give you concrete feedback about your plan. Which areas are strongest? Which areas need strengthening? How can your plan be strengthened?

# PUTTING YOUR ADVOCACY ACTION PLAN INTO ACTION

After you have set your plan, it is time to put your plan into action. The following are some key points to keep in mind as you move into and through your advocacy action:

- **Advocacy actions can be challenging, personal work.** How will you care for yourself throughout the duration of your plan? How will you "recharge" when feeling depleted?
- **Advocacy actions require tenacity.** What will allow you to stick with your action until it's complete? Whom will you reach out to for support?
- **Advocacy actions command us to know ourselves and to continue to learn about ourselves.** How will you keep yourself open and nonjudgmental so you can continue to learn and grow?
- **Advocacy actions often have setbacks.** How do you tend to deal with setbacks? How will you deal with setbacks in this process?
- **Advocacy actions require your strengths.** Remember when you wrote down your strengths? Use them continuously throughout your process! How can you remind yourself of your strengths?

# POST-ADVOCACY ACTION

Evaluation is an integral part of advocacy action because it gives you insight into what worked well and what can be adjusted for future advocacy plans. Consider each of these questions thoroughly, and use the information you gain to hone your next Advocacy Action Plan.

1. What action steps were most effective to effect change?
2. In what areas of my action plan was I most strong? (*List at least three!*)
3. What is *one* way I can nuance future action plans?
4. Whom can I invite to advocate with me next time?

## ADVOCACY EXAMPLES

- Public policy work (lobbying, letter writing, "legislative days," meeting with elected officials)
- Increasing client services/working with folks who have the power to increase client services
- Educating clients about their rights
- Educating clients about how to get the services they need
- Educating community members about social justice issues
- Working with clients to encourage/teach them to advocate for themselves
- Partnering with your clients in advocacy efforts
- Supervising clinicians from a social justice perspective (see Glosoff & Durham, 2010)
- Organizing helping professionals to work together on advocacy efforts

## REFERENCES AND SELECTED READING

Chung, R. C., & Bemak, F. P. (2012). *Social justice counseling*. Thousand Oaks, CA: Sage Publications.

Glosoff, H. L., & Durham, J. C. (2010). Using supervision to prepare social justice counseling advocates. *Counselor Education & Supervision, 50*(2), 116–129. doi:10.1002/j.1556-6978.2010.tb00113.x

Johnson, A. G. (2006). *Privilege, power, and difference* (2nd ed.). New York, NY: McGraw Hill.

Lee, C. C., & Rodgers, R. A. (2009). Counselor advocacy: Affecting systemic change in the public arena. *Journal of Counseling and Development, 87*(3), 284–287. doi:10.1002/j.1556-6678.2009.tb00108.x

Ratts, M. J. (2008). A pragmatic view of social justice advocacy: Infusing microlevel social justice advocacy strategies into counseling practices. *Counseling and Human Development, 41*(1), 1–8.

Ratts, M. J., Singh, A. A., Nassar-McMillian, S., Butler, S. K., & McCullough, J. R. (2015). *Multicultural and social justice counseling competencies*. Retrieved from www.multiculturalcounseling.org/index.php?option=com_content&view=article&id=205:amcd-endorses-multicultural-and-social-justice-counseling-competencies&catid=1:latest&Itemid=123

Roysircar, G. (2009). The big picture of advocacy: Counselor, heal society and thyself. *Journal of Counseling and Development, 87*(3), 288–294. doi:10.1002/j.15566678.2009.tb00109.x

# CHAPTER 21

# #Dismantling Islamophobia
## A Technology-Based Experiential Activity to Increase Awareness and Empathy Toward Muslims

*Minnah W. Farook and Roberto L. Abreu*

## Course Recommendations

| SOCIAL JUSTICE AND ADVOCACY PRINCIPLES | CORE CACREP STANDARDS | COUNSELING SPECIALIZATION |
|---|---|---|
| ☑ Social Constructs of Oppression and Privilege | ☑ Social and Cultural Diversity | ☑ Clinical Mental Health Counseling<br>☑ School Counseling<br>☑ Student Affairs and College Counseling |

## TOPIC

The goal of this activity is to increase awareness of Islamophobia, or biases against Muslims, and reflect on how individuals can become allies of Muslims in their communities.

## LEARNING OBJECTIVES

1. Increase awareness of biases against Muslims and Islam in the United States.
2. Identify misconceptions about Muslims and Islam in the United States.
3. Develop empathy among students, staff, faculty, and community members toward Muslims.

## TARGET POPULATION

Students, professionals, and anyone over the age 12

## GROUP SIZE

5–20 people

# TIME REQUIRED

Depending on the size of the group, prior knowledge of the topic, and setting (i.e., graduate course on multiculturalism, ally training and workshops, community settings), this activity requires 15–30 minutes to complete, including presentation and written activity. An additional 30 minutes or more should be reserved for discussions and debriefing of presentation and experiential activity. Overall, this activity should not last less than 45 minutes.

# SETTING

The ideal location for this activity is in a classroom or conference room setting where participants have access to the Internet on either their own electronic devices or computers made available by the facility or presenter. Depending on the ages and socioeconomic backgrounds of the participants, participants may or may not have smartphones or Internet access.

# MATERIALS NEEDED

- Smartphone with Internet access or computer with Internet access
- Writing materials (e.g., paper, pencil, pen) for notes if desired
- PowerPoint slides of different pictures of Muslims and non-Muslims
- Overhead projector to display the PowerPoint slides

Note: the facilitator should walk around the room to make sure participants are actively working on the activity and not engaged in other activities on their smartphones or computers. It is crucial for participants to not be distracted by outside stimuli in order for an emotional connection to the material to take place.

# INSTRUCTIONS FOR CONDUCTING ACTIVITY

Ask participants to search Muslims or Islam on Twitter and share a picture/post/article that is included in the top search results. Ask participates to reflect on the following questions:

1. What thoughts, feelings, and images came up for you when you saw the picture/post/article?
2. Does the picture/post/article match your perceptions of Muslims or Islam? How so?
3. Does it invoke positive/negative/neutral thoughts, feelings, and images for you?

For this part of the activity, allow participants 5–10 minutes to find the picture/post/article and reflect on the preceding questions. It is important for participants to not share their impressions with the other participants or presenter.

Present participants with PowerPoint slides of different pictures of Muslims and non-Muslims. Based on what participants found and learned on Twitter about Muslims or Islam ask them to identify whether people depicted in the images are Muslims or non-Muslims. The presenter must make sure that the images reflect the diversity of Muslims in America and other parts of the world. That is, the presenter must be careful not to only chose pictures that are consistent with stereotypical images of how Muslims are depicted in the media. Considering people are likely to encounter and interact with Muslims in their communities who look like the people in the images, a representation of Muslims and Islam as a diverse community must be included in the selected images. For example, Muslims are usually represented as Arabs with brown skin. Women are usually covered with a hijab or burqa. Men are often depicted as oppressive, religious zealots, and terrorists. In reality, a large population of American Muslims are Black, and Islam has been in the U.S. since the transatlantic slave trade as some African slaves were practicing Muslims (Ahmed & Reddy, 2007). Additionally, the majority of Muslims in the world are not Arab nor from the Middle East (Ibrahim & Dykeman, 2011). Muslims express varying levels of religiosity and diverse practices depending on acculturation, racial/ethnic background, culture of origin, etc. (Ibrahim & Dykeman, 2011). Therefore, images used in this activity should reflect the diversity of American Muslim communities.

Ask volunteers to share whether they think the image is of a Muslim. After some participants share their responses, review whether they correctly or incorrectly guessed the religion of the person in the image.

# DISCUSSION

Encourage participants to share their thoughts and feelings if they are comfortable. Facilitate the discussion using questions that prompt participants to think about their own biases and knowledge of Muslims and Islam. The discussion should focus on encouraging participants to explore their own thoughts and feelings about Muslims. This exercise is intended to increase participants' curiosity about Muslims and Islam, as many Americans have not met Muslims or do not have Muslim friends and family members. In addition, guiding questions should be used to challenge some of the participants' initial thoughts and perceptions from the pictures/posts/articles they found on Twitter at the beginning of this activity. The following questions may be used to facilitate the discussion:

- What do you know about Muslims or Islam?
- What thoughts, feelings, or images come up for you when you think about Muslims or Islam?
- What are some stereotypes or biases about Muslims in our society?
- Where did you learn the information that you know about Muslims?
- Do you personally know any Muslims? If so, do they fit the description that was shared by others in the group?
- Are there similarities and differences between what participants shared?
- Which of the descriptions are true and which are false?
- Do the images represent the images you have of Muslims or images portrayed in the media?
- Is there anything that surprised you about the images of Muslims presented in the slides? If so, what surprised you?
- Were you surprised by the number of images you were able to identify correctly? Explain.
- What are the similarities and differences between Muslims and Islam compared to people of other faiths (e.g., Christians, Jews, Hindus, Buddhists, etc.)?

If this activity takes place in a course, the activity can be followed with a discussion or lecture on stereotypes about Muslims, common narratives of Muslims portrayed in the media, and how such biases can influence our perceptions of Muslims and Islam. Provide information about values of Islam and the five pillars of Islam, common religious and cultural practices among Muslims, history of Muslims in America, Islamophobia and its impact on Muslims and non-Muslims, and how to dismantle these biases, empower Muslim clients, and be an ally.

## Supplemental Activity

Depending on the setting, time availability, and commitment from participants the presenter should consider asking participants to fill out the Islamophobia Scale (IS; Lee, Gibbon, Thompson, & Timani, 2009), a 16-item measure of an individual's fear-based attitudes toward Muslims, at the beginning of the activity (i.e., before asking them to search for pictures/posts/articles on Twitter), at the end of the discussion, and three months after the presentation/workshop has taken place. This will allow the presenter to measure the effectiveness of the experiential activity at two different stages, immediately after the discussion and three months after.

# BIBLIOGRAPHY

Munoz, L., Miller, R., & Poole, S. M. (2016). Professional student organizations and experiential learning activities: What drives student intentions to participate? *Journal of Education for Business, 91*, 45–51. doi:10.1080/08832323 .2015.1110553

Yokoyama, K., Magraw, S., Miller, J., & Hecht, L. (2011). Interrupting oppression: Finding ways to speak out against overt oppression and everyday microaggressions. In M. Pope, J. S. Pangelinan, & A. D. Coker (Eds.), *Experiential activities for teaching multicultural competence in counseling* (pp. 197–198). Alexandria, VA: American Counseling Association.

# SUGGESTED BACKGROUND READING

Ahmed, S., & Reddy, L. A. (2007). Understanding the mental health needs of American Muslims: Recommendations and considerations for practice. *Journal of Multicultural Counseling & Development, 35*, 207–218.

Alsultany, E. (2012). *Arabs and Muslims in the media: Race and representation after 9/11.* New York: New York University Press.

Ibrahim, F. A., & Dykeman, C. (2011). Counseling Muslim Americans: Cultural and spiritual assessments. *Journal of Counseling & Development, 89*, 387–396.

Lee, S. A., Gibbon, J. A., Thompson, J. M., & Timani, H. S. (2009). The Islamophobia Scale: Instrument development and initial validation. *International Journal for the Psychology of Religion, 19*, 92–105.

Nadal, K. L., Griffin, K. E., Hamit, S., Leon, J., Tobio, M., & Rivera, D. P. (2012). Subtle and overt forms of Islamophobia: Microaggressions toward Muslim Americans. *Journal of Muslim Mental Health, 6*, 15–37. doi:10.3998/ jmmh.10381607.0006.203

Sue, D. W., & Sue, D. (2016). Counseling Arab Americans and Muslim Americans. In *Counseling the culturally diverse: Theory and practice* (7th ed., pp. 573–590). Hoboken, NJ: John Wiley & Sons, Inc.

# CHAPTER 22

## Service-Learning Ideas for Universities and Graduate School

*Judith Justice*

### Course Recommendations

| SOCIAL JUSTICE AND ADVOCACY PRINCIPLES | CORE CACREP STANDARDS | COUNSELING SPECIALIZATION |
|---|---|---|
| ☑ Strategies for Change | ☑ Career Development<br>☑ Helping Relationships<br>☑ Social and Cultural Diversity | ☑ School Counseling |

## TOPIC

Multicultural awareness, advocacy, and social justice can be taught through service-learning projects, which use practical learning with higher order thinking to benefit the community. Students-in-training are required to design a service-learning project as a major project.

## LEARNING OBJECTIVES

- Students participate in helping youth to contribute to communities.
- Students advocate for a cause to help others.
- Students relate to, assist, and/or collaborate with those different than themselves.
- Students write proposals and search funding for projects.
- Students organize groups to assist others.

## TARGET POPULATION

Class of graduate students

## GROUP SIZE

5–20 students assisting groups of people (5–500)

# TIME REQUIRED

Student projects should take 5–20 hours to complete for class, though the actual projects could take 2 hours (workshop or dance) or months (on-going adopt a grandparent project).

# SETTING

Students present in their class, but the projects can take place in nursing homes, city parks, nursery schools, or wherever the student chooses.

# MATERIALS NEEDED

For students' presentation, a typical classroom is needed, including computers and screens for presentations. Students will supply their varied materials for class, and the actual projects will require volunteers, popcorn, juice-packs, face paints, etc.

# INSTRUCTIONS FOR CONDUCTING ACTIVITY

The first order of business is to ensure that university students know what service learning means and how they must fulfill the requirements of their project. This assignment will teach them how to get their K–12 students on board in regard to assisting others while learning, advocating, and practicing social justice.

Service learning is a great way to encourage students to learn early, while they are practicing social justice. Multicultural awareness, advocacy, and social justice can be gained as service-learning projects use practical learning to benefit the community. Their projects might include visiting and serving at a homeless shelter, visiting and serving at a nursing home, volunteering for the Red Cross, cooking and serving at the neighborhood soup kitchens, cleaning or gardening at local parks, tutoring at schools or churches, or other such activities.

Students-in-training are required to design a service-learning project as a major portion of one of their School Counseling courses. Students work with school counselors in their area and/or run a needs assessment to determine an area of need. They research the issues and determine their project, which includes a proposal, a paper, and a presentation.

University students write their proposal (similar to what they might include in grant-writing or other proposals) as if to propose the project to a possible organization. The proposal includes the service-learning plan and what will be achieved; its effect on community members; the students' learning (academic, social, etc.); and how the project will be implemented. Included in the proposal is research, the cost and funding, timeline, those who will benefit, those who will do the work, an evaluation tool (of what worked and what should be changed in the future), and plans for continuation of the project.

A scholarly APA, five- to eight-page paper is also required and is graded on the depth of the proposal plan, quality of the idea, and references. The presentation of the project reflects on the summary of the proposal, contemporary knowledge of the need, comprehensive concern of the specific issues, implications of counseling, respect of multicultural issues, and applied advocacy for social justice. Additional points are granted to those who implement their project. A Service-Learning Grading Rubric is included herein.

University students seem to love this assignment. They are encouraged with the skills they attain with this project, especially if they put it into action and see the actual results.

# DISCUSSION

Students will present their projects in class and lead class discussions on areas of strength and areas of improvement.

# BIBLIOGRAPHY

Students will present their project to their classmates for ideas on improvement. The required evaluation of the project will help students to gain insight should they actually do the project.

# SUGGESTED BACKGROUND READING

Students are required to research their topic and project. Ruby Payne's *Understanding Poverty* is helpful.

**HANDOUT**

# Handout 22.1: Service-Learning Project Rubric for Evaluation of Performance

Name_____     Date _____     _____/100

1. **Proposal** (5 points per item) /30
   a. Rationale (plan, implantation, effect on students' learning and community members)
   b. Cost and funding
   c. Who will benefit
   d. Who will work
   e. Continuation of project (after initial implementation)
   f. Evaluation
2. **Paper** (5 points per item) /20
   a. Scholarly depth of the justified proposal plan and quality of the idea
   b. APA six standards
   c. Five to eight pages
   d. Minimum of eight references
3. **Presentation: Project Content** (5 points each) /30
   *One to two slides each, summarizing content*
   a. Summary of proposal
   b. Demonstrates contemporary knowledge
   c. Comprehensive concern of the specific issue
   d. Implications of counseling
   e. Respectful and mindful of multicultural issues
   f. Applied advocacy for social justice
4. **Overall presentation** (4 points each) /20
   a. Presentation remained within the 15–20 minute parameter.
   b. Presentation was arranged well, had eye appeal, and was comprehensive.
   c. Presentation used discussion, hands-on learning activities, music, and/or movement.
   d. Eye contact, voice quality and volume, and variety of presentation held participants' interest.
   e. Presentation remained on topic, was timely, and flowed sensibly.

**+5. Bonus for implementing project and/or presenting to public**

# CHAPTER 23

# The Intersectionality of Dawn

*Kristine Ramsay-Seaner, Amber Letcher, Brandi Schmitt, and Courtney Ballard*

## Course Recommendations

| SOCIAL JUSTICE AND ADVOCACY PRINCIPLES | CORE CACREP STANDARDS | COUNSELING SPECIALIZATION |
|---|---|---|
| ☑ Intersections of Oppression | ☑ Helping Relationships<br>☑ Professional Counseling Orientation and Ethical Practice<br>☑ Social and Cultural Diversity | ☑ Clinical Mental Health Counseling<br>☑ Marriage, Couple, and Family Counseling |

## TOPIC

The purpose of this case study is to provide students with an opportunity to consider future counseling practice with a marginalized client. Moreover, students are encouraged to consider how their values and social privileges impact their ethical and/or diagnostic impression of the clients with whom they will work.

## LEARNING OBJECTIVES

As a result of this activity, students will:

1. Identify how personal values may impact the counseling process with future clients.
2. Increase their awareness of the complexity and intersectionality of issues presented by future clients.
3. Discuss ethical, multicultural, and/or diagnostic considerations when working with clients.

## TARGET POPULATION

This case study is most appropriate for master's-level graduate students enrolled in Ethics, Clinical Diagnosis, Multicultural Counseling, Couples and Family Counseling, Practicum, or Internship.

## GROUP SIZE

Students should be divided into small groups of three to four to discuss and process this case study.

## TIME REQUIRED

Students should be given 20–30 minutes to discuss and process the case study. An additional 30–45 minutes of class time should be set aside to discuss the case study as a large group.

## SETTING

The classroom should be arranged in a manner that allows for small group discussion. It is recommended that the case study be used in a classroom equipped with moveable chairs and tables in order to facilitate small group participation and discussion.

## MATERIALS NEEDED

- Copies of the case study
- 2014 American Counseling Association Code of Ethics (depending on objective of the activity)
- *Diagnostic Statistical Manual of Mental Disorders*, 5th Edition (depending on objective of the activity)
- Pen
- Paper

## INSTRUCTIONS FOR CONDUCTING ACTIVITY

The facilitator should divide the students into small groups of three to four students. It is encouraged that the facilitator be conscious of diversity when arranging the group, as increased group diversity will aid in the process and discussion of the case study. Students should be provided with a copy of the handout and instructed to consider the implications of working with Dawn. Depending on the objectives of the facilitator as well as the skills of the students, students may be encouraged to consider ethical, diagnostic, multicultural, and/or counseling implications. Students should be instructed to consider how their values and beliefs may impact their future work with marginalized clients in a community agency setting.

## DISCUSSION

Students should be encouraged to consider the following questions as they process the case study:

1. How did you picture Dawn as you were reading the case study?
2. What other assumptions might you have made about Dawn's identity as you were reading? For instance, would you describe Dawn as spiritual? Why or why not?
3. How would your own biases impact your work with Dawn?
4. Consider the concept of intersectionality. How do you foresee intersectionality impacting Dawn's development?
5. In what ways and at what different levels can you advocate for Dawn?
6. What other questions would you like to ask or information would you like to gather from Dawn in order to better understand her experiences and to provide adequate support?

Potential additional questions to add depending on course objectives:

- What is your diagnostic impression of Dawn based on the information provided? Please provide additional support for your diagnostic impression based on the information provided in the case study.

- What ethical considerations should be taken into account in working with Dawn? Do you have any presenting ethical concerns based on the information provided? What steps would you take to resolve any ethical concerns that you may have?

## BIBLIOGRAPHY

Carter, R. (1991). Cultural values: A review of empirical research and implications for counseling. *Journal of Counseling & Development, 70,* 164–173.

Dollarhide, C., & Oliver, K. (2014). Humanistic professional identity: The transtheoretical tie that binds. *Journal of Humanistic Counseling, 53,* 203–217.

Mallicoat, W. (2014). Counselors' perception of sexuality in counseling: A pilot study [the practitioner scholar]. *Journal of Counseling and Professional Psychology, 70,* 63–81.

## SUGGESTED BACKGROUND READING

American Counseling Association. (2014). *ACA code of ethics.* Arlington: VA: Author.

American Psychiatric Association. (2013). *Diagnostic and statistical manual of mental disorders* (5th ed.). Arlington, VA: American Psychiatric Publishing.

Sue, D., & Sue, D. (2013). *Counseling the culturally diverse: Theory and practice* (7th ed.). New York: J. Wiley.

**HANDOUT**

# Handout 23.1: The Intersectionality of Dawn

Dawn is a 21-year-old woman who is seeking counseling services after being referred by her doctor. Dawn reveals she is currently taking antidepressants and that her doctor has suggested she supplement this treatment with counseling. Dawn is also currently unemployed and receives governmental aid, including food stamps. Therefore, Dawn is seeking services at a community agency that provides low-income counseling services based on a sliding scale fee.

Dawn is the mother of three children, aged 4 years, 2 years, and 9 months old. Dawn reveals that she is currently in a custody battle with the father of her 9-month-old son, whom she is no longer in a romantic relationship with. She states she is concerned for her son's safety, as the father has a history of physical abuse toward the child.

When asked about social supports, Dawn states that she has her mother, with whom she and her three children currently live. Dawn, however, describes her relationship with her mother as strained and explains that her mother has a history of alcohol abuse, mental illness, and negligent behavior (Dawn was repeatedly taken away from her mother by child protective services when she was a child). Dawn's children are often left at home alone with Dawn's mother, because, Dawn says, "Sometimes I just need a break from my kids." Dawn also explains that her mother has recently threatened to kick her and her children out of the home, which has caused Dawn a great deal of stress.

Dawn reveals that she tends to use sex as a means of coping with stress in her life, which is a pattern she can trace back over the last four or five years. She explains that sex "helps me forget everything else that's happening around me," and describes feeling a thrill or a rush when she encounters new sexual partners. Dawn goes on to report that she engages in consensual sex with an average of three to six unfamiliar men per week, meeting them by happenstance in various areas of the community (e.g., truck stops, convenience stores, etc.). Dawn rarely brings men back to her own home, and states she will most often have sex "wherever it's convenient" (e.g., in vehicles, public restrooms, etc.). Dawn also states she is interested in BDSM. She has had a number of "doms" (i.e., the dominant person in a BDSM relationship or encounter) over the years, including the father of her 9-month-old son.

Dawn reports she has recently made multiple attempts to minimize her sexual behaviors, but that she has experienced great difficulty doing so. When describing her relapses to the therapist, Dawn will physically retreat, hide her face in her hands, and respond using baby talk. While Dawn expresses feeling shame in her difficulty to control her sexual impulses, she does report she has made some recent progress in other areas of her life. She has been studying to take the GED and has described an interest in signing up for parenting classes at a local church.

## Discussion Questions

1. How did you picture Dawn as you were reading the case study?
2. What other assumptions might you have made about Dawn's identity as you were reading? For instance, would you describe Dawn as spiritual? Why or why not?
3. How would your own biases impact your work with Dawn?
4. Consider the concept of intersectionality. How do you foresee intersectionality impacting Dawn's development?
5. In what ways and at what different levels can you advocate for Dawn?
6. What other questions would you like to ask or information would you like to gather from Dawn in order to better understand her experiences and to provide adequate support?

## Potential Additional Questions to Add Depending on Course Objectives

1. What is your diagnostic impression of Dawn based on the information provided? Please provide additional support for your diagnostic impression based on the information provided in the case study.
2. What ethical considerations should be taken into account in working with Dawn? Do you have any presenting ethical concerns based on the information provided? What steps would you take to resolve any ethical concerns that you may have?

# CHAPTER 24

## Aiming for Success

*Jayna Bonfini*

### Course Recommendations

| SOCIAL JUSTICE AND ADVOCACY PRINCIPLES | CORE CACREP STANDARDS | COUNSELING SPECIALIZATION |
|---|---|---|
| ☑ Social Constructs of Oppression and Privilege | ☑ Human Growth and Development<br>☑ Social and Cultural Diversity | ☑ Clinical Mental Health Counseling<br>☑ Student Affairs and College Counseling |

## TOPIC

This activity concerns the reality of economic mobility and demonstrates what being economically disadvantaged means, particularly in the context of upward mobility.

## LEARNING OBJECTIVES

1. Increase awareness about privilege and social mobility.
2. Identify problems faced by those lacking privilege.
3. Strategize ways to create equitable conditions in the classroom and counseling environments.

## TARGET POPULATION

Undergraduate or graduate classes in human development or multicultural awareness

## GROUP SIZE

This activity is adaptable to a classroom or group of any size. However, 15–25 participants are optimal for discussion after the activity.

## TIME REQUIRED

25 minutes total (5–10 minutes for activity; 15–20 minutes to process and discuss activity)

# SETTING

Classroom or other large group instruction space

# MATERIALS NEEDED

Sheet of paper for each participant; waste receptacle or recycling bin (preferred)

# INSTRUCTIONS FOR CONDUCTING ACTIVITY

1.  Provide each participate with a piece of paper and ask them to crumple up the paper into a ball. Move the waste receptacle or recycling bin to the front of the room.
2.  Explain to the participants that in our society, we all have a chance for upward mobility. In order to move up to the upper echelons of society, all they must do is throw their crumpled-up ball into the receptacle.
    a.  This should elicit reactions from those farthest away! Typically, those closest to the receptacle keep quiet and size up the distance to make an accurate throw.
3.  Ask the participants to take aim and throw their ball. Note to the participants that the closer they are to the receptacle, the better the odds for upward mobility. This is what privilege looks like.

# DISCUSSION

There was not an option of moving the chairs to the front, and participants had to figure out how to make their shot from their seats. Why? No one can change the circumstances that they are born into. The only thing that can be done is to figure out how to take a shot from where you are to the best of your ability. For children, the stakes are especially high given what we know about psychosocial development and the importance of high quality early childhood education.

We could hypothesize that the seating arrangements might represent different class elements, and one could layer on other things like gender or race into this activity. This is not to say that a wealthy, Caucasian, straight male will automatically succeed, but his struggle might not be as onerous due to his close proximity to the receptacle.

## Process Questions

- How did you feel doing this activity?
- How was it to consider your starting position and your likelihood of success?
- How was it to notice the starting position of others around you?
- What does it feel like to have or not have certain privileges?
- How do you think the back-row starting point relates to children who are afflicted by poverty?
- What if a person in the front row had an arm injury or disability that prevented that person from throwing?
- What are potential solutions to enable more people to have a successful shot? Some examples may be to expand the middle rows at the cost of the front rows, block the throws from the front rows, make the target larger, or add additional targets.

# BIBLIOGRAPHY

Dvorak, P. (2010, October 1). The grinding reality of growing up poor. *The Washington Post*. Retrieved from www.washingtonpost.com/wp-dyn/content/article/2010/09/30/AR2010093006864.html

Evans, G. W., & English, K. (2002). The environment of poverty: Multiple stressor exposure, psychophysiological stress, and socioemotional adjustment. *Child Development, 73*, 1238–1248. doi:10.1111/1467-8624.00469

Pyle, N. (2014, December 9). *BuzzFeed presents: Students learn a powerful lesson about privilege*. Retrieved from www.youtube.com/watch?v=2KlmvmuxzYE

# CHAPTER 25

## #LearningIn140Characters
## Twitter as a Pedagogical Tool for Social Justice

*Hector Y. Adames and Nayeli Y. Chavez-Dueñas*

### Course Recommendations

| SOCIAL JUSTICE AND ADVOCACY PRINCIPLES | CORE CACREP STANDARDS | COUNSELING SPECIALIZATION |
|---|---|---|
| ☑ What Is Social Justice and Advocacy?<br>☑ Intersections of Oppression<br>☑ Strategies for Change | ☑ Assessment and Testing<br>☑ Career Development<br>☑ Group Work<br>☑ Helping Relationships<br>☑ Human Growth and Development<br>☑ Professional Counseling Orientation and Ethical Practice<br>☑ Social and Cultural Diversity | ☑ Career Counseling<br>☑ Clinical Mental Health Counseling<br>☑ Marriage, Couple, and Family Counseling<br>☑ School Counseling<br>☑ Student Affairs and College Counseling |

## TOPIC

The activity aims to enhance student engagement with topics related to social justice and expand learning beyond the classroom by creating better continuity of content between class times.

## LEARNING OBJECTIVES

As a result of this activity students will:

1. Understand and identify ways that different social groups (e.g., immigrants, refugees, ethnic and racial minority groups, trans-community) engage in social justice related activities though social media.
2. Develop comprehension around the impact of systemic oppression on the lives of diverse individuals and communities; become aware of how experiences of oppression and marginalization may impact clinical work with members of minority groups; and learn how to utilize social media platforms as tools of social justice advocacy.

# TARGET POPULATION

Undergraduate and graduate students in counseling, psychology, social work, and the helping professions in general

# GROUP SIZE

The exercise can be used with 2–50 participants. It is optimal to have enough people to help generate content and interactions on social media.

# TIME REQUIRED

- This activity will require 10 to 20 minutes, either at the beginning or end, of each class meeting to reflect on content created and/or shared on Twitter.
- Participants will also need time outside of class to read and post content on Twitter on social justice endeavors that relate to the course content (e.g., research methods, assessment, theories, lifespan).

# SETTING

This activity is conducted online. Discussion around content generated on Twitter can be discussed at either the beginning or ending of class.

# MATERIALS NEEDED

1. Have or create a Twitter account.
2. Instructor creates a hashtag represented by the pound sign (#) that organizes and aggregates information created by topics.
3. Participants become familiar with how to get started with Twitter. Individuals not familiar with the social media platforms may visit: https://support.twitter.com/articles/215585#.

# INSTRUCTIONS FOR CONDUCTING ACTIVITY

Overview: the classrooms of the 21st century are predominately filled with a generation of tech-savvy students accustomed to being digitally connected around the clock (Adames, Chavez-Dueñas, Goertz, & Perez-Chavez, 2016). Their approach to learning, communicating, and engaging is evident in their increased usage of social media platforms including Instagram, Snapchat, Twitter, and the like. Overall, the current generation of graduate students is more likely to value exploratory learning, convenience, as well as the personalization and customization of education (Sweeney, 2006). Research suggests that using social media in the classroom can enhance student engagement, expand learning beyond the classroom, and create better continuity of content between class times (Adames et al., 2016; Domizi, 2013; Evans, 2014; Wright, 2010). Lastly, social media can help instructors track students' comprehension of how the course content is related to social justice by assessing how they connect what they are learning in the course with real-life examples.

1. Discuss the importance of balancing ethics, professionalism, and social media use as mental health providers. Read and discuss the articles listed in the "Required Background Reading" section.
2. Ask participants to create a Twitter account.
3. Explain the social media requirement and share the hashtag for the semester (e.g., #Fall17SocialJustice AndHealth, #Spring2018EquityAndCounseling).
   a. Decide ahead of time the number of tweets (posts) they are required to produce and share between classes. Of note, tweets are posts of 140 characters or less published on Twitter that can include text, images, or short video. Tweets are shown on users' timelines and are publicly made available to both users and nonusers.
   b. Provide students with clear expectations. A version of the following instructions can be included in the syllabus or provided at the beginning of the semester.

Instructions: Twitter is an increasing method employed by academics to share research, theory, best practices, and the like. Please sign up for a free Twitter account if you currently do not have one.

1. As part of this course, we will all participate in a Twitter activity throughout the semester. At a minimum, you are required to tweet once per day (minimum of seven tweets per week) in addition to retweeting, favoriting, and responding to content generated from members in the class.
2. Please keep in mind that all tweets must be accompanied by the class hashtag in order for us to follow what we are producing and sharing as a class. Our hashtag for the semester is, e.g., #Fall17SocialJusticeAndHealth.
3. Tweets should be relevant to content discussed during class sessions and connected to social justice. Lastly, if you start a message with "@" it will only be seen by that person and the followers you share. So never start a tweet with the @ symbol. For example, Dr. Adames' Twitter address is @HYAdames.

## DISCUSSION

During the beginning of each class, set aside 10–20 minutes for participants to share how the material produced and shared on Twitter is connected to social justice and the course content. The following are some questions to help ignite classroom discussions on the implications of the course content to social justice:

• What are you learning about social justice from the information shared this past week on Twitter?
• How does this new learning/new knowledge impact the work we are doing together here in the classroom?
• In what ways does this learning impact your interest in and commitment toward social justice?
• What are some of the personal reactions you are having while you review the content shared on Twitter?
• What social groups or topics have you noticed are under addressed in our Twitter discussions?

## BIBLIOGRAPHY

Adames, H. Y., Chavez-Dueñas, N. Y., Goertz, M. T., & Perez-Chavez, J. G. (2016). #DigitalLearning: Twitter as a pedagogical tool in psychology, a comparative study. *PsycEXTRA*.

Domizi, D. P. (2013). Microblogging to foster connections and community in a weekly graduate seminar course. *TechTrends*, *57*(1), 43–51.

Evans, C. (2014). Twitter for teaching: Can social media be used to enhance the process of learning? *British Journal of Educational Technology*, *45*(5), 902–915.

Sweeney, R. (2006). *Millennial behaviors and demographics*. Retrieved from https://certi.mst.edu/media/administrative/ certi/documents/Article-Millennial-Behaviors.pdf

Wright, N. (2010). Twittering in teacher education: Reflecting on practicum experiences. *Open Learning*, *25*(3), 259–265.

# REQUIRED BACKGROUND READING

Antheunis, M. L., Tates, K., & Nieboer, T. E. (2013). Patients' and health professionals' use of social media in health care: Motives, barriers and expectations. *Patient Education and Counseling, 92*(3), 426–431.

Hwang, H., & Kim, K. (2015). Social media as a tool for social movements: The effect of social media use and social capital on intention to participate in social movements. *International Journal of Consumer Studies, 39*(5), 478–488.

Kolmes, K., & Taube, D. O. (2014). Seeking and finding our clients on the internet: Boundary considerations in cyberspace. *Professional Psychology: Research and Practice, 45*(1), 3–10.

# CHAPTER 26

## Creating Change
### Social Justice Advocacy Group Project

*Cort Dorn-Medeiros*

### Course Recommendations

| SOCIAL JUSTICE AND ADVOCACY PRINCIPLES | CORE CACREP STANDARDS | COUNSELING SPECIALIZATION |
|---|---|---|
| ☑ Strategies for Change | ☑ Helping Relationships<br>☑ Professional Counseling Orientation and Ethical Practice<br>☑ Social and Cultural Diversity | ☑ Addiction Counseling<br>☑ Clinical Mental Health Counseling<br>☑ School Counseling |

## TOPIC

This small group activity provides master's-level counseling students a real world experience in creating an advocacy plan focused on community collaboration grounded in social justice theory. Students assess community needs via discussions with community members and mental health professionals in the fields of mental health and and/or addiction counseling, identify potential gaps in mental health and/or addiction counseling services, and create an advocacy plan to address the gap in needed services.

## LEARNING OBJECTIVES

1. Students will learn culturally sensitive and non-oppressive strategies for assessing community needs.
2. Students will learn necessary, developmentally appropriate skills for the creation of an advocacy plan to address community and agency identified gaps in mental health and/or addiction services.
3. Students will learn interpersonal and organizational skills to work as a group to effectively plan change in their current community.

## TARGET POPULATION

This activity is intended for master's-level counseling students in clinical mental health.

## GROUP SIZE

This activity is intended for groups of three to four students.

# TIME REQUIRED

This activity is intended to take place over the course of a 10–15 week academic class. The extended length of this activity is to allow the student groups sufficient time to identify a target mental health and/or addiction counseling agency or specific underserved population for their advocacy plan, debrief ongoing progress with the class instructor and peers, and present a final advocacy plan to the class.

# SETTING

This activity is intended to take place in the classroom, out in the community as students gather supporting information for justifying their advocacy plan, and outside the classroom wherever students plan to meet. While students are given two or three 30-minute sessions during class to meet and debrief with the course instructor, they are expected to spend significant time outside the classroom working on their project.

# MATERIALS NEEDED

Instructors will not need any specific materials. Student groups would benefit from the following:

1. Laptop or desktop computer with Internet access.
2. Notepad and pen or pencil or tablet or laptop to take field, interview, and group notes.
3. Library with access to academic journals, including journals focusing on mental health, counseling, and addictions.
4. Access to a word processing program and a presentation program such as Microsoft PowerPoint, Prezi, or Google Slides.

# INSTRUCTIONS FOR CONDUCTING ACTIVITY

1. Before students divide up into small groups, invite them to brainstorm on their own for 10–15 minutes about a social justice topic or area of focus that is meaningful for them. Some examples of topics are homelessness and housing insecurity, racial and ethnic equality, immigration and refugee services, post-prison populations, etc. These topics should be able to relate, in some way, to the field of professional mental health and/or addictions counseling.
2. After individual reflection, invite students to verbally share their personal topics with the entire class.
3. Students are then instructed to divide themselves up into groups of three or four based on a social justice related area of interest. As not all topics will directly align with each other, provide students approximately 20–30 minutes to talk to each other and decide, as a group, one area of interest on which they would like to focus.
4. Groups are given three weeks to narrow down their topic to one critical issue within their target area. Examples of critical issues could be addressing limited access to mental health counseling for children of lower-income families, providing addiction treatment services within correctional facilities, increasing availability of culturally appropriate counseling services, and creating an outreach program to offer counseling support to those experiencing homelessness or housing insecurity. Groups must be able to justify their critical issue through completing the following actions:
    a. Review the current literature on their selected topic. Does the literature point to any current needs or gaps in counseling services related to their topic?
    b. Research specific resources in their community, such as agencies, community centers, churches, and private practitioners that contain members of the target population or provide services for their target population.

c.  Get out in the community and talk to people! Contact a minimum of three of the preceding outside resources. Ask them about their current areas of need. Example questions to ask are, If you or your agency/center/church could have any counseling-related service made available, what would it be? and What do your clients say they are currently lacking in their treatment, care, or supportive services?

5.  After conducting a literature review and getting input from community resources, student groups will begin creating an advocacy plan around their critical issue using the provided template (see handout). Advocacy plans should be as detailed as possible and include items such as addressing basic budget and funding, service delivery, and sustainability. Groups will be given four weeks to complete this portion of the project.

6.  Instructors should allow two to three opportunities for groups to consult and debrief in class with both the instructor and peers during these four weeks.

7.  Each group must collectively write one ten-page paper to submit to the instructor. This paper should address the following:

a.  A clear statement of the identified critical issue and evidence of said issue through literature review and interviews with community resources.

b.  A discussion of systemic and cultural attitudes toward the critical issue.

c.  Identification of a specific target location for the advocacy plan. If you were to implement this plan, where would you be advocating and to whom?

d.  Specific advocacy plan including timeline, budget and financial concerns, strategies for implementation, and needed additional resources.

e.  Brief discussion of why this specific plan will be effective.

f.  Identification of one or two obstacles to implementation and potential strategies to address these should they arise.

8.  This activity is concluded with in-class group presentations. Each group will give a 30-minute presentation of their advocacy plan to the class. Presentations must include a visual element using a presentation program such as PowerPoint, Prezi, or Google Slides.

# DISCUSSION

Following group presentations, students will engage in a semi-structured discussion regarding their group process and the project's impact on their understanding of social justice and advocacy work. Depending on time limitations of the class, this discussion may take place immediately following the group presentations or the class directly following. Some examples of prompt questions include:

• What did you learn about social justice and advocacy work during this project?

• How does your advocacy plan translate to the greater counseling profession? What does it mean to be a social justice oriented counselor?

• What surprised you during your interactions with community resources? Did you learn anything unexpected?

• Share a bit about your group process during this project. What was difficult? What went better than expected? How did you address conflicts or disagreements?

# BIBLIOGRAPHY

Lewis, J. A., Ratts, M. J., Paladino, D. A., & Toporek, R. L. (2011). Social justice counseling and advocacy: Developing new leadership roles and competencies. *Journal for Social Action in Counseling and Psychology*, 3(1), 5–16.

Myers, J. W., Sweeney, T. J., & White, V. E. (2002). Advocacy for counseling and counselors: A professional imperative. *Journal of Counseling and Development: JCD*, 80(4), 394.

# SUGGESTED BACKGROUND READING

Goodman, R. D., Williams, J. M., Chung, R. C. Y., Talleyrand, R. M., Douglass, A. M., McMahon, H. G., & Bemak, F. (2015). Decolonizing traditional pedagogies and practices in counseling and psychology education: A move towards social justice and action. In *Decolonizing "multicultural" counseling through social justice* (pp. 147–164). New York: Springer.

Ratts, M. J., & Hutchins, A. M. (2009). ACA advocacy competencies: Social justice advocacy at the client/student level. *Journal of Counseling and Development, 87*(3), 269–275.

Ratts, M. J., Singh, A. A., Nassar-McMillan, S., Butler, S. K., McCullough, J. R., & Hipolito-Delgado, C. (2015). *Multicultural and social justice counseling competencies*. Alexandria, VA: AMCD.

Ratts, M. J., Toporek, R. L., & Lewis, J. A. (2010). *ACA advocacy competencies: A social justice framework for counselors.* American Counseling Association.

# Handout 26.1: Creating Change: Advocacy Plan

1. *Describe the problem your plan will address.*
2. *What is the target location of your advocacy plan?* Be specific. This should be a local agency, community center, church, etc. where your plan would be implemented.
3. *In a few sentences, state the evidence your group collected to justify the identified problem.* This includes any relevant literature and conversations with local agencies, community centers, churches, community members and leaders.
4. *In two to three paragraphs, describe how your group plans to advocate with your target location and/or population.* Provide a narrative overview of your step-by-step plan.
5. *Write out step-by-step action items to implement your plan.* Be sure to specify who will be responsible for each action item.
6. *Provide a general overview of budget and funding.* What do you estimate is the cost of implementing your plan? Where would you get necessary funds?
7. *Briefly discuss sustainability of your plan.* What resources does your group need to ensure your plan could continue in the future after your initial implementation?
8. *What challenges do you anticipate in implementing your plan or in the sustainability of your plan?* How would you address these challenges?

# CHAPTER 27

# Songs for Social Justice and Advocacy
## Songs Make Me Want to Fight or Just Do Something

*Charles Edwards*

## Course Recommendations

| SOCIAL JUSTICE AND ADVOCACY PRINCIPLES | CORE CACREP STANDARDS | COUNSELING SPECIALIZATION |
|---|---|---|
| ☑ What Is Social Justice and Advocacy?<br>☑ Strategies for Change | ☑ Professional Counseling Orientation and Ethical Practice<br>☑ Social and Cultural Diversity | ☑ Addiction Counseling<br>☑ Clinical Mental Health Counseling<br>☑ Marriage, Couple, and Family Counseling<br>☑ School Counseling |

## TOPIC

Sharing songs of freedom and justice: music and songs and important tools in the fight against oppression

## LEARNING OBJECTIVES

1. Students will identify songs that motivate them to act or fight against injustices (general or specific). Students will connect specific songs with specific social justice causes.
2. Students will discuss the significance of songs for promoting social justice issues.
3. Students will share and listen to music that highlights different forms of oppression.

## TARGET POPULATION

This activity is best suited for students in graduate counseling programs and for counseling professionals seeking to reinforce their commitment to social justice and advocacy.

## GROUP SIZE

This activity is suited for a class or group of 15–20 participants who will work in subgroups of four to five.

# TIME REQUIRED

In a class of 15–20 students this activity should take 60–75 minutes. Time may be adjusted based on variations in the number of students. Give an overall time estimate that is needed to complete the activity. Suggested distribution of time is as follows:

Introduction: 5–10 minutes
Group work: 25 minutes
Group presentations and discussion: 25–30 minutes, 5 minutes each
Summary evaluation: 5–10 minutes

# SETTING

This activity is suited for a classroom that is large enough to accommodate 15–20 participants. There should be sufficient space to allow groups of four to five participants to work together. Classrooms and venues should allow participants to easily move into groups and return to their positions for presentation. The size of the group may be adjusted downward depending on the size of the room. Rooms suited for individuals with varying physical disabilities would be ideal.

# MATERIALS NEEDED

Paper, pencil, or pen will be needed for this activity. The room should also be equipped with audio visual and online technologies. Participants may be permitted to use cell phones to complete the group activity. Participants should be asked to put away cell phones during presentations.

# INSTRUCTIONS FOR CONDUCTING ACTIVITY

1. Introduction. Instructor will begin by seeking to activate participants' prior knowledge of the importance of music and songs in highlighting social justice issues. Instructor may ask students to quickly identify songs that motivate individuals and groups to take action regarding a specific or general cause. Instructor may give examples to enhance students' understanding. Instructor will help students make a connection between music, social justice, oppression, and advocacy.
2. Instructor will inform students that they will be working in groups of four or five members to brainstorm and identify five songs that have motivated them to take some kind of action on a specific or general issue. Let students know that actions may include a number of things such as speaking out, changing ones behavior, or demonstrating. Let students know that they will be asked to present their songs and talk about their process to the class.
3. Instructor will model examples for the students by selecting and playing a song that motivates him/her to take action against an injustice. Instructor will model the process of selecting the song, stating why the song was selected and how it motivated her/him to take action. For example, the song "Get Up Stand Up" by Bob Marley may be used as a song that promotes resistance and advocacy. The presenter then plays the song with lyrics displayed on a large screen. Students are then asked to reflect on the song, stating their own feelings, thoughts, and associations.
4. Instructor will randomly place students in groups by counting from one to four (or five). All ones, twos, threes, and so on will form working groups. Encourage groups to allow for maximum space between each other in order to lessen distractions.
5. Ask the groups to begin working; inform them that they will be working for 25 minutes. Each subgroup will brainstorm and come up with a minimum of three songs and decide which of these songs they will play for the entire class.

6. Provide students with paper and pen/pencil.
7. Inform students that they may use cell phones and headphones to assist in completing the task. Inform students that they will need to put away cell phones when presentations begin.
8. Encourage students to work collaboratively and dip into their reservoirs of songs to complete the task.
9. Provide support to the group as need. Let students know when they have 10 and 5 minutes left to complete the task.
10. When all groups have completed the task determine quickly the order of presentations.
11. Each group will present their songs and speak about their process, feelings, thoughts, and associations. Each group will play one of the three songs selected for entire class. One or two questions or comments may follow each presentation.
12. Lead the entire class into an applause after each group presents.
13. Discussion will follow after all groups have presented. The discussion will focus on students' thoughts, feelings, associations, and other reactions to the presentations. In order to support the discussion the instructor will ask the following questions:
    • What are your thoughts, feelings, and associations regarding the songs presented today?
    • How do the presentations support or deepen your understanding of the connection between music, social justice, and advocacy.
14. Summary and conclusion. Instructor should thank all the groups for their presentations and emphasize the following points:
    • Social justice, oppression, and multiculturalism are not just constructs found in textbooks; they are real issues that are explored in popular music forms. Music can be conceptual as a tool that can serve to liberate and also to oppress (Clonal & Johnson, 2002). Any given song may also be subjected to multiple interpretations and usage. The songs that were presented served as motivational tools for advocacy. Carefully consider also the connection between empathy and advocacy (Fischlin & Heble, 2003).

## DISCUSSION

Instructor will implement strategies to encourage thought and discussion. Before each presentation group members should be asked to talk about the process involved in selecting their songs and why the songs were selected. Group members should be encouraged to explore thoughts, feelings, and associations related to their selections. Participants will then play one of the songs they feel best represents the specific type of oppression they identified. The song will be played for the entire class with lyrics displayed on large smart board screen. The instructor will inform students that an important component of the class is the ability to listen to each group's presentation. Listening will be highlighted as an important counseling skill.

## BIBLIOGRAPHY

Clonal, M., & Johnson, B. (2002). Killing me softly with his song: An initial investigation into the use of popular music as a tool of oppression. *Popular Music, 21*(1), 27–39.

Fischlin, D., & Heble, A. (2003). *Rebel musics: Human rights, resistant sounds, and the politics of music making* (p. 11). Montreal: Black Rose.

## SUGGESTED BACKGROUND READING

Adams, M., & Bell, L. A. (Eds.). (2016). *Teaching for diversity and social justice*. New York: Routledge.

Ratts, M. J., Singh, A. A., Nassar-McMillan, S., Butler, S. K., McCullough, J. R., & Hipolito-Delgado, C. (2015). *Multicultural and social justice counseling competencies*. Alexandria, VA: AMCD.

Schmitz, C., Stakeman, C., & Sisneros, J. (2001). Educating professionals for practice in a multicultural society: Understanding oppression and valuing diversity. *Families in Society: The Journal of Contemporary Social Services, 82*(6), 612–622.

# CHAPTER 28

## Personal Perspectives
### A Social Justice and Religion/Spirituality Developmental Timeline

*Timothy Hanna*

## Course Recommendations

| SOCIAL JUSTICE AND ADVOCACY PRINCIPLES | CORE CACREP STANDARDS | COUNSELING SPECIALIZATION |
|---|---|---|
| ☑ What Is Social Justice and Advocacy?<br>☑ Cycle of Socialization and Liberation<br>☑ Social Constructs of Oppression and Privilege<br>☑ Intersections of Oppression | ☑ Human Growth and Development<br>☑ Social and Cultural Diversity | ☑ Addiction Counseling<br>☑ Career Counseling<br>☑ Clinical Mental Health Counseling<br>☑ Marriage, Couple, and Family Counseling<br>☑ School Counseling<br>☑ Student Affairs and College Counseling |

## TOPIC

This activity involves an exploration of the counselor trainee's developmental timeline in terms of their religious and spiritual worldviews that intersect with social justice perspectives.

## LEARNING OBJECTIVES

1. Gain insight into how one's religious and spiritual identifications contribute to one's social justice understandings.
2. Identify key religious and spiritual influences on one's orientation to social justice.
3. Recognize the developmental sequence of such influences, from youth to present day.

## TARGET POPULATION

Counselor trainees and/or current practitioners, regardless of religious or spiritual affiliation

# GROUP SIZE

1–15—this can be done individually, but would benefit from a sharing component. In classroom settings, the activity can start with individual reflection, and then break up into small groups of two to four for sharing, followed by bringing it back to the large group.

# TIME REQUIRED

The personal reflection component of this activity can be augmented by assigning extra time ahead of the subsequent interaction, e.g., one week, one day, 1 hour; or, if done in class, should be given at least 15 minutes. Ongoing reflection post-activity can be expected and encouraged.

When involving small groups, the sharing component should allow at least 5 minutes per group member. So, for example, a class of 15 students can be broken into five groups of three students each, with 15–20 minutes total for small group discussion.

In classroom settings, subsequent large group discussion should be given another 15–30 minutes, at least.

# SETTING

Personal reflection can be done ahead of time at home or in class, or students can be allowed to find a comfortable space nearby to reflect individually (with more time allotted accordingly).

Small group sharing can be done either in class or in nearby breakout rooms/other private, quiet spaces.

Large group sharing should be done in a setting that allows for all to hear and participate, with teacher facilitating discussion—e.g., classroom.

# MATERIALS NEEDED

Paper and pencil/pen (per student)

# INSTRUCTIONS FOR CONDUCTING ACTIVITY

This is an activity to help you understand how your religious and spiritual identities impact your social justice perspectives. It essentially involves developing a personal timeline that traces different religious and spiritual influences on your social justice perspectives across your lifespan. The activity applies to everyone, regardless of religious or spiritual affiliation. Even if you do not currently identify as religious or spiritual, this activity can reveal important aspects of your worldview, as these influences can come through from various points in your life. The idea is to really reflect on what those different religious and/or spiritual influences have been, as they impact your social justice perspectives. Even if you currently identify as atheist, agnostic, or even a-spiritual, you can reflect on your past religious/spiritual influences as well as your current and past core principles and guiding beliefs regarding personal and societal purpose, meaning, and significance.

1.  Before attending to the specifics of this activity, you should familiarize yourself with the essential concepts of social justice—especially the fundamentals of systemic privilege and oppression, marginalization and disenfranchisement, and the social justice emphasis on active engagement to redress unjust sociopolitical structures. These fundamentals are further unpacked in some of the following "Suggested

Background Readings," especially the Johnson (2017) text, and are also summarized in the "handout" addendum to this activity.

2.  Having familiarized yourself with the aforementioned, find a quiet place where you can now reflect on your religious and spiritual views on social justice matters. For instance, what do you believe about how people are created? How are you called to respond to inequality and injustice in the world? What is your ultimate purpose? How are you called to live in community with others? What other aspects of your religious and/or spiritual identity bear on your views of social justice issues? (5–30 minutes)

3.  Think about where these views come from, and how they have changed across your lifetime. Have there been important experiences in your life that shaped those views? Important religious or spiritual texts, congregations, or leaders that shaped those views? How has your family impacted those religious and spiritual orientations to social justice? How have your friends? How have you related to those different social messages that came to you through religious and spiritual formats? (5–30 minutes)

4.  Either starting with where you currently are, or at any other key point in your timeline that strikes you first, begin to trace your timeline of religious and spiritual influences on your social justice perspectives. For instance, you might note that you currently belong to a certain church that espouses certain views on matters related to social justice, and might note that you personally do not agree 100 percent with those views or perhaps agree wholeheartedly with them and draw a great sense of identity and belonging from those communal ideas. Mark that down somewhere toward the bottom of your paper, and then start tracing back to other key points in your lifespan where you recall having important religious and/or spiritual views/experiences/conversations that impacted your orientation toward social justice matters. (5–30 minutes)

5.  By the end, you should have outlined the key religious and spiritual influences on your social justice perspectives across your lifetime, to date. Looking back over the timeline, what stands out to you? What are the most important moments that impacted your views? Has there been substantial change or relative constancy in your views? Are there any patterns or common themes that you notice with regard to your views or the religious/spiritual influences on them? Is there anything else that comes up for you that you feel needs to be added or mentioned with regard to your timeline? (5–15 minutes)

6.  Having reflected on your own journey, gather in small groups of two to four, and share with each other what came up for you. You do not have to share anything you do not feel comfortable sharing, and can share as much as you like. In particular, share what were the main sources of religious/spiritual influence on your social justice views? How have they shifted or changed, or not? How does the timeline connect with what your views are today on social justice? (5–10 minutes per group member)

7.  After sharing in small groups, return to your large group setting, where your designated leader/instructor will facilitate a large group discussion/debriefing. (15–30 minutes)

# DISCUSSION

1.  What were the main sources of religious and/or spiritual influences for you on your views pertaining to social justice? Did you notice any particularly influential experiences, texts, congregational leaders, family influences, friend influences, or personal experiences?

2.  Have you noticed significant changes in your religious/spiritual views on social justice matters across your lifespan? To what do you attribute those changes?

3.  What is it like for you to consider these sources of religious and/or spiritual influence? Does it feel personal? Sacred? Vulnerable?

4.  How do you feel about the level of impact/influence that those religious/spiritual identities and experiences have had on your social justice perspectives? Do they seem insignificant? Essential? Moderately influential? Worthwhile considerations?

5.  How do you feel future changes in your social justice perspectives might interact with your religious/spiritual views? Will one have to change for the other? If such changes prove challenging, how would you navigate such changes? What sources might you draw upon to cope with any associated stressors?

6. A final layer to consider, if it has not already come up in discussion or reflection, is the privilege of religious group membership itself. How much sociopolitical power has been attributed to your own religious group, past and present? How has that privilege or marginalization impacted your orientation toward social justice initiatives? How might you envision advocating for clients and individuals who belong to less privileged religious groups? What accommodations might you make in your clinical work settings to foster greater mental health access and equity for members of various religious/spiritual groups and identities?

# BIBLIOGRAPHY

American Counseling Association (2014). *ACA code of ethics*. Alexandria, VA: Author.

Ammerman, N. T. (2013). Spiritual but not religious? Beyond binary choices in the study of religion. *Journal for the Scientific Study of Religion, 52*(2), 258–278. doi:10.1111/jssr.12024

Beer, A., Spanierman, L., Greene, J., & Todd, N. (2012). Counseling psychology trainees' perceptions of training and commitments to social justice. *Journal of Counseling Psychology, 59*(1), 120–133. doi:10.1037/a0026325

Buser, J. K., Buser, T. J., & Peterson, C. H. (2013). Counselor training in the use of spiritual lifemaps: Creative interventions for depicting spiritual/religious stories. *Journal of Creativity in Mental Health, 8*(4), 363–380. doi:10.1080/15401383.2013.844659

Caldwell, J., & Vera, E. (2010). Critical incidents in counseling psychology professionals and trainees' social justice orientation development. *Training and Education in Professional Psychology, 4*, 163–176. doi:10.1037/a0019093

Crethar, H., & Winterowd, C. (2012). Values and social justice in counseling. *Counseling and Values, 57*, 3–9. doi:10.1002/j.2161-007X.2012.00001.x

Curry, J. R. (2009). Examining client spiritual history and the construction of meaning: The use of spiritual timelines in counseling. *Journal of Creativity in Mental Health, 4*(2), 113–123. doi:10.1080/15401380902945178

Hanna, T. S. (2016). *Counselor Conscientization: Exploring religious and spiritual identities in the development of a critical consciousness in counselor trainees* (Unpublished doctoral dissertation). Loyola University Maryland, Baltimore, MD.

Johnson, A. (2017). *Privilege, power, and difference*. Boston, MA: McGraw-Hill.

Manis, A. (2012). A review of the literature on promoting cultural competence and social justice agency among students and counselor trainees: Piecing the evidence together to advance pedagogy and research. *The Professional Counselor: Research and Practice, 2*(1), 48–57. Retrieved from http://tpcjournal.nbcc.org

Miller, M., & Sendrowitz, K. (2011). Counseling psychology trainees' social justice interest and commitment. *Journal of Counseling Psychology, 58*, 159–169. doi:10.1037/a0022663

Parikh, S., Post, P., & Flowers, C. (2011). Relationship between a belief in a just world and social justice advocacy attitudes of school counselors. *Counseling and Values, 56*, 57–72. doi:10.1002/j.2161-007X.2011.tb01031.x

Singh, A., Hofsess, C., Boyer, E., Kwong, A., Lau, A., McLain, M., & Haggins, K. (2010). Social justice and counseling psychology: Listening to the voices of doctoral trainees. *Counseling Psychologist, 38*, 766–795. doi:10.1177/0011000010362559

Todd, N., McConnell, E., & Suffrin, R. (2014). The role of attitudes toward white privilege and religious beliefs in predicting social justice interest and commitment. *American Journal of Community Psychology, 53*(1–2), 109–121. doi:10.1007/s10464-014-9630-x

Todd, N., & Rufa, A. (2013). Social justice and religious participation: A qualitative investigation of Christian perspectives. *American Journal of Community Psychology, 51*, 315–331. doi:10.1007/s10464-012-9552-4

# SUGGESTED BACKGROUND READING

Caldwell, J., & Vera, E. (2010). Critical incidents in counseling psychology professionals' and trainees' social justice orientation development. *Training and Education in Professional Psychology, 4*, 163–176. doi:10.1037/a0019093

Crethar, H., & Winterowd, C. (2012). Values and social justice in counseling. *Counseling and Values, 57*, 3–9. doi:10.1002/j.2161-007X.2012.00001.x

DeYoung, C. (2007). *Living faith: How faith inspires social justice*. Minneapolis, MN: Fortress Press.

Johnson, A. (2017). *Privilege, power, and difference*. Boston, MA: McGraw-Hill.

Kiesling, C., Sorell, G., Montgomery, M., & Colwell, R. (2006). Identity and spirituality: A psychosocial exploration of the sense of spiritual self. *Developmental Psychology, 42*, 1269–1277. doi:10.1037/0012-1649.42.6.1269

Lee, C., & Hipolito-Delgado, C. (2007). Introduction: Counselors as agents of social change. In C. Lee (Ed.), *Counseling for social justice* (2nd ed., pp. xiii–xxviii). Alexandria, VA: American Counseling Association.

McAdams, D. (2001). The psychology of life stories. *Review of General Psychology, 5*, 100–122. doi:10.1037/1089-2680.5.2.100

Singh, A., Hofsess, C., Boyer, E., Kwong, A., Lau, A., McLain, M., & Haggins, K. (2010). Social justice and counseling psychology: Listening to the voices of doctoral trainees. *Counseling Psychologist, 38,* 766–95. doi:10.1177/0011000010362559

Todd, N., & Rufa, A. (2013). Social justice and religious participation: A qualitative investigation of Christian perspectives. *American Journal of Community Psychology, 51,* 315–331. doi:10.1007/s10464-012-9552-4

Wink, P., Adler, J., & Dillon, M. (2012). Developmental and narrative perspectives on religious and spiritual identity for clinicians. In J. Aten, K. O'Grady, & E. Worthington, Jr. (Eds.), *The psychology of religion and spirituality for clinicians: Using research in your practice* (pp. 39–68). New York: Routledge.

# HANDOUT

# Handout 28.1: Social Justice Definitions

## UNDERSTANDING DIVERSITY, VALUE CONFLICTS, MULTICULTURAL SENSITIVITY, SOCIAL JUSTICE, AND ADVOCACY IN COUNSELING

Remember that multicultural competency is a dynamic, ongoing process. It is not something that is ever "fully" realized or actualized, but something that we are always working on and attending to . . . because, after all, it hinges on a key principle that we are all unique and different, and those differences require continuous attention and learning. An attitude of openness and curiosity allows us to continue in humble support of the "worth, dignity, potential, and uniqueness of people within their social and cultural contexts" (ACA, 2014, Code of Ethics Preamble). There are a handful of constructs to be distinguished within this overarching aim:

1. First, one might note the importance of *diversity, value conflicts*, and *multicultural sensitivity* in counseling. Remember that our counseling profession has certain embedded cultural values. They are largely "Western," with certain emphases that may vary from other cultures. For instance, East Asian, Middle Eastern, South American, and Sub-Saharan African cultures often include more collectivistic values; but the more general message here is to be mindful that our clients' viewpoints may differ from our own in ways that are very important to the therapeutic endeavor. Important differences exist between any given counselor and client that may influence one's ability to understand their struggles and to offer the most effective treatment strategies. Understanding our own multicultural identities and those of our clients, and fostering ways of learning through open curiosity and consultation, can enhance our benevolent aims of treating each individual in a more cooperative and helpful manner.

2. When we start to consider more closely the diversity of human identities, experiences, values, etc., we start to recognize a second facet of this overarching emphasis on multicultural competency—namely, the experience of *marginalization* and corresponding call to *social justice*. Social justice recognizes that certain groups of ("marginalized") individuals experience less access to resources and avenues that would secure their well-being than other groups (e.g., access to education, financial resources such as loans, political recognition and/or representation, etc.). This is called "disenfranchisement," and relates to a concrete lack of access and lack of sociopolitical power within the structures of our society. It is connected to racism/sexism/ageism, etc.; but whereas those "-isms" pertain to personal views, social justice is more attuned to the systemic, sociopolitical structures that maintain a certain status quo, maintaining the power and privilege of those who have it, while inhibiting the advancement or rightful claim to power of those who lack it. So, attending to matters of social justice means examining and ultimately altering the social structures that inhibit access to resources for marginalized and disenfranchised groups. Those groups have historically (and contemporarily) included people of color, women, members of the LGBT community, some religious minorities, the elderly, the physically or mentally disabled, the poor, and non-native language speakers.

3. From here, we can move more easily into the third and final facet of this overarching value of multiculturalism—namely, *advocacy*. Advocacy is about taking action to help bring attention to a lack of equity, power, or recognition experienced by certain groups. As counselors, we see first hand the disenfranchisement experienced by women, people of color, members of the LGBT community, etc. It is part of our professional identity to respond to that inequity by taking action to facilitate changes in the sociopolitical structures that keep such groups sociopolitically oppressed. This action includes an

element of "active citizenship" wherein we can participate in organizations and/or contact our local, state, and national representatives to advocate for more just and equitable policies. Such engagement can also occur on more immediate levels, for instance, by advocating for more equitable policies at our clinical work settings (e.g., access for individuals with disabilities, language translation access for non-English speakers, transportation services for individuals with fewer financial resources, etc.). Both immediate and larger, more systemic interventions contribute to our professional aims by promoting client welfare through access to mental health care and other vital resources.

## REFERENCE

American Counseling Association (ACA) (2014). *ACA code of ethics*. Alexandria, VA: Author.

# CHAPTER 29

## Teaching African American Male Counselors-in-Training
### Perspective and Bias Management

*Courtney R. Boddie*

## Course Recommendations

| SOCIAL JUSTICE AND ADVOCACY PRINCIPLES | CORE CACREP STANDARDS | COUNSELING SPECIALIZATION |
|---|---|---|
| ☑ Cycle of Socialization and Liberation<br>☑ Social Constructs of Oppression and Privilege | ☑ Helping Relationships<br>☑ Professional Counseling Orientation and Ethical Practice<br>☑ Social and Cultural Diversity | ☑ Clinical Mental Health Counseling<br>☑ Marriage, Couple, and Family Counseling<br>☑ Student Affairs and College Counseling |

## TOPIC

This activity is designed to teach counselor educators-in-training about working effectively with master's students who identify as African American men. As an act of social justice, this activity serves to model ways in which counselor educators-in-training can use their position and voice to advocate for the use of equitable practices. The overarching goal of this activity is to develop a working theory about African American male counselors-in-training based on the extant literature. The working theory is intended to create or enrich a lens that enables counselor educators-in-training to formulate instructional approaches that are culturally responsive. Learning to do so with regard to this population is expected to establish a protocol for developing culturally responsive approaches with other marginalized and underserved groups. Additionally, this work to rectify unjust instructional practices can serve as fodder to apply the same approach to advocate for more socially just institution-level practices.

## LEARNING OBJECTIVES

- To develop a working theory about African American male counselors-in-training
- To understand the sociohistorical and sociopolitical context in which African American men approach graduate-level training
- To recognize specific barriers (e.g., in the classroom) one may encounter when working with counselors-in-training who identify as African American men
- To deepen awareness of personal triggers related to work with counselors-in-training who identify as African American men

- To notice, respond to, and prevent biased communication in interactions with counselors-in-training who identify as African American men

## TARGET POPULATION

Counselor educators-in-training

## GROUP SIZE

5–15

## TIME REQUIRED

2 hours

## SETTING

This activity will be best served by being conducted in a classroom or conference room. It is recommended for use in courses on counselor education and supervision, university teaching, teaching and learning in counselor education, curriculum and instruction, pedagogy, theories of learning, or advanced multicultural counseling. All suggested courses are doctoral level.

## MATERIALS NEEDED

- Articles
- PowerPoint presentation
- Pencils

## INSTRUCTIONS FOR CONDUCTING ACTIVITY

In this activity, students will give a short lecture, interact as part of a process group, and develop a written action plan. The lectures will provide a didactic component that addresses learning objectives two and three. The group experience will provide a process component that addresses learning objectives four and five.

### Lecture

For efficiency, the following recommendations are made for the course instructor. The instructor should assign topics either individually for small class sizes or in pairs for larger class sizes. For ease, the instructor should also set a predetermined order for the presentations. All presenters will be asked to provide slides with space to take notes. Additionally, all presentations should be emailed to the instructor prior to the session during which the activity will take place. This will enable the instructor to load the presentations all at once at the beginning of class.

## Topics Include

- The myth of anti-intellectualism (Cokley, 2014)
- The myth of acting white (Fordham & Ogbu, 1986)
- The relationship between racial scripting (Williams, 2007) and academic self-concept (Cokley, 2000)
- The role of Toms, coons, mulattoes, and bucks in historical and modern media portrayal of African American men (Bogle, 2001).
- The invisibility syndrome (Franklin & Boyd-Franklin, 2000) and Cool Pose (Majors & Billson, 1992)
- The relationship between racial identity development (Cross, 1971) and stereotype threat (Steele & Aronson, 1995)
- Data
  - Representation of African American men in the field of counselor education (CACREP, 2016)
  - General challenges African American men face approaching academic tasks (Cokely, 2014)
  - Overrepresentation of African American men in special education (Bolden, 2009)
  - Impact of racism on well-being (Clark, Anderson, Clark, & Williams, 1999)
- Use of non-Eurocentric pedagogical approaches
  - Liberation psychology (Burton, 2013; Friere, 2000)
  - Critical race theory (Ladson-Billings, 1998  )

## Criteria for Presentations

- Instructors should allot 1 hour for the five presentations.
- Each presentation should be 10 minutes (timed).
- Slide sequence:
  - Title
  - Raw disclosure of academic and personal perspectives on African American men
  - Agenda
  - Ten body slides
  - Reference slide

Note: each slide should include: (a) parenthetical or in-text citations and (b) three to four bullet points and/or one to two images.

## Process Group

For the remaining time in class (approximately 1 hour), students will process what they have learned: Suggested allocation of group time
Topic: check-in on content (10 minutes).

- What questions did you have about any of the presentations?
- What are your thoughts and feelings about the content discussed in the five presentations? What did you notice about your attitudes, beliefs, and values regarding this population?

Topic: I noticed friction (10 minutes).
    For this segment, students will process feelings of dissonance that arose in response to the presented information.

- What does it mean to have recognized a barrier to working with this population?

Topic: What does working through my personalizations with regard to this population entail (20 minutes)?
    For this segment, students will actively process the biases, stereotypes, and ingroup favoritism that may negatively affect their work with African American men.
Topic: I can commit to working through my personalizations by . . . (20 minutes).

For this segment, students will develop the initial components of an action plan that includes the following. Students are encouraged to take notes in preparation for the action plan paper due the following class period:

- Strategy used to monitor biases as they arise
- Use of reflection-in-action
- Three ways to offer yourself some grace when personalizations occur
- With whom will you consult if you have a need to process?
- Paper: action plan. Write a three to five page paper in APA Style (excluding title page, references, and applicable appendices).
  - Key elements of this plan should include the following:
    - Identify a social injustice with regard to African American men in general, and its impact on African American men in your department's training program.
    - Establish a plan to correct the injustice you have identified. You should detail ways your plan redistributes resources in such a way that African American men experience parity with other populations in your program.
    - Create a strategy to communicate your findings, including a timeline and ways to implement departmental accountability.

## DISCUSSION

See "Process Group."

## BIBLIOGRAPHY

Brooks, M., & Steen, S. (2010). "Brother where art thou?" African American male instructors perceptions of the counselor education profession. *Journal of Multicultural Counseling and Development, 38*(3), 142–153. doi:10.1002/j.2161-1912.2010.tb00122.x

Harper, S. R. (2014). (Re)setting the agenda for college men of color: Lessons learned from a 15-year movement to improve Black male student success. In R. A. Williams (Ed.), *Men of color in higher education: New foundations for developing models for success* (pp. 116–143). Sterling, VA: Stylus.

Haskins, N., Whitfield-Williams, M., Shillingford, M. A., Singh, A., Moxley, R., & Ofauni, C. (2013). The experiences of black masters counseling students: A phenomenological inquiry. *Counselor Education & Supervision, 52*, 162–177. doi:10.1002/j.1556-6978.2013.00035.x

## SUGGESTED BACKGROUND READING

Bogle, D. (2001). *Toms, coons, mulattoes, mammies, and bucks: An interpretive history of blacks in American films* (4th ed.). London, UK: Bloomsbury Academic.

Bolden, A. J. (2009). *An examination of teacher bias in special education referrals based upon student race and gender* (Doctoral dissertation). Retrieved from ProQuest.

Boysen, G. A., & Vogel, D. L. (2009). Bias in the classroom: Types, frequencies, and responses. *Teaching of Psychology, 36*, 12–17. doi:10.1080/00986280802529038

Boysen, G. A., Vogel, D. L., Cope, M. A., & Hubbard, A. (2009). Incidents of bias in college classrooms: Instructor and student perceptions. *Journal of Diversity in Higher Education, 2*(4), 219–231. doi:10.1037/a0017538

Burton, M. (2013). *Liberation psychology: A constructive critical praxis. Estudos de Psicologial Campinas, 30*(2), 249–259. doi:10.1590/S0103–166X2013000200011

Clark, K., & Clark, M. (1950). The negro child in the American social order. *The Journal of Negro Education, 19*(3), 341–350.

Clark, R., Anderson, N. B., Clark, V. R, & Williams, D. R. (1999). Racism as a stressor for African Americans: A biopsychosocial model. *American Psychologist, 5*, 805–816. doi:10.1037//0003-066X.54.10.805

Cokley, K. (2000). An investigation of academic self-concept and its relationship to academic achievement in African American college students. *Journal of Black Psychology, 26*(2), 148–164. doi:10.1177/0095798400026002002

Cokley, K. (2014). *The myth of black anti-intellectualism: A true psychology of African American students*. Westport, CT: Praeger.

Counsel for Accreditation of Counseling and Related Educational Programs [CACREP]. (2016). *2016 standards for accreditation*. Alexandria, VA: Author.

Cross, W. E., Jr. (1971). The Negro-to-black conversion experience. *Black World, 20*(9), 13–27.

Fordham, S., & Ogbu, J. U. (1986). Black students' school success: Coping with the "burden of acting White". *The Urban Review, 18*(3), 176–206. doi:10.1007/BF01112192

Franklin, A. J., & Boyd-Franklin, N. (2000). Invisibility syndrome: A clinical model of the effects of racism on African American males. *Journal of Orthopsychiatry, 70*, 33–41. doi:10.1037/h0087691

Friere, P. (2000). *Pedagogy of the oppressed* (30th anniversary ed.). New York: Bloomsbury.

Harper, S. R. (2010). An anti-deficit framework for research on students of color in stem. In S. R. Harper & C. B. Newman (Eds.). *Students of color in stem: Engineering a new research agenda*. New Directions for Institutional Research (pp. 63–74). San Francisco: Jossey-Bass.

Harper, S. R. (2012). *Black male student success in higher education: A report from the national black male college achievement study*. Philadelphia: University of Pennsylvania, Center for the Study of Race and Equity in Education.

Johnson-Ahorlu, R. N. (2013). "Our biggest challenge is stereotypes": Understanding stereotype threat and the academic experiences of African American undergraduates. *The Journal of Negro Education, 82*(4), 382–392. doi:10.7709/jnegroeducation.82.4.0382

Ladson-Billings, G. (1998). Just what is critical race theory and what's it doing in a nice field like education? *Qualitative Studies in Education, 11*, 7–24. Retrieved from https://ezproxy.umsl.edu/login?url=http://search.ebscohost.com/login.aspx?direct=true&db=eoah&AN=307797&site=ehost-live&scope=site

Majors, R., & Billson, J. M. (1992). *Cool pose: The dilemmas of black manhood in America*. New York: Touchstone.

National Center for Education Statistics. (2012). *Higher education: Gaps in access and persistence study*. Washington, DC: National Center for Education Statistics, Institute of Education Sciences, U.S. Department of Education.

Rosenberg, M. (1979). *Conceiving the self*. Malabar, FL: Robert E. Krieger.

Shavelson, R. J., Hubner, J. J., & Stanton, G. C. (1976). Self-concept: Validation of construct interpretations. *Review of Educational Research, 46*, 407–441. Retrieved from https://ezproxy.umsl.edu/login?url=http://search.ebscohost.com/login.aspx?direct=true&db=eoah&AN=48132487&site=ehost-live&scope=site

Solarzano, D., Ceja, M., & Yosso, T. (2000). Critical race theory, racial microaggressions, and campus racial climate: The experiences of African American college students. *The Journal of Negro Education, 69*(1/2), 60–73. Retrieved from https://ezproxy.umsl.edu/login?url=http://search.ebscohost.com/login.aspx?direct=true&db=psyh&AN=2002-10183-005&site=ehost-live&scope=site

Steele, C. M., & Aronson, J. (1995). Stereotype threat and intellectual test performance of African Americans. *Journal of Personality and Social Psychology, 69*(5), 797–811. doi:10.1037/0022-3514.69.5.797

Sue, D. W., Lin, A. I., Torino, G. C., Capodilupo, C. M., & Rivera, D. P. (2009). Racial microaggressions and difficult dialogues on race in the classroom. *Cultural Diversity and Ethnic Minority Psychology, 15*(2), 183–190. doi:10.1037/a0014191

Williams, R. L. (2007). *Racism learned at an early age through racial scripting*. Bloomington, IN: AuthorHouse.

Woodland, M. H. (2008). A validity study of scores on the personal and academic self-concept inventory based on a sample of black college males. *Journal of Black Psychology, 34*(4), 452–478. doi:10.1177/0095798408316795

**HANDOUT**

# Handout 29.1: Culturally Responsive Teaching With African American Male Trainees: An Action Plan

- Identify a social injustice with regard to African American in general and its impact on African American men in your department's training program.
  - Counselor Education is a discipline that emerged from cultural roots, responding to a shift in American culture from agrarian to predominately industrialized. Despite this grounding in cultural reflexivity, Counselor Education, like its sibling Counseling Psychology, is built upon the perspectives, insights, data, and practices of white identified individuals. When attempting to properly meet the needs of the current cohort of students, existing practices fall short, particularly with regard to counselors-in-training who identify as African American men. Of primary concern is the preponderance of African American students who report incidences of biased communication in classroom settings. There is evidence this may contribute to attrition and a continued dearth of African American men who are practicing as professional counselors. This action plan is designed to rectify this imbalance by identifying specific ways in which biased communication toward African American men shows up in the classroom as well as ways to notice, respond to, and prevent it. It is a means of redistributing this educational resource toward equitable treatment. The implications of this action plan also have benefits to public health. Discrimination is one of a number of social determinants of health. Systemic injustices, including those along the educational pipeline, may account for the dearth of African American men who are clinical practitioners. This can negatively affect the public by the lack of needed services to clients who may prefer an African American male provider, or they may not perceive counseling to be "for" them. This plan may assist with increasing the availability of this provider population.
- Establish a plan to correct the injustice you have identified. You should detail ways your plan redistributes resources in such a way that African American men experience parity with other populations in your program.
  - What needs to take place in order for corrective action to be seen?
    - Bias management
      - Operationalize bias and bias management
        - Bias is . . .
        - Bias management is . . .
      - Monitoring my bias
        - Self-care in bias management
      - Consultation
        - Describe the significance of consultation in bias management.
        - With whom can I consult to manage my biases? Name three individuals and include a rationale for why you selected them.
- Create a strategy to communicate your findings, including a timeline and ways to implement departmental accountability.
  - Advocacy
    - Conduct an inventory of the textbooks, articles, videos, and handouts used in your department to train master's students. Document these findings to share with core faculty members.
    - Do images and language present in course readings reflect the experiences of African American men? If not, describe actions taken to rectify.
      - It was identified that very little reflected the experiences of men of African descent.
    - What is the timeline for this project?
      - One semester

- Who will help to hold you accountable for your progress?
  - The members of my doctoral cohort
- What format and approach will you use to convey your findings to faculty in your program?
  - A PowerPoint and executive summary will be crafted to convey findings.
- Describe specific actions taken to address bias in your department.
  - I will meet with the course instructor, doctoral program coordinator, and department chair to discuss these concerns with all parties present at this meeting.
- Identify the extent to which these themes are present in the broader college/university community and develop a graduate student task force designed to resolve or remediate the identified concerns.
  - Connect with other doctoral students in your college and through your institution's overarching graduate school or program as a means of connecting with other doctoral students on campus.
  - Seek to establish a task force through the graduate program or school.
    - Identify members of this task force.
      - One doctoral student from each of the college/university's schools
      - One tenured professor
      - One person with clearly defined administrative responsibilities who identifies themselves to be a student advocate (i.e., Director of the Multicultural Center)
    - Establish meeting times, locations, and objectives. This must involve discernment of the key administrators to invite or with whom you will share your findings.
      - For example, meetings will be held in the student union at noon every third Wednesday, at the same time that key administrators meet so that relevant conversations can be had with these individuals during an identified, mutually available moment.
    - Upon communication of concerns with key parties, a plan will be collaboratively designed to establish mutual accountability and communication between members of the task force and those in a position of power at your institution.

# CHAPTER 30

# Using Creativity to Explore Socially Constructed Narratives as a Way to Promote Personal Liberation and Agency

*Mariaimeé Gonzalez and Dani Baker*

## Course Recommendations

| SOCIAL JUSTICE AND ADVOCACY PRINCIPLES | CORE CACREP STANDARDS | COUNSELING SPECIALIZATION |
|---|---|---|
| ☑ Strategies for Change | ☑ Career Development<br>☑ Helping Relationships<br>☑ Human Growth and Development<br>☑ Professional Counseling Orientation and Ethical Practice<br>☑ Social and Cultural Diversity<br>☑ Theories | ☑ Clinical Mental Health Counseling<br>☑ Marriage, Couple, and Family Counseling<br>☑ School Counseling<br>☑ Student Affairs and College Counseling |

## TOPIC

Many people are denied social resources, rights, and opportunities as a result of multifaceted, interconnected systems of oppression that exploit social power and privilege and are maintained by three contextual levels: individual knowing and behaviors, institutional expectations and norms, and social/cultural beliefs and practices (Hardiman, Jackson, & Griffin, 2007).

The purpose of this activity is to explore and promote the externalization of socially constructed narratives or stories through the use of imagery and magazine collage. Using creative approaches, such as collage, creates a contained structure, while also promoting personal agency and choice via non-verbal expression (Stallings, 2016, 2009; Elkis-Abuhoff, 2008; Foster, 1992; Vick, 1999). Combining personal stories and creativity allows for the exploration of internal and external narratives of cultural oppression, specifically, oppressive *isms* such as sexism, racism, ageism, and heterosexism, all of which are influential determinants in many individuals' lives. A narrative approach that integrates imagery allows each student the freedom to focus on a specific oppression(s), externalize and deconstruct the oppression(s), and reconstruct or restory their personal narrative, ultimately helping each group member establish a newfound sense of agency and self-worth.

Finally, this activity allows the student, with the support of the group, to share their story of how a specific oppression(s) has impacted their constructed meaning of self and others, and will empower the student member to be their own agent of change (White, 2007).

## LEARNING OBJECTIVES

1. Learn how to foster mental liberation.
2. Learn how creative approaches, such as collage, create a contained structure, while also promoting personal agency and choice via non-verbal expression.
3. Explore how forms of oppression identified by counselors-in-training might impact the counselor-client relationship.

## TARGET POPULATION

Graduate students in Counselor Education Program

## GROUP SIZE

15–20 maximum including students, faculty, or volunteers

## TIME REQUIRED

One class period or typically 1.5–2.5 hours including a 10-minute break

## SETTING

During one class session with a room big enough for all the participants and preferably a table on which to place the materials

## MATERIALS NEEDED

- Chairs and tables in a space big enough for the number of people involved in the activity
- Magazine images of people or faces (images pulled from magazines and prepared ahead of group, spread out on a table for participants to view and choose from)
- Two 8.5"× 11" sheets of blank paper
- Scissors (if working with a population where scissors are not allowed, participants can tear images to achieve their desired shape or size)
- Glue sticks
- Sharpies (light and dark colors that will show up on magazine images) and a pen or pencil

## INSTRUCTIONS FOR CONDUCTING ACTIVITY

Prior to class period or group, lay out all materials, such as precut magazine images, on a large table with space for participants to view from all angles and a separate space or table with paper, scissors, glue sticks, sharpies, and pens/pencils. Next, follow these steps:

1. Ask participants to review magazine imagery and ask them to pull any five images that speak to them (10 minutes).*

2. Ask participants to find a space to work (table or floor) and cut or tear and glue images in any way to one of the blank papers (10 minutes).*

3. Ask participants to label each image with a sharpie or identify any oppressive construct(s) they represent (5 minutes).*

4. Once collage is created, ask participants, "What do you see when you look at your collage?" Next, using the other blank sheet of paper, ask the participants to externalize what they see or the oppressive constructs that have been revealed in their collage by free writing, via stream of consciousness, their story on the additional blank paper (5 minutes).

5. In a short session, lead the participants in a large group discussion (30 minutes). In a longer session (2.5 to 3 hours), break into small group discussions and transition back to a large group discussion (see processing questions in the "Discussion" section).**

6. Provide a "recap of the learning" based on the large group discussion and then lead the participants in a short wrap-up/grounding exercise.

\* For class periods longer than 1.5 hours, add time accordingly. For example, add 5 minutes to steps 1 and 3 and 10 minutes to steps 2 and 5.

\*\* For larger groups and if time allows, modify step 5 by asking group members to break into small group discussions, sharing their collage image and thoughts with other members before coming back to a large group for processing and discussion.

# DISCUSSION

1. The facilitator asks the participants to sit in a circle with their collage and shares that the purpose of the activity is to explore our stories, new insights, and lessons learned regarding personal narratives and socially constructed labels through collage.

2. Begin by inviting each participant to share at least one *ism* that is represented in their collage image. Each participant willing to share will then volunteer one at a time.

3. Ask the participants to look at their collage image. Encourage the group to choose a social label or social construct that has been oppressive to them that they would like to explore with the group. Participants are asked to pick only one oppressive *ism* that they feel has impacted their life in a negative way. For example, "As a person of color who identifies as a woman, you may have experienced some forms of sexism or racism that you would like to explore."

4. Ask the participant to take on the persona of the oppression. For example, "So Marie, I want you to take on the persona of sexism. When we ask you a question, answer the question as if you were sexism and discuss the ways you have impacted Marie." Marie is then to take on the persona of sexism and refer to herself (Marie) in the third person. If group members are hesitant to take on the persona of their *ism*, a secondary externalization option would be, "Marie, as you look at the part of your collage that represents sexism, use your imagination and tell us what the image is saying."

5. At this time, group members are encouraged to pose questions to sexism about its impact on Marie. For example, the leader could start the conversation by asking, "So sexism, when did Marie first notice you in her life?" Marie is to respond to questions through the persona of sexism; she might respond, "Marie noticed me when she turned 9 and people started treating her differently."

6. This continues until allotted time is complete. After each group member has been given the option to share (all group members have the right to pass, if they are not ready to share their *ism* within the large group), ask the group members to reflect on the experience and how these scripts have impacted their life story, and to identify one way they feel empowered to be their own agent of change.

7. As the group is coming to an end, the group leader provides a synopsis of the group process by validating individual experiences of oppression, the group's external expression of social construct themes and *isms*, discoveries, lessons learned, and new ways the members are encouraged to lean more fully into their persona/identity as empowered agents of personal change and transformation.

8. Finally, in the last few minutes of group, the group leader facilitates a short exercise such as deep breathing, setting a supportive intention, or guided visualization to wrap up the session for the members so that they leave group feeling grounded in their bodies and fully present to move back into the world.

Debriefing is largely conducted during the final portion of the activity when all participants are joined in one larger circle. Suggested questions could include:

- What did you learn about yourself and your life story?
- What part of this process was most impactful? In what way?
- How did it feel to hear your group members ask your *ism* questions on your behalf? Which question stood out the most?
- What was it like to talk directly to your *ism* images? Did anything shift or change as a result of your conversation with your *ism* images?
- How will you reconstruct your life story to benefit you outside of this group?

Educators/supervisors should feel free to ask additional questions taking into consideration the needs of their particular students/audience.

## BIBLIOGRAPHY

Elkis-Abuhoff, D. I. (2008). Art therapy applied to an adolescent with Asperger's Syndrome. *The Arts in Psychotherapy*, *35*, 262–270.

Foster, M. T. (1992). Experiencing a "creative high". *The Journal of Creative Behavior, 26*(1), 29–39.

Hardiman, R., Jackson, B., & Griffin, P. (2007). Conceptual foundations for social justice education. In M. Adams, L. A. Bell, & P. Griffin (Eds.), *Teaching for diversity and social justice* (2nd ed., pp. 35–66). New York: Routledge.

Stallings, J. W. (2009). Collage as a therapeutic modality for reminiscence in patients with dementia. *Art Therapy: Journal of the American Art Therapy Association, 27*(3), 136–140.

Stallings, J. W. (2016). Collage as an expressive medium in art therapy. In D. E. Gussak & M. L. Rosal (Eds.), *The Wiley handbook of art therapy* (pp. 163–170). MA: John Wiley & Sons.

Vick, R. M. (1999). Utilizing prestructured art elements in brief group art therapy with adolescents. *Art Therapy: Journal of the American Art Therapy Association, 16*(2), 68–77.

White, M. (2007). *Maps of narrative practice*. New York: W. W. Norton & Company.

White, M., & Epston, D. (1990). *Narrative means to therapeutic ends*. New York: W. W. Norton & Company.

# SECTION 2

# Core CACREP Standards

In section two, the educator or supervisor will find social justice and advocacy experiential activities in chapters that are aligned with the CACREP core standards: assessment and Testing, Career Development, Group Work, Helping Relationships, Human Growth and Development, Professional Counseling Orientation and Ethical Practice, Research and Program Evaluation, Social and Cultural Diversity, and Theories.

## ASSESSMENT AND TESTING

*These activities address how assessment and testing intersect with social justice and advocacy tenets. Activities will provide learning opportunities to explore the power complexities around assessments and testing in regard to environmental factors or personal attributes that are treated by others in an unfair fashion. Activities will promote the examination of cultural influences when conducting assessment and testing and safeguards to allow an empowering voice in the assessment and testing process that may affect one's life.*

## CAREER DEVELOPMENT

*These activities examine the world of work, sources of career information, and the concepts of vocational development in a social justice and advocacy context. Activities will also include themes surrounding world poverty, economic inequality, oppressive labor practices, and global economic injustices impacting marginalized populations including short-/long-term impact.*

## GROUP WORK

*These activities examine group interactions and social justice and advocacy tenets. Activities will provide learning opportunities to explore group complexities around power, privilege, inclusion, and empowerment. Activities will generate an understanding of, and appreciation for, social justice counseling and advocacy among group participants.*

## HELPING RELATIONSHIPS

*These activities examine the philosophic bases of counseling and the helping relationship, focusing on the foundational and theoretical concepts necessary for working with individuals, groups, children, and families in a social justice and advocacy context. Activities will provide learning opportunities to explore relationship building complexities and elements to create opportunities for safe alliances and rapport building in order to establish a personal social justice compass.*

## HUMAN GROWTH AND DEVELOPMENT

*These activities examine the dynamic aspects of human growth and development over the lifespan and historical and current theories of human nature and human individuality in a social justice and advocacy context. Activities will provide learning opportunities to explore the intersections between human development, human nature, and the influence of oppressive systemic factors.*

# PROFESSIONAL COUNSELING ORIENTATION AND ETHICAL PRACTICE

*These activities examine the legal, ethical, and professional choices faced by mental health practitioners within a social justice and advocacy context, including, but not limited to, the role of racial, ethnic, and cultural heritage, nationality, socioeconomic status, family structure, age, gender, sexual orientation, religious and spiritual beliefs, occupation, physical and mental status, and equity issues in different systemic settings.*

# RESEARCH AND PROGRAM EVALUATION

*These activities promote informed students and clients of psychological and service research to examine these tenets within a social justice and advocacy context. Participants will be able to identify various research approaches and the strengths and limitations associated with oppression and systemic power. These activities will also encourage participants to conduct research in the human services/community counseling field within a social justice and advocacy context.*

# SOCIAL AND CULTURAL DIVERSITY

*These activities promote concepts and paradigms used in counseling diverse populations within a social justice and advocacy context. Activities will include examining current theories, trends, and issues in counseling special populations; domestic and international human rights; relevant social justice skills to work with diverse populations; personal privilege; nature of oppression; advocacy strategies for studying and changing personal agency, organization, and communities; and understanding, attitudes, and behaviors toward multicultural groups.*

# THEORIES

*These activities focus on the major theories of personality and related counseling approaches and will help participants create their personal approach therapy within a social justice and advocacy context. Participants will examine, through activities, the intersections of the personality, social constructs, and counseling theories in depth, clearly elucidate their personal values by examining them through the lens of an oppressive system, and finally integrate these into their own concept of personality, counseling, and social justice and advocacy.*

# CHAPTER 31

# An Unleveled Playing Field

## *Alexandria Kerwin and Sumedha Therthani*

### Course Recommendations

| SOCIAL JUSTICE AND ADVOCACY PRINCIPLES | CORE CACREP STANDARDS | COUNSELING SPECIALIZATION |
|---|---|---|
| ☑ Social Constructs of Oppression and Privilege | ☑ Social and Cultural Diversity | ☑ Clinical Mental Health Counseling<br>☑ Marriage, Couple, and Family Counseling<br>☑ School Counseling<br>☑ Student Affairs and College Counseling |

## TOPIC

This activity is designed to facilitate awareness and advocacy skills regarding systemic inequalities in socioeconomic status (SES).

## LEARNING OBJECTIVES

As a result of this activity, students will:

1. Be able to acknowledge that their privileged and marginalized status provides advantages and disadvantages in society.
2. Discuss the dynamics of privilege and marginalization.
3. Better understand the influence of socioeconomic status.

## TARGET POPULATION

Master's- or doctoral-level counselor education students

## GROUP SIZE

5–15 people. If an instructor has more than 15 people, students may break into groups of two to three.

# TIME REQUIRED

45 minutes (may take longer with larger groups)

# SETTING

Classroom

# MATERIALS NEEDED

- Manila envelopes
- Paper and pencil
- A variety of arts and crafts supplies of your choice (markers, crayons, glitter, stickers, stencils, poster board, clay, paint, etc.)

# INSTRUCTIONS FOR CONDUCTING ACTIVITY

Although a reading assignment is not necessary to conduct this activity, *The Myth of the Level Playing Field* by Jerry Fowler may be an appropriate book to give context to this activity.

Prior to class you will need to stuff the manila envelopes (one for each student) with craft supplies. The amount of supplies in each envelope will vary and should somewhat represent wealth and resource distribution. For example, some envelopes should contain only pencil and paper, while others contain a mixture of various arts and crafts supplies. One envelope should be stuffed with all craft supplies to represent the 1 percent.

The activity begins by having each student take one stuffed envelope. Instruct the students to create something with the art supplies provided to them. For example, the instruction could be that everyone make a poster depicting what social justice advocacy means to them. It is important to note that the creative prompt is NOT the focus of the activity, so it can be anything the instructor chooses. The objective is that everyone be asked to accomplish the same task with differing resources. Be clear that they are to only use the supplies in their envelope and no sharing is allowed. Encourage them to imagine this is an assignment for a grade or a contest with a cash prize. Ask them to pay attention to their thoughts and feelings as they create their work of art.

Give students 10–15 minutes to complete their project. Then, bring the group together to process their experiences of being asked to accomplish the same task with different resources.

# DISCUSSION

Have the students reflect on the activity. This activity is designed to generate awareness of systemic inequalities, foster compassion for those less fortunate, and encourage social justice advocacy. The following are examples of process questions:

- What was it like to be expected to do the same task with different resources?
- How did it feel to have an abundance, scarcity, or moderate amount of resources?
- How can the advice to "pull yourself up by the bootstraps" be harmful?
- Is there a difference between equity and equality?
- Did the thought of earning a grade or cash prize impact your experience?
- How did this exercise relate to issues of privilege and marginalization?

- What are some ways you can advocate for clients lacking in resources?
- How, as a counselor, can you use your skills and knowledge to facilitate change at the individual, community, and societal levels?
- Ask the students with an abundance of craft supplies how they would advocate for individuals struggling with low SES. Also ask students who had fewer craft supplies how they would advocate for themselves at a lower SES?
- Invite students to share their experiences of any roadblocks and barriers as well as strategies and skills they used to overcome the obstacles. How would they help their clients to overcome similar obstacles?
- Encourage students to reflect and share one social justice advocacy experience in which they have already engaged; it could be personal or professional.

## BIBLIOGRAPHY

Arthur, N., & Achenbach, K. (2002). Developing multicultural counseling competencies through experiential learning. *Counselor Education and Supervision, 42,* 2–14.

Kim, B. S. K., & Lyons, H. Z. (2003). Experiential activities and multicultural counseling competence training. *Journal of Counseling & Development, 81,* 400–408.

## SUGGESTED BACKGROUND READING

Fowler, J. (2016). *The myth of the level playing field.* New York, NY: Page Publishing.

# CHAPTER 32

# Getting Personal With Immigrants and Refugees
## Advocacy and Social Justice Counseling Concerns

*Kevin C. Snow, Joy Mwendwa, and John Harrichand*

## Course Recommendations

| SOCIAL JUSTICE AND ADVOCACY PRINCIPLES | CORE CACREP STANDARDS | COUNSELING SPECIALIZATION |
|---|---|---|
| ☑ Strategies for Change | ☑ Career Development<br>☑ Helping Relationships<br>☑ Human Growth and Development<br>☑ Professional Counseling Orientation and Ethical Practice<br>☑ Social and Cultural Diversity<br>☑ Theories | ☑ Clinical Mental Health Counseling<br>☑ Marriage, Couple, and Family Counseling<br>☑ School Counseling<br>☑ Student Affairs and College Counseling |

## TOPIC

Throughout U.S. history there have been shifting views on immigrants/refugees and their places in our society, the contributions they bring to it, and the many needs they may have once they arrive. This activity connects students to current events concerning this population and encourages them to examine their own views and the potential roles counselors/educators have when working in personal ways with immigrants and refugees to America.

## LEARNING OBJECTIVES

1. Students will identify the needs of immigrants/refugees in present-day America relating to counseling.
2. Students will apply the knowledge/awareness, skills, and action of multicultural counseling, social justice, and advocacy to immigrant/refugee populations.
3. Students will examine information highlighting current challenges and barriers to health that immigrants/refugees face in America as well as address their own biases, assumptions, prejudices, and stereotypes connected to these populations.

4. Students will evaluate how their counselor-in-training (or counselor educator-in-training) identity along with concepts/skills of social justice and advocacy can influence their work with immigrants/refugee populations.
5. Students will conduct personal interviews and create presentations highlighting the challenges immigrant/refugee interviewees face in America and explore social justice and advocacy steps to meet the needs of these populations.

## TARGET POPULATION

Counseling master's and/or Counselor Education doctoral Students from any of the CACREP specialty areas

## GROUP SIZE

10–25 students

## TIME REQUIRED

Part 1: 30–90 minutes in class depending on group size, number of participants, or participant demographics (for example rural vs. urban classrooms may have different diversity levels and may need additional time to explore the issue, depending on participant make-up). More or less time can be used, depending on needs of instructor and/or depth of discussion. Video clips vary in size, not longer than 10 minutes (but this too can be altered as needed). At least 20 minutes of discussion is considered average for this activity in addition to watching at least one video clip.

Part 2: 10–15 minutes per presentation per student in class, generally taking one or two class periods depending on class size and presentation size. Students should be expected to meet outside of class time with participants for no more than 30–60 minutes, to respect interviewees' time. Presentation size and content expectations can be altered as needed too.

## SETTING

Part 1: Any standard classroom area, especially one that permits students in large groups to sit in a circle or other format to see each other and/or a space that permits small group formation. This can be modified for synchronous distance learning environments via specified chat rooms and other tools using video conferencing and course management systems. For asynchronous distance learning environments, similar video conferencing or chat rooms can be used with students at pre-scheduled meeting times, via discussion boards, or via other standard video conferencing and course management system tools. Instructors can modify based on their own or student needs.

Part 2: Interviews will take place outside of class in various community-based or other settings, depending on comfort and through agreement with interviewees. For example, at the discretion of interviewee and interviewer, students could conduct interviews in available campus meeting spaces (e.g., classrooms, offices) that would permit some privacy or could conduct interviews in nearly any community setting that seems best suited to doing a 30–60 minute interview. Presentations would then be shared in a designated class in either traditional face-to-face or distance learning environments. Distance learning presentations can be done synchronously or asynchronously (via recorded presentations) in various ways depending on instructor needs and course management or presentation tools available. Instructors can modify based on their own or student needs.

# MATERIALS NEEDED

Part 1: The instructor will need technology to play videos with sound and/or access to the Internet to show video clips, a suitable classroom space (whether in-person or virtual, for distance learning), and their preferred format to display or present guiding questions for discussion for this activity. The authors prefer to use PowerPoint or other presentation software to create this activity, but little more is needed than to show the videos and ask questions of students (or make use of the many distance learning tools and formats to do similar). Questions and/or video links could be shared via handouts, or in other ways, if desired. The instructor will provide the students with either hardcopies or online links to reading materials needed to prepare for the discussion, prior to watching video clips in class. Students will read the materials before class. All video clips should be tested ahead of time, especially those located online, as websites change, links become lost, etc., and thus additional videos beyond those offered in this activity may need to be located. Instructors can modify based on their own or student needs.

Part 2: Students will interview participants, located by either themselves or the instructor. Students could record interviews (audio or video) with permission of participants or take notes by hand, or both. If recording, students would need appropriate recording technology, readily available on any smartphone or other mobile devices. Students will use PowerPoint, Prezi, or other instructor preferred programs or methods to develop a presentation for class. Depending on technology available for in-person or virtual classrooms, modifications to presentation tools and formats will need to be made. Students are asked to be certain their presentations are compatible with available classroom technology, especially if they intend to show any video recordings or other audiovisual materials. Instructors can modify based on their own or student needs.

# INSTRUCTIONS FOR CONDUCTING ACTIVITY

Part 1: leading a discussion via video clips with or without required readings.

1. Students are expected to prepare for this activity by reading Meyer's (2016) *Counseling Today* article "Immigration's Growing Impact on Counseling." This article could be optional, but using it as a required reading prior to this activity enhances the discussion and begins the process of students exploring their self-awareness of issues raised in this activity. It is not essential to use it, but highly recommended. Other or additional readings may be used at instructor's discretion.
2. (With required reading) Students will read assigned resources on immigrants and refugees and consider some of the following aspects:
   a. Purposes immigrants/refugees have for moving to America.
   b. Social, religious, political, and economic beliefs or values, and other cultural underpinnings, associated with different immigrant/refugee populations.
   c. Personal values, biases, beliefs, assumptions, stereotypes, and/or prejudices about immigrant/refugee populations.
3. Instructors may use one or more videos, depending on their preferences. Introduce the selected video(s):
   "We will be watching a short video(s) about immigrants/refugees in America. Pay attention to obvious and covert details about potential counseling issues for this population as well as your own personal reactions as you watch it. We will hold a discussion afterward, in either one large or several small groups."
4. Play the selected video(s).
5. After the video(s), lead the class in an interactive discussion, in either one large or several small groups, using some or all of the following questions:
   a. What are some key things you have learned about immigrants/refugees after watching this video(s)?

b.  What surprised you about the immigrants/refugees, their situations, and the issues represented in this video(s)?

c.  What impressions did you have regarding immigrants/refugees in America prior to today's class and how were those impressions met or changed after seeing the video(s)?

d.  What are some key things (e.g., emotional reactions, thoughts, and awareness of bias or beliefs) you learned about yourself in response to this video(s)?

e.  As you consider your own cultural background, why do you think you responded in the ways you did to this video(s)?

f.  What are some specific potential issues related to counseling presented in the video(s)?

g.  What barriers did you observe that these individuals may have to overcome to achieve health and success connected to the aforementioned issues?

h.  What social justice principles apply to working with immigrants/refugees?

i.  What are concrete, potential strategies that counselors could employ to advocate for this cultural group?

j.  Based on your knowledge or review of the various counseling competencies, guidelines, and ethical codes connected to working with advocacy and social justice issues in counseling, what would treatment planning and counseling sessions look like when working with immigrants/refugees?

Note: this is a suggested list of questions, and instructors are encouraged to modify or add other questions to suit their needs. Instructors could also pair this discussion with a review before or within class of one or more of the various counseling documents connected to advocacy and social justice, if desired. If done in small groups, it is recommended to bring the class back together and briefly wrap up the activity by exploring some of the highlights of the discussion. A group secretary can be used in the small groups to record responses, and the instructor is encouraged to wander between the small groups to help facilitate the discussions and listen to students' responses.

Part 2: conducting immigrant or refugee interviews and presentations

1.  Each student group will conduct a 30–60 minute interview with an immigrant/refugee.

2.  Students are encouraged to locate and contact potential participants on their own, or instructors may assist with this process, as they feel necessary. Depending on location, potential participants can be contacted through local organizations or local branches of regional/national organizations working with immigrant/refugee populations. Such organizations exist in rural, suburban, and urban areas throughout the U.S. Research can be conducted online to locate such organizations, and may include local faith groups (e.g., churches, mosques, synagogues), refugee services done by larger faith-based organizations (e.g., Lutheran Social Services or Catholic Charities networks), nonprofit groups (e.g., Refugee Services of Texas, International Rescue Committee), or government agencies (e.g., U.S. Office of Refugee Resettlement). These are suggestions, and options will vary by locality.

3.  Contact a selected organization and respectfully explain the purpose of this assignment and the parameters of the interview (to learn about immigrant/refugee individuals' needs in America first hand and explore potential issues for counselors working with this population in a brief interview). Request a referral to interview an individual and discuss the details of the interview (e.g., possible times, locations to meet, whether it will be recorded or not, and any other logistics of the interview). It is often beneficial for activities like this to prepare a consent form or informational sheet with the instructor's professional affiliation and contact information so participants can know this is an official course assignment and address any questions or concerns directly to the course instructor. Students or instructors can give this sheet to organizations and participants as part of the process of securing an interview.

4.  Students are encouraged to find different individuals from different immigrant/refugee groups to allow for multiple experiences to be collected and shared with their peers during the presentations. Furthermore, students' knowledge gained from Part 1, as well as their sense of their interviewee, will guide them in how personal they can get with their questions. Different immigrant/refugee groups and individuals vary on how private they are, and interviewers should be respectful to

participants at all times. Students should use their interviewee's feedback regarding what areas they can probe during the interview. If the person is very open, go deeper. If not, then students should respect that cultural boundary and ask why this boundary is there.

Issues that students may wish to explore during the interview include, but are not limited to, the following:

a. Early childhood experiences and parental values in the immigrant/refugee process
b. Earliest memories of recognizing membership in a culturally different group
c. The role of religion/spirituality in the participant's life
d. Immigration/refugee experiences (e.g., transitions, work, or life in general)
e. Similarities/differences between family interactions in the U.S. compared to the person's original culture
f. School experiences as a member of a non-dominant culture
g. Experiences with subtle racism or discrimination
h. Experiences with overt racism or discrimination
i. Ways the person chose his/her career or makes career choices (or barriers to getting jobs within the U.S. and pursuing careers)
j. The experience of being culturally different
k. Attitudes about the "dominant" culture
l. Impact of assimilation to dominant cultural attitudes, values, and lifestyles
m. Feelings of oppression
n. Feelings of anger toward dominant culture
o. From the person's cultural background, the biggest concerns, challenges, and barriers to being an immigrant/refugee in America
p. Strengths identified from the person's cultural background that help him/her cope with living in the U.S. and transitioning to life here

5. Once students complete their interview, they will develop a 10–15 minute presentation on their immigrant/refugee interviewee and the experience of interacting with them. Presentations will be given in-person or can be done via many options for distance learning presenting. Grades will be based on the depth of the experience, clarity of information presented, creativity, and cohesive integration of the material. Presentations and grading criteria can be modified to instructor needs. The following are some potential guiding questions to help students create their presentation, but students are to be creative in their presentations and use these guidelines or new ones the instructor develops, or develop their presentations on their own.

Once students complete their interview, they will answer the following questions to prepare their presentation:

1. What (if at all) are barriers that this immigrant/refugee has to overcome? How do you think these barriers impact the community?
2. How did you come to know of the barriers? Share the process of how you identified these barriers and the ease/difficulty of this process.
3. What are two social justice strategies that counselors could employ to advocate for this cultural group?
4. How does your overall experience of this project shape your counseling theory and social justice and advocacy perspective regarding the immigrant/refugee population?
5. How does your overall experience of this project influence your perspective on the potential roles counselors can have with the immigrant/refugee population?
6. What would an advocacy plan for your immigrant/refugee cultural group look like? Develop an outline of your plan and include specific, executable social justice and advocacy actions (include this outline in your presentation: one to three slides and notes).

Note: this two-part activity could be modified easily to focus on many different specialized courses. For example, students could explore career development and counseling with immigrant and refugee populations. Or students could explore couples and family counseling, or school counseling, or student affairs and college counseling issues, barriers, challenges, and related constructs as they impact immigration and refugee populations. This activity could be modified for nearly any counseling course at the master's or doctoral level, and expectations could be increased or decreased as needed for that course or graduate student level. Additionally, although it is our intention both parts will be used, instructors can easily use either Part 1 or 2 independently as activities.

## DISCUSSION

Part 1: debriefing is a built in process of the activity. Questions have been built into the preceding instructions. Please refer to the instructions for Part 1 of this activity to review potential discussion questions.

Part 2: debriefing is encouraged to flow naturally from the class and instructor based on student presentations and is not specifically built into the activity.

## BIBLIOGRAPHY

BBC World News America (Producer). (2010, July 22). *Ethnic diversity in America heartland* [Video file]. Retrieved from www.youtube.com/watch?v=J96G2yD1Zmw

Jeffries, A. (Producer). (2017, February 1). *Where the refugees go: America's refugee cities are now in middle America* [Video file]. Retrieved from https://theoutline.com/post/985/where-the-refugees-go-lancaster-pennsylvania-immigration

Meyers, L. (2016). Immigration's growing impact on counseling. *Counseling Today, 58*(8), 22–31.

The National Child Traumatic Stress Network (Producer). (2005). *Children of war: A video for educators* [Video file]. Retrieved from www.nctsn.org/products/children-war-video-educators-2005

## SUGGESTED BACKGROUND READING

Bemak, F., & Chung, R. C. (2016). Counseling immigrants and refugees. In P. B. Pedersen, W. J. Lonner, J. G. Draguns, J. E. Trimble, & M. R. Scharron-del Rio (Eds.), *Counseling across cultures* (7th ed., pp. 323–346). Thousand Oaks, CA: Sage Publications.

Bemak, F., Chung, R. C., & Pedersen, P. (2003). *Counseling refugees: A psychosocial approach to innovative multicultural interventions.* Westport, CT: Greenwood Publishing Group.

Chung, R. C.-Y., Bemak, F., Ortiz, D. P., & Sandoval-Perez, P. A. (2008). Promoting the mental health of immigrants: A multicultural/social justice perspective. *Journal of Counseling & Development, 86*(3), 310–317. doi:10.1002/j.1556-6678.2008.tb00514.x

The National Child Traumatic Stress Network Refugee Trauma Working Group Children of War Production Committee. (2005). *Children of war: A video for educators' resource guide.* Retrieved from www.nctsn.org/sites/default/files/assets/pdfs/Children_of_War.pdf

Nilsson, J. E., Schale, C. L., & Khamphakdy-Brown, S. (2011). Facilitating trainees' multicultural development and social justice advocacy through a refugee/immigrant mental health program. *Journal of Counseling & Development, 89*(4), 413–422. doi:10.1002/j.1556-6676.2011.tb02838.x

Sue, D. W., & Sue, D. (2013). *Counseling the culturally diverse: Theory and practice* (6th ed., pp. 457–470). Hoboken, NJ: John Wiley & Sons.

Villalba, J. A. (2009). Addressing immigrant and refugee issues in multicultural counselor education. *Journal of Professional Counseling, Practice, Theory, & Research, 37*(1), 1–12. Retrieved from http://search.proquest.com.ezproxy.liberty.edu/docview/212449396?pq-origsite=summon&http://search.proquest.com/psychology?accountId=12085

Yakushko, O., Backhaus, A., Watson, M., Ngaruiya, K., & Gonzalez, J. (2008). Career development concerns of recent immigrants and refugees. *Journal of Career Development, 34*(4), 362–396. doi:10.1177/0894845308316292

# CHAPTER 33

# Experiencing Government Assistance

*Carrie VanMeter and Azra Karajic Siwiec*

## Course Recommendations

| SOCIAL JUSTICE AND ADVOCACY PRINCIPLES | CORE CACREP STANDARDS | COUNSELING SPECIALIZATION |
|---|---|---|
| ☑ Social Constructs of Oppression and Privilege | ☑ Helping Relationships<br>☑ Social and Cultural Diversity | ☑ Clinical Mental Health Counseling<br>☑ Marriage, Couple, and Family Counseling<br>☑ School Counseling<br>☑ Student Affairs and College Counseling |

## TOPIC

This assignment gives students the opportunity to explore government assistance through the lens of a counselor and challenges them to face biases they may have about populations that seek government assistance.

## LEARNING OBJECTIVES

1. Interpret the impact of power, privilege, and oppression within student's life and the lives of his/her client(s).
2. Illustrate advocacy processes needed to address institutional and social barriers that impede access, equity, and success for clients.
3. Distinguish strategies for working with and advocating for diverse populations (including multicultural competence).
4. Differentiate counselors' roles in developing cultural self-awareness and promoting cultural social justice.

## TARGET POPULATION

Master's-level counseling students

# GROUP SIZE

This is an individual assignment but is discussed in the class.

# TIME REQUIRED

30–45 minutes for classroom discussion after assignment is completed. Student will be required to schedule time outside of class to perform the required 1-hour observation of chosen site.

# SETTING

Real world experience

# MATERIALS NEEDED

No materials needed

# INSTRUCTIONS FOR CONDUCTING ACTIVITY

The following instructions are given to the students in a written format. This project requires some time to be set aside at the beginning of the course for explicit verbal explanation and overview of the requirements. It is important that the students seek out these resources on their own; no list of agencies is provided.

The purpose of this assignment is to have students experience what clients must go through in order to receive government assistance such as welfare, Medicare, Medicaid, or food stamps, using public transportation, etc. Students are to visit a government agency of their choice for a minimum of 1 hour. During that time students are required to try and obtain information on eligibility for that program. The rest of the hour will be spent respectfully observing what occurs in the office (how everyone is treated, how quickly people are helped, the overall atmosphere of the office, etc.). Students may also attempt to navigate the public transportation in their area for a minimum of 1 hour. Students will observe their surroundings and determine how easy or difficult the system is to use, what are the benefits and downfalls of the system, etc. At no point should students be on their cell phone or any other device to pass the time.

You may feel uncomfortable completing this assignment. If you feel unsafe, you may, however, take another student or person with you, but the expectation is that you will not sit beside this person during your hour of observation, whether you are in a government office or on the bus. I want you to embrace this experience individually so you can empathize with your clients who are going through this and see if you can identify ways you could advocate for this population.

Prior to your experience you must complete a write up (one to one-and-a-half pages) where you explore any personal feelings and biases you may have regarding the population you believe you will encounter during this experience or the environment you are going to be visiting. Take time to explore how your worldview and other influences have shaped your opinions such as your own cultural identities.

After the experience write a three to four page paper on this experience that includes responses to the following prompts: (1) type of activity/event and date, (2) thoughts, feelings, and behaviors during attendance of activity/event, (3) any observations of others including perceived reactions to your attendance, (4) reflection on how this experience relates to your development of two or more of the Association for Multicultural Counseling and Development (AMCD) Multicultural Counseling Competencies, (5) discussion of how you think the Multicultural Counseling Competencies can assist you in the future as you try to develop strategies to work with and develop treatment goals for diverse populations, (6) details of how you could advocate to address institutional and social barriers that impeded access, equity, and success for a client who was going through the government assistance program you chose to observe, and (7) comparison with your write up regarding your biases before your experience.

Please note that you will not be required to share these papers with fellow students and are encouraged to reflect on actual thoughts, feelings, and behaviors rather than present beliefs that are considered politically correct.

In order to develop and learn, you must first complete an honest assessment of where you are at now and where you have been. Keep in mind that we all have prejudices. It is how we manage these thoughts and our behaviors that makes the difference. Although it may be difficult, I encourage you to take a risk here, in terms of both the activity you select and your level of disclosure.

## DISCUSSION

After the assignments are completed 30–45 minutes of class time would be used to facilitate a reflective discussion. Discussion takes place in two phases.

Phase one: students are grouped with peers who observed similar services (e.g., all students who explored food stamps are in a group). In these small groups students discuss with one another their experiences, comparing similarities and differences, and how these experiences elucidated the stated aims of the project. Phase two: instructor leads the discussion, going around the room asking each small group to share their insights with the group at large.

Questions instructor might pose during phase two:

- What happened in your experience that you did not anticipate?
- Given your experiences what changes could be advocated for in order to make these services more accessible or inclusive?
- This project was geared toward experiencing government services that you may not have knowledge about. What other activities might you engage in to hone your multicultural competences?

## BIBLIOGRAPHY

Council for Accreditation of Counseling and Related Educational Programs. (2009). *CACREP accreditation manual.* Alexandria, VA: Author.
Sue, D. W., Arredondo, P., & McDavis, R. J. (1992). Multicultural competencies/standards: A pressing need. *Journal of Counseling & Development, 70,* 477–486.

## SUGGESTED BACKGROUND READING

Faculty member needs to be up-to-date on the government agencies in their area.

# CHAPTER 34

## Combatting Ableism
### Advocacy in the Real World for Persons With Disabilities

*Toni Saia*

### Course Recommendations

| SOCIAL JUSTICE AND ADVOCACY PRINCIPLES | CORE CACREP STANDARDS | COUNSELING SPECIALIZATION |
|---|---|---|
| ☑ Strategies for Change | ☑ Professional Counseling Orientation and Ethical Practice <br> ☑ Social and Cultural Diversity | ☑ Addiction Counseling <br> ☑ Clinical Mental Health Counseling <br> ☑ Marriage, Couple, and Family Counseling <br> ☑ School Counseling <br> ☑ Student Affairs and College Counseling |

## TOPIC

The focus of this activity is to highlight advocacy strategies to decrease barriers within the disability community, specific to the Americans With Disabilities Act (ADA Title III, Public Accommodations).

## LEARNING OBJECTIVES

1. To identify strategies to ensure the rights of people with disabilities under the ADA
2. To identify your advocacy style and approach as an advocate
3. To identify your role as an advocate

## TARGET POPULATION

Students (future professionals within the field of counseling)

## GROUP SIZE

Group size does not impact the activity, because students will break into four groups. The more students, the more students in each group.

141

# TIME REQUIRED

1 hour—group size/number of participants does not impact the time. Make sure at least 20 minutes are left for discussion/debriefing.

# SETTING

Any classroom or space that is large enough for four groups to discuss a specific scenario.

# MATERIALS NEEDED

- Colored sticky notes (one color for each group)
- Writing utensils (markers are best) for students to write on the sticky notes.
- Paper (give the scenario on a piece of paper to the assigned group)

# INSTRUCTIONS FOR CONDUCTING ACTIVITY

1. Divide students into four groups.
2. Give each group one of the following scenarios.
   Scenario 1:
   > You use a wheelchair. Some of your friends invite you to a new pub. There is, however, a high step at the entrance. What are your options? (Both short-term and long-term solutions.)
   Scenario 2:
   > You are blind. You recently tried having lunch at a new restaurant, near your house. The diner did not, however, have a Braille menu, and the server refused to read it, saying she was too busy. What are your options? (Both short-term and long-term solutions.)
   Scenario 3:
   > You have a disability that affects your speech. You and your attendant recently went shopping, and several sales associates as well as the store manager would only talk to your attendant. What are your options? (Both short-term and long-term solutions.)
   Scenario 4:
   > You are deaf. You were in a minor car accident and had to go to the emergency room. The emergency room refused to provide an American Sign Language (ASL) interpreter, and you had difficulty communicating with the doctor and nurses. What are your options? (Both short-term and long-term solutions.)
3. Instruct the group members to put one option/approach per sticky note. For example, if the option is to "leave" that would be written on a sticky note, and they would move to the next option.
4. The facilitator will go around and collect the sticky notes as the group continues to come up with options.
5. The facilitator will display the sticky notes (on the board or wall depending on what is available).
6. The facilitator will group the sticky note based on style/approach given (this is across all four scenarios). For example, the facilitator will group together indirect approaches like contact the media and call the manager and direct approaches like boycotts and protests.
7. The idea is to highlight all the approaches that can be used across all scenarios. The sticky notes create a great visual. It is always interesting to see if the group picks more approaches that put the burden on the person with the disability. For example, in scenario 2, one option that someone might give is for the person who is blind to create a Braille menu for the restaurant.

# DISCUSSION

1. How can advocacy address broader social justice issues for people with disabilities?
2. What option/approach would YOU be most comfortable doing?
3. What option/approach would YOU be least comfortable doing?
4. How can a local Center for Independence or other disability organization help to actively confront the social injustices that loom over people with disabilities?
5. What types of advocacy are the groups using?
6. Are more direct or indirect approaches listed? Why or why not?
7. What would you do as a counselor if your client came to you with one of the issues highlighted in the scenarios?

# BIBLIOGRAPHY

Colker, R. (2000). ADA Title III: A fragile compromise. *Berkeley Journal of Employment and Labor Law, 21*(1), 377–412.

Ratts, M. J., & Hutchins, A. M. (2009). ACA advocacy competencies: Social justice advocacy at the client/student level. *Journal of Counseling & Development, 87*(3), 269–275.

# CHAPTER 35

## Universal Language, Different Responses
### Using Music to Teach Multiculturalism

*Carrie Sanders and Dannette Gomez Beane*

### Course Recommendations

| SOCIAL JUSTICE AND ADVOCACY PRINCIPLES | CORE CACREP STANDARDS | COUNSELING SPECIALIZATION |
|---|---|---|
| ☑ What Is Social Justice and Advocacy? | ☑ Group Work<br>☑ Professional Counseling Orientation and Ethical Practice<br>☑ Social and Cultural Diversity | ☑ Clinical Mental Health Counseling<br>☑ School Counseling<br>☑ Student Affairs and College Counseling |

## TOPIC

This activity provides an introduction for conversations about individual perspectives. Each participant will have an opportunity to share a unique perspective of a shared group experience while identifying similarities and differences within the peer group.

## LEARNING OBJECTIVES

- Participants will identify their thoughts, feelings, images, and overall reactions to a wide variety of music genres.
- Participants will recognize that individual perceptions of the same information will have similarities and differences.
- Participants will increase an awareness of their own perceptions and preferences based on worldview.
- Participants will develop an awareness of the importance of seeking to understand the perspective of others.

## TARGET POPULATION

The target population for this activity is any group who is exploring considerations when working with or counseling diverse populations.

# GROUP SIZE

This activity can be done with any size group; however, to facilitate rich dialogue and connect with individual members, we recommend a group of 8–12 participants.

# TIME REQUIRED

The time required depends on the number of participants as well as the number of music sample clips selected. In general, we recommend estimating about 30 seconds for each music clip, 10 minutes for individual reflection/response, 30 minutes for sharing reactions and revisiting content, and 15 minutes for debriefing the exercise. To summarize, if you select ten music clips, we estimate your activity will take an hour.

# SETTING

This activity can take place in any quiet space that can accommodate the number of people in the group comfortably. Participants need a surface to write on or an alternative way to document their responses and reactions during the activity.

# MATERIALS NEEDED

Each student will need a piece of paper or handout and a writing utensil. If creating a handout, the instructor could include prompts such as:

1. What thoughts and feelings do you have when you listen to this song?
2. Describe images that come to mind when you hear this music.
3. Rate the song on a scale of 1–10 (with 10 representing a very strong positive response).

The instructor will need to prepare 10–12 30-second sample clips of a variety of musical genres. In order to deliver the music clips, the instructor needs the appropriate audio capabilities for students to have a clear and audible experience. If you have participants with audio or visual disabilities consider alternate ways to experience the musical vibrations and document reactions.

# INSTRUCTIONS FOR CONDUCTING ACTIVITY

Preparation work: Instructor can choose music from various genres. Recommendations would be to use a mix of familiar and unfamiliar songs, to include both with and without lyrics; for example, jazz, blues, opera, rap, country, reggae, blue grass, etc.
Some examples: Bob Marley: "One Love," Allison Krauss: "Oh, Atlanta," Hank Williams: "Lovesick Blues," Pyotr Ilyich Tchaikovsky: "The Nutcracker Suite," Idina Menzel: "Let It Go," etc.

To facilitate the activity follow the following steps:

1. Prepare the students for the activity by informing them at the beginning of class that they will be listening to music samples and reacting to them during the class. (We recommend this activity to take place about midway through the class meeting and after a short break.)
2. Provide students a sheet of paper to document responses and reactions to the music.

3. Prior to beginning the activity, explain the entire activity to the participants by describing each step and what is expected. (They will listen and respond individually to each clip, then they will be invited to share with the class their responses after the class has heard all music clips.)
4. The instructor plays each clip for 30 seconds, allowing time in between for students to write.
5. After all songs are played, ask the group how they felt about the assignment; specifically, ask, Were there songs you liked and did not like?
6. Go back and play each song for 1–3 seconds to remind the students of the tune and invite students to share their responses based on the prompts.
7. Encourage students to notice similarities and differences in their preferences for the music selections.
8. After each song is replayed and comments shared, ask the students how this activity relates to multiculturalism.

For more seasoned scholars, an instructor can use the music selection to emphasize how the arts have influenced social justice movements by selecting pieces that have been associated with war, oppression, freedom, etc.

Examples of songs could be Public Enemy's "Fight the Power," Mary Lambert's "She Keeps Me Warm," or Dolly Parton's "9 to 5."

## DISCUSSION

Reflection for this exercise can be rich and go in many directions. An instructor can follow up by asking questions such as the following:

- Was this activity fun?
- What emotions did you have?
- How does this activity relate to diversity and advocacy?
- How can music help us connect to one another?
- What can we learn about ourselves and others through this activity?
- How does music communicate social justice issues?
- In what ways can music promote social justice?

It is important to stress to the students that there is no wrong or right answer; each person feels and imagines different things based on their own experiences and worldview. This time can be spent talking through differences in age, geographic locations, cultures, politics, class, etc.

## BIBLIOGRAPHY

DeLorenzo, L. C. (2016). *Giving voice to democracy in music education: Diversity and social justice.* New York, NY: Routledge.
Pearsons, M., & Wilson, H. (2009). *Using expressive arts to work with mind, body and emotions: Theory and practice.* Philadelphia, PA: Jessica Kingsley Publishers.

## SUGGESTED BACKGROUND READING

Cloudhuri, D., Santiago-Rivera, A., & Garrett, M. (2012). *Counseling and diversity.* Belmont, CA: Brooks/Cole, Cengage Learning.

**HANDOUT**

# Handout 35.1: Universal Language Musical Reactions

Take a moment to write down your responses/reactions to each of the music clips that will be played for you. Include the thoughts, feelings, and images that come to mind when you listen to each selection. Also, indicate on a scale from 1 to 10 (with 10 = very strongly) how the song resonates with you.

1.  Thoughts & Feelings:
    Images:
    Scale (1–10):
2.  Thoughts & Feelings:
    Images:
    Scale (1–10):
3.  Thoughts & Feelings:
    Images:
    Scale (1–10):
4.  Thoughts & Feelings:
    Images:
    Scale (1–10):
5.  Thoughts & Feelings:
    Images:
    Scale (1–10):
6.  Thoughts & Feelings:
    Images:
    Scale (1–10):
7.  Thoughts & Feelings:
    Images:
    Scale (1–10):
8.  Thoughts & Feelings:
    Images:
    Scale (1–10):
9.  Thoughts & Feelings:
    Images:
    Scale (1–10):
10. Thoughts & Feelings:
    Images:
    Scale (1–10):

# CHAPTER 36

## Social Justice Scenes

*Alison Phillips Sheesley*

| Course Recommendations | | |
|---|---|---|
| **SOCIAL JUSTICE AND ADVOCACY PRINCIPLES** | **CORE CACREP STANDARDS** | **COUNSELING SPECIALIZATION** |
| ☑ Social Construct of Oppression and Privilege | ☑ Helping Relationships<br>☑ Social and Cultural Diversity | ☑ Addiction Counseling<br>☑ Clinical Mental Health Counseling |

## TOPIC

Exercises adapted from the practice of improv comedy can provide a foundation for powerful experiential classroom activities. This activity focuses on broadening counseling students' empathy for clients of various socioeconomic/class statuses.

## LEARNING OBJECTIVES

1. Develop empathy through embodying clients of various socioeconomic/class statuses.
2. Utilize the tenets of improv comedy to increase comfort with spontaneous therapeutic responses to clients.

## TARGET POPULATION

Master's-level counseling students

## GROUP SIZE

There should be approximately six to eight participants per group, but multiple groups can run simultaneously.

## TIME REQUIRED

Approximately 20–30 minutes are required, but could be shorter or longer depending on the instructor's needs.

## SETTING

A classroom environment is ideal for this activity.

## MATERIALS NEEDED

One deck of playing cards

## INSTRUCTIONS FOR CONDUCTING ACTIVITY

In this activity, two students at a time will enact an improv scene for 3–5 minutes, while the other students watch. If students are very uncomfortable acting in front of the class, this activity can be done in pairs.

When introducing the activity, the instructor should provide a brief explanation of improv comedy as follows:

> Improv (i.e., improv comedy or improvisational theater) refers to any theatrical performance occurring without a script. The foundation of all improv scenes is an exercise called, "Yes, and . . ." (as cited in Phillips Sheesley, Pfeffer, & Barish, 2016). Two improvisers stand or sit facing each other. The first improviser starts with a premise, a single statement as simple or complicated as desired (e.g., "The sky is blue"). The second improviser responds with "Yes, and . . .," adding to the premise (e.g., "Yes, and there is a cloud in the sky that looks like an elephant"). In turn, each improviser continues to respond to the other with "Yes, and . . .," building on each other's ideas. The crucial component of this exercise as explained by Salinsky and Frances-White (2008) is the absence of rejection: "Saying yes to your partner's idea represents a risk. You have to let an alien idea in and, if you have to build on it, you have to let it influence you" (p. 61).

The improv scenes that you (the student) will be doing with your partner today can take place anywhere that you would like and can begin however you would like. If you just keep in mind that you are trying to say "yes, and . . ." to your partner, I'm sure you will not have any problems.

At this point, depending on how much time you (the instructor) have reserved for this activity, you can allow students to practice the activity "Yes, and . . ." before adding the high status, low status component.

When you are ready to proceed, have students form a seated circle. Have each student pick a playing card while telling all students that the card rank corresponds to how they carry themselves and expect to be treated (Mullaney, 2015). Then, have students stand in front of the group in pairs (or sit together more privately) and enact 3–5 minute improv scenes while embodying this "status." Instruct students to focus on creating realistic scenes and that the goal is not to be funny or entertaining.

Students may benefit from more guidance as to the content of their scenes, and so you could also employ the following social justice "scene starters," with or without the use of cards:

1. At times, women are marginalized. Create a scene where one character is a woman employee of a large company and the other character is an older man who is her boss. Start with the line, "I am feeling like you do not value my contribution to the company" and build the conversation from there using the "Yes, and . . ." technique. Remember that, "In feminist theory, resistance means the refusal to merge with dominant cultural norms and to attend one's own voice and integrity" (Gilligan, Rogers, & Tolman, 1991, as cited in Brown, 1994).
2. There are people we will counsel who have struggles that we do not know personally. For example, a counselor may be privileged to not have personal experiences with poverty, but may be working with clients of low socioeconomic status. Re-enact a situation where one person is the counselor and the other person is explaining his/her struggles with poverty. Start with the line, "I am so worried that I will not be able to make my rent payment" and build the conversation from there using the "Yes, and . . ."

technique. The person who is a counselor should draw upon his/her knowledge of the *multicultural and social justice counseling competencies* (Ratts, Singh, Nassar-McMillan, Butler, & McCullough, 2015).

3. White identity development as discussed by Helms (1990) progresses through six stages. Re-enact a scene in which one character identifies with *Stage 4—Pseudo-Independent Status* and one character identifies with *Stage 5—Immersion-Emmersion Status*. For example, two friends could be discussing the recent removal of Confederate monuments, while responding from these two perspectives.

4. Sue and Sue (2013) discuss the Racial/Cultural Identity Development Model (R/CID) as a five-stage process in which minorities move from a white frame of reference to a positive minority frame of reference. Re-enact a scene in which one character identifies with *Stage 1—Conformity* and one character identifies with *Stage 3—Resistance and Immersion*. For example, two friends could be discussing the *Black Lives Matter* movement.

Throughout this activity, it is important to remind students that "Experiential learning is not intended to emulate another individual's exact experience; the intention is to develop awareness and accuracy around the viewpoints of others and to move out of a culturally encapsulated view of the world" (Pedersen & Ivey, 1993, as cited in Arthur & Achenbach, 2002).

Provide these instructions to all students before beginning scenes: "I want you to imagine that you are truly this person and fully embody this individual. What is your history? Why do you believe that you deserve to be treated this way? Does this belief impact how you treat others? Once students have had time to imagine and create the individuals they will be embodying, scenes can begin."

After each scene, you can provide some processing time for comments from the participants and audience members. However, remind students that you will be processing this experience as a group at the end.

Additional variations:

Tell students that the card corresponds to how they should treat the other person (i.e., the perceived status of their scene partner). You can also give students two cards, one card representing how they see themselves and one card representing how they see their scene partner. Another variation is to have students do a scene in which they know the status of their scene partner, but not their own status. Then, you can have students explore how they perceived their own statuses based on cues from their partner.

# DISCUSSION

The instructor can facilitate a meaningful discussion of socioeconomic and class status following the completion of this activity. Questions that could be posed to students include:

- What was the most challenging part of this activity for you?
- How did you know if someone was so-called high status? What does the word "status" mean to you?
- What card numbers did you consider to be high status, and what card numbers did you consider to be low status?
- Was it more difficult for you to embody someone of high status or low status? What about your own background made it more difficult?
- Was it more difficult for you to respond to someone of high status or low status? What about your own background made it more difficult?
- How might a client's socioeconomic/class status affect their mental health?
- How will you respond if a client comes into your office clearly displaying his or her perceived and/or actual socioeconomic/class status, low or high? Do you think it will be as obvious as in these scenes, or could it be more subtle?

# BIBLIOGRAPHY

Arthur, N., & Achenbach, K. (2002). Developing multicultural counseling competencies through experiential learning. *Counselor Education & Supervision, 42*(1), 2–14.

Brown, L. S. (1994). *Subversive dialogues: Theories in feminist therapy.* New York, NY: Basic Books.

Helms, J. E. (1990). *Black and white racial identity: Theory, research, and practice.* Westport, CT: Greenwood.

Gilligan, C., Rogers, A. G., & Tolman, D. T. (1991). *Women, girls, & psychotherapy: Reframing resistance.* New York, NY: Routledge.

Mullaney, K. (2015). *Status exercises in improv.* Retrieved from https://kevinmullaney.com/2015/11/16/status-exercises-in-improv/

Phillips Sheesley, A., Pfeffer, M., & Barish, B. (2016). Comedic improv therapy for the treatment of social anxiety disorder. *Journal of Creativity in Mental Health, 11*(2), 157–169. doi:10.1080/15401383.2016.1182880

Pedersen, P. P., & Ivey, A. E. (1993). *Culture-centered counseling and interviewing skills: A practical guide.* West Port, CT: Praeger.

Ratts, M. J., Singh, A. A., Nassar-McMillan, S., Butler, S. K., & McCullough, J. R. (2015). Multicultural and social justice counseling competencies. *Association for Multicultural Counseling and Development, 44,* 28–48.

Salinsky, T., & Frances-White, D. (2008). *The improv handbook: The ultimate guide to improvising in comedy, theatre, and beyond.* New York, NY: Continuum International Publishing Group.

Sue, D. W., & Sue, D. (2013). *Counseling the culturally diverse: Theory and practice* (6th ed.). New York, NY: John Wiley & Sons.

# SUGGESTED BACKGROUND READING

Belle, D. (1990). Poverty and women's mental health. *American Psychologist, 45*(3), 385–398.

Leonard, K., & Yorton, T. (2015). *Yes, and: How improvisation reverses "No, But" thinking and improves creativity and collaboration lessons from The Second City.* New York, NY: Harper Collins Publishers.

Smith, L., Li, V., Dykema, S., Hamlet, D., & Shellman, A. (2013). "Honoring somebody that society doesn't honor": Therapists working in the context of poverty. *Journal of Clinical Psychology, 69*(2), 138–151. doi:10.1002/jclp.21953

# CHAPTER 37

## Room for All
## An Introductory Activity in Empathy

*Elizabeth Keller-Dupree, Karlie Collins, Jenifer Cortes Gray, and Jordan Westcott*

### Course Recommendations

| SOCIAL JUSTICE AND ADVOCACY PRINCIPLES | CORE CACREP STANDARDS | COUNSELING SPECIALIZATION |
|---|---|---|
| ☑ What Is Social Justice and Advocacy? <br> ☑ Social Constructs of Oppressional and Privilege <br> ☑ Intersections of Oppression | ☑ Career Development <br> ☑ Group Work <br> ☑ Helping Relationships <br> ☑ Human Growth and Development <br> ☑ Professional Counseling Orientation and Ethical Practice <br> ☑ Social and Cultural Diversity <br> ☑ Theories | ☑ Addiction Counseling <br> ☑ Career Counseling <br> ☑ Clinical Mental Health Counseling <br> ☑ School Counseling |

## TOPIC

Room for All is an inviting introductory activity for group experiences in which group members are encouraged to deconstruct their personal identities and select salient descriptors of their unique personal selves that they bring to the group experience. The group will then process these individual personal identities to develop a group, or collective, reconstructed identity.

## LEARNING OBJECTIVES

- Participants will explore three elements of their constructed identity brought to the group experience.
- Participants will examine ways that dissimilar individual identities can coexist in a collective learning experience.
- Participants will investigate the relationship between empathy, social justice, and advocacy.
- Participants will understand how experiential group activities can be facilitated in clinical or school counseling settings.

# TARGET POPULATION

This activity is appropriate for a variety of participants including clinical populations, students in school counseling settings, and graduate counselor training. Within graduate counselor training, this activity is uniquely suited as an introductory activity in courses such as Counseling Foundations, Counseling Diversity, Group Counseling, Practicum, and Internship. Room for All is best used in a process-oriented setting, which promotes constructivism in learning. The target population would value connecting with and learning from others, their experiences, and their appropriately disclosed vulnerabilities.

# GROUP SIZE

Room for All is a group activity suited for small groups (five to eight people) or large groups (potentially up to 30 participants).

# TIME REQUIRED

Time requirement for this activity will vary depending on the number of group members or participants in the learning environment. For small group application, 45 minutes is appropriate. For larger group application, 90 minutes may be needed.

# SETTING

A classroom or counseling setting is ideal for conducting the Room for All activity. Participants in the activity need a place to sit and a place to write, thus allowing a variety of venues to be suitable for appropriate facilitation of this activity.

# MATERIALS NEEDED

Preparing this activity involves gathering the following resources:

- One or two packets of cardstock of various sizes and colors (100+ card stocks per packet)
- One piece of poster board (size depending on number of participants)
- Various colored markers (one box per two to four participants)
- Scissors (one pair per two to four participants)
- Tape

Cardstock sizes should be a minimum of 3 × 3 inches and not to exceed 5 × 5 inches (approximate) in size.

# INSTRUCTIONS FOR CONDUCTING ACTIVITY

All individuals have a unique identity that is constructed of characteristics in which they were born, historical experiences that have impacted their personal self, and elements of their identities that are not necessarily known to others (Arredondo et al., 1996). When individuals explore the richness and complexity of their individually constructed selves, group identities then become richer and more complex in their construction as well! The following activity is designed to help individuals explore their unique identities and to share and connect that unique self with the larger group.

# Step-by-Step Directions

After students/participants (subsequently referred to as "participants" throughout this explanation) have an understanding of constructed identities (Arredondo et al., 1996), the facilitator will explain that participants are invited to participate in a group learning experience.

1. The group facilitator will first hang a piece of poster board at the front of the classroom that is purposefully smaller than the number of cardstocks anticipated to be placed on it (see steps 2 and 3). For example, a large poster board (size 20 × 30 inches) would be appropriate for a class size of ten or more participants. A small poster board (size 11 × 14 inches) would be appropriate for a class/group of five or fewer.

2. The group facilitator will begin distributing the supplies needed for the activity. Supply distribution should involve dispersing several different sized and colored cardstock piles to participants in the class, along with markers (one box per two to four participants) and scissors (one pair per two to four participants). For example, a table of four participants could have 30 different pieces of cardstock with varying sizes and colors, along with one or two pairs of scissors. After supplies have been distributed, participants will then receive the following instructions: in front of you, you will see several pieces of cardstock, along with markers, and scissors. Take a few minutes and consider your identity. What makes you? What elements of your personality, life experience, or dimensions of yourself, perhaps even not noticeably recognizable to others, lead you to be the person that you are in this class, in this profession, and in this society? Begin deconstructing that identity. Next, select three pieces of cardstock that stand out to you, considering size, shape, and color, which reflect your self-identifiers. Feel free to modify or transform the cardstock by altering it if it needs to be a different size or shape to represent a certain dimension of your individual self. Lastly, write a word or phrase on each of the three pieces of selected cardstock that reflects the three parts of your personal identity that came to mind.

3. Facilitator's note: some participants may need to see a visual to have an understanding of the expectation of the activity. So, select a piece of colored cardstock that stands out to you (the facilitator) and write a word or phrase on it that represents a part of your constructed identity. For example, if a core piece of the facilitator's identity is college graduate, then the facilitator could select an appropriate cardstock and write that element of identity on the cardstock. Then, the facilitator could verbally share the following: for those of you who need an example, I am going to select this red cardstock because it stands out to me as bold and strong. I am going to write First-Generation College Graduate on this cardstock, as education is a vital element of my individually constructed identity. I would then select two other colors of cardstock and write two more words/phrases on them to complete this part of the activity. Does anyone have questions?

4. Allow approximately 10–15 minutes for individuals to complete this part of the activity. The facilitator should participate in this part of the activity as well.

5. After all participants have selected three pieces of cardstock to represent three pieces of their constructed identities, the facilitator will begin the next phase of this experiential activity by making the following statement: now that we have all deconstructed our personal identities and have identified three meaningful pieces of whom we are, next we are going to use these identities to create a new collective group identity. We all bring something unique and special to our interpersonal relationships. Sometimes those pieces of ourselves may seem small, and sometimes they may seem core to whom we are. But regardless, we all bring something. Now, we are going to take turns coming up to this blank poster board, explaining our three pieces of ourselves to our group, and taping our pieces of our identity to the poster board. I will go first as an example.

6. Facilitator's note: use this time to model and explain appropriate disclosure to your group. Share meaningful pieces of your constructed identity while also considering how to model the length of time of disclosure and the depth of revealing/sharing. For example, in modeling how to share constructed identity, one might say the following: it is important to consider how you share pieces of your constructed identity to the class as this is a form of self-disclosure. I will go first to model

appropriate disclosure for this activity. Many people know me as Dr. [fill in the blank], and that title reflects education as a core component of identity for me. I am a first-generation college graduate (tape First-Generation College Graduate to poster board). Other elements of my identity are female (tape Female to poster board). And I am a wife to my husband (tape Wife to poster board). Who would like to go next? Continue to tear off pieces of tape as members of the class come up to the poster board and share their pieces of their constructed identity.

7. Invite each participant to share their pieces of identity and encourage each person to take a brief moment to explore their card (for example, why that color or size represents that piece of identity). Thank each person as they share their pieces with the group.

8. When the construction of the group identity nears the end (with two to three participants left to share), the poster board should become increasingly full. Group members left to share will have to consider how to attach their pieces of identity to the board while respecting those that are already on the board.

9. Facilitator's note: patience in problem-solving is key to this part of the activity. Refrain from offering suggestions as to how the remaining participants can get their pieces of identity to fit onto the board. Eventually, the group will figure it out. They will either overlap pieces of paper (which they may have already begun doing), add an additional portion of poster board, or determine another strategy for making room for all on the constructed group identity.

10. After all participants have had the opportunity to individually process their constructed pieces of identity and collage them on the group poster board (approximately 30 minutes depending on group size), proceed to the following post-activity processing questions/discussion points.

# DISCUSSION

Following the group experience of deconstructing pieces of our identity and reconstructing the group identity, take 15–20 minutes to process the activity as a whole. The following section offers suggested dialogue for facilitating the group processing.

1. Script to read to the group: "We began this lesson by exploring how all people bring something to an interpersonal experience. In fact, in counseling, we will sit across from people every day who are uniquely different than us, and at the same time, we each contribute rich and unique pieces to that interpersonal relationship, much in the same way to how we created this rich and complex group identity here today. Let's spend some time processing this activity and its impact on you personally and collectively."

2. Suggested processing questions:
   - How did you decide what were the most meaningful pieces of your deconstructed identity to put on the cardstock?
   - What was it like to share your pieces of identity with the group?
   - How did you decide when you should share your pieces of identity with the group?
   - How is the way in which you processed your pieces of identity with the group similar or dissimilar to how you share pieces of your life with people in the real world?
   - What was most challenging for you? How did you address that challenge?
   - What happened when the poster board became too full?
   - How is this poster board similar to or dissimilar from the way in which our society operates?
   - How is this poster board reflective of the counseling profession?
   - What does this poster board symbolize for our group?
   - What themes do you notice within our constructed group identity? What themes are missing?
   - As future helping professionals, how could you see this group activity being used in future clinical/school counseling settings?
   - What type of client/person might struggle with this activity?
   - How can counseling professionals help all people feel safe in participating in this group activity?

- How does society make room for diverse identities?
- How would you challenge stereotypes and labels associated with an individual's identity?
- How have you had to advocate for different parts of your identity that you disclosed?
- When have you felt unsafe or uncertain to disclose about your identity?
- How do you advocate for someone who is reluctant, scared, or uncertain about sharing pieces of their identity?
- What causes prejudicial thinking? What causes discriminatory behavior?
- How can an individual overcome prejudicial thinking and discriminatory behavior?
- How can making room for multiple identities combat oppression and injustice?
- What steps can individuals take to continue to make room for all people and their identities?

3. End the processing with a statement that bridges this activity to the greater goal of the course, counselor training, advocacy, social justice issues, or the helping profession in general. For example, the facilitator could say something similar to the following: as the facilitator of this course, I know that each of you brings so much to this group classroom experience. Imagine what it would be like if there was a piece of your identity that felt compromised, unappreciated, or undervalued. Can you imagine the impact that those feelings may have on your readiness, willingness, and comfort with collectively engaging with others? Throughout the semester, we will have lots of time to learn together, grow together, unite in our similarities, and stretch each other in our differences. What is most important is that we always value the space for adding more or making room for all persons to feel part of the collective group experience. Sometimes we may disagree, and sometimes we may struggle to see eye-to-eye. This happens in counseling, too. But empathy is not about liking or agreeing with someone; it is about seeking to understand their perspective. Today, we have learned about many perspectives, many pieces of identities that are here, present, in this room. I know that we will be a richer, more complex group because of those identities.

# BIBLIOGRAPHY

Arredondo, P., Toporek, R., Brown, S. P., Jones, J., Locke, D. C., Sanchez, J., & Stadler, H. (1996). Operationalization of the multicultural competencies. *Journal of Multicultural Counseling and Development, 24*, 42–78.

Mezirow, J. (1997). Transformative learning: Theory to practice. In P. Cranton (Ed.), *Transformative learning in action: Insights from practice* (pp. 5–13). San Francisco: Jossey-Bass. http://dx.doi.org/10.1002/ace.7401

Robinson-Wood, T. L. (2013). *The convergence of race, ethnicity, and gender: Multiple identities in counseling* (4th ed.). Upper Saddle River, NJ: Pearson.

# SUGGESTED BACKGROUND READING

Anderson, R. D., & Price, G. E. (2001). Experiential groups in counselor education: Student attitudes and instructor participation. *Counselor Education and Supervision, 41*(2), 111–119.

Arredondo, P., Toporek, R., Brown, S. P., Jones, J., Locke, D. C., Sanchez, J., & Stadler, H. (1996). Operationalization of the multicultural competencies. *Journal of Multicultural Counseling and Development, 24*, 42–78.

Auxier, C. R., Hughes, F. R., & Kline, W. B. (2003). Identity development in counselors-in-training. *Counselor Education and Development, 43*, 25–38. http://dx.doi.org/10.1002/j1556-6978.2003.tb01827.x

Gibson, D. M., Dollarhide, C. T., & Moss, J. M. (2010). Professional identity development: A grounded theory of transformational tasks of new counselors. *Counselor Education and Supervision, 50*, 21–38. http://dx.doi.org/10.1002/j.1556-6978.2010.tb00106.x

# CHAPTER 38

## Self-Care
### Advocacy for Therapists' Needs

*Kristin Vincenzes, Jenny Benson, and Dionne Sterner*

---

### Course Recommendations

| SOCIAL JUSTICE AND ADVOCACY PRINCIPLES | CORE CACREP STANDARDS | COUNSELING SPECIALIZATION |
|---|---|---|
| ☑ Social Constructs of Oppression and Privilege<br>☑ Strategies for Change | ☑ Group Work<br>☑ Helping Relationships<br>☑ Human Growth and Development<br>☑ Professional Counseling Orientation and Ethical Practice | ☑ Addiction Counseling<br>☑ Career Counseling<br>☑ Clinical Mental Health Counseling<br>☑ Marriage, Couple, and Family Counseling<br>☑ School Counseling<br>☑ Student Affairs and College Counseling |

---

## TOPIC

As counselor educators, it is important to facilitate discussions on self-care throughout the curriculum (CACREP, 2016, Standard F.1.l). When we practice self-care, we can reduce the potential for impairment through burnout, compassion fatigue, and vicarious trauma (Skovholt & Trotter-Mathison, 2011).

## LEARNING OBJECTIVES

1. Students/participants will gain an awareness of the importance of self-care and how it may impact one's personal and professional life.
2. Students/participants will demonstrate an ability to achieve empowerment and assertiveness with regard to one's self-care as a means to gain a more fulfilling and meaningful life.
3. Students/participants will reflect on the Personal Bill of Rights (Bourne, 2015) as it relates to their own personal lives.
4. Students/participants will create a minimum of one personal goal and action plan to optimize one's self-care.

# TARGET POPULATION

This activity is utilized effectively in a face-to-face graduate group counseling class, specifically in the processing group that students are required to attend; however, the activity can be used with a wide array of groups to include psychoeducational groups, processing groups, and/or psychotherapy groups. Regardless of an individual client's mental health needs, wellness and prevention are pertinent counseling goals (CACREP, 2016). It is important to note that this activity does require the group members to utilize insight and reasoning; therefore, it may not be appropriate for younger children and/or individuals with cognitive impairment. Lucock, Gillard, Adams, Simons, White, and Edwards (2011) synthesized a meta-analysis and identified populations in which self-care has been effective. These populations included adolescents and adults, both male and female, the chronically mentally ill (i.e., those with schizophrenia, reactive psychosis, manic depression, paranoia), those in recovery from long-term mental health issues, homeless individuals with a mental illness, and mental health consumers. In addition to graduate counseling students and/or clients who may benefit from this activity, it could also be used in group supervision with current mental health professionals. This activity would support the need for the professional to engage in self-care activities to help minimize the potential for impairment through burnout, compassion fatigue, and vicarious trauma (ACA, 2014; Skovholt & Trotter-Mathison, 2011).

# GROUP SIZE

The suggested number of participants for the activity is 2–12.

# TIME REQUIRED

Approximately 35–45 minutes depending on the size of the group. The bigger the group the more time that will need to be allotted.

# SETTING

This activity can be conducted face-to-face in a classroom or at a counseling practice. This activity also has been successfully conducted in an online format. While it can be completed via a phone conference, the optimal success would be to conduct the group session via a synchronous learning platform such as Blackboard Collaborate or Digital Samba. The group leader needs to provide participants with a copy of the Personal Bill of Rights via email ahead of time or other accessible online tools that are readily accessible during the group session. In addition, each participant should be made aware of the essential materials in order to complete this activity in a timely manner (e.g., paper and pen/pencil).

# MATERIALS NEEDED

To prepare for the group activity, the group leader should arrange the chairs in a circle so that all participants can be seen and heard. Each participant is encouraged to be actively engaged in the activity. Each participant should be provided with a handout of the Personal Bill of Rights, a blank sheet of paper, and a pencil/pen for writing.

# INSTRUCTIONS FOR CONDUCTING ACTIVITY

To begin the process of introducing this particular activity, it would be essential for the group leader to discuss the definition of self-care and who should practice self-care. It would also be beneficial for the leader to facilitate a discussion on each group member's perspective of self-care to include current self-care strategies each member uses in their daily life.

Step-by-step directions:

1. Facilitate a group discussion surrounding the following questions:
   a. What does self-care mean to you?
   b. What self-care strategies do you currently use in your daily life?
   c. Who should practice self-care?
2. Provide each group member/participant with a copy of the Personal Bill of Rights (Bourne, 2015).
3. The group leader reads aloud the Personal Bill of Rights to the group.
4. After the group leader reads all 30 rights to the group participants, ask each group member to square or circle the ones that they could say more often.
5. Ask group members to share a few (preferably two or three) rights that they could say more often. (It is important for facilitators to pay attention to group members' non-verbal behavior.)
6. Ask the group members to put a star next to the one most troublesome to them.
7. Ask the group members to write down the rights that they chose as most troublesome at the top of a blank sheet of paper. Underneath it, members are asked to identify potential challenges or obstacles that may make the item troublesome. Then ask the members to create a self-care goal focusing on that right. Remind the members to create a concrete, measurable, and observable goal.
8. Ask the group members to create an action plan underneath the goal to integrate that goal. Ideas may include: who will be involved in this self-care goal? How will this goal be carried out? How often will the self-care strategy be integrated into one's life? What additional support may be necessary for this goal to be accomplished?
9. After the group leader assesses the group members' non-verbal cues and feels that the members have completed their self-care goals to include their action plans, ask each member to share their personal challenges or obstacles, goals, and action plans with the group. Further prompt each member to think about how they will be consistent with their self-care plans.
10. Once all students share, the facilitator can ask how this activity could be used with diverse clients. Discussions could focus on individual clients as well as how the activities may compare to counseling couples, families, and various groups.

Helpful hints for observing non-verbal behavior (Corey, Corey, & Corey, 2014):

1. A member who is talking about a painful experience while smiling
2. A member who speaks very softly and proclaims that nobody listens to him/her
3. A client who is verbally expressing positive feelings yet is very constricted physically
4. A person who says that he/she really wants to work and to have group time but consistently waits until the end of a session before bringing up concerns
5. A participant who claims that he/she feels comfortable in the group and really likes members yet sits with his/her arms crossed tightly and tends to look at the floor
6. A member who displays facial expressions and gestures but denies having any reactions

## DISCUSSION

After each group member shares his/her goal and action plan with the group, the leader facilitates a discussion around self-care to process the activity. The group leader notes themes within the group to include potential obstacles that may arise when trying to meet one's self-care goal. In addition, the group leader facilitates a discussion on the importance of self-care as it relates to both one's personal life and professional life (i.e., burnout, compassion fatigue, vicarious trauma, ACA Code of Ethics). At the end of the activity, each participant will be able to demonstrate an ability to achieve empowerment, identify their own personal basic human rights, process potential obstacles inhibiting their self-care, demonstrate how to effectively achieve assertiveness with regard to their personal self-care needs, and implement their personal self-care plan.

## Performance Indicators/Evaluation

At the end of the aforementioned activity, the success of each objective will be measured by observation and level of group member participation in the activity/discussion. The group member's personal self-care goal will be evident through self-report and sharing with the group. At the conclusion of the group session, the leader can facilitate a round robin closure asking the following question: "What is the most prominent concept, idea, or reflection that you are taking away from this group session?" It is highly recommended that the next time the group meets, the leader reinforces the activity by following up on everyone's self-care plan.

S.L.O. #1: students/participants will gain an awareness of the importance of self-care and how it may impact one's personal and professional life.
a. Success will be measured by in-session discussion and participation.

S.L.O. #2: students/participants will demonstrate an ability to achieve empowerment and assertiveness with regard to one's self-care as a means to gain a more fulfilling and meaningful life.
b. Success will be measured by self-report during in-session discussion and closing take away statement.

S.L.O. #3: students/participants will reflect on the Personal Bill of Rights as it relates to their own personal lives.
c. Success will be measured by in-session participation and sharing with the group their two to three rights they want to say more often.

S.L.O. #4: students/Participants will create a minimum of one personal goal and action plan to optimize one's self-care.
d. Success will be measured by active participation in writing down one's goal/action plan as well as self-report when asked to share with the group.

## BIBLIOGRAPHY

American Counseling Association. (2014). *ACA code of ethics and standards of practice*. Retrieved from www.counseling.org/Resources/aca-code-of-ethics.pdf

Bourne, E. J. (2015). *The anxiety and phobia workbook* (6th ed.). Oakland, CA: New Harbinger Publications, Inc.

Corey, M. S., Corey, G., & Corey, C. (2014). *Groups process and practice* (9th ed.). Belmont, CA: Brooks/Cole, Cengage Learning.

Council for Accreditation of Counseling and Related Educational Programs [CACREP]. (2016). *2016 standards for accreditation*. Alexandria, VA: Author.

Lucock, M., Gillard, S., Adams, K., Simons, L., White, R., & Edwards, C. (2011). Self-care in mental health services: A narrative review. *Health and Social Care in the Community, 19*(6), 602–616. doi:10:1111/j.1365-2524.2011.01014.x

Skovholt, T. M., & Trotter-Mathison, M. J. (2011). *The resilient practitioner: Burnout prevention and self-care strategies for counselors, therapists, teachers, and health professionals* (2nd ed.). Boston, MA: Allyn & Bacon.

# SUGGESTED BACKGROUND READING

Figley, C. (Ed.). (2002). *Treating compassion fatigue*. Philadelphia, PA: Brunner and Routledge.

Newel, J. M., & MacNeil, G. A. (2010). Professional burnout, vicarious trauma, secondary traumatic stress, and compassion fatigue: A review of theoretical terms, risk factors, and preventive methods for clinicians and researchers. *Best Practices in Mental Health: An International Journal*, 6(2), 57–68.

Newsome, S., Chambers Christopher, J., Dahlen, P., & Christopher, S. (2006). Teaching counselor's self-care through mindfulness practices. *Teaching College Record*. Retrieved from www.tcrecord.org/content.asp?contentid=12686

Richards, K. C., Campenni, C., & Muse-Burke, J. L. (2010). Self-care and well-being in mental health professionals: The mediating effects of self-awareness and mindfulness. *Journal of Mental Health Counseling*, 32(3), 247–261.

Warren, J., Morgan, M. M., Morris, L. B., & Morris, T. M. (2010). Breathing words slowly: Creative writing and counselor self-care-the writing workout. *Journal of Creativity in Mental Health*, 5(109), 109–124. doi:10.1080/15401383.2010 .485074

## HANDOUT

# Handout 38.1: Personal Bill of Rights

1. I have the right to ask for what I want or need.
2. I have the right to say no to requests or demands I can't meet or choose not to follow.
3. I have the right to express all my feelings, positive or negative.
4. I have the right to make mistakes and not have to be perfect.
5. I have the right to follow my own values, standards, and beliefs.
6. I have the right to say no to anything when I feel I am not ready, it is unsafe, or it violates my values.
7. I have the right to determine my own priorities.
8. I have the right not to be responsible for others' behavior, actions, feelings, or problems.
9. I have the right to expect honesty from others.
10. I have the right to be angry with someone I love.
11. I have the right to be uniquely myself.
12. I have the right to feel scared and say, "I'm afraid."
13. I have the right to say, "I don't know."
14. I have the right not to give excuses for my behavior.
15. I have the right to make decisions based on my own feelings.
16. I have the right to my own needs for personal space and time.
17. I have the right to be playful.
18. I have the right to be healthier than those around me.
19. I have the right to be in a nonabusive environment.
20. I have the right to make friends and be comfortable around people.
21. I have the right to change and grow.
22. I have the right to have my needs and wants respected by others.
23. I have the right to be treated with dignity and respect.
24. I have the right to be happy.
25. I have the right to maintain my dignity by being properly assertive—even if the other person feels hurt, as long as I do not violate the other person's basic human rights.
26. I have the right to be left alone.
27. I have the right to get what I paid for.
28. I have the right to change my mind.
29. I have the right to be successful and independent.
30. I have the right NOT to feel guilty in making decisions that are in my best interest. It is my responsibility to take care of my needs.

# CHAPTER 39

# Justice for All
## Utilizing Drama Therapy to Increase Empathy and Promote Social Justice With Marginalized Populations

*Abigail Nedved, Dasha Carver, Acacia Douglas, and Dixie Meyer*

## Course Recommendations

| SOCIAL JUSTICE AND ADVOCACY PRINCIPLES | CORE CACREP STANDARDS | COUNSELING SPECIALIZATION |
|---|---|---|
| ☑ Cycle of Socialization and Liberation<br>☑ Social Construct of Oppression and Privilege<br>☑ Intersection of Oppression<br>☑ Strategies for Change | ☑ Career Development<br>☑ Group Work<br>☑ Helping Relationships<br>☑ Human Growth and Development<br>☑ Social and Cultural Diversity | ☑ Clinical Mental Health Counseling<br>☑ Marriage, Couple, and Family Counseling<br>☑ School Counseling<br>☑ Student Affairs and College Counseling |

## TOPIC

The project calls for students to interview someone from any marginalized population, present in class the content of the interview, and enact stories of the interviewee. The goal of the activity is to understand the lived experiences of marginalized populations and recreate an alternate outcome to unjust experiences.

## LEARNING OBJECTIVES

The objectives of the activity are to:

1. Increase awareness of the experiences of individuals from a variety of cultures.
2. Develop a clearer understanding of common microaggression experiences by marginalized populations daily.
3. Brainstorm ways to create justice in an unjust society.
4. Increase empathy for marginalized populations through acting out the experiences of marginalized populations.
5. Explore preconceived expectations of marginalized populations and understand that each person does not represent the marginalized population but that each person has their own unique perspectives.

# TARGET POPULATION

The activity can be utilized with high school students to graduate students.
Students may consider some of the following groups as examples of marginalized populations:

- Women in STEM-related fields
- Men and women from the Muslim community (or other religions)
- Syrian and other refugees, migrants, or immigrants
- Sexual minorities (LGB, transgender, intersex individuals)
- Individuals who have a mental disorder, physical disability, or developmental delay
- Single parents (mothers and fathers) or students who are parents
- American Indians or Native Americans
- Ex-offenders (male and female) and families of inmates
- Former victims of human-trafficking
- War veterans
- Individuals in recovery from substance abuse

# GROUP SIZE

This activity is best executed in classes with a minimum of four students.

# TIME REQUIRED

This activity will take approximately three weeks to complete. Students will need a minimum of one week to interview someone, one week to present the content and what they learned from the interview, and one week to facilitate the enactments. More time may be needed depending on the class size.

Students will want to interview their volunteer for at least 45 minutes. Presentations should last 15–30 minutes. Enactments should take 30 minutes to complete. Included in the enactment is the selection of a story from the interview, selection of students to play the roles identified in the story, the enactment, brainstorming alternative outcomes that recreate the situation to become a just situation, and the alternative ending enactment.

# SETTING

Interviews can be discussed anywhere the student and the chosen individual feel comfortable. The presentations and enactments can be conducted in a classroom with access to technology such as PowerPoint and plenty of space for the enactment.

# MATERIALS NEEDED

No materials will be needed. Students can have the freedom to bring in any materials that represent either their chosen individual or their specific population. Students must be able, however, to state why a particular material is important to their overall discussion about what they learned from interviewing someone of a marginalized population (e.g., a photograph of the individual, something that they both have in common, etc.).

# INSTRUCTIONS FOR CONDUCTING ACTIVITY

The instructor and/or the class can identify a specific time for the interviews, class presentations, and enactments.

The interview: the process will begin by the students selecting an individual from a marginalized population. The students will need to conduct a minimum of a 45-minute interview with someone from a marginalized population. Example questions to ask in the interview include: will you share with me your story? How is your life different from the typical person in our society? Have you had any experiences where you felt your experiences were different because of whom you are or because of what you could do? Have you ever felt generalized because of some part of your identity? Have you witnessed lack of power influence your life or someone you know? Have you experienced microaggressions? Have you witnessed someone on the receiving end of microaggressions? What impact did those microaggressions have on the way you live your day-to-day life? Are there certain places/people you avoid? What has society taught you about whom you are and how you should behave? Do you feel you have power to break free from those stereotypes?

The presentation: students will present what they learned from their interview. Presentations should last 15–30 minutes. Presentations should cover demographic information about the interviewee, stories unique to that person, how that person's life has been affected by unjust situations, and what you learned from the interviewee.

The enactment: after the presentation, invite the students to act out the experiences they heard discussed by those they interviewed. Students will share the stories from their interviewee during the presentation. Then the interviewer will select one story for the class to act out. Students in the class will be selected by the interviewer to play each role in the story. The interviewer will ensure each player understands the story of the interviewee. After a clear understanding is established, the enactment of the event will occur. After the enactment, the class will discuss how the situation could have been different if it had promoted social justice. The students will be encouraged to identify what was unfair about the story and identify ideas that would have made the situation fair. After the class decides on a new manner in which the situation could have played out, the players will re-enact the scene. After the scene, the players will have an opportunity to discuss how the scene felt different each time.

# DISCUSSION

This activity not only brings awareness about social justice concerns, but encourages students to actively decide on choices they can make to create equality in our society. To facilitate learning about social justice, the instructor will need to engage the students in a meaningful conversation after the activity. Some helpful questions to propose to students may include: what did you learn from this assignment? What expectations or misconceptions did you have going into the assignment? How has this assignment changed your thinking about your assigned population? What other populations have changed your initial expectations and misconceptions? What microaggressions did the assigned population discuss experiencing on a daily basis? How has understanding another population's microaggression made you culturally aware of your own interactions with people who are culturally different from yourself? How does it feel to be doing this project? What do those feelings or that self-reflection tell you about your own beliefs, values, and experiences? How might these feelings be different than the feelings of the person you are interviewing? What was it like to see/experience the enactments? What does social justice mean to everyone, and what informs that definition? How will the definition that you carry influence your experience in this class? This project? Your life?

# BIBLIOGRAPHY

Baden, A. L. (2016). Do you know your real parents? And other adoption microaggressions. *Adoption Quarterly*, *19*(1), 1–25.

Dupper, D. R., Forrest-Bank, S., & Lowry-Carusillo, A. (2015). Experiences of religious minorities in public school settings: Findings from focus groups involving Muslim, Jewish, Catholic, and Unitarian Universalist youths. *Children & Schools*, *37*(1), 37–45.

Nadal, K. L., Davidoff, K. C., Davis, L. S., Wong, Y., Marshall, D., & McKenzie, V. (2015). A qualitative approach to intersectional microaggressions: Understanding influences of race, ethnicity, gender, sexuality, and religion. *Qualitative Psychology*, *2*(2), 147–163.

Reyers, M. E. (2011). Unique challenges for women of color in STEM transferring from community colleges to universities. *Harvard Educational Review*, *81*(2), 241–263.

Strayhorn, T. L., Johnson, R. M., & Barrett, B. A. (2013). Investigating the college adjustment and transition experiences of formerly incarcerated black male collegians at predominately white institutions. *Spectrum: A Journal on Black Men*, *2*(1), 73–98.

Sue, D. W. (Ed.). (2010). *Microaggressions and marginality: Manifestation, dynamics, and impact*. Hoboken, NJ: John Wiley & Sons.

Sue, D. W. (2010). *Microaggressions in everyday life: Race, gender, and sexual orientation*. Hoboken, NJ: John Wiley & Sons.

Suzuki, L. A., & Ponterotto, J. G. (Eds.). (2007). *Handbook of multicultural assessment: Clinical, psychological, and educational applications*. Hoboken, NJ: John Wiley & Sons.

# SUGGESTED BACKGROUND READING

Compton-Lilly, C. (2015). Reading lessons from Martin: A case study of one African American student. *Language Arts*, *92*(6), 401.

Giesler, M. (2013). Teaching Note: Cultural immersion in the classroom: Using consciousness-raising groups to enhance diversity competence. *Journal of Baccalaureate Social Work*, *18*(1), 173–181.

Williams, S. A., & Conyers, A. (2016). Race pedagogy: Faculty preparation matters. *Administrative Theory & Praxis*, *38*(4), 234–250.

Yosso, T. J., & Garcia, D. G. (2010). From Ms. J. to Ms. G.: Analyzing racial microaggressions in Hollywood's urban school genre. In B. Frymer, T. Kashani, A. J. Nocella II, & R. Van Heertum (Eds.), *Hollywood's exploited: Public pedagogy, corporate movies, and cultural crisis* (pp. 85–103). New York: Palgrave Macmillan.

# CHAPTER 40

# The Wellness Tree
## Branches of Support or Oppression?

*Nicole Randick and Solange Ribeiro*

## Course Recommendations

| SOCIAL JUSTICE AND ADVOCACY PRINCIPLES | CORE CACREP STANDARDS | COUNSELING SPECIALIZATION |
|---|---|---|
| ☑ What Is Social Justice and Advocacy?<br>☑ Social Constructs of Oppression and Privilege | ☑ Career Development<br>☑ Helping Relationships<br>☑ Professional Counseling Orientation and Ethical Practice<br>☑ Social and Cultural Diversity | ☑ Career Counseling<br>☑ Clinical Mental Health Counseling<br>☑ School Counseling |

## TOPIC

The primary focus of this activity is to introduce how the environment is a factor in marginalization and privilege, directly impacting equitable opportunities to access resources for wellness.

## LEARNING OBJECTIVES

1. Students will identify oppressive environmental factors that can become a barrier to a person's wellness.
2. Students will describe different resources that can be used to improve the conditions that foster wellness.
3. Students will demonstrate how having attainable resources is vital in supporting wellness and empowering others.
4. Students will identify the different parts of the environment that can either sustain marginalization or nurture privilege.
5. Students will identify specific strategies to empower clients.

## TARGET POPULATION

This activity would be used as an introduction to the concepts of marginalization and privilege for beginning counselors.

# GROUP SIZE

Group size should range between two and four students per group. A co-facilitator is recommended if the group size exceeds a 1:12 faculty:student ratio.

# TIME REQUIRED

Adequate time should be given to process the questions at the end of this activity. Processing this activity can be done in an hour depending on the makeup of the classroom. The more diverse the students the richer the discussion may become; therefore, proper preparation is needed to become familiar with the diversity and experience of the students.

# SETTING

This activity can be done in a classroom setting. It is important to reinforce and encourage a safe environment that allows students to guide the process in a way that is meaningful to the group and lesson.

# MATERIALS NEEDED

Pencil, Wellness Tree worksheet, tables to work on or desks pushed together to form a table, copies of the questions for each group

# INSTRUCTIONS FOR CONDUCTING ACTIVITY

The instructor begins the activity by explaining:

Our wellness orientation helps us to conceptualize our clients through a non-pathological lens. Counselors assess people in several areas to see what is hindering them from meeting their maximum potential of wellness. Counselors must also be able to actively advocate for underrepresented people and develop, coordinate, and initiate support systems to improve the conditions that foster wellness. When counselors fail to see clients through a wellness lens they fail to empower their clients. Counselors can determine, by looking at the following areas, what area(s) of holistic functioning require(s) further empowerment in order to facilitate wellness.

a. Work/occupation: how we use our unique qualities to construct our own lives; the ability to work with others to accomplish the goals of contributing and creating a better life for ourselves and others in our community
b. Love: our ability to construct and maintain significant, intimate relationships
c. Friendship: how we cooperate with others in our community; includes our ability to have positive relationships with others
d. Self: our sense of meaning and purpose in life; can include gender, cultural identity, spirituality, physical health, and self-care

The instructor then explains:

The class will be going on a journey to discover the hidden (or not so hidden) factors in our environment that contribute to marginalization and privilege. This journey will be done together in groups as we all belong to and contribute to our environment.

The instructor then asks the group to help define the following terms:

1. Marginalization
2. Privilege
3. Environment: make sure to discuss the impact of society, culture, and context

After the group discussion:

1. Divide the class in groups of two to four students.
2. Provide each student with a copy of the Wellness Tree worksheet.
3. Explain each part of the worksheet:
   a. Kite: represents wellness and is hidden in the tree
   b. Tree branches: keep the kite in place; represents factors/forces that contribute to marginalization or to privilege and prevent the individual from reaching it
   c. Ladder: represents a path for the individual to reach the kite (wellness), with each step contributing to changes in the forces that impact the individual and facilitating movement toward wellness
4. Give groups approximately 15 minutes to discuss their own experiences of privilege and marginalization, using the tree branches to identify the positive and negative environmental forces that have framed (supported or hindered) these experiences and impacted their functioning and wellness.
5. After the 15 minutes have passed, ask the small groups to use the ladder to create a path toward wellness, with each step representing an advocacy strategy or a personal resource that can help marginalized individuals move toward wellness.
6. Follow the small group activity with large group processing.

# DISCUSSION

The following questions are offered as suggestions for large group processing and discussion.

- What are some of the societal forces that result in marginalization?
- What historical events, current issues, and powers contribute to the societal forces you mentioned in the previous item?
- What are some of the advantages experienced by those in a position of privilege?
- If one were to think of each quadrant of the kite as representative of one life task (quadrant 1 = work; quadrant 2 = love; quadrant 3 = friends; quadrant 4 = self), how would the different forces of marginalization and privilege affect each of these quadrants?
- What are some of the strategies identified in the small groups as part of the ladder leading to a path toward wellness? Are these attainable by all people or just some people? What more is needed to make these attainable?
- What are some specific ways in which counselors can empower their clients to fight the forces of marginalization?
- How can counselors serve as advocates for and with clients in order to promote equal access to the resources necessary to promote a movement toward wellness?
- What advocacy interventions can counselors do at the intrapersonal, interpersonal, institutional, community, public policy, and international/global levels?

## Extension Questions

### Ladder Questions

- Is the ladder supported enough to stand on its own? When using a ladder is more than one person needed to keep it in place?
- The first step appears high. What supports should be put in place to reach the first step (to begin your advocacy efforts)?

- Once the top of the ladder is reached it appears that more is needed to reach the kite. What more can be added for ongoing support?

### Kite Questions

- Is the kite hiding in the tree, too overwhelmed to come out?
- Is the kite resting, taking a break from life?
- Is the kite getting ready to take flight? Where would it go?
- Is the kite quite content with its status and supports?

### Tree Questions

- If you were to name each branch as a force of privilege or a force of marginalization what would each branch be named? And why that particular branch?
- The tree has several knotholes. What would each of these knotholes represent? How do these knotholes contribute to overall wellness? Is there anything hiding in these knotholes?
- What kind of tree is this? Does it bear fruit? There is a bushel at the bottom of the tree. Would the fruit go into this bushel? What else might go into this bushel? Are there certain tools needed for this journey?

## BIBLIOGRAPHY

Ratts, M. J., Singh, A., Nassar-McMillan, S., Buttler, S. K., & McCullough, J. F. (2016). Multicultural and social justice counseling competencies: Guidelines for the profession. *Journal of Multicultural Counseling and Development, 44,* 28–48.

Witmer, J. M., & Sweeney, T. J. (1992). A holistic model for wellness and prevention over the life span. *Journal of Counseling & Development, 71,* 140–148.

## SUGGESTED BACKGROUND READING

Chang, C. Y., Crethar, H. C., & Ratts, M. J. (2010). Special issue: Social justice: A national imperative for counselor education and supervision. *Counselor Education and Supervision, 50,* 82–87.

Lewis, J., Arnold, M., House, R., & Toporek, R. (2002). *ACA advocacy competencies.* Retrieved from http://counseling.org/docs/competencies/advocacy_competencies.pdf?sfvrsn=3

Myers, J. E., & Sweeney, T. J. (2005). *Counseling for wellness: Theory, research, and practice.* Alexandria, VA: American Counseling Association.

# HANDOUT

# Handout 40.1: Wellness Tree

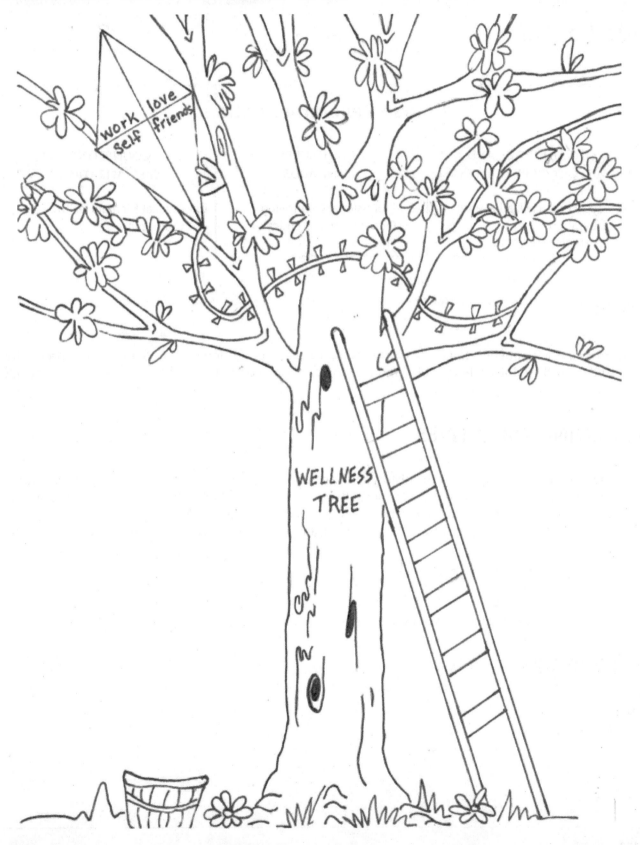

# CHAPTER 41

## Counselor Professional Identity
### The Advocate

*Marisa White*

---

### Course Recommendations

| SOCIAL JUSTICE AND ADVOCACY PRINCIPLES | CORE CACREP STANDARDS | COUNSELING SPECIALIZATION |
|---|---|---|
| ☑ Cycle of Socialization and Liberation<br>☑ Strategies for Change | ☑ Professional Counseling Orientation and Ethical Practice | ☑ Clinical Mental Health Counseling |

---

## TOPIC

The Advocate assignment is to facilitate the development of a professional counselor identity. Specifically, the student will explore different roles and responsibilities of counselors and how each role can include advocacy.

## LEARNING OBJECTIVES

1. The student will describe how the history of the counseling profession has been impacted by advocacy.
2. The student will analyze and illustrate how advocacy can be a part of each of the roles and responsibilities of counselors (counselor, researcher, author, supervisor, educator, etc.).
3. The student will develop an advocacy plan that they intend to implement within one year.

## TARGET POPULATION

Students in a counselor education training program

## GROUP SIZE

Any size

# TIME REQUIRED

This assignment could be done in stages or as a final project for a class.

- During week one, the student will describe how the history of the counseling profession has been impacted by advocacy.
- During week two, the student will analyze and illustrate how advocacy can be a part of each role and responsibility (counselor, researcher, author, supervisor, educator, etc.).
- During week three, the student will develop an advocacy plan and present this information to the class.

# SETTING

The research and writing would occur outside of the classroom.
   A presentation of the advocacy plan will take place in a classroom setting/forum.

# MATERIALS NEEDED

Should the presentation be in PowerPoint, the student would need a computer with PowerPoint.

# INSTRUCTIONS FOR CONDUCTING ACTIVITY

1. In week one, the students will research the history of the counseling profession and how advocacy played a part in the development of the counseling profession. Complete a three-page paper summarizing at least five ways in which advocacy impacted the development of the counseling profession.
2. In week two, the student will write a three-page paper that illustrates how at least four different counselor roles (clinician, researcher, author, supervisor, educator, etc.) incorporate advocacy for social justice.
3. In week three, the student will develop an advocacy plan and timeline that demonstrates how they will incorporate at least two advocacy activities that they intend to implement within the next year. This plan will be presented to the class via PowerPoint presentation in week three.
   a. Remember to consider the time, energy, cost, resources, and allies needed to execute your advocacy project.
   b. Advocacy plan and timeline can be constructed like a treatment plan. You will indicate a problem that needs advocacy. You will then establish a goal to address the identified problem. Next, you will develop a plan for how you will accomplish your goal. These are the objectives. Please have at least three objectives per goal. Additionally, please indicate the time that you think it will take you to complete each objective.
      i. Problem: _____ (cause about which you are advocating)
      ii. Goal: _____
      iii. Objective A: _____ (what you will do to reach your goal)
      iv. Objective B: _____
      v. Objective C: _____

# DISCUSSION

Social justice and advocacy discussions should be continuously woven into the curriculum of all counseling courses. However, it is important for beginning students to not only define advocacy and social justice, but also identify how it is a part of the professional identity of a counselor. To help students gain an understanding of the importance, they need to examine the history of the counseling profession. Historical exploration will help students understand the uniqueness of counselor identity (separate from social work and psychology), why/how counselor licensure was established, and why/how counselors continue to incorporate advocacy into their work.

It is also helpful for students to recognize that advocacy is identified as a responsibility in the ACA Code of Ethics (2014) and in accreditation standards (CACREP, 2009). Knowledge of history and ethical standards is intended to help students conceptualize how/why the different roles of a counselor incorporate advocacy. Kennedy and Arthur (2014) state that all helping professionals have a responsibility to consider how their professional education, research, and practice improve the lives of people they serve (p. 187). Overall, this assignment will help students identify how the counseling profession has developed from advocacy efforts and how the profession continues to require social justice advocacy to address the changing culture of the world and the counseling profession.

# BIBLIOGRAPHY

American Counseling Association. (2014). *ACA code of ethics*. Alexandria, VA: Author.

Council for Accreditation of Counseling and Related Educational Programs [CACREP]. (2009). *2009 standards for accreditation*. Alexandria, VA: Author.

Kennedy, A. B., & Arthur, N. (2014). Social justice and counselling psychology: Recommitment through action justice. *Canadian Journal of Counselling and Psychotherapy*, *48*(3), 186–205.

# SUGGESTED BACKGROUND READING

Brott, P. E., & Myers, J. E. (1999). Development of professional school counselor identity: A grounded theory. *Professional School Counseling*, *2*(5), 339–348.

Cutler, D. L., Bevilacqua, J., & McFarland, B. H. (2003). Four decades of community mental health: A symphony in four movements. *Community Mental Health Journal*, *39*(5), 381–398. https://doi.org/10.1023/A:1025856718368

Gladding, S. T. (2011, Fall). Courtland Lee: A global advocate for counseling. *Journal of Counseling & Development*, *89*(4), 493. https://doi.org/10.1002/j.1556-6676.2011.tb02847.x

Kaplan, D. M., & Gladding, S. T. (2011). A vision for the future of counseling: The 20/20 principles for unifying and strengthening the professionals. *Journal of Counseling and Development*, *89*(3), 367–372. https://doi.org/10.1002/j.1556-6678.2011.tb00101.x

King, J. H. (2011). Three paradoxes of the counseling social justice movement. *Counseling Today*, *54*(3), 46.

Kiselica, M. S., & Robinson, M. (2001). Bringing advocacy counseling to life: The history, issues, and human dramas of social justice work in counseling. *Journal of Counseling & Development*, *79*(4), 387–397. https://doi.org/10.1002/j.1556-6676.2001.tb01985.x

Lee, C. C. (2007). *Social justice: A moral imperative for counselors (ACAPCD-07)*. Alexandria, VA: American Counseling Association.

Marbley, A. F., Bonner, F. I., Robinson, P. A., Stevens, H., Li., J., Phelan, K., & Huang, S. (2015). Voices from the field of social justice: Defining moments in our professional journey. *Multicultural Education*, *23*(1), 45–51.

Myers, J. E., Sweeney, T. J., & White, V. E. (2002). Advocacy for counseling and counselors: A professional imperative. *Journal of Counseling & Development*, *80*(4), 394–408. https://doi.org/10.1002/j.1556-6678.2002.tb00205.x

Ratts, M. J. (2009). Social justice counseling: Toward the development of a fifth force among counseling paradigms. *Journal of Humanistic Counseling, Education and Development*, *48*(2), 160–172. https://doi.org/10.1002/j.2161-1939.2009.tb00076.x

Roysircar, G. (2009). The big picture of advocacy: Counselor, heal society and thyself. *Journal of Counseling & Development*, *87*(3), 288–294. https://doi.org/10.1002/j.1556-6678.2009.tb00109.x

Toporek, R. L., Lewis, J. A., & Crethar, H. C. (2009). Promoting systemic change through the ACA advocacy competencies. *Journal of Counseling and Development*, *87*(3), 260–268. https://doi.org/10.1002/j.1556-6678.2009.tb00105.x

White, M. L. (2005, July). Unleash a counselor, unveil an advocate. *Counseling Today*, p. 24.

Additional reading for doctorate-level students:

Chang, C. Y., Crethar, H. C., & Ratts, M. J. (2010). Social justice: A national imperative for counselor education and supervision. *Counselor Education and Supervision, 50*(2), 82–87. https://doi.org/10.1002/j.1556-6978.2010.tb00110.x

Odegard, M. A., & Vereen, L. G. (2010). A grounded theory of counselor educators integrating social justice into their pedagogy. *Counselor Education and Supervision, 50*(2), 130–149. https://doi.org/10.1002/j.1556-6978.2010.tb00114.x

Zalaquett, C. P., Foley, P. F., Tillotson, K., Dinsmore, J. A., & Hof, D. (2008). Multicultural and social justice training for counselor education programs and colleges of education: Rewards and challenges. *Journal of Counseling and Development, 86*(3), 323–329. https://doi.org/10.1002/j.1556-6678.2008.tb00516.x

# CHAPTER 42

# Photovoice
## Teaching and Learning About Social Justice Through Research

*Mazna Patka, Rieko Miyakuni, and Candice Robbins*

## Course Recommendations

| SOCIAL JUSTICE AND ADVOCACY PRINCIPLES | CORE CACREP STANDARDS | COUNSELING SPECIALIZATION |
|---|---|---|
| ☑ What Is Social Justice and Advocacy?<br>☑ Cycle of Socialization and Liberation<br>☑ Strategies for Change | ☑ Research and Program Evaluation<br>☑ Social and Cultural Diversity | ☑ Clinical Mental Health Counseling<br>☑ School Counseling<br>☑ Student Affairs and College Counseling |

## TOPIC

PhotoVoice (PV; Wang & Burris, 1997), a modified version of a community-based participatory research method, is a powerful tool for counselors-in-training to learn how to take action to create social change through photos. This activity is useful for research and program evaluation courses and/or social and cultural diversity classes.

## LEARNING OBJECTIVES

1. Develop way(s) to centralize the marginalized voices: critical consciousness.
2. Learn how to use PV to create opportunities for advocacy and activism for social and policy changes.
3. Engage in the research process as both a researcher and participant.
4. Learn about how to conduct qualitative research.

## TARGET POPULATION

Counselors-in-training

## GROUP SIZE

The maximum group size for this activity is eight, and the minimum group size is four.

# TIME REQUIRED

This modified version of PV allows the instructor and students flexibility. Each PV process is referred to as a cycle, which involves five steps: (1) identify a research question, (2) generate a photograph and interpretation, (3) discuss the photographs and interpretations in a focus group, (4) transcribe focus groups, and (5) analyze transcriptions (Patka, Miyakuni, & Robbins, in press). Students can engage in three PV cycles throughout the semester or one cycle as a single activity during the term. In this chapter, we describe the steps for a PV activity that can be completed in a single cycle during a semester.

For a single activity (one PV cycle)
First week of PhotoVoice
1. Learn about PV. Allocate 45 minutes to an hour for lecture. Students will be assigned to generate research questions to bring to the following class meeting.
Second week of PhotoVoice
2. Form a group to discuss their questions and develop a theme of photographs. Allocate 45 minutes to an hour for the first focus group.
Third week of PhotoVoice
3. Students will have one week (or two weeks) to take three pictures and write descriptions and post on Blackboard (or other online learning platform).
Fourth week of PhotoVoice
4. In the following week (or in two weeks), the second focus group will be held in which students will discuss their pictures and interpretations. Allocate 90 minutes to 2 hours for this focus group.
Fifth week of PhotoVoice
5. The activity can expand to a campus event. Students can compile the findings from the second focus group, which include photos, descriptions, and themes, and display on campus or at a public event. This may be an outside of the class activity.

# SETTING

Lecture and focus group will take place in class. Photos are taken outside of the classroom.

# MATERIALS NEEDED

A digital camera, a digital recorder, online platform (e.g., Blackboard) to share the pictures and text descriptions, transcription software, and qualitative analysis software (e.g., Dedoose).

When taking pictures, students must exercise their judgment about where, when, how, and what/whom they are taking pictures of. An emphasis will be placed on what they cannot take a picture of (e.g., someone's face and anything else that would reveal their identities). Students can be creative, and take a picture of hands or other body parts to try to describe what they intend to capture.

# INSTRUCTIONS FOR CONDUCTING ACTIVITY

This modified version of PV allows the instructor and students flexibility. This activity can be utilized throughout the semester or conducted as a single activity. For this publication, we will focus on a single activity. If the instructor chooses to conduct PV throughout the semester, these steps can be repeated.

For a single activity:

1. Students learn about PV and the project. The PowerPoint lecture will introduce (1) the history of PV, (2) its various uses with sociopolitical minorities, and (3) a rationale for why it is being used in class (Patka et al., in press). During this introductory stage, students will be assigned to read multiple articles that utilize PV in different contexts (e.g., Booth & Booth, 2003; Carlson, Engebretson, & Chamberlain, 2006; Cook & Buck, 2010; Wang & Burris, 1997). At the end of the PowerPoint lecture on PV, students will be assigned to generate three to five questions. These questions will be discussed in a following class meeting to develop a collective theme of photographs, which will be the research question. At this stage, confidentiality and the ACA Code of Ethics should be reviewed. At the end of the class, students complete anonymous exit cards on which they write questions, concerns, areas of confusion and improvement, as well as what went well and what they learned. Exit cards are incorporated at the end of each class meeting throughout the semester as a way to engage students in reflecting and debriefing on learning activities.

2. Students will return to class with potential research questions. First, the instructor has the members write down the questions they generated prior to the class on the whiteboard. An example research question may include, "What are obstacles and barriers that students from low socioeconomic status face in higher education during degree completion?" Students cast their votes to narrow down the number of research questions. Once the questions are reduced to two or three, students form the first focus group to discuss these questions to determine a single research question through consensus building (Patka et al., in press). It is important that the research question be broad enough to pertain to each member's life experiences (Patka et al., in press). Once the research question is determined, the theme of the photograph is identified. For example, the group members may identify the theme of "obstacles and barriers" from the preceding research question, from which the group generates a broad research question, such as "What are my obstacle and barriers?"

3. The group members will have one week (or two weeks) to take three pictures and write descriptions (two to three paragraphs) of each picture and post on Blackboard (or other online learning platform). With the previous example, the group members will take photos that capture their experiences of obstacles and barriers in their lives and prepare narratives of their pictures.

4. In the following week (or in two weeks), the second focus group will be held in which the group members will share their photographs and interpretations to engage in dialogue and critical reflection with other group members (Patka et al., in press). It is advised that the instructor of the course will take a role of facilitator. First, the facilitator may ask the members to volunteer presenting their photograph, and the photograph chosen for discussion can be projected on a screen. The group members sit in a semi-circle to view the projector and each other. After a few minutes to view the picture and reflect, group members will be encouraged to share their impressions and insights for 10 to 15 minutes. Then, the interpretation of the picture will be projected on the screen, and a group member may volunteer to read the narrative of the photo. Then, the author of the picture will provide additional context to the picture, which will expand the group discussion through asking the author of the picture questions and sharing their own interpretations of the picture, as well as their own life experiences. This discussion may take 15 minutes to 30 minutes. The instructor highlights that their pictures represent their views of the world (e.g., various forms of oppression and marginalization); being exposed to other students' perspectives about the world and their realities is critically important for counselors-in-training, which will be transferred to counseling and advocacy skills.

5. Focus group will be audio recorded via smartphone or voice recorder. It is important that the group continue to revisit confidentiality of the information obtained through the focus group as well as ethical responsibilities as counselors-in-training and researchers. Each student will be assigned to transcribe the audio recording. Depending on the class size, assignment of the transcription role can be left to the instructor's discretion. The group members will be encouraged to take field notes to record moments that stood out for further exploration and clarification and nonverbal expressions (Patton, 2015). The group members post their field notes on Blackboard (or other online learning platform) for other students to view and utilize to assist in data analysis.

6. Qualitative analyses will be conducted on the transcripts to look for common themes among participants by utilizing Poland's (1995) process. Transcribers listen to the audio recording and type each

word stated and sounds transmitted by the group members during the second focus group. Then, the members review each other's transcript to ensure the accuracy of transcripts (Patka et al., in press). All transcriptions will be uploaded onto Blackboard (or other online platform) for students to utilize during the analysis process.

7.  Analyses will be interpreted and discussed by each participant.
8.  The activity can expand to a campus event or public event. Compiled photos, descriptions, and themes can be displayed at a cultural program that is consistent with the themes of each PV. For example, the authors displayed the photos and descriptions that addressed a research question "what is my gender identity?" during the "Transformation exhibit" that featured photos of transgender persons by a trans-gender photographic artist.
9.  At the end of PV, the instructor and the entire group reflect on and debrief the entire process.

Note: the activity can stop after the first cycle, although the entire PV process can take three cycles throughout the semester, with two more different research questions and themes for photos. The number of cycles should be left to the instructor's choice. This activity may need alteration for online course.

# DISCUSSION

Incorporating PV to teach qualitative research methods in a research and program evaluation course will provide counselors-in-training with the opportunity to develop social justice advocacy skills. Such skills include teamwork, communication, and problem-solving through running focus groups. As researchers and participants in PV within the class and training environment, students can develop skills to gather information about social issues and analyze the data to identify social needs from individuals' experiences that are captured by photos and perceived meanings that are depicted through the author's interpretation of their photos. Therefore, PV improves understanding the intended meaning of the author of the photo. Through developing perspective-taking abilities, students can develop critical thinking skills, centralize marginalized voices, and influence social change through presenting their findings in class and on campus, all of which will transfer to social justice advocacy and leadership skills, by expanding the products for public knowledge by disseminating the photos' policymakers (Patka et al., in press).

Students reflect on the PV process throughout the course. At the end of a focus group, students will take a few minutes to reflect on the discussion. PV requires students to open up and share their photos and perceived meanings they attach to their photos in the group. It is critical that students feel comfortable sharing their thoughts and feelings because controversial subjects may be discussed during focus groups. One way to address it is to review and discuss the Belmont Principle of Justice (U.S. Department of Health & Human Services, n.d.) as well as the ACA Code of Ethics (ACA, 2014) when engaging in discussion that involves topics that may be controversial (Patka et al., in press). Another way of debriefing is the use of exit cards. Exit cards provide the instructor with a way to address unanswered questions, areas of confusion, and areas of improvement. The instructor asks students to write a brief reflection of the activity at the last few minutes of PV activity. Students can remain anonymous. Prompts may include: (1) what went well? (2) what went poorly? (3) what do I need help with more? (4) how may I apply one concept learned from today? and (5) what am I confused about?

The central tenet of the constructivist paradigm is to understand how individuals understand their social world and researchers who operate from the paradigm engage in reflexivity (Patka et al., in press). Because one's sociopolitical context often influences and shapes one's knowledge, ideas, and beliefs (Patton, 2015), counselors actively engage in examining the source of and application of their knowledge, ideas, and beliefs. By engaging in reflexivity throughout the learning process, counselors-in-training can improve their understanding about how others make sense of their reality, identify social needs, and eventually take action for social justice advocacy (Patka et al., in press).

# BIBLIOGRAPHY

American Counseling Association. (2014). *The ACA code of ethics.* Alexander, VA: Author.

Booth, T., & Booth, W. (2003). In the frame: Photovoice and mothers with learning difficulties. *Disability & Society*, 18, 431–442.

Carlson, E. D., Engebretson, J., & Chamberlain, R. M. (2006). Photovoice as a social process of critical consciousness. *Qualitative Health Research, 16*(6), 836–852.

Cook, K., & Buck, G. (2010). Photovoice: A community-based socioscientific pedagogical tool. *Science Scope*, 35–38.

Patka, M., Miyakuni, R., & Robbins, C. (in press). Experiential learning: Teaching research methods with PhotoVoice. *Journal of Counselor Preparation and Supervision.*

Patton, M. Q. (2015). *Qualitative research and evaluation methods* (4th ed.). Thousand Oaks, CA: Sage Publications.

Poland, B. D. (1995). Transcription quality as an aspect of rigor in qualitative research. *Qualitative Inquiry, 1*(3), 290–310. doi:10.1177/107780049500100302

US Department of Health & Human Services. (n.d.). *The Belmont report: Ethical principles and guidelines for the protection of human subjects of research.* Retrieved from www.hhs.gov/ohrp/humansubjects/guidance/belmont.html

Wang, C., & Burris, M. A. (1997). Photovoice: Concept, methodology, and use for participatory needs assessment. *Health Education & Behavior, 24*(3), 369–387. doi:10.1177/109019819702400309

# SUGGESTED BACKGROUND READING

Agee, J. (2009). Developing qualitative research questions: A reflective process. *International Journal of Qualitative Studies in Education, 22*(4), 431–447.

Booth, T., & Booth, W. (2003). In the frame: Photovoice and mothers with learning difficulties. *Disability and Society, 18*(4), 431–442.

Braun, V., & Clarke, V. (2006). Using thematic analysis in psychology. *Qualitative Research in Psychology, 3*(2), 77–101.

Brydon-Miller, M. (2001). Education, research, and action: Theory and methods of participatory action research. In D. L. Toleman & M. Brydon-Miller (Eds.), *From subjects to subjectives: A handbook of interpretive and participatory methods* (pp. 76–89). New York, NY: New York University Press.

Carlson, E. D., Engebretson, J., & Chamberlain, R. M. (2006). Photovoice as a social process of critical consciousness. *Qualitative Health Research, 16*(6), 836–852.

Cook, K., & Buck, G. (2010). Photovoice: A community-based socioscientific pedagogical tool. *Science Scope*, 35–38.

Jason, L. A. (2013). *Principles of social change.* New York, NY: Oxford University Press.

Oliver, M. (1992). Changing the social relations of research production? *Disability, Handicap & Society, 7*(2), 101–114.

Patka, M., Miyakuni, R., & Robbins, C. (in press). Experiential learning: Teaching research methods with PhotoVoice. *Journal of Counselor Preparation and Supervision.*

Poland, B. D. (1995). Transcription quality as an aspect of rigor in qualitative research. *Qualitative Inquiry, 1*(3), 290–310.

Smith, J. A. (1995). Semi-structured interviewing and qualitative analysis. In J. A. Smith, R. Harre, & L. Van Langenhove (Eds.), *Rethinking methods in psychology* (pp. 9–26). Thousand Oaks, CA: Sage Publications.

Wang, C., & Burris, M. A. (1997). Photovoice: Concept, methodology, and use for participatory needs assessment. *Health Education & Behavior, 24*(3), 369–387. doi:10.1177/109019819702400309

# CHAPTER 43

# If You Listen Carefully to This Song Maybe You Will Better Understand Me

## Charles Edwards

### Course Recommendations

| SOCIAL JUSTICE AND ADVOCACY PRINCIPLES | CORE CACREP STANDARDS | COUNSELING SPECIALIZATION |
|---|---|---|
| ☑ What Is Social Justice and Advocacy?<br>☑ Cycle of Socialization and Liberation | ☑ Group Work<br>☑ Helping Relationships<br>☑ Social and Cultural Diversity | ☑ Clinical Mental Health Counseling<br>☑ Marriage, Couple, and Family Counseling<br>☑ School Counseling<br>☑ Student Affairs and College Counseling |

## TOPIC

Empathic listening: using songs to improve our understanding of oppressed individuals and groups

## LEARNING OBJECTIVES

1. Participants will identify and share songs that support their understanding of oppressed individuals and groups.
2. Participants will practice empathic listening skills.
3. Participants will improve their capacity to empathize with oppressed groups and individuals.

## TARGET POPULATION

This activity is suited for demographically diverse graduate counseling students and professional counselors who are to deepen or reinforce empathic skills needed to improve cultural competence and advocacy.

## GROUP SIZE

Groups of 15–20, working in subgroups of four to five

# TIME REQUIRED

In a class of 15–20, working in smaller groups of four to five students, this activity should take 60–75 minutes. Time may be adjusted based on variations in the number of students. Give an overall time estimate that is needed to complete the activity.

Suggested distribution of time is as follows:

Introduction: 5–10 minutes
Group work: 25 minutes
Group presentations: 25–30 minutes
Summary evaluation: 5–10 minutes

# SETTING

This activity is suited for a classroom or workshop space that is large enough to accommodate 15–20 participants. There should be sufficient space to allow all four or five groups to work efficiently. Spaces that allow participants to easily move into groups and return to their original positions for presentations would be ideal. The size of the group may be adjusted downward depending on the size of the room. Rooms suited for individuals with varying physical disabilities would also be ideal.

# MATERIALS NEEDED

Paper and pencil or pen will be needed for this activity. The room should also be equipped with audio visual and online technologies. Participants may be permitted to use cell phones to complete the group activity. To allow for active and emphatic listening, participants should be asked to put away all cell phones during presentations.

# INSTRUCTIONS FOR CONDUCTING ACTIVITY

1. Introduce the topic and objectives and activate participants' prior knowledge of the importance of songs in highlighting social justice issues. Instructor may ask students to quickly identify a song where the artist expressed concerns or outrage regarding a specific issue or a number of issues. Instructor may give examples to enhance students' understanding. Instructor will help students make a connection between music, social justice, oppression, and advocacy. Instructor may share the following: social justice, privilege, oppression, and multiculturalism are constructs that have been explored in popular music. Songs have been used to support social justice movements, advocate for specific causes, inspire people to take action, and create awareness, among other things. Some of the music associated with Nina Simone, Bob Marley, and Bob Dylan has been identified as social commentary on human social, economic, and political realities. Music and songs can used as tools to support the journey of becoming culturally competent counselors.

2. Inform students that they will be working in groups of four or five members to brainstorm and identify five songs that have motivated them to take some kind of action on a specific or general issue. Let students know that actions may include a number of things such as speaking out, changing one's behavior, or demonstrating. Let students know that they will be asked to present their songs and talk about their process to the class.

3. The instructor will provide examples for the students by selecting and playing a song that motivates him/her to take action against an injustice. The instructor will model the process of selecting the song, stating why the song was selected and how it motivated her/him to take action. For example the

song "Get Up Stand Up" by Bob Marley may be used as a song that promotes resistance and advocacy. The presenter then plays the song with lyrics displayed on a large screen. Students are then asked to reflect on the song, stating their own feelings, thoughts, and associations.

4. The instructor will randomly place students in groups by counting off from one to four (or five). All ones, twos, threes, and so on will form working groups. Encourage groups to allow for maximum space between each other in order to lessen distractions.

5. Ask the groups to begin working; informing them that they will be working for 25 minutes. Each sub-group will brainstorm and come up with a minimum of three songs and decide which of these songs they will play for the entire class.

6. Provide students with paper and pen/pencil.

7. Inform students that they may use cell phones and head phones to assist in completing the task. Inform students that they will need to put away cell phones when presentations begin.

8. Encourage students to work collaboratively and dip into their reservoirs of songs to complete the task.

9. Provide support to the groups as needed. Let students know when they have 10 and 5 minutes left to complete the task.

10. When all groups have completed the task determine quickly the order of presentations.

11. Each group will present its songs and speak about its process, feelings, thoughts, and associations. Each group will play one of the three songs selected for the entire class. One or two questions or comments may follow each presentation.

12. Lead the entire class into an applause after each presents.

13. Discussion will follow after all groups have presented. The discussion will focus on students' thoughts, feelings, associations, and other reactions to the presentations. In order to support the discussion the instructor will ask the following questions:
   - What are your thoughts, feelings, and associations regarding the songs presented today?
   - How do the presentations support or deepen your understanding of the connection between music, social justice, and advocacy?

14. Summary and conclusion: thank all the groups for their presentations and emphasize the following points:
   - Social justice, oppression, and multiculturalism are not just constructs found in textbooks. They are real issues that are explored in popular music forms. Music can be seen as tool that can serve to liberate and also oppress (Clonal & Johnson, 2002). Any given song may also be subjected to multiple interpretations and usages.
   - Songs that focus on oppression can be useful tools in enhancing our understanding of others, reinforcing our own beliefs in social justice, and supporting our journey toward empathic understanding and multicultural competence (Fischlin & Heble, 2003).

## DISCUSSION

The instructor will implement strategies to encourage thought and discussion. Before each presentation group members should be asked to talk about the process involved in selecting their songs and why the songs were selected. Group members should be encouraged to explore feelings, thoughts, and associations related to their selections. Participants will then play one of the songs that best represents the specific type of oppression they identified. The song will be played for the entire class, with lyrics displayed for the entire class. The instructor will inform the students that an important component of the class is the ability to listen to each group's presentation. Listening will be highlighted as an important counseling skill. The capacity to listen to musical selections of others also demonstrates empathy.

# REFERENCES

Clonal, M., & Johnson, B. (2002). Killing me softly with his song: An initial investigation into the use of popular music as a tool of oppression. *Popular Music, 21*(1), 27–39.

Fischlin, D., & Heble, A. (2003). *Rebel musics: Human rights, resistant sounds, and the politics of music making* (p. 11). Montreal: Black Rose.

# SUGGESTED BACKGROUND READING

Adams, M., & Bell, L. A. (Eds.). (2016). *Teaching for diversity and social justice*. New York: Routledge.

Ratts, M. J., Singh, A. A., Nassar-McMillan, S., Butler, S. K., McCullough, J. R., & Hipolito-Delgado, C. (2015). *Multicultural and social justice counseling competencies*. Alexandria, VA: AMCD.

Schmitz, C., Stakeman, C., & Sisneros, J. (2001). Educating professionals for practice in a multicultural society: Understanding oppression and valuing diversity. *Families in Society: The Journal of Contemporary Social Services, 82*(6), 612–622.

# CHAPTER 44

# Exploring White Fragility
## An RCT Approach to Cultural Competency

*Angela Schubert and Jessica Z. Taylor*

## Course Recommendations

| SOCIAL JUSTICE AND ADVOCACY PRINCIPLES | CORE CACREP STANDARDS | COUNSELING SPECIALIZATION |
|---|---|---|
| ☑ Social Constructs of Oppression and Privilege <br> ☑ Intersections of Oppression <br> ☑ Strategies for Change | ☑ Helping Relationships <br> ☑ Human Growth and Development <br> ☑ Social and Cultural Diversity | ☑ Clinical Mental Health Counseling |

## TOPIC

The purpose of the activity is to help engage students in a meaningful and radically respectful dialogue and project on the topic of white fragility, as defined by Robin DiAngelo's (2011) theory. By focusing on the subjective experiences of the students' beliefs toward white fragility and racism, students may strengthen mutuality, relational growth, and their ability to build a meaningful therapeutic relationship with clients.

## LEARNING OBJECTIVES

1. Address how learning about white fragility, institutional racism, and white supremacy can actually help counselors become better prepared to address sensitive cultural issues, both personally and professionally, with clients.
2. Explore how white racial insulation protects and hinders white identified counselors from understanding the depth of racism, and as a result, possibly limits their ability to connect with clients of color.
3. Help white counselors identify ways to become more multiculturally competent and increase competency related to social justice as a result of addressing their own whiteness and exploring individual and systemic privileges bestowed upon them as a result of their skin color.
4. Apply what students learn during the in-class exercise toward facilitating a community awareness project on white privilege with a non-counseling student population to assist others in developing understanding of white fragility and racism.

## TARGET POPULATION

Counseling students

## GROUP SIZE

10–20

## TIME REQUIRED

2 hours—first class; 1 hour—second class

## SETTING

- Classroom setting at first for discussion and group conversation. The instructor will need to coordinate with the appropriate campus representative to select an appropriate place for the poster display.
- Facilitators may need to incorporate more time for students to reflect on and write their thoughts prior to inviting students into discussion, in pairs or in a large group. The size of groups may be left up to the instructor's discretion and familiarity with the interpersonal dynamics within the classroom.

## MATERIALS NEEDED

PowerPoint on white fragility and oppressed language; poster boards; markers

## INSTRUCTIONS FOR CONDUCTING ACTIVITY

1. The PowerPoint presentation will take approximately 45–60 minutes. Allow 5–10 minutes for students to reflect upon and write down their internal affective and cognitive reactions to the concept of the PowerPoint material.
2. Allow 15–20 minutes for students to discuss in pairs their reactions to the PowerPoint.
3. For the remainder of the allotted time, each student pair will form a group with another student pair (no more than four students to a group) to brainstorm examples of white fragility.
   a. The instructor will assist students in identifying specific terms to use on the posters, on which they will be asked to write down a term related to white fragility and an example or quote of the term.
   b. Students will write down their initial thoughts regarding how the campus student body might react to the posters once displayed. The instructor will work with the counseling center (if the appropriate department) to identify a space to place the posters.
4. During the next class period, students will spend approximately 1 hour to discuss the results of the poster display.
   a. In-class discussion and reflection on terms and concepts related to white fragility discussed in the PowerPoint material. Students brainstorm examples of white fragility in class in small groups.
   b. During the same class period, students create posters based on their brainstormed examples.
      - At the top: a term related to white fragility.
      - Main body of poster: a quote or example of the term.
      - With school's permission, students put posters up in common areas around campus.
5. Students spend a week observing what they see happen to the posters, what they hear about the posters, how they see people react to the posters, and how they feel about having put up the posters.
6. In the next class period, students debrief about observations/reactions to the posters for the week and how this influences their understanding of clients who are racist, oppressive, conservative, or religious, or who may have trouble acknowledging the privilege of being white.

7.  In small groups (two to three students), identify specific ways to actively dismantle racism and how the students may be advocates for their future clients of color and those clients who struggle with white fragility.

Facilitators will want to have established the classroom space as a safe and nonjudgmental space prior to initiating this activity. Ideally, students will have had time to start forming supportive interpersonal connections with one another to allow for a safe space for personal assumptions and discomfort to be voiced, heard, and respected. Facilitators may want to encourage students to do personal process check-ins before responding to others.

# DISCUSSION

1.  What is your internal reaction to the posters and how they were approached by the college community?
2.  How does your reaction influence your impression of the student body?
3.  What systemic factors related to race, gender, and power may be contributing to your reaction toward the posters?
4.  How might your own privilege or marginalized status be influencing your internal reaction to the posters?
5.  How might white fragility interfere with one's ability to engage in mutuality, authenticity, and growth?
6.  How might we, as counselors, actively pursue ways to dismantle racism and white fragility?

# BIBLIOGRAPHY

DiAngelo, R. (2011). White fragility. *International Journal of Critical Pedagogy, 3*(3), 54–70.

Jordan, J. V. (2010). *Relational-cultural therapy*. Washington, DC: American Psychological Association.

Ratts, M. J., Singh, A. A., Nassar-McMillan, S., Butler, S. K., & McCullough, J. R. (2016, January 1). Multicultural and social justice counseling competencies: Guidelines for the counseling profession. *Journal of Multicultural Counseling and Development, 44*(1), 28–48.

# SUGGESTED BACKGROUND READING

DiAngelo, R. (2011). White fragility. *International Journal of Critical Pedagogy, 3*(3), 54–70.

Jordan, J. V. (2010). *Relational-cultural therapy*. Washington, DC: American Psychological Association.

Ratts, M. J., Singh, A. A., Nassar-McMillan, S., Butler, S. K., & McCullough, J. R. (2016, January 1). Multicultural and social justice counseling competencies: Guidelines for the counseling profession. *Journal of Multicultural Counseling and Development, 44*(1), 28–48.

Schwartz, E. Q. (2011). Promoting social justice advocacy through service-learning in higher education. *Journal of Student Affairs at New York University, 7*, 12–27.

# HANDOUT

# Handout 44.1: White Privilege PPT

## What is White Privilege and How do People React?

### White Privilege is...

- Is insulated (Finn, 1997)
- Encompasses economic, political, social, and cultural structures, actions, and beliefs that systematize and perpetuate an unequal distribution of privileges, resources, and power (Feagin, 2006)
- The direction of power flows one way... (Feagin, 2006)
- Dynamic, relational, and operational at all times (DiAngelo, 2011)
- "If privilege is defined as a legitimization of one's entitlement to resources, it can also be defined as permission to escape or avoid any challenges to this entitlement" (Vodde, 2001, p.3).

### Common Reactions to Privilege Discussion

- Anger
- Cognitive Dissonance
- Guilt
- Arguing
- Withdrawal
- Emotional incapacitation
- Overcompensation
- Over-identification

## FACTORS RELATED TO WHITE FRAGILITY

- Growing up in segregated environments
  - Quality of white space = absence of people of color

- Individualism & Universalism
  - Uniqueness is valued and buffers from any affects of racial messages in the culture
  - White people are taught to value individuality rather than a racially socialized group
  - Everyone is the same
  - Whiteness remains outside of culture
  - Entitlement to Racial Comfort
  - Developed unchallenged expectations to remain racially comfortable
  - No need to defend whiteness

- Entitlement to Racial Comfort
  - Developed unchallenged expectations to remain racially comfortable
  - No need to defend whiteness

- Racial Arrogance
  - Ideological racism
  - Cannot validate other racial experiences because "you don't know what you don't know"

- Racial Belonging
  - White racial image is constantly reflected back in US culture

- Psychic Freedom
  - Whites don't bear the burden of race

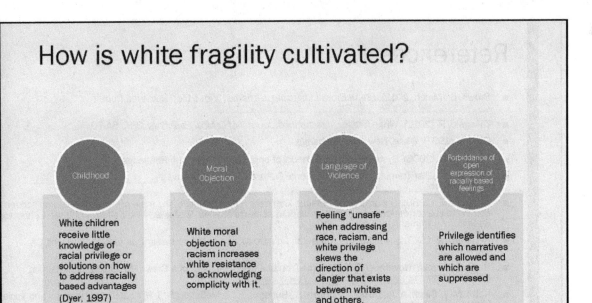

## How is white fragility cultivated?

**Childhood**
White children receive little knowledge of racial privilege or solutions on how to address racially based advantages (Dyer, 1997)

**Moral Objection**
White moral objection to racism increases white resistance to acknowledging complicity with it.

**Language of Violence**
Feeling "unsafe" when addressing race, racism, and white privilege skews the direction of danger that exists between whites and others.

**Forbiddance of open expression of racially based feelings**
Privilege identifies which narratives are allowed and which are suppressed

Di'Angelo, 2011

## Why Should Counselors Understand White Fragility?

**Activities to discuss racism, power, and privilege may be the best way to start a conversation...**

Other Articles or Videos by:

- Aamer Rahmen - https://www.youtube.com/watch?v=dw_mRalHb-M
- Tim Wise - https://www.youtube.com/watch?v=hOB_ix10--l
- Brene Brown - https://www.youtube.com/watch?v=psN1DORYYV0
- Child Race Doll Test - https://www.youtube.com/watch?v=tkpUyB2xgTM
- Jane Elliott - https://www.youtube.com/watch?v=Nqv9k3jbtYU

# References

- Brown, B. (March, 2012). *Brene Brown: Listening to shame* [Video file]. Retrieved from https://www.ted.com/talks/brene_brown_listening_to_shame
- DiAngelo, R. (2011). White fragility. *International Journal of Critical Pedagogy, 3(3)*, 54-70.
- Dyer, R. (1997). White. New York: Routledge.
- Feagin, J. R. (2006). Systemic racism: A theory of oppression. New York: Routledge.
- Jean Baker Miller Training Institute. Relational Cultural-Theory. Retrieved from https://www.jbmti.org/Our-Work/relational-cultural-theory
- McIntosh, P. (1988). Unpacking the invisible knapsack. White privilege and male privilege: A personal account of coming to see correspondences through work in women's studies. Wellesley, MA: Wellesley College, Center for Research on Women.
- Neukrug. (2015). The world of the counselor: An introduction to the counseling profession. Belmont, CA: Brooks/Cole.
- Rahman, Aamer. (November, 2013). Home [Youtube Channel]. Fear of a Brown Planet - Reverse Racism. Retrieved from https://www.youtube.com/watch?v=dw_mRaIHb-M/
- Ratts, M. J., Singh, A. A., Nassar-McMillan, S., Butler, S. K., & McCullough, J. R. (2016). Multicultural and social justice counseling competencies: Guidelines for the counseling profession. Journal of Multicultural Counseling and Development, 44(1), 28-48.
- Vodde, R. (2001). De-centering privilege in social work education: Whose job is it anyway? Journal of Race, Gender and Class, 7(4), 139-160.

# CHAPTER 45

# A Thousand Miles in Their Shoes
## Learning About Social Justice Through Narratives

*Nayeli Y. Chavez-Dueñas and Hector Y. Adames*

| Course Recommendations | | |
|---|---|---|
| **SOCIAL JUSTICE AND ADVOCACY PRINCIPLES** | **CORE CACREP STANDARDS** | **COUNSELING SPECIALIZATION** |
| ☑ Social Constructs of Oppression and Privilege<br>☑ Intersections of Oppression<br>☑ Strategies for Change | ☑ Group Work<br>☑ Helping Relationships<br>☑ Social and Cultural Diversity | ☑ Clinical Mental Health Counseling<br>☑ Marriage, Couple, and Family Counseling<br>☑ School Counseling<br>☑ Student Affairs and College Counseling |

## TOPIC

The activity aims to provide participants with the opportunity to enter the experiential reality of individuals who belong to oppressed groups by exposing them to their narratives and stories as a way to increase their commitment to social justice.

## LEARNING OBJECTIVES

As a result of this activity students will:

1. Understand and have concrete examples of how people's behavior, affect, and cognition are impacted by their sociocultural context.
2. Develop comprehension around the impact of systemic oppression on the lives of diverse others.
3. Become aware of how such experiences may impact their clinical work with members of minority communities.

## TARGET POPULATION

Undergraduate and graduate students in counseling, psychology, social work, and the helping professions in general, as well as mental health practitioners

# GROUP SIZE

The exercise can be used with one to 15 people. It is optimal to have enough people to help generate discussions in a group setting.

# TIME REQUIRED

This activity will require time in at least two or three class meetings as well as time spent outside of the class. Participants will need ample time outside of the class to read the assigned narratives.

# SETTING

No specific room design is required.

# MATERIALS NEEDED

- Assigned narratives
- List of questions outlined in the "Instructions for Conducting Activity" section

# INSTRUCTIONS FOR CONDUCTING ACTIVITY

This activity is based on the Multiracial/Multiethnic/Multicultural Competency Building (M3CB) training model developed by White and Henderson (2008) and used by several mental health professionals to help inform practice and social justice advocacy (e.g., Adames & Chavez-Dueñas, 2017; Henderson, Horton, Saito, & Shorter-Gooden, 2016). The M3CB seeks to offer a way for both European/American and multicultural minority mental health professionals and students to progress on their multicultural competence and social justice advocacy journey (p. 24) by explicitly articulating the role of emotional processing and planful action on the development of multicultural competency and a professional who is engaged in social justice.

This activity can be integrated throughout the course or as part of a weekend workshop.

1. Assign participants the narrative (e.g., biography, autobiography, novel) of an individual that represents a dimension of diversity (e.g., race, ethnicity, sexual orientation, gender, religion, immigration status, ableness). Please see "Suggested Background Reading" for exemplars.
2. As participants go through their assigned reading, they are asked to give a brief, 5-minute update of their book to the group. During these brief presentation updates, participants are asked to discuss three main areas including:
   a. Describe the area of the diversity that the protagonist in your assigned narrative represents.
   b. Discuss how the sociopolitical context and systemic oppression impact the lives and access to resources of the protagonist.
   c. Explain how the content of the book relates to the various social group identities you hold (e.g., race, gender, sexual orientation).
3. After participants complete their assigned reading, they are asked to present their clinical impressions on the protagonist of the narrative they read using a psychological or counseling theory. This should be done in a 25–30 minute presentation. During this activity, students are asked to address the following components:

a. Provide a brief synopsis of the book discussing the main thesis of the book and describe the area of diversity that the protagonist in your narrative represented.
b. Provide the social history and a potential presenting problem, if any, the protagonist may discuss in therapy.
c. Conceptualize the individual from any of the classic theories (e.g., cognitive, psychodynamic, systems) you have learned.
d. Conceptualize the character from a multicultural perspective.

# DISCUSSION

The following set of questions is offered as a way for participants to reflect and debrief on the activity "A Thousand Miles in Their Shoes":

- What did you learn about diversity and social justice from this narrative?
- How does this new learning/new knowledge impact the work you do or will engage in as a mental health professional?
- How does this learning impact your interest and commitment toward social justice?
- What are some of the personal reactions you had as you were reading the book?
- How did the book change your perspectives on the area of diversity your book addressed and on social justice work?

# BIBLIOGRAPHY

Adames, H. Y., & Chavez-Dueñas, N. Y. (2017). *Cultural foundations and interventions in Latino/a mental health: History, theory, and within-group differences.* New York, NY: Routledge.

Henderson, S. J., Horton, R. A., Saito, P. K., & Shorter-Gooden, K. (2016). Validation of assessment vignettes and scoring rubric of multicultural and international competency in faculty teaching. *Multicultural Learning and Teaching, 11*(1), 53–81.

White, J. L., & Henderson, S. J. (2008). The browning of America: Building a new multicultural, multiracial, multiethnic paradigm. In J. L. White & S. J. Henderson (Eds.), *Building multicultural competency: Development, training and practice* (pp. 17–49). New York, NY: Rowman & Littlefield Publishers.

# SUGGESTED BACKGROUND READING

Below, please find a list of narratives that can be assigned for this exercise. The list is not exhaustive; instead, we hope to stimulate ideas for participants to learn about diversity and social justice.

Alexie, S. (2007). *The absolutely true diary of a part-time Indian.* New York, NY: Little, Brown, and Company.

Allende, I. (2011). *The island beneath the sea.* New York, NY: Harper Perennial.

Diaz, J. (2007). *The brief and wondrous life of Oscar Wao.* New York, NY: Riverhead Trade.

Malcolm, X., Haley, A., & Shabazz, A. (1992). *The autobiography of Malcolm X: As told to Alex Haley.* New York, NY: Random House.

Mandela, N. (1995). *Long walk to freedom.* New York, NY: Back Bay Books.

Matsuda Gruenewald, M. (2005). *Looking like the enemy: My story of imprisonment in Japanese American Internment Camps.* Troutdale, OR: New Sage Press.

Menchu, R. (2010). *I, Rigoberta Menchu: An Indian woman in Guatemala.* Brooklyn, NY: Verso.

Shepard, J. (2009). *The meaning of Matthew: My son's murder in Laramie, and a world transformed.* New York, NY: Hudson Street Press.

Wise, T. (2011). *White like me.* Berkeley, CA: Soft Skull Press.

Yousafzai, M. (2015). *I am Malala: The girl who stood up for education and was shot by the Taliban.* London, UK: Orion Publishing Group.

# CHAPTER 46

# Classroom Without Borders
## Service Learning Experiences in Developing Multicultural and Social Justice Counseling Competencies

*Thomas Field*

## Course Recommendations

| SOCIAL JUSTICE AND ADVOCACY PRINCIPLES | CORE CACREP STANDARDS | COUNSELING SPECIALIZATION |
|---|---|---|
| ☑ Strategies for Change | ☑ Assessment and Testing<br>☑ Career Development<br>☑ Group Work<br>☑ Helping Relationships<br>☑ Human Growth and Development<br>☑ Professional Counseling Orientation and Ethical Practice<br>☑ Social and Cultural Diversity | ☑ Addiction Counseling<br>☑ Career Counseling<br>☑ Clinical Mental Health Counseling<br>☑ Marriage, Couple, and Family Counseling<br>☑ School Counseling |

## TOPIC

Integrating service learning experiences into core counselor education courses, to provide exposure to multicultural, social justice, and advocacy issues within the local community

## LEARNING OBJECTIVES

1. Learners will engage in direct service to multicultural, social justice, and advocacy issues that exist within the local community.
2. Learners will identify barriers that exist for people within the local community, and apply principles of multicultural and social justice counseling competencies to identify potential advocacy action steps to address barriers.
3. Learners will evaluate their attitudes and beliefs about the role of the counselor within the community, through reflecting on their personal responses to the service learning experience.
4. Learners will identify areas in which they can grow in relation to the multicultural and social justice counseling competencies, based on their experiences of participating in service learning.

## TARGET POPULATION

Graduate counseling students in their first year of study

## GROUP SIZE

Can be used with courses that have an enrollment between four and 30 students.

## TIME REQUIRED

The instructor can determine the number of hours of service learning that students must complete as part of their course grade. Students log time on a timesheet. The hours must be substantial enough for the student to have an immersive experience, without overburdening the student. For a three semester credit course (five quarter credits), 20 hours is recommended.

## SETTING

The setting can vary, depending on the nature of the service learning activity. Suggested settings include:

- Supportive employment centers for people who are homeless
- Vocational rehabilitation services for people with developmental disabilities
- Career fairs at high schools that are under resourced
- Support groups for people who are in recovery from addiction
- Free clinics that provide free mental health screenings as part of comprehensive medical services

## MATERIALS NEEDED

It is important to develop documents that structure the service learning experience. The following documents are recommended:

- Timesheet
- Instructions about the nature of activities the student is expected to engage in, with psychotherapy services prohibited unless under live supervision of the attending faculty member
- Lecture handouts that are presented prior to the service learning experience that address the following:
  - The multicultural and social justice counseling competencies, with an actual copy of the competencies provided to each student
  - Potential barriers that exist within the community, such as discrimination and oppression
  - Examples of advocacy action steps
- A course assignment within the syllabus that requires a written reflection paper. Reflection questions should address:
  - Potential barriers that exist in the community
  - Advocacy action steps
  - Self-evaluation of attitudes and beliefs about the role of the counselor within the community
- Evaluative criteria (rubrics, etc.) for assessing student participation and ethical behavior at the service learning site, alongside demonstrated self-awareness.

# INSTRUCTIONS FOR CONDUCTING ACTIVITY

Setting up and executing successful service learning projects require an extended amount of work (Burnett, Hamel, & Long, 2004; Jett & Delgado-Romero, 2009). The payoff is worth the investment, as these experiences assist students to develop multicultural and social justice counseling competencies (Midgett & Doumas, 2016). The following procedure is recommended when setting up service learning projects within core counselor education courses.

1. Meet with someone on the campus who has local knowledge of potential service learning sites, and the university's relationship with such sites in the past. Some universities have outreach offices with dedicated staff members to service learning projects, while others do not. Sometimes, a departmental faculty member will be the best resource for locating site possibilities in the community. Conducting individual searches through 211 may be useful when looking for a very specific type of site. For example, researching vocational rehabilitation services could be useful when teaching a Career Counseling course. Search results may feature sites that the instructor was initially unaware of, such as sites that provide vocational rehabilitation services to adults with developmental disabilities. The university may not have prior connections with such a site, requiring the faculty member to reach out directly after locating contact information on 211. Often, schools, community agencies, and organizations are more than happy to accept volunteer support from students.

2. Once a potential site has been identified, ask the outreach office about whether to reach out directly or have it reach out on the instructor's behalf. Meeting with the site director in-person can be very helpful, and should occur at least two to three months in advance of the course. This allows for the instructor to assess whether the site is appropriate for students, and developing relationships with the directors of the program is an important first step in the process. During the initial meeting, discuss ideas about the service learning project, and ask about needs at the site. Ideally, the instructor and site director will collaboratively identify on-site activities that benefit both the student and the site. Ensure that the site agrees to the time commitment outlined. Identify the on-site point of contact for students, in case an issue arises. After the meeting, write up a summary and send it to the contact person from the site. Directors of community programs or schools are very busy people and will often forget the details of the arrangement afterward. A summary can be helpful to avoid this potential issue.

3. Ensure that site agreements are completed before the first day of the course. Consider securing an additional agreement with a second site, particularly if the class size is greater than ten students. This provides students with a choice, which is often well-received. If the course contains students from different specialties (e.g., school counseling, clinical counseling), it can be helpful to provide choices that reflect each specialty (e.g., a school-based site and a community agency).

4. At the beginning of the course, anticipate taking at least an hour to explain the nature of the service learning requirement and allow students plenty of time to ask questions. Invite the director of the service learning site to visit with the students early in the course, within the first two or three weeks. Consider arranging a site visit early in the course, so that students can see the site and meet with the director. If there are two site agreements, ensure that students visit both sites before making a decision about where they would like to complete their service learning requirement. The site will usually want to provide a brief orientation of its facility to the students, along with important information about the mission and scope of the program.

5. If possible, give students at least a week after the site visit to reflect on which placement they would like to commit to (if there are two possibilities). Note that some sites can only take a certain number of students, and thus those slots can be more competitive among students. If you have more interested students than slots, this issue can be resolved by selecting finalists randomly from a hat, for the purpose of fairness.

6. Once students have finalized their choice of sites, require that they sign a form that outlines ethical expectations and their role at the site, along with the contact information of the site supervisor and the instructor in case an issue arises. Before students begin their service learning experience, it is important for the instructor to go over the materials needed for the project, which include the timesheet,

lecture handouts about multicultural and social justice counseling competencies, barriers, and advocacy action steps, associated course assignments such as reflection papers, and evaluative criteria for student participation at the site. Once all of these preparatory tasks have been completed, students are permitted to begin their service learning experiences. At this point, the instructor's role is to check in with each student and the site supervisor periodically, to ensure that the service learning experience is going as planned. Toward the conclusion of the term, hold a closing meeting with the site supervisor and the students who completed their hours at the site.

## DISCUSSION

Often, students complete their hours over the course of several weeks. When students are completing hours, ask each student for a brief report of their activities at the site during each class period. This provides students with faculty support. When teaching about other topics, try to connect the topic to the student's experiences at the site that they have reported. This often brings richness and vitality to the topic being covered that day.

Toward the conclusion of the course, set up a discussion group so that students can process their experiences with each other. Each discussion group should have no more than eight students. Provide students with structured discussion prompts about their awareness of attitudes and beliefs during their service learning experiences; if possible, use the same prompts from their self-reflection paper. Examples of prompts include: (1) discuss barriers that exist within the community for the people that you have worked with during the service learning experience, (2) identify advocacy action steps that address those barriers, and (3) evaluate your attitudes and beliefs about the role of the counselor within the community that you observed during the service learning experience.

Encourage students to give direct feedback to each other. This provides students with the opportunity to compare and contrast their experiences, and also to identify areas in which they can grow. Allow at least 60 minutes for this discussion group. If there are multiple discussion groups occurring simultaneously, ask each of the discussion groups to share a summary of their discussion. In feedback to student self-reflection papers, be sure to highlight student areas of growth related to the multicultural and social justice counseling competencies during their experience, in addition to identifying areas for further growth.

After the course has concluded, meet again with the site director and process the experience. This is usually a very helpful discussion, as it typically evolves into a brainstorming discussion about how to improve the service learning experience the next time around. It is worth noting that some sites are not worth returning to for a second time, for a variety of reasons. However, some sites will hopefully become consistent partners for future courses. This is useful as the instructor will already have a good sense of what the student's experience is likely to be at the service learning site, and it reduces the amount of preparatory work to set up the site placement. It is worth noting that staff turnover can result in the instructor needing to establish contact with the next site supervisor, and so maintaining regular contact with the site is recommended.

## BIBLIOGRAPHY

Burnett, J. A., Hamel, D., & Long, L. L. (2004). Service learning in graduate counselor education: Developing multicultural counseling competency. *Journal of Multicultural Counseling and Development, 32*(3), 180–191. doi:10.1002/j.2161-1912.2004.tb00370.x

Jett, S. T., & Delgado-Romero, E. A. (2009). Prepracticum service learning in counselor education: A qualitative case study. *Counselor Education and Supervision, 49*(2), 106–121. doi:10.1002/j.1556-6978.2009.tb00091.x

Midgett, A., & Doumas, D. M. (2016). Evaluation of service-learning-infused courses with refugee families. *Journal of Multicultural Counseling and Development, 44*(2), 118–134. doi:10.1002/jmcd.12041

## SUGGESTED BACKGROUND READING

Alvarado, M., & Gonzalez, P. A. (2013). Experiences in service learning among counselor education students. *Vistas 2013*, *79*, 1–9. Retrieved from www.counseling.org/docs/default-source/vistas/experiences-in-service-learning-among-counselor-education-students.pdf

Dockery, D. J. (2011). A guide to incorporating service learning into counselor education. *Vistas 2011*, *34*, 1–11. Retrieved from http://counselingoutfitters.com/vistas/vistas11/Article_34.pdf

Oliver, B., Abel, N. R., Keller, T., Myers, M., & McAulay, A. (2014). Service learning in counselor education: Learning outside the classroom. *Scholarship and Professional Work Education*, *33*. Retrieved from http://digitalcommons.butler.edu/coe_papers/33

# CHAPTER 47

# Enhancing Research Competencies to Promote Social Justice and Multiculturalism

*Jennifer Austin Main, Kassie Terrell, and Sumedha Therthani*

## Course Recommendations

| SOCIAL JUSTICE AND ADVOCACY PRINCIPLES | CORE CACREP STANDARDS | COUNSELING SPECIALIZATION |
|---|---|---|
| ☑ What Is Social Justice and Advocacy? | ☑ Helping Relationships<br>☑ Professional Counseling Orientation and Ethical Practice<br>☑ Research and Program Evaluation<br>☑ Social and Cultural Diversity | ☑ Clinical Mental Health Counseling<br>☑ Marriage, Couple, and Family Counseling<br>☑ School Counseling<br>☑ Student Affairs and College Counseling |

## TOPIC

The purpose of this activity is to enhance students' ability to select appropriate research to inform ethical, multicultural, and social justice practices, especially since a range of mental health disorders are diagnosed worldwide using the DSM 5 (e.g., depression, anxiety, obsessive compulsive disorder, anorexia, bulimia, post-traumatic stress disorder, schizophrenia, and bipolar disorder). To build multicultural competencies and promote social justice advocacy in interpreting and utilizing research, students need to be mindful of the research they are using to inform their practice.

## LEARNING OBJECTIVES

1. Upon completion of this activity, students will be able to identify at least two cultural factors related to mental health counseling.
2. Upon completion of this activity, students will be able to critique at least two empirically based research articles that enhance social justice and multicultural awareness.
3. Upon completion of this activity, students will be able to identify at least three ethical and culturally relevant strategies for conducting research.
4. Upon completion of this activity, students will be able to describe at least two ways in which he or she will be able to advocate for a client within his or her community.

## TARGET POPULATION

The target population for this activity is master's- and doctoral-level students enrolled in a counseling program.

## GROUP SIZE

This activity is appropriate for individual or group activity. Size of the groups can vary depending on the objectives of the counselor educator and needs of the students.

## TIME REQUIRED

- This activity will take place over at least one to two class periods to allow for student presentations and class discussion.
- Counselor educators should allow adequate time to process questions and debrief after the activity.
- The time for this activity can be altered to the counselor educator's desire and number of students enrolled in the class.
- Online instructors should allow at least one week for submission and discussion.

## SETTING

- This activity will take place in two settings, inside the classroom (e.g., signup of diagnosis, student presentations, and class discussion) and outside of the classroom (e.g., searching for research articles and developing presentation).
- This activity can be altered for an online class. Students will sign up for the diagnosis he or she wants to research, upload relevant material to the online forum (e.g., two articles), and upload a paper detailing the results of his or her investigation. Additionally, to facilitate class discussion students may post questions to the Learning Management System (e.g., Blackboard) used by the university. Students are then required to respond to at least three different questions posed by the instructor or other students on the discussion board.

## MATERIALS NEEDED

- Paper and pen
- Access to research databases and/or empirically reviewed research journals
- Computer, email, printer, PowerPoint/Prezi, and the Internet

## INSTRUCTIONS FOR CONDUCTING ACTIVITY

1. Students will select one DSM 5 diagnosis of interest and find two empirically reviewed research articles that study the selected diagnosis in two different populations and/or cultures.
   a. Students are encouraged to review and compare best practices and appropriate interventions of the different populations and/or cultures.
   b. Students are instructed to prepare a 10- to 15-minute presentation highlighting their findings; students should be able to identify independent and dependent variables, research design, methodology, theoretical foundation, population and/or culture studied, intervention used (if applicable), results of the study, and implications.

    c.  Students should be able to articulate how this research deepens their multicultural understanding and how this could empower students, individuals, and groups to confront injustices and inequalities within their communities.

2.  Once students have completed the presentations the counselor educator will lead an open dialogue with students using discussion questions.

# DISCUSSION

Once students have completed the presentations the counselor educator will lead an open dialogue with students using the following prompts:

1.  With your increased awareness of issues of diversity and social justice, how can you be more effective with advocating for the clients you serve?
2.  How did these research articles inform your practice?
3.  How did the articles enhance your understanding of a mental health diagnosis in this particular population and/or culture?
4.  After reading these articles, what will you do differently?
5.  After reading these articles, what misconceptions or assumptions did you have about the population or diagnosis?
6.  How has reading the articles changed or altered your assumptions or misconceptions?
7.  How did the researchers demonstrate culturally competent research strategies?
8.  Based on your classmate's presentations, what new knowledge have you gained?
9.  How will you integrate this new knowledge into your practice?

# BIBLIOGRAPHY

Durham, J. C., & Glosoff, H. L. (2010). From passion to action: Integrating the ACA advocacy competencies and social justice into counselor education and supervision. In M. J. Ratts, R. L. Toporek, & J. A. Lewis (Eds.), *ACA advocacy competencies: A social justice framework for counselors* (pp. 139–149). Alexandria, VA: American Counseling Association.

Hook, J. N., Davis, D. E., Owen, J., Worthington, E. L., Jr., & Utsey, S. O. (2013). Cultural humility: Measuring openness to culturally diverse clients. *Journal of Counseling Psychology, 60,* 353–366. doi:10.1037/a0032595

Nassar-McMillan, S. C. (2014). A framework for cultural competence, advocacy, and social justice: Applications for global multiculturalism and diversity. *International Journal for Educational and Vocational Guidance, 14,* 103–118. doi:10.1007/s10775-014-9265-3

Ratts, M. J., Singh, A. A., Nassar-McMillan, S., Butler, S. K., & McCullough, J. R. (2016). Multicultural and social justice counseling competencies: Guidelines for the counseling profession. *Journal of Multicultural Counseling and Development, 44,* 28–48. doi:10.1002/jmcd.12035

# SUGGESTED BACKGROUND READING

Chen, E. C., Kakkad, D., & Balzano, J. (2008). Multicultural competence and evidence-based practice in group therapy. *Journal of Clinical Psychology, 64,* 1261–1278. doi:10.1002/jclp.20533

Collins, N. M., & Pieterse, A. L. (2007). Critical incident analysis based training: An approach for developing active racial/cultural awareness. *Journal of Counseling and Development, 85,* 14–23. http://dx.doi.org/10.1002/j.1556-6678.2007.tb00439.x

Corrigan, P. W., & Miller, F. E. (2004). Shame, blame, and contamination: A review of the impact of mental illness stigma on family members. *Journal of Mental Health, 13,* 537–548. doi:10.1080/09638230400017004

Miller, M. J., & Sendrowitz, K. (2011). Counseling psychology trainees' social justice interest and commitment. *Journal of Counseling Psychology, 58,* 159–169. http://dx.doi.org/10.1037/a0022663

Ratts, M. J., Singh, A. A., Nassar-McMillan, S., Butler, S. K., & McCullough, J. R. (2015a). *Multicultural and social justice counseling competencies.* Retrieved from www.counseling.org/docs/defaultsource/competencies/multicultural-and-social-justice- counseling-competencies.pdf?sfvrsn=20

# CHAPTER 48

# Assessment Effectiveness

## Mary-Anne Joseph and DeAnna Henderson

### Course Recommendations

| SOCIAL JUSTICE AND ADVOCACY PRINCIPLES | CORE CACREP STANDARDS | COUNSELING SPECIALIZATION |
|---|---|---|
| ☑ Strategies for Change | ☑ Assessment and Testing<br>☑ Professional Counseling Orientation and Ethical Practice<br>☑ Research and Program Evaluation | ☑ Career Counseling<br>☑ Clinical Mental Health Counseling |

## TOPIC

This activity is intended to assist participants identify potential social justice issues with assessment instruments.

## LEARNING OBJECTIVES

1. To identify potential social justice issues with assessment instruments
2. To identify appropriate strategies to advocate for one's clients to be assessed with cultural relevant instruments

## TARGET POPULATION

This activity is suited for counseling students and/or counselor trainees.

## GROUP SIZE

This activity is well suited for groups of 8–12 participants.

## TIME REQUIRED

This activity takes approximately 30–45 minutes. The length of time needed to complete the activity may be impacted by the number of members in the group.

## SETTING

This activity can be conducted in a general classroom setting. The classroom should be divided into two or three groups of three to five. State how setting could be altered by participant demographics.

## MATERIALS NEEDED

- Advocacy and assessment case study
- Handout
- Pen/pencil

## INSTRUCTIONS FOR CONDUCTING ACTIVITY

1. Participants are to be divided into two or three groups of three to five.
2. Each team is to be provided the case study and the handout.
3. Each team will have 20–30 minutes to review the case study and answer the questions on the handout.
4. Each team must support their responses with relevant ACA or CRC Code of Ethics or other scholarly materials.
5. Students are to utilize current peer reviewed research and the ACA and/or CRC Code of Ethics to support their debate points.

## DISCUSSION

- Each team will have 5–10 minutes to present their perspective regarding the social justice issues with the case study and the assessment instrument.
- Was there information or an idea presented that you hadn't considered?

## BIBLIOGRAPHY

Brown, K. M. (2005). Leadership for social Justice and equity: Evaluating a transformative framework and andragogy. *Educational Administration Quarterly, 42*(5), 700–745. doi:10.1177/0013161X06290650

Nelson, M. L., & Neufeldt, S. A. (1998). The pedagogy of counseling: A critical examination. *Counselor Education and Supervision, 38*(2), 70–89.

Wyatt, G. E., & Parham, W. D. (1985). The inclusion of culturally sensitive course materials in graduate school and training programs. *Psychotherapy: Theory, Research, Practice, Training, 22*(2S), 461–468.

## SUGGESTED BACKGROUND READING

Arredondo, P., Tovar-Blank, Z. G., & Parham, T. A. (2008). Challenges and promises of becoming a culturally competent counselor in a sociopolitical era of change and empowerment. *Journal of Counseling and Development, 86*(3), 261–268.

Baltussen, B., Mikkelsen, E., Tromp, N., Hurtig, A., Byskov, J., Olsen, A., . . . Norheim, O. F. (2013). Balancing efficiency, equity and feasibility of HIV treatment in South Africa: Development of programmatic guidance. *Cost Effectiveness & Resource Allocation, 11*(1), 26–43. doi:10.1186/1478-7547-11-26

Banham, D., Lynch, J., & Karnon, J. (2011). An equity-effectiveness framework linking health programs and healthy life expectancy. *Australian Journal of Primary Health, 17*(4), 309–319. doi:10.1071/PY11034

Brown, K. M. (2005). Leadership for social Justice and equity: Evaluating a transformative framework and andragogy. *Educational Administration Quarterly, 42*(5), 700–745. doi:10.1177/0013161X06290650

Capuzzi, D., & Stauffer, M. D. (2016). *Counseling and psychotherapy: Theories and interventions* (6th ed.). Upper Saddle River, NJ: Pearson Merrill and Prentice Hall.

Carey, J., & Dimmitt, C. (2012). School counseling and student outcomes: Summary of six statewide studies. *Professional School Counseling, 16*(2), 146–153.

Chopra, P. (2014). Seeking conditions of possibility: (Re)conceptualising democratic discursive practices in a rights-based approach to adult education. *Compare: A Journal of Comparative & International Education, 44*(3), 335–355. doi:10.1080/03057925.2012.757149

Ginns, P., Loughland, A., Tierney, R. J., Fryer, L., Amazan, R., & McCormick, A. (2015). Evaluation of the learning to teach for social justice beliefs scale in an Australian context. *Higher Education Research & Development, 34*(2), 311–323. doi:10.1080/07294360.2014.956701

Kraehe, A., Acuff, J., & Travis, S. (2016). Equity, the arts, and urban education: A review. *Urban Review, 48*(2), 220–244. doi:10.1007/s11256-016-0352-2

Loewenson, R. (2007). Exploring equity and inclusion in the responses to AIDS. *AIDS Care, 19*(1), 2–11.

Nelson, M. L., & Neufeldt, S. A. (1998). The pedagogy of counseling: A critical examination. *Counselor Education and Supervision, 38*(2), 70–89.

Romero, D., & Chan, A. (2005). Profiling Derald Wing Sue: Blazing the trail for the multicultural journey and social justice in counseling. *Journal of Counseling and Development, 83*(2), 202–213.

Szalacha, L. A. (2004). Educating teachers on LGBTQ issues: A review of research and program evaluations. *Journal of Gay & Lesbian Issues in Education, 4*(1), 67–79.

Wyatt, G. E., & Parham, W. D. (1985). The inclusion of culturally sensitive course materials in graduate school and training programs. *Psychotherapy: Theory, Research, Practice, Training, 22*(2S), 461–468.

## HANDOUT

# Handout 48.1: Assessment Effectiveness Case Studies

## CASE SCENARIO 1: THE CASE OF KRIS

Kris was scheduled to have an on the job vocational assessment to determine if he was suited to work in an emergency call center as a dispatcher. Upon arriving at the evaluation site Kris found that the accommodations he requested, an ergonomic keyboard and a screen magnification and reader, were not provided. He was asked to improvise with the materials and tools provided. After Kris completed the on the job evaluation, the evaluator informed Kris' rehabilitation counselor that she did not believe Kris would be suited to work as a dispatcher. Kris stated that he believes the evaluator was wrong and he was not given a fair chance to succeed.

## CASE SCENARIO 2: THE CASE OF CYNTHIA

Cynthia is a 17-year-old African American female who has been experiencing some familial and social challenges. She has been suspended from school on numerous occasions for fighting, and despite multiple attempts, Cynthia's teachers and school counselor have been unable to help her change her behavior. Cynthia also has a visual impairment and was diagnosed with ADHD as a child. Cynthia's school counselor believes that her disabilities have something to do with her behaviors. Thus, Cynthia was referred to a psychologist by her school counselor for additional assessment. During one of their early sessions the psychologist administered the Rorschach test. Based on the assessment results, the psychologist indicated that Cynthia had a diagnosis of schizophrenia. Cynthia argues that the psychologist does not know what he is talking about and he doesn't understand her as an African American.

## CASE SCENARIO 3: THE CASE OF BRIAN

Brian is a 19-year-old Hispanic male. He has been diagnosed with a learning disability. Brian has been diagnosed with both dyslexia and dysgraphia. Brian is preparing for college and has sat for the SAT and ACT on two occasions. His scores on both tests continue to be quite low. Brian's mother is concerned that his disability is hampering his ability to be successful. She thinks he should be provided with alternative means of completing the assessments outside of a rigidly timed and isolated environment. Brian's mother believes that he should receive time and a half and be able to take these assessments in his counselor's office.

## CASE SCENARIO 4: THE CASE OF TOMMY

Tommy is a 22-year-old senior college student. Tommy is a first-generation student who hails from a small American Indian town in Montana. Tommy was recently convicted of a DUI and was court ordered to join the Substance Abuse program provided through the university he attends. Upon admission to the program, Tommy was asked to take a substance abuse questionnaire. Upon evaluating Tommy's responses the university counselor stated that she believed that Tommy had a significant substance abuse problem. Tommy argues that in his culture, drinking is a social activity and everyone partakes.

# CHAPTER 49

# Build, Explore, and Consider Career Interventions (BECCI) Case Study

*Shamire Rothmiller and Jessica Henry*

## Course Recommendations

| SOCIAL JUSTICE AND ADVOCACY PRINCIPLES | CORE CACREP STANDARDS | COUNSELING SPECIALIZATION |
|---|---|---|
| ☑ Social Constructs of Oppression and Privilege | ☑ Career Development | ☑ Career Counseling |

## TOPIC

BECCI case studies are designed to create a simulation of potential social justice issues that may arise and create barriers within career counseling sessions. The goal is to prevent social injustice within career counseling (Sampson, Dozier, & Colvin, 2011). This specific activity highlights the limitations of interest inventories (e.g., SDS).

## LEARNING OBJECTIVES

1. To explore careers associated with Holland's Typology using O*Net
2. To explore how our assumptions/beliefs about our clients can create barriers to successful outcomes
3. To explore potential stereotypes, implicit biases, or prejudices in career counseling
4. To explore social justice issues that may arise in career counseling
5. To explore the limitations of career intervention by considering external factors
6. To explore possible interventions to confront barriers

## TARGET POPULATION

Master's students

## GROUP SIZE

Six

# TIME REQUIRED

It will take approximately 40 minutes to complete this activity. The amount of time depends on the amount of discussion that will take place during debriefing.

# SETTING

This activity can be conducted in any classroom. It may include individuals or small groups.

# MATERIALS NEEDED

For this activity the instructor will need paper, blank male and female templates, pencils, desk space, scissors, small container or zip lock bags and access to the Internet (O*NET) and/or relevant reference (e.g., Holland's Typology). Color pencils or markers are optional.

# INSTRUCTIONS FOR CONDUCTING ACTIVITY

Preface: discussing sensitive topics such as race, sexual orientation, religion, etc. can provoke uncomfortable emotions; participants are encouraged to be aware and respectful of others and considerate in their response. Participants should feel free to discontinue participating in the activity if they no longer feel like engaging.

Preparation:
1. Print male and female body templates from the Internet.
2. Using a blank sheet of paper, write down various demographic factors that have implications for social justice (e.g., race, SES, religion, sexual orientation, geographic location).
3. Cut and fold those factors and place them separately in containers or zip lock bags. For example: one container/bag could be gender and another age. The instructor can add as many variables as they like.

Part 1:
- Using O*NET participants will secure a career for their client.
- Break into small groups using the Realistic, Investigative, Artistic, Social, Enterprising, and Conventional (RIASEC) Typology by John Holland. Group #1 is RIA, and Group #2 is SEC.
- Provide each group with a male and female template and inform them of their client's name (e.g., RIA or SEC).
- Participants will have the ability to create the client that they would like to work with. Taking into consideration concepts such as Holland's Typologies and PE Fit, they will bring their client to life (give that individual a personality including personal characteristics, e.g., wears glasses, doesn't like ___, etc.). The only thing that is "fixed" is their typology (synonymous with their name, either RIA or SEC). They may choose the clothes and gender of the client.

Part 2: social justice variables:
- Using the same the person (RIA or SEC) participants will pull different demographic variables.
- Groups will build on their previous client, by randomly drawing associations related to social justice. Students should write their variable on their sheet.

Participants will then work together to explore how these implications may/may not create barriers.

- Finally, participants will consider innovative ways to help their client.
- After groups finish, they will present their intervention plans.

- Participants are strongly encouraged to use the Sampson et al., 2011, article and to be as creative as possible (think outside of the box).

# DISCUSSION

1. Discussion will occur between group members first. Participants should discuss why they chose specific genders and personal characteristics. They should be prepared to present their rationale to the rest of the class.
2. Part 1 discussion:
   a. These are ideal cases; they do not take into consideration external factors. This is also an opportunity to explore assumptions related to what a person should look like in different positions (e.g., gender), or how individuals with certain personalities may dress (e.g., artistic vs. realistic interests).
   b. Helpful guiding question: how can our assumptions/beliefs about our clients create barriers to successful outcomes?
3. Part 2 discussion:
   a. BUILD: what external factors were pulled and how do they help or hinder?
   b. EXPLORE: what barriers and options are/are not available?
   c. CONSIDER: what plan of action could best assist the client?
   d. CAREER INTERVENTION: create and share a holistic intervention that infuses social justice concepts.
   e. Helpful guiding questions:
      i. What are some social justice issues that may not be considered when using interest inventories?
      ii. What research study could be conducted that considers social justice interventions as well as connects theory to practice?
      iii. In what ways could you advocate on behalf of your client?

# BIBLIOGRAPHY

Gottfredson, G. D. (1999). John L. Holland's contributions to vocational psychology: A review and evaluation. *Journal of Vocational Behavior, 55*(1), 15–40. http://doi.org/10.1006/jvbe.1999.1695

Sampson, J. P., Dozier, V. C., & Colvin, G. P. (2011). Translating career theory to practice: The risk of unintentional social injustice. *Journal of Counseling & Development, 89*(3), 326–337. doi:10.1002/j.1556-6678.2011.tb00097.x

# SUGGESTED BACKGROUND READING

Gottfredson, G. D., & Johnstun, M. L. (2009). John Holland's contributions: A theory ridden approach to career assistance. *The Career Development Quarterly, 58*(2), 99–107. doi:10.1002/j.2161-0045.2009.tb00050.x

Miller, M. J., & Miller, T. A. (2005). Theoretical application of Holland's theory to individual decision-making styles: Implications for career counselors. *Journal of Employment Counseling, 42*(1), 20–28. doi:10.1002/j.2161-1920.2005.tb00895.x

# CHAPTER 50

# Eugenics and Early Assessment

*Tyler Wilkinson*

## Course Recommendations

| SOCIAL JUSTICE AND ADVOCACY PRINCIPLES | CORE CACREP STANDARDS | COUNSELING SPECIALIZATION |
|---|---|---|
| ☑ What Is Social Justice and Advocacy?<br>☑ Social Constructs of Oppression and Privilege | ☑ Assessment and Testing | ☑ Addiction Counseling<br>☑ Clinical Mental Health Counseling<br>☑ Marriage, Couple, and Family Counseling<br>☑ School Counseling |

## TOPIC

The focus of this activity is to teach individuals greater awareness of how assessment results, specifically intelligence testing, have been used to impact individuals and sociopolitical outcomes in our culture. This leads individuals into conversations about language, constructs, and biases in testing/assessment.

## LEARNING OBJECTIVES

- Describe how early testing in the United States was used to identify "feeblemindedness."
- Discuss the impact of sterilization laws as a result of early testing.
- Consider ways in which current cultural values influence how we consider the language used with individuals to describe themselves as a result of assessment.

## TARGET POPULATION

Master's level counseling students

## GROUP SIZE

Class size of 20–25. Groups of three to four.

## TIME REQUIRED

60–90 minutes

## SETTING

Traditional classroom setting or online synchronous/asynchronous discussion

## MATERIALS NEEDED

Readings prior to course discussion. Paper or computer for taking notes/reflection.

## INSTRUCTIONS FOR CONDUCTING ACTIVITY

1.  Assign students to read items from the "Suggested Background Reading" section.
2.  Provide a brief history lecture on the emergence of intelligence testing in Paris and the impact of Goddard translating and bringing intelligence testing to the United States in the early 1900s.
3.  Have students discuss the language of "feeblemindedness," "moron," and "idiot." This language was initially used as diagnostic labels to categorizes levels of intelligence. Have them discuss how language is used today and its impact on individuals (e.g., Mental Retardation was a diagnostic category).
4.  Allow students to read the definition of the "socially inadequate classed" in Laughlin's (1922) model law. A "feebleminded" individual would meet the criteria of eugenical sterilization.
5.  Point out to the students that the Harry Laughlin model legislation lead to the notable U.S. Supreme Court case *Buck v. Bell* in 1927 in which the Court ruled in favor of legal sterilization of the social inadequate class, in which feebleminded individuals were included. Justice Oliver Wendell Holmes wrote the decision, in which he stated, "It is better for all the world, if instead of waiting to execute degenerate offspring for crime, or to let them starve for their imbecility, society can prevent those who are manifestly unfit from continuing their kind. The principle that sustains compulsory vaccination is broad enough to cover cutting the Fallopian tubes. Three generation of imbeciles is enough" (Ekland-Olson & Blicken, 2012, p. 1).
6.  Have students get into small groups of three to four to discuss their reactions to the assigned readings and to learning about involuntary sterilization as a result of an intelligence test. The instructor then discusses with the entire class.
7.  Students then discuss their thoughts regarding the way in which cultural systems continue to use assessment data to make decisions about individuals. Students are encouraged to apply this to the counseling context.
8.  This activity can then move discussions to begin looking at counseling ethics, testing biases, and the impact of language/constructs on the assessment process. Students are encouraged to be mindful of collaborative efforts to fully maximize understanding their clients, working with clients to co-create meaning in session.

## DISCUSSION

Participants are provided some questions and prompts to consider to facilitate discussion. Participants are encouraged not just to reflect on the history of the United States but to consider ways in which testing and assessment do not promote social justice with clients.

Some possible prompts/questions:

*   Describe your reactions to learning about the earliest uses of testing in the United States.
*   What is your reaction in learning that some of the sterilization laws were on the books until the 1960s and 1970s?

- How does this impact the way in which you think about assessment today? Specifically, in working with individuals in counseling?
- Describe ways in which you can work to minimize reductive practices and consider the complexity (values, cultures, beliefs) of the individuals with whom you work?
- Discuss how language and construct can be useful tools in working to create meaning in a session with clients.

# BIBLIOGRAPHY

Buck v. Bell, 274 U.S. 200 (1927).

Ekland-Olson, S., & Blicken, J. (2012). *How ethical systems change: Eugenics, the final solution, bioethics*. New York, NY: Routledge.

Farreras, I. (2014). Clara Harrison Town and the origins of the first institutional commitment law for the "feebleminded": Psychologist as expert diagnostician. *History of Psychology, 17*(4), 271–281. doi:10.1037/a0036123

Gregory, R. (2013). *Psychological testing: History, principles, and applications* (7th ed.). Boston, MA: Pearson.

Laughlin, H. H. (1922). *Eugenical sterilization in the United States*. Chicago, IL: Psychopathic Laboratory of the Municipal Court of Chicago.

Neukrug, E. S., & Fawcett, R. C. (2015). *Essentials of testing ad assessment: A practical guide to counselors, social workers, and psychologists* (3rd ed.). Stamford, CT: Cengage.

# SUGGESTED BACKGROUND READING

Students are provided with a copy of Harry Laughlin's (1922) "Model Eugenical Sterilization Law" (p. 446) and the Clara Harrison Town article (Farreras, 2014) prior to the discussion activity. The instructor is encouraged to read Eklan-Olson and Blicken (2012) for a primer on Laughlin, eugenics, and sterilization. Gregory (2013) and Neukrug and Fawcett (2015) provide an overview of eugenics and early intelligence testing in the United States.

# CHAPTER 51

# Teaching Radical Respect
## Increasing Empathy for Stigmatized Groups Through a Relational-Cultural Theoretical Lens

*Angela Schubert and Jessica Z. Taylor*

## Course Recommendations

| SOCIAL JUSTICE AND ADVOCACY PRINCIPLES | CORE CACREP STANDARDS | COUNSELING SPECIALIZATION |
|---|---|---|
| ☑ Cycle of Socialization and Liberation<br>☑ Strategies for Change | ☑ Group Work<br>☑ Social and Cultural Diversity<br>☑ Theories | ☑ Clinical Mental Health Counseling |

## TOPIC

The purpose of this activity is to help counseling students identify, explore, and potentially eliminate barriers, prejudices, and processes of intentional and unintentional oppression and discrimination toward socially stigmatized and devalued groups of people.

## LEARNING OBJECTIVES

1. Reflect on their own relational images and how they influence students' internal reactions to clients who may have behaved contrary to their own personal value systems.
2. Develop radical respect and understanding for clients who have behaved contrary to their own personal value systems.
3. Understand how systemic factors related to race, gender, and power may have contributed to clients behaving in ways that go against student personal values systems.
4. Apply what they learn during the in-class exercise toward facilitating a psychoeducational group with a non-counseling student population to assist others in developing understanding and radical respect for stigmatized groups.

## TARGET POPULATION

Counseling students

# GROUP SIZE

10–20

# TIME REQUIRED

1 hour for the in-class activity and 1 hour for the psychoeducational campus activity (this may be altered based on group size and the number of presentations the student desires to engage in)

# SETTING

A classroom will be most suitable to teach the activity, especially one that can accommodate several groups of one to three students and one large group. The setting of the psychoeducational group depends on the availability offered by the college campus.

# MATERIALS NEEDED

- Client scenarios set A
- Client scenarios set B
- Stigmatized Psychoeducation Group Facilitation instructions

# INSTRUCTIONS FOR CONDUCTING ACTIVITY

Timing: allow 10–20 minutes per group for students to discuss the first set of client scenarios. Allow 5–10 minutes for students to reflect upon and write down their reactions to the second set of client scenarios. Allow 20–30 minutes per group for students to discuss the processing questions after the second set of client scenarios. Spend the remainder of allotted time in large group discussion reflecting on the processing questions and their applicability to their work as future counseling professionals. For the psychoeducational group activity following the classroom component, allow for approximately an hour per group topic.

1. Have students read through the first set of client scenarios.
2. Have students arrange themselves in small groups of three to four students to discuss their thoughts about the client scenarios and what therapeutic goals they may see as relevant for working with the client.
3. After students have had time to discuss each client scenario, provide students with the second set of client scenarios.
4. Encourage students to be silent and focus on their internal affective, behavioral, and cognitive states as they read through the second set of client scenarios.
5. After students have focused on their internal states, encourage students to write down their reactions and thoughts.
6. After students have had time to write down their thoughts, have students discuss in their small groups the processing questions.
7. After each student has had the opportunity to discuss the processing questions within a small group, invite students into large group discussion to continue discussing the processing questions and applications to their work as future counseling professionals.

8.  After students have debriefed the in-class exercise, have each small group select one of the stigmatized group topics pertaining to the client scenarios (e.g., bisexuality, adultery, swinging, polyamory, abortion, end-of-life decisions for terminal illness). Have the members of each small group learn about their selected topic and develop a psychoeducational group focused on the topic.

On-campus psychoeducational activity (date and time dependent on campus availability; it would be ideal for the instructor to collaborate with the university counseling center prior to the activity to establish predesignated dates and times):

*   In collaboration with the university counseling center, have each student group facilitate a psychoeducational group to interested members of the general student body.
*   Have students incorporate an awareness-raising component as well as a teaching component into their psychoeducational group.

Post-facilitation discussion:

*   After students have facilitated their psychoeducational group, have them reflect upon and discuss the post psychoeducational facilitation process questions in class.

## DISCUSSION

Initial classroom activity discussion questions:

*   How does this additional piece of the client's story change your impression of the individual and the potential therapeutic goals you developed?
*   What is your internal reaction to learning this additional piece of the client's story?
*   How do your personal experiences with others influence your internal reaction and ability to work effectively with the client?
*   What systemic factors related to race, gender, and power may have contributed to the client behaving in a way that may go against your personal value system?
*   How would you be able to overcome this internal reaction to avoid negatively influencing the counseling relationship?

Post psychoeducational group facilitation discussion questions:

*   Which client scenario did you choose and why?
*   Reflecting on the experience itself, what was it like for you to facilitate a group on such a topic?
*   What systemic factors related to race, gender, and power may have influenced how you approached this group?
*   In what ways did your personal experiences with others influence your internal reaction and ability to effectively facilitate the psychoeducational group on the chosen topic?

## BIBLIOGRAPHY

Comstock, D. L., Hammer, T. R., Strentzsch, J., Cannon, K., Parsons, J., & Salazar, G. (2008). Relational-cultural theory: A framework for bridging relational, multicultural, and social justice competencies. *Journal of Counseling & Development, 86*(3), 279–287. doi:10.1002/j.1556-6678.2008.tb00510.x

Jordan, J. V. (2010). *Relational-cultural therapy*. Washington, DC: American Psychological Association.

# SUGGESTED BACKGROUND READING

Comstock, D. L., Hammer, T. R., Strentzsch, J., Cannon, K., Parsons, J., & Salazar, G. (2008). Relational-cultural theory: A framework for bridging relational, multicultural, and social justice competencies. *Journal of Counseling & Development, 86*(3), 279–287. doi:10.1002/j.1556-6678.2008.tb00510.x

Jordan, J. V. (2010). *Relational-cultural therapy*. Washington, DC: American Psychological Association.

Molnar, C., Ritz, T., Heller, B., & Solecki, W. (2011). Using higher education-community partnerships to promote urban sustainability. *Environment: Science and Policy for Sustainable Development, 53*(1), 18–28. doi:10.1080/00139157.2011.539944

Schwartz, E. Q. (2011). Promoting social justice advocacy through service-learning in higher education. *Journal of Student Affairs at New York University, 7*, 12–27. Retrieved from http://steinhardt.nyu.edu/josa/

## HANDOUT

# Handout 51.1: Stigmatized Psychoeducational Group Facilitation

As part of this assignment, students (in small groups of no more than four) are to select a stigmatized group previously identified in the earlier activity (e.g., bisexuality, adultery, swinging, polyamory, abortion, end-of-life decisions for terminal illness). Group members will learn about the selected group and identify an awareness-raising component to help educate the university student body community and encourage community conversation on the topic. In collaboration with the university counseling center, each student group will facilitate a psychoeducational group to interested members of the general student body. The student group should prepare an informative flyer and module for the psychoeducational group. The developed group facilitation module should incorporate the following aspects:

1. Identify an awareness-raising component on behalf of the identified group.
2. Introduce a teaching component with evidence based facts and scholarly literature on the topic.
3. Incorporate a culturally meaningful activity.
4. Note the materials needed.

# Handout 51.2: RCT and Stigmatized Groups Scenario A

## CLIENT SCENARIOS—SET A

**Jane**—Growing up, I was a pretty happy kid. I was the oldest of five kids. One brother and three sisters. My parents divorced when I was the age of 6, and I felt the need to take on the responsibilities of the missing parent from time to time. We were poor but we had a roof over our head. I remember in third grade, I went over to a friend's house. Her mother said it was okay to take a bath together. Bella was my dearest friend. But to see her naked was surprising. She had breasts. We were 9. I don't know if I was jealous or if I was attracted to her but something felt different. I let it go and pushed it off as jealousy and regret about my underdeveloped body.

**Grace and Harold**—We met through his roommate who was my boyfriend at the time. Well, I guess you could say we were just dating. Harold was in a long-distance relationship with a girl who was getting her doctorate three states away. We immediately connected one night after a game of darts. My "boy-friend" was upstairs asleep. After that night, we were inseparable. Harold broke up with his girlfriend, and I broke it off with the "boyfriend," and for months we had fun bar hopping and enjoying our time. Shortly after becoming exclusive, I found out Harold was still dating his so-called ex-girlfriend. A week after that discovery, I found out I was miscarrying. It brought us back together again, and Harold officially broke up with the other girl. It was a very tough week. We were engaged a few months later and married shortly after. Everything was going well, but I still didn't feel like the marriage was enough. I wanted more. I wanted to feel the connection I felt with Harold when we first met. We were never sexually conservative, but when we married something changed for Harold that didn't necessarily become clear to me. I found myself feeling rejected by him, and I started pulling away in a nagging kind of way.

I tried to talk to Harold about it, but he would shut me down whenever I would try to talk about our marriage.

**Daniel and Marquita**—We have had quite the life these past 25 years! There were ups and downs, but it was all full of love, and respect was our foundation. We met at a Super Bowl party. We are pretty sure at this point, we were set up by friends. It just seemed too good to be true that we just so happened to be at the same Super Bowl party and that we hit it off so well. We married three months later. We just knew it. Hell, I think I knew it the moment I saw her wearing the opposing team's jersey and sexy hair. She was gorgeous. Her family was Baptist, and my family was Catholic, but religion wasn't a big deal for us. We had our first daughter two years after we married. She was the sparkle in our eyes. Shortly, we had our son, Brandon. We were so stressed and worn out and happy. For the next 18 years, we raised our kids in the same home with principles we valued and family and respect as our pillars. We were so proud of both of them! But, we found our life together feeling empty after both of our children moved away to college.

**Jeb and Hannah**—I knew as a young child that being raised Mormon, I would one day meet my soul mate; that God himself would choose the right woman for me. Think of it. Handpicked by God himself. So many people in life go through this fumbling process without any direction in life. But I was not that person. When the church elder shared with me that Hannah dreamt God had told her to marry me, I wasn't surprised. I had visions prior to this event that God was preparing the way for something beautiful to happen in my life. I prayed for patience, and I prayed for her. She was 19, and I was 20. In this case it could be seen that the church arranged the marriage, but it was God. We were soon married, and we were very much in love.

**Laurel**—I was a 20-year-old college student. I was so excited to move away from home and learn new things about myself and life. I was a pretty busy student. I was in a sorority and a few clubs on campus. I had straight As, and all of my teachers were very supportive. Tough but supportive. I had never dated really anyone before college. You can say I jumped in feet first. It was exciting to be with my friends and party at the fraternity houses. I didn't really see a point to be in an actual relationship because there wasn't any time for one. I would hook up occasionally with a frat guy every now and then, but we didn't label it anything but friends with benefits. All around, I suppose I was just trying to have the fun that I never really got a chance to have before college due to being so involved with taking care of my younger siblings while my parents were at work.

**Molly**—I knew that things would be hard after getting divorced from the man whom I had thought was my soul mate, but I never knew things would be this hard. About two years after having our second child, I was experiencing abnormal vaginal bleeding that just wouldn't stop. I went to see the doctor to figure out why I was bleeding so much, and that's when I found out I had cervical cancer. When I told my husband, Frederick, he freaked out. He called me a whore and accused me of cheating on him. He said the only thing that causes cervical cancer is HPV, which he said he doesn't have since he's never had any symptoms. Nothing I said calmed him down, and that's when he left me. Leaving me to raise our two small children on my own while also trying to go through medical treatment. Thankfully, my mom was able to move in and help take care of the kids and the house while I went through treatment. Although treatment seemed to be working alright, I guess it's true what they say that it's a long time before you can consider yourself "cured." After four years seemingly cancer-free, I found out last week that the cancer has come back, and this time it has spread.

# Handout 51.3: RCT and Stigmatized Groups Scenario B

## CLIENT SCENARIOS—SET B

**Jane**—Growing up, I was a pretty happy kid. I was the oldest of five kids. One brother and three sisters. My parents divorced when I was the age of 6, and I felt the need to take on the responsibilities of the missing parent from time to time. We were poor, but we had a roof over our head. I remember in third grade, I went over to a friend's house. Her mother said it was okay to take a bath together. Bella was my dearest friend. But to see her naked was surprising. She had breasts. We were 9. I don't know if I was jealous or if I was attracted to her, but something felt different. I let it go and pushed it off as jealousy and regret about my underdeveloped body.

- Later, when all of my girlfriends were dating boys, I didn't think of myself as exclusively into boys. Yes, they were dreamy and I would write their names down in my notebook, but I would still think back to what I felt in the bath with Bella. During the summer before sixth grade, I found myself again confronted with girl parts. We hung out in the public pool all summer. Sometimes, my friend Posey would suggest that I go under water and look for her. Surprisingly, she would expose herself to me. I didn't know if she was trying to be funny, but again, I couldn't tell if I was nervous because she was naked or because of this attraction I felt for her in that moment. Was it because she was wild? A daredevil? Although I dated only boys in high school, I couldn't help but desire to kiss one of my girlfriends. Or at least to be held.

**Grace and Harold**—We met through his roommate who was my boyfriend at the time. Well, I guess you could say we were just dating. Harold was in a long-distance relationship with a girl who was getting her doctorate three states away. We immediately connected one night after a game of darts. My "boyfriend" was upstairs asleep. After that night, we were inseparable. Harold broke up with his girlfriend, and I broke it off with the "boyfriend," and for months we had fun bar hopping and enjoying our time. Shortly after becoming exclusive, I found out Harold was still dating his so-called ex-girlfriend. A week after that discovery, I found out I was miscarrying. It brought us back together again, and Harold officially broke up with the other girl. It was a very tough week. We were engaged a few months later and married shortly after. Everything was going well, but I still didn't feel like the marriage was enough. I wanted more. I wanted to feel the connection I felt with Harold when we first met. We were never sexually conservative, but when we married something changed for Harold that didn't necessarily become clear to me. I found myself feeling rejected by him, and I started pulling away in a nagging kind of way. I tried to talk to Harold about it, but he would shut me down whenever I would try to talk about our marriage.

- Maybe it was because every family member in my life had divorced at least once in my lifetime. Maybe I was not confident in my choice of Harold, or maybe I wasn't ready. I was only 26 when we married. Conversations were going nowhere with Harold, and I had asked for counseling as a solution to my problem. Harold shut that down really quick. One night, while at a company event, I ran into an old boyfriend. I drank too much, but I knew what I was doing. I wanted someone to appreciate me and enjoy me for so long. To give me what I was no longer experiencing within my marriage and unable to even talk to Harold about. I chose to have sex with him that night.

**Daniel and Marquita**—We have had quite the life these past 25 years! There were ups and downs, but it was all full of love, and respect was our foundation. We met at a Super Bowl party. We are pretty sure at this point, we were set up by friends. It just seemed too good to be true that we just so happened to be at the same Super Bowl party and that we hit it off so well. We married three months later. We just knew it. Hell, I think I knew it the moment I saw her wearing the opposing team's jersey and sexy hair. She was gorgeous. Her family was Baptist, and my family was Catholic, but religion wasn't a big deal for us. We had our first daughter two years after we married. She was the sparkle in our eyes. Shortly, we had our son, Brandon. We were so stressed and worn out and happy. For the next 18 years, we raised our kids in the same home with principles we valued and family and respect as our pillars. We were so proud of both of them! But, we found our life together feeling empty after both of our children moved away to college.

- After they both left for college, Marquita started to question my happiness in the bedroom. At first I was confused, but then we talked about it. We talked and talked and talked. We researched the pros and cons of other couples who were swingers. From what we learned, we knew that we had to come up with two lists: the Absolutely Not list and the Green Light list. We talked about each rule and created clear definitions. Our first time was terrifying. Marquita chose a woman, Alicia, that we both were attracted to. Nothing happened the first date. Or even the second date. Or the third date. We just talked about our rules and how to communicate needs and desires. We didn't want anything to fall in the gray area of communication. Alicia turned out to be a wonderful woman. She was so considerate and kind. And we both really appreciated how much she liked to please Marquita.

**Jeb and Hannah**—I knew as a young child that being raised Mormon, I would one day meet my soul mate; that God himself would choose the right woman for me. Think of it. Handpicked by God himself. So many people in life go through this fumbling process without any direction in life. But I was not that person. When the church elder shared with me that Hannah dreamt God had told her to marry me, I wasn't surprised. I had visions prior to this event that God was preparing the way for something beautiful to happen in my life. I prayed for patience, and I prayed for her. She was 19, and I was 20. In this case it could be seen that the church arranged the marriage, but it was God. We were soon married, and we were very much in love.

- After two years passed, we had a child on the way, and God spoke to me again. Hannah and I prayed about what God had told me for a very long time. We heard God's truth, and we both knew the direction God wanted our relationship to go in. With the blessing of the church elder, I asked Elizabeth if I could court her. After a brief courtship, I married Elizabeth, and she joined our family.

**Laurel**—I was a 20-year-old college student. I was so excited to move away from home and learn new things about myself and life. I was a pretty busy student. I was in a sorority and a few clubs on campus. I had straight As, and all of my teachers were very supportive. Tough but supportive. I had never dated really anyone before college. You can say I jumped in feet first. It was exciting to be with my friends and party at the fraternity houses. I didn't really see a point to be in an actual relationship because there wasn't any time for one. I would hook up occasionally with a frat guy every now and then, but we didn't label it anything but friends with benefits. All around, I suppose I was just trying to have the fun that I never really got a chance to have before college due to being so involved with taking care of my younger siblings while my parents were at work.

- During winter break, I found out I was pregnant. Before then, I thought I was pro-life. I had even protested outside of an abortion clinic one time with a group from church when I was in high school. But when I sat down and reviewed my current situation, I felt sorry for myself and the pregnancy. I didn't have any money. I lived in the dorms. There wasn't a permanent other in my life. I had no family nearby. I had dreams of attending medical school after college. And I was a kid. How could I raise a kid? It was six weeks into the pregnancy, and I knew an abortion was the only way to go.

**Molly**—I knew that things would be hard after getting divorced from the man whom I had thought was my soul mate, but I never knew things would be this hard. About two years after having our second child, I was experiencing abnormal vaginal bleeding that just wouldn't stop. I went to see the doctor to figure out why I was bleeding so much, and that's when I found out I had cervical cancer. When I told my husband Frederick, he freaked out. He called me a whore and accused me of cheating on him. He said the only thing that causes cervical cancer is HPV, which he said he doesn't have since he's never had any symptoms. Nothing I said calmed him down, and that's when he left me. Leaving me to raise our two small children on my own while also trying to go through medical treatment. Thankfully, my mom was able to move in and help take care of the kids and the house while I went through treatment. Although treatment seemed to be working alright, I guess it's true what they say that it's a long time before you can consider yourself "cured." After four years seemingly cancer-free, I found out last week that the cancer has come back, but this time it has spread.

- I haven't told anyone. The doctor said that the cancer is very advanced, and that even with aggressive treatment, I have maybe four months. I remember how sick treatment made me feel the first time, and I can't bear that being how my children remember me at the end of my life. I've done a lot of soul searching, and I've made the decision to forego medical treatment. I'd rather enjoy the time I have left with my children, family, and friends, than spend it sick and going through invasive medical treatments that won't do me much good long-term. I've made peace with my decision.

# CHAPTER 52

## Career Counseling Case Study and Letter Project

*Katherine Nordell Fort*

### Course Recommendations

| SOCIAL JUSTICE AND ADVOCACY PRINCIPLES | CORE CACREP STANDARDS | COUNSELING SPECIALIZATION |
|---|---|---|
| ☑ Intersections of Oppression<br>☑ Strategies for Change | ☑ Career Development | ☑ Career Counseling<br>☑ Clinical Mental Health Counseling<br>☑ Student Affairs and College Counseling |

## TOPIC

A case study follow-up letter, culminating the student's understanding of conceptualization, assessment, theory, application, and recommendations utilized in the career counseling process. Students will create an informed consent, conduct a career assessment interview, gather information for a genogram, and discuss the intersecting identities and co-cultures of the client before writing a final letter to the client summarizing assessment results and information gathered with next step recommendations for the client's career exploration process.

## LEARNING OBJECTIVES

As a result of this assignment, students will be able to:

1.  Describe how social, cultural, and political factors influence career decision-making processes (CACREP Professional Identity G.4.d & g; G.2. a., b., & f, G.5 a, b, & c; CACREP Clinical Mental Health Counseling D.5; E.1 & F.3; CACREP Career Counseling E.1,2,4,5).
2.  Identify interrelationships among and between work, family, and other life roles and factors including the role of diversity and gender in career development (CACREP Professional Identity G.4.d & g; G.2. a., b., & f, G.5 a, b, & c; CACREP Clinical Mental Health Counseling D.5; E.1 & F.3; CACREP Career Counseling E.1,2,4,5).
3.  Complete assessment instruments and techniques that are relevant to career planning and decision making (CACREP Professional Identity G.4.b & f).
4.  Understand career counseling processes, techniques, and resources, including those applicable to specific populations (CACREP Professional Identity G.4.d & g; G.2. a., b., & f, G.5 a, b, & c; CACREP Clinical Mental Health Counseling D.5; E.1 & F.3; CACREP Career Counseling E.1,2,4,5).

5. Operationalize career and educational planning, placement, follow-up, and evaluation (CACREP Professional Identity G.4.c & e; CACREP Career Counseling A.3 & 4).

## TARGET POPULATION

Clients for this assignment should identify as different in gender, gender identity, race, ethnicity, sexual orientation, age, ability, or other cultural background, as compared to the student. Students are recommended to choose a participant for this case study from an underserved/underrepresented population in connection to those in need of career counseling at a local mental agency, community college, and/or the student's practicum/internship site. Students completing this activity should be master's level counseling students taking a Career Counseling course.

## GROUP SIZE

16–30 students

## TIME REQUIRED

Four to eight weeks

## SETTING

A Career Counseling course setting, in combination with an on-site interview conducted at a local community mental health agency or community college, or with an internship/practicum client.

## MATERIALS NEEDED

- Access to a formal career counseling assessment, such as the MBTI, Strong Interest Inventory, OR an informal assessment such as a career focused/related card sort (professional card sort or one created by the student for use with this specific client).
- Word processor and ability to deliver a confidential, hard-copy letter back to the client.

## INSTRUCTIONS FOR CONDUCTING ACTIVITY

1. Create an informed consent for completion of a career assessment and information-gathering career interview, to be signed by the client for this case study. Include the parameters of confidentiality, a description of the nature of the assignment, and contact information for the professor (should the client have any questions). Include a space for the client to give signed permission to be audio/video recorded.
2. Choose and conduct an appropriate career assessment (formal or informal) such as the MBTI, Strong Interest Inventory, or card sort.
3. Interview the client and gather information regarding the following:
   a. Work experience, education, and training, recreational and leisure interests and activities, and strengths and obstacles related to work.

    b.  Gender, cultural, and personal issues that may affect this interviewee in his/her career. Include a complete description of the client's identified salient cultures and intersecting identities.

    c.  A family history genogram.

    d.  A career genogram.

4.  Write up an eight-page case summary of the interview, aligning the paper to the preceding listed sections. De-identify the client, use direct quotes from the interview to support your work, and cite any relevant career theories.

    In addition to summarizing the interview sections, discuss the following:

- What were the impacts/implications of the client's cultures, family backgrounds, and intersecting identities on their career history and exploration process? For example, access to education, job search/exploration process, job interviewing process, overall knowledge of career options/access.
- What were the impacts/implications of the client and counselor differences in culture and identity on the career counseling process and therapeutic alliance?

5.  Write a two-page letter to the client, comprising the student's understanding of case study conceptualization, assessment, theory, application, and recommendations utilized in the career counseling process and summarizing the assessment results and information gathered in the interview:

6.  Theorize the client's Holland Code, MBTI results, or other assessment related theoretical considerations. Provide evidence from the interview to support the theory.

7.  Apply other career theories (career stage, personality type, multicultural considerations, identity development formation) that are most relevant to this client. Provide evidence from the interview to support your suggestions.

8.  Develop a career action plan that identifies next steps and suggests homework assignments and appropriate goals for the client moving forward. Include any recommendations for additional assessment, evaluation, or research tools. Be creative!

9.  Submit a copy of the letter to the professor for final approval/recommendations/feedback before providing a copy to the client.

# DISCUSSION

Discuss the prompts listed in the case summary paper as a class, along with the following prompts:

- A self-evaluation of readiness to conduct career assessments.
- Student's comfort with the career counseling process.
- What the student felt that they did well in the assessment, interview, and recommendation process.
- What the student felt they could improve upon in the assessment, interview, and recommendation process.
- What did the student learn from the overall career counseling process?
- What did the student learn in regard to the impact of systems of power, privilege, and oppression and the client's access to and experiences with the education system? The job market?
- What did the student learn in regard to the impact of social justice advocacy in the context of helping their client's career exploration process?
- What are some of the most important steps that counselors can take in facilitating the career exploration process from a social justice advocacy perspective?
- What were the impacts/implications of the client's cultures, family backgrounds, and intersecting identities on their career history and exploration process? For example, access to education, job search/ exploration process, job interviewing process, and overall knowledge of career options/access, and HOW aware was the student to these impacts/issues before working with this client? What has the student learned as a result?

- What were the impacts/implications of the client and counselor differences in culture and identity on the career counseling process and therapeutic alliance, and HOW could the student improve upon this alliance in the future?

## BIBLIOGRAPHY

Gysbers, N. C., Heppner, M. J., & Johnston, J. A. (2014). *Career counseling: Holism, diversity, & strengths* (4th ed.). Boston, MA: Allyn and Bacon.

Hays, P. A. (2008). *Addressing cultural complexities in practice* (2nd ed.). Washington, DC: American Psychological Association.

Swanson, J., & Fouad, N. (2010). *Career theory and practice: Learning through case studies* (3rd ed.). Thousand Oaks, CA: Sage Publications.

# CHAPTER 53

# Using Songs to Teach About Oppression and Privilege

*Charles Edwards*

## Course Recommendations

| SOCIAL JUSTICE AND ADVOCACY PRINCIPLES | CORE CACREP STANDARDS | COUNSELING SPECIALIZATION |
| --- | --- | --- |
| ☑ What Is Social Justice and Advocacy?<br>☑ Social Constructs of Oppression and Privilege | ☑ Group Work<br>☑ Social and Cultural Diversity | ☑ Addiction Counseling<br>☑ Clinical Mental Health Counseling<br>☑ Marriage, Couple, and Family Counseling<br>☑ Student Affairs and College Counseling |

## TOPIC

This activity will serve to heighten students' awareness of social justice issues by looking at its presence in popular music. Students will work in groups to select five songs related to five different types of oppression.

## LEARNING OBJECTIVES

1. Students will develop an increased awareness of social justice issues through popular music.
2. Students will be able to identify specific types of oppression being addressed in different songs.
3. Students will deepen their empathic and listening skills by participating in an experiential activity that involves listening to the song selection of other group members and providing feedback.

## TARGET POPULATION

This activity is suited for demographically diverse graduate counseling students and professional counselors seeking to improve or reinforce their understanding of oppression and privilege.

## GROUP SIZE

This activity is suited for a group of 15–20 participants working in subgroups of four to five.

# TIME REQUIRED

In a class of 15–20 students this activity should take 60–75 minutes. Time may be adjusted based on variations in the number of students. Give an overall time estimate that is needed to complete the activity. State if required time to complete the activity will be altered by group size, number of participants, or participant demographics. Instructor may observe the following time schedule:

Introduction: 5–10 minutes
Group work: 25 minutes
Group presentations: 25–30 minutes
Summary evaluation: 5–10 minutes

# SETTING

This activity is suited for a classroom that is large enough to accommodate 15–20 participants. There should be sufficient space to allow groups of four to five participants to work together. Classrooms/venues should allow participants to easily move into groups and return to their positions for presentation. The size of the group may be adjusted depending on the size of the room and number of participants. Rooms suited for individuals with varying physical disabilities would be ideal.

# MATERIALS NEEDED

Paper and pencil or pen will be needed for this activity. The room should also be equipped with audio visual and online technologies. Participants may be permitted to use cell phones to complete the group activity. Cell phones will need to be put away during presentations.

# INSTRUCTIONS FOR CONDUCTING ACTIVITY

1. Inform students about the topic and objectives of the activity. Provide an overview connection between music, the arts, and social justice. The issues that concern counselors are issues that are of concern to others, and songs provide an outlet for social justice concerns.
2. Instructor will inform students that they will be working in groups of four or five members to brainstorm and identify five songs that they believe best represent five different types of oppression. Let students know that they will be asked to present their songs and talk about their process to the class.
3. The instructor will model examples for the students by selecting and playing a song that she/he associates with a specific type of oppression. The instructor will model the process of selecting the song and why the song was selected, and identify the specific oppression associated with the song. For example, the instructor may talk about "Redemption Song" by Bob Marley, giving reasons for selection, and identify that he/she associates the song with slavery, racism, and colonialism. Beyoncé's "If I Were a Boy" may serve as an example of sexism. The presenter then plays the song with lyrics displayed on a large screen. Students are then asked to reflect on the song, stating their own feelings, thoughts, and associations.
4. Instructor will randomly place students in groups by counting off from one to four or five. All ones, twos, threes, and so on will form working groups. Encourage groups to allow for maximum space between each other to lessen distractions.
5. Ask the groups to begin working; inform them that they will be working for 25 minutes. Let them know that they will use the worksheet provided to identify five songs that address specific types of oppression. Let students know that of these five songs they will be asked to play one for the entire class.
6. Provide students with paper and pen/pencil.

7. Inform students that they may use their cell phones and head phones to assist in completing the task. Inform students that they will need to put away cell phones when presentations begin.

8. Encourage students to work collaboratively, dipping into their reservoirs of songs to complete the task.

9. Provide support to the group as needed. Let students know when they have 10 and 5 minutes left to complete the task.

10. When all groups have completed the task quickly determine the order of presentations.

11. Each group will present their five songs, stating the type of oppression associated with each. Group members will speak about their selection process, feelings, thoughts, and associations. One or two questions or comments may be allowed after each presentation.

12. Lead the entire class into an applause after each group presents.

13. Discussion will follow after all groups have presented. The discussion will focus on students' thoughts, feelings, associations, and other reactions to the presentations. In order to support the discussion the instructor will ask the following questions:
    - What are your thoughts, feelings, and associations regarding the songs presented today?
    - How do the presentations support or deepen your understanding of the nature of oppression faced by specific groups of individuals?

14. Summary and conclusion: thank all the group members for their presentation and emphasize the following points:
    - Social justice, oppression, and multiculturalism are not just constructs found in textbooks; they are real issues that are explored in popular music forms. Music can be conceptual as a tool that can serve to liberate and also to oppress (Clonal & Johnson, 2002). Any given song may also be subjected to multiple interpretations and usages. In your daily consumption of music and songs carefully consider their connections to social, political, and economic realities.
    - Songs that focus on oppression can be useful tools in enhancing our understanding of others, reinforcing our own beliefs in social justice, and supporting our journey toward multicultural competence (Fischlin & Heble, 2003).

## DISCUSSION

Instructor will implement strategies to encourage thought and discussion. Before each presentation group members should be asked to talk about the process involved in selecting their songs and why the songs were selected. Group members should be encouraged to explore thoughts, feelings, and associations related to their selections. Participants will then play one of the songs they feel best represent the specific type of oppression they identified. The song will be played for the entire class with lyrics displayed on large smart board screen.

## BIBLIOGRAPHY

Adams, M., Bell, L. A., & Griffin, P. (Eds.). (1997). *Teaching for diversity and social justice: A sourcebook*. New York: Routledge.

Clonal, M., & Johnson, B. (2002). Killing me softly with his song: An initial investigation into the use of popular music as a tool of oppression. *Popular Music, 21*(1), 27–39.

Fischlin, D., & Heble, A. (2003). *Rebel musics: Human rights, resistant sounds, and the politics of music making* (p. 11). Montreal: Black Rose.

## SUGGESTED BACKGROUND READING

Ratts, M. J., Singh, A. A., Nassar-McMillan, S., Butler, S. K., McCullough, J. R., & Hipolito-Delgado, C. (2015). *Multicultural and social justice counseling competencies*. Alexandria, VA: AMCD.

Schmitz, C., Stakeman, C., & Sisneros, J. (2001). Educating professionals for practice in a multicultural society: Understanding oppression and valuing diversity. *Families in Society: The Journal of Contemporary Social Services, 82*(6), 612–622.

## HANDOUT

# Handout 53.1: Identifying Different Types of Oppression Reflected in Songs

**Instruction**: work in groups of four to five to identify five songs that can be associated with any five different types of oppression. Please provide working definitions for the types of oppression that your group identifies. Note also that associations may be direct or indirect. Song choices may also be protesting, reinforcing, or highlighting a particular type of oppression.

| Type of Oppression (Ism) | Song Choice (Artist and Title) |
|---|---|
| ableism | |
| adultism | |
| ageism | |
| classism | |
| cisgenderism/transphobia | |
| colorism | |
| ethnocentrism | |
| heterosexism | |
| lookism | |
| racism | |
| sexism | |
| sizeism | |
| systemic forms of religious intolerance | |

# CHAPTER 54

# Lifeline

*Erika R. N. Cameron*

## Course Recommendations

| SOCIAL JUSTICE AND ADVOCACY PRINCIPLES | CORE CACREP STANDARDS | COUNSELING SPECIALIZATION |
|---|---|---|
| ☑ What Is Social Justice and Advocacy?<br>☑ Social Constructs of Oppression and Privilege | ☑ Human Growth and Development<br>☑ Social and Cultural Diversity | ☑ Clinical Mental Health Counseling<br>☑ School Counseling |

## TOPIC

Experiencing how privilege and oppression operate in everyday situations

## LEARNING OBJECTIVES

1. Sensitizing students to what life is like for an oppressed group with which they do not personally identify, experiencing how privilege and oppression operate in everyday situations, and observing the coping strategies that oppressed groups utilize when they experience discrimination
2. Utilizing the knowledge of a particular culture to develop and implement culturally appropriate advocacy strategies for a client within a family or community.

## TARGET POPULATION

Counseling students taking a Human Development Course

## GROUP SIZE

15–30 class members

## TIME REQUIRED

Varies according to the number of students; 30–45 minutes

# SETTING

Large classroom

# MATERIALS NEEDED

Name tags, application forms (one with gibberish and one that is readable), pens, complaint forms, and Lysol

# INSTRUCTIONS FOR CONDUCTING ACTIVITY

In this exercise, several students are selected to stay in the classroom before the class begins, while the remaining students are instructed to wait in the hallway until they are called in. The students who stay in the classroom become the workers in three stations (bank, jobs, housing), a sheriff, an escort, a complaints desk attendant, the name tag distributor, and the distributor of the finished letters. The workers are given written instructions with suggestions of what they could say to a participant, depending on his or her name tag, and they are instructed to remain in role and to refrain from informing the participants about the meaning of the letters and colors on the name tags. The name tag distributor (usually the instructor) calls the students into the classroom one at a time. Each student is given a name tag with three letters (symbolizing socioeconomic class, race/ethnicity, and gender) and age, and some of the name tags have a brown, yellow, or red line, which indicates to the worker whether the participant is a Muslim, lesbian/gay man, or person using a wheelchair. The name tag given to a student should provide for a different experience and identity than he or she usually has in life. A white, male, heterosexual student, for example, may receive a name tag that indicates a Black, female lesbian. Participants do not know what their name tags mean or the reasons why they are being treated as they are throughout the game.

The two white male and female upper-income (35–50 years old) participants are escorted to the front of each station, regardless of who is waiting, often getting a mansion, high-status jobs, and vacation homes, and then they are seated in a VIP section, away from the other participants.

Those who end up in "jail" are often low-income persons of color, persons with disabilities, those who are lesbian or gay, or those who are 18–26 years old. They may or may not make it out of jail before the exercise ends.

There may be one or two low-income people over the age of 65 who fail to get past the first station (bank) because they do not understand the gibberish application form that was given to them to get money, which they need for the jobs and housing stations.

Other low-income participants look over at the application the middle-income participants receive and try to answer their forms based on what they can see.

Those without privilege who attempt to file a complaint at the complaint desk may witness the worker crush the complaint form and pretend to throw it away.

A couple of lesbian or gay participants may be seated far away from other participants, and a worker at a station may pretend to spray Lysol on their seat when they vacate it. They may have also been told that they are not suitable for a job that would involve teaching children.

Asian and Hispanic men and women may be asked very slowly and condescendingly if they "speak English."

Participants using a wheelchair or are 65 or older are told by the name tag distributor that they are not to attempt to go anywhere without the escort's assistance, and the workers speak to them very slowly and in a loud voice as if their need to use an assistive device means that they also are deaf or cognitively disabled.

# DISCUSSION

In a fishbowl format. Students who were the "participants" and went through the exercise will discuss their experiences in the ways they were treated. Encourage them to discuss their feelings and how they reacted (or wanted to react). Flip the fishbowl and have the "oppressors" discuss what it was like to treat students differently based on their name tag.

Depending on the stage of life, discussion questions can be tailored: For instance, older adult lifespan development: elder abuse, disabilities, lack of resources available, and utilizing technology could be discussed to heighten students' awareness of how systemic tasks can marginalize individuals who are over the age of 65.

# BIBLIOGRAPHY

Blando, J. (2014). *Counseling older adults*. New York: Routledge.
Johnson, C. V., & Friedman, H. L. (Eds.). (2014). *The praeger handbook of social justice and psychology* (3 vols.). ABC-CLIO.

# SUGGESTED BACKGROUND READING

In the case of graduate counseling students, they would have had the prerequisite human development knowledge about each developmental period and relevant skill processes.

Dilworth-Anderson, P., Pierre, G., & Hilliard, T. S. (2012). Social justice, health disparities, and culture in the care of the elderly. *The Journal of Law, Medicine & Ethics, 40*(1), 26–32.

# SECTION 3

# Social Justice and Advocacy Issues in Specific Counseling Specialty Settings

In section three, educators and supervisors are introduced to activities that promote the social justice and advocacy lens in the different counseling specialties. These chapters will be composed of activities, to be used in the classroom or out in the field, that address the specific knowledge and awareness that are required by counselors to counsel, advocate, or assist in making systemic changes for individuals who have experienced oppression or marginalization in the specialties of Addiction Counseling; Career Counseling; Clinical Mental Health Counseling; Marriage, Couples, and Family Counseling; School Counseling; and Student Affairs and College Counseling.

## ADDICTION COUNSELING

*These activities address issues related to the etiology and treatment of substance use disorders within a social justice and advocacy context. Addictions can also come in various forms such as, but not limited to, illicit drugs, prescription drugs, alcohol, tobacco, caffeine, gambling, or sex. The purposes of these activities are to be able to discuss abuse, addiction, and co-dependence so that this problem can be appropriately addressed with clients and students using social justice applications. The activities will include the intersection of oppression, culture, family and friends, and addictions.*

## CAREER COUNSELING

*These activities address issues related to career/vocational development in the framework of the counseling process and strategies for facilitating optimum development over the lifespan within a social justice and advocacy context. Activities will include awareness surrounding the intersections of cultural oppressive factors impacting and limiting career development and career seeking. In addition, activities will include advocacy tenets to enhance current career programs, individual counseling, and student learning.*

## CLINICAL MENTAL HEALTH COUNSELING

*These activities address the scope and methods of counseling in community and agency settings within a social justice and advocacy context. Practical applications include the development of methods for assessing community needs for counseling services and providing rationales for use of various theoretical approaches in those settings using a social justice paradigm. The activities will focus specifically on the application of social justice community counseling theoretical applications and advocacy problem-solving within the community and agency setting.*

# MARRIAGE, COUPLES, AND FAMILY COUNSELING

*These activities examine concepts of family life cycle, intergenerational patterns, and how these patterns intersect with social inequalities including race, class, gender, and sexuality, when working with clients' relationships within a social justice and advocacy context. Activities will recognize ways in which family history has been influenced by an oppressive system and how professionals and educators can utilize current social justice applications when working with families and relationships.*

# SCHOOL COUNSELING

*These activities provide professionals, students, and clients with an examination of the profession of school counseling within a social justice and advocacy context. Activities will include examination of current oppressive systemic concerns in schools and in education, as well as enhancing advocacy in counseling programs for P–12 students and the national model and standards for school counseling programs. In addition, methods of advocacy to dismantle oppressive factors impacting students in schools P–12 will include a sensitivity to the role of the following intersections: racial, ethnic, cultural, nationality, socioeconomic, family structure, age, gender, sexual orientation, religious and spiritual beliefs, occupation, physical and mental status, and equity issues in school counseling, and will be illuminated with a variety of social justice activities.*

# STUDENT AFFAIRS AND COLLEGE COUNSELING

*These activities examine the theories, skills, and research in college counseling and student services work within a social justice and advocacy context. Activities will include topics within the specialty fields of student affairs, including current and future issues, problems, and trends with a focus on college counseling. Topics will be infused with functions and organizational patterns of student affairs programs, the interaction of the academic and student services areas, and legal and ethical issues, all within an advocacy context.*

# CHAPTER 55

# Passionate Advocacy
## Instilling Advocates Through Poster Presentations

*Azar Karajic Siwiec and Carrie VanMeter*

### Course Recommendations

| SOCIAL JUSTICE AND ADVOCACY PRINCIPLES | CORE CACREP STANDARDS | COUNSELING SPECIALIZATION |
|---|---|---|
| ☑ Strategies for Change | ☑ Social and Cultural Diversity | ☑ Addiction Counseling |
| | | ☑ Career Counseling |
| | | ☑ Clinical Mental Health Counseling |
| | | ☑ Marriage, Couple, and Family Counseling |
| | | ☑ School Counseling |
| | | ☑ Student Affairs and College Counseling |

## TOPIC

Development of advocacy initiatives for counseling students to work with a selected population of their choosing

## LEARNING OBJECTIVES

1. Recognition and development of social justice initiatives
2. Promotion and empowerment of human development
3. Understanding and deeper appreciation of advocacy efforts

## TARGET POPULATION

Master's-level counseling students

## GROUP SIZE

1–20

## TIME REQUIRED

Depending on the size of class, at least 2 hours. Provide 2–3 hours for presentation of all students' advocacy posters followed by group discussion.

## SETTING

A classroom big enough to display all students' posters in a simulated conference setting

## MATERIALS NEEDED

Students will need a poster board to display their advocacy information. Students choose how to display their information. Some choose to display it by printing PowerPoint pages, and others develop their own creative way to present the information. Optional: provide students with evaluation forms to facilitate standardized peer critiques.

## INSTRUCTIONS FOR CONDUCTING ACTIVITY

Students are given the following instructions and made aware of this assignment on the first night of the course.

### Content Directions

1. Identify the setting (school, church, community agency programing, community group, employer, etc.) for which the activity is designed (be specific).
2. Spend time at the location and find out needs of the people attending/living at this selected location.
3. Research the population needs and create an advocacy poster that will reflect two sets of information: anecdotal and research validated.
4. In your poster, describe the target audience (age; educational level; cultural diversity/gender/personal history background as relevant)
5. Provide a detailed, step-by-step description of the advocacy project and details regarding training requirements, materials, time, finances, etc.
6. Address advocacy processes needed to address institutional and social barriers that impede access, equity, and success for clients and how to promote mental health programs.
7. Distinguish individual, couple, family, group, and community strategies for working with and advocating for diverse populations.
8. Be sure to differentiate counselors' roles in developing cultural self-awareness and promoting cultural social justice, advocacy, and conflict resolution.
9. Address counselors' roles in eliminating biases, prejudices, and processes of intentional and unintentional oppression and discrimination.
10. Examine theories and models of individual, cultural, couple, family, and community resilience and discuss them.
11. Distinguish appropriate and effective methods for client advocacy at all levels and the promotion and support of mental health programs.
12. Examine impact of recent public policy on availability and accessibility of MH services.
13. Provide a rationale for the activity. Explain how the project relates to the barriers of treatment and how you aim to address these barriers. (How can you eliminate biases, prejudices, and processes of intentional and unintentional oppression and discrimination?)
14. Discuss resilience aspects of your target population and how can you build on these.

15. Discuss the inherent limitations of the project and suggest why this advocacy project would be beneficial (e.g., advantages).
16. Provide two professional research reference sources (other than the text) that support your project. It is alright if only one piece of the advocacy proposal is supported and not the complete proposal.

**Process Directions**

- The poster must be displayed on the assigned date in the syllabus to consider the assignment completed.
- At times, we may possibly invite other classes taking place that are in our counseling program, so be prepared to discuss this project with peers who may not be as familiar with the topic.
- Creativity is welcome. In the end the expectation is that you will at least prepare between 12–16 PowerPoint slides, which will be attached to the poster boards provided.
- Presenting someone else's project is not accepted.

# DISCUSSION

Describe the process by which the participants will debrief the activity. Include helpful questions or prompts for the participants.

- What was it like putting this presentation together?
- What did you learn about the project?
- What did you learn about the population?
- What did you learn about yourself?
- How possible will it be for you to execute this project (maybe in some modified manner) in an internship? What will you need? How do you make this a success later?

# BIBLIOGRAPHY

Bandura, A. (1997). *Self-efficacy: The exercise of control*. New York: W. H. Freeman.
Council for Accreditation of Counseling and Related Educational Programs. (2009). *CACREP accreditation manual*. Alexandria, VA: Author.
Sue, D. W., Arredondo, P., & McDavis, R. J. (1992). Multicultural competencies/standards: A pressing need. *Journal of Counseling & Development, 70*, 477–486.

# SUGGESTED BACKGROUND READING

Shaules, J. (2007). *Deep culture: The hidden challenges of global living*. Clevedon: Multilingual Matters.
Shaules, J. (2010). *A beginner's guide to the deep culture experience: Beneath the surface*. Boston, MA: Intercultural Press.
Sue, D. W., Arredondo, P., & McDavis, R. J. (1992). Multicultural competencies/standards: A pressing need. *Journal of Counseling & Development, 70*, 477–486.

# CHAPTER 56

# In the Shoes of a Person Struggling With Addiction
## A Game

*Lauren Wilson, Brendon Alaniz, and Dixie Meyer*

## Course Recommendations

| SOCIAL JUSTICE AND ADVOCACY PRINCIPLES | CORE CACREP STANDARDS | COUNSELING SPECIALIZATION |
|---|---|---|
| ☑ Social Constructs of Oppression and Privilege<br>☑ Intersections of Oppression<br>☑ Strategies for Change | ☑ Group Work<br>☑ Helping Relationships<br>☑ Human Growth and Development<br>☑ Social and Cultural Diversity | ☑ Addiction Counseling<br>☑ Clinical Mental Health Counseling<br>☑ Marriage, Couple, and Family Counseling<br>☑ School Counseling<br>☑ Student Affairs and College Counseling |

## TOPIC

This activity asks students to explore their attitudes about addictions by engaging in an interactive simulation game. The goal of the game is to increase understanding about lived experiences of people struggling with addictions to promote attitudes of empathy and social justice and advocacy. The first player to 25 points wins.

## LEARNING OBJECTIVES

The objectives of the activity are to:

1. Increase awareness of the experiences of individuals with addictions from a biopsychosocial-spiritual perspective to increase empathy.
2. Develop a clearer understanding of common day-to-day experiences of someone living with an addiction in various dimensions of life and stages of change, including risk and protective factors.
3. Develop understanding of the social issues associated with addiction and the way to be an advocate.
4. Engage in self-reflection to identify previously held biases, attitudes, stereotypes, or stigmas about people with addictions.

# TARGET POPULATION

The activity can be utilized with a range of educational levels: from high school to graduate students. Educators or trainers may also consider the following audiences or populations:

- Behavioral/mental health providers
- Health care providers (e.g., family physicians, pediatricians, etc.)
- Youth athletic clubs
- Parents
- Churches, spiritual/religious congregations, etc.
- Community/neighborhood associations

# GROUP SIZE

This activity is best executed in groups of two to four people.

# TIME REQUIRED

Dependent on the facilitator's discretion, the game can be played in one sitting or over the course of several meetings until a player reaches 25 points. Following completion of the game, students will engage in a dialogue and spend time journaling about their own and others' simulated life experiences.

# SETTING

This activity can be carried out in classroom or conference room settings where students can be comfortable to gather around the game deck.

# MATERIALS NEEDED

Color printer (compatible for double-sided printing) for game cards, scissors or paper cutter for game cards, paper to record points, and a journal or computerized word document for individual reflections. Prizes (of both meaningful value and pointless necessity) to be administered at the facilitator's discretion. No other materials will be needed. Students and teachers have the freedom to bring in additional materials that may enrich overall dialogue of the experiential activity. For example, documentaries or DVDs about addiction can be powerful. Other examples include guest speakers with specialized experience (e.g., person in recovery, substance abuse counselor, family members, etc.), attending a 12-step meeting, etc.

# INSTRUCTIONS FOR CONDUCTING ACTIVITY

Students pick a random number, and the student with the closest number to the number identified by the instructor will go first in clockwise rotation. Various colors of the cards represent scenarios guided by SAMHSA's 8 Dimensions of Wellness (emotional, environmental, financial, intellectual, occupational, physical, social, and spiritual). Points are designated for each dimension on a spectrum of risk and protective factors, as well as celebratory accomplishments or natural consequences (e.g., prison time or death). Scenarios also represent how motivated a person may be to change, using the Transtheoretical Model (Prochaska & DiClemente, 1982). The objective of the game is to be the first student to 25 points.

After each scenario, the players will have an opportunity to discuss how the situations felt different each time.

## DISCUSSION

The game was developed to help individuals view the dangers associated with continued drug use more realistically. The game simulates what can happen to a person's health/sanity, social support network, self-concept, and financial/legal situation if he or she were to continue abusing drugs. Some observations, discussion dialogue, and journal reflections may include the following topics:

- Identify and discuss the various stages of change represented in the scenarios.
- Identify and discuss the social justice disparities among those who struggle with addiction.
- Identify previous attitudes and beliefs held about individuals struggling with addictions. Identify any attitudes that have changed as a result of the game.
- Identify how risk/protective factors change outcomes for individuals facing addictions.
- Identify how poor health, legal problems, impaired relationships, job losses, withdrawal, and discomfort may trigger relapse.
- Identify ways to implement social justice and advocacy with those who are struggling with addiction.

## BIBLIOGRAPHY

Insel, P., & Roth, W. (2012). *Wellness worksheets*. New York City, NY: McGraw-Hill Companies, Inc. Retrieved from www.integration.samhsa.gov/health-wellness/wellness-strategies/wellness.pdf

Prochaska, J. O., & DiClemente, C. C. (1982). Transtheoretical therapy: Toward a more integrative model of change. *Psychotherapy: Theory, Research & Practice, 19*(3), 276.

Substance Abuse and Mental Health Services Administration (SAMHSA). (2017, October 24). *The eight dimensions of wellness*. Retrieved from www.samhsa.gov/wellness-initiative/eight-dimensions-wellness

Warren, J. A., Hof, K. R., Mcgriff, D., & Morris, L. B. (2012). Five experiential learning activities in addictions education. *Journal of Creativity in Mental Health, 7*(3), 272–288. doi:10.1080/15401383.2012.710172

Youth.gov. (n.d.). *Risk & protective factors*. Retrieved from https://youth.gov/youth-topics/substance-abuse/risk-and-protective-factors-substance-use-abuse-and-dependence

## SUGGESTED BACKGROUND READING

Rollo, T. (2002). *99 days and a get up: A guide to success following release for inmates and their loved ones* (3rd ed.). Dallas, TX: Offender Preparation and Education Network (OPEN), Inc.

Zehr, H. (2002). *The little book of restorative justice*. Intercourse, PA: Good Books.

## HANDOUT

# Handout 56.1: Game Cards

| | |
|---|---|
| Emotional | Emotional |
| Emotional | Emotional |
| Emotional | Emotional |
| Emotional | Emotional |

## Emotional

You have exceptional emotional self-regulation, high self-esteem, good coping skills, and problem-solving skills!

+4

## Emotional

You experienced childhood trauma, insecure parent attachment, parental modeling of drug/alcohol use and constant self-protection from abuse, harm, and fear.

-4

## Emotional

You see a counselor weekly and attend peer support meetings several times a week.

+3

## Emotional

You experienced cold and unresponsive parental behavior, unreliable support and discipline from caregivers, and a severe lack of structure that contributed to your early involvement with addiction.

-3

## Emotional

You have made attempts to repair ruptured relationships with healthy friends and family, although it has been an emotionally slow and strenuous process.

+2

## Emotional

You ran into an old acquaintance who was not a substance abuser and felt terrible for lying, manipulating, and stealing from them.

-2

## Emotional

You find it easy to relax and express your feelings freely, while successfully fighting the urge to use substances to cope with hardships.

+1

## Emotional

You experienced an insecure attachment with caregiver and family of origin issues making current relationships difficult.

-1

BACK

ENVIRONMENT

ENVIRONMENT

ENVIRONMENT

ENVIRONMENT

ENVIRONMENT

ENVIRONMENT

ENVIRONMENT

ENVIRONMENT

### Environment

You feel physically and psychologically safe; away from potential environmental triggers.
+4

### Environment

You live in an impoverished, drug-ridden community with little safety and resources to survive (e.g., food desert, no public transit, militarized policing, etc.)
-4

### Environment

You are engaged and connected in two or more of the following contexts: at school/work, with peers, in athletics, employment, religion, culture, etc.
+3

### Environment

Mainstream medical/health care culture is sometimes impossible to access and few medical providers in the immediate area provide services.
-3

### Environment

Stable, secure attachment to childcare providers/caregivers and regulatory systems that support high quality of care for little ones in the family/extended family.
+2

### Environment

Your parents were heavy substance users, which contributed to lack of adult supervision and poor attachment with caregivers.
-2

### Environment

The local police department has Crisis Intervention Trained (CIT) officers to help specifically with mental health or substance abuse concerns. A relapse crisis occurred, a CIT officer and team of providers helped.
+1

### Environment

You intentionally made plans with an old acquaintance whom you previously used drugs with; however, because of your willingness to change, you explain you could no longer associate with that friend.
-1

BACK

INTELLECTUAL

INTELLECTUAL

INTELLECTUAL

INTELLECTUAL

INTELLECTUAL

INTELLECTUAL

INTELLECTUAL

INTELLECTUAL

## Intellectual

You are aware of the neuroscience of addiction and how it impacts brain functioning and ultimately, behaviors.
+4

## Intellectual

You experience substance-induced psychosis on a daily basis from years of abusing substances and sometimes cannot tell reality from fiction.
-4

## Intellectual

You pursue and retain knowledge, think critically about issues, make sound decisions, identify problems, and find solutions (e.g., common sense, creativity, curiosity).
+3

## Intellectual

Persistent substance abuse has begun damaging your brain, causing symptoms such as poor decision-making, poor memory information and retention, and intense mood swings. This makes maintaining healthy relationships especially challenging.
-3

## Intellectual

You completed secondary schooling as well as obtained some college experience.
+2

## Intellectual

You dropped out of high school.
-2

## Intellectual

After hours of dedication, you have mastered age-appropriate academic skills (math, reading, writing, etc.)
+1

## Intellectual

You were born with a cognitive impairment due to your mother using substances while pregnant.
-1

BACK

PHYSICAL

PHYSICAL

PHYSICAL

PHYSICAL

PHYSICAL

PHYSICAL

PHYSICAL

PHYSICAL

## Physical

You maintain overall physical health and engage in appropriate physical activity five to six days per week (e.g., stamina, strength, flexibility, healthy body composition).
+4

## Physical

Because of an open and infected injection wound site, you have been in the hospital for more than a week and medication assistance to help with withdrawl is not sufficient, so you cannot wait to use again.
-4

## Physical

You do exercises to develop muscular strength and endurance at least twice a week.
+3

## Physical

Relationship guilt and the consistent urge to use again have resulted in major changes in sleeping habits.
-3

## Physical

You've always had a perfectly healthy diet, but never worked out or engaged in much physical activity.
+2

## Physical

You recognize smoking a pack of cigarettes per day has negative health outcomes, but you are not ready to quit.
-2

## Physical

You eat fast food about three times a week, but otherwise try to eat healthy foods.
+1

## Physical

You have a terrible toothache, but access to affordable dental services is impossible.
-1

BACK

SOCIAL

SOCIAL

SOCIAL

SOCIAL

SOCIAL

SOCIAL

SOCIAL

SOCIAL

## Social

You have made an entirely new circle of friends free from addiction to help support you through your recovery.
+4

## Social

You have no contact with family members, and thus no support system because relationships were drastically damaged during the height of your addiction.
-4

## Social

You are engaged and connected in two or more of the following contexts: at school/work, with peers, in athletics, employment, religion, culture, etc.
+3

## Social

Mainstream medical/health care culture is sometimes impossible to access and few medical providers in the immediate area provide services.
-3

## Social

You have a great relationship with your sponsor who helps you abstain from using.
+2

## Social

Your partner asked for a separation because you have chosen to feed your addiction and ignore how it impacts other people in your life.
-2

## Social

For the first time in a long time, you feel welcomed at a family function as you have been making progress in recovery.
+1

## Social

You happen to have an appointment in a community where you previously used drugs and ran into an old buddy who influenced your decision to relapse and use again.
-1

BACK

FINANCIAL

FINANCIAL

FINANCIAL

FINANCIAL

FINANCIAL

FINANCIAL

FINANCIAL

FINANCIAL

## Financial

You have a sense of adult status and future orientation of achievement. You are motivated to become self-sufficient and financially independent.

+4

## Financial

You have stolen guns and engage in identity theft for profits to help feed your addiction.  You are still repaying your financial wrongdoings which will take years to pay off.

-4

## Financial

You were able to save some money to purchase a small gift for someone who means a lot to you.

+3

## Financial

You are thousands of dollars in debt with the court system and still owe monthly court costs.

-3

## Financial

You inherited a substantial amount of money from an extended family member, however, it goes straight to paying off debt.

+2

## Financial

You cannot afford to live independently so you found a roommate. However, they use substances and it's tempting.

-2

## Financial

Despite the hard work, you are slowly making progress repairing your credit score and borrowing eligibility for loans.

+1

## Financial

You have exhausted all natural support systems for temporary loans and choose to steal food from the store.

-1

BACK

OCCUPATIONAL

OCCUPATIONAL

OCCUPATIONAL

OCCUPATIONAL

OCCUPATIONAL

OCCUPATIONAL

OCCUPATIONAL

OCCUPATIONAL

## Occupational

You have found a meaningful career helping people with addictions by sharing lived experiences.
+4

## Occupational

You were fired because of an accident while on the job due to the fact that you were high and someone was badly injured.
-4

## Occupational

You have been employed for over a year with an employer who appreciates your hard work ethic.
+3

## Occupational

The small network of employers in your industry area have heard from references and other connections about your struggles with maintaining employment while being addicted to drugs.
-3

## Occupational

You have been awarded "employee of the month"!
+2

## Occupational

You have taken several aptitude tests for possible job placements, but interviewers continually explain how they are looking for someone with a more expansive skillset and more work history.
-2

## Occupational

You were courageous enough to be honest and forthcoming with a potential employer about past felonies and mistakes. Because you were able to eloquently explain lessons learned from those mistakes, the interviewer hires you for the job!
+1

## Occupational

You have a job interview, but are wondering if the interviewer will ask you about the "felony checkbox" on the application.
-1

BACK

SPIRITUAL

SPIRITUAL

SPIRITUAL

SPIRITUAL

SPIRITUAL

SPIRITUAL

SPIRITUAL

SPIRITUAL

## Spiritual

Your new spiritual congregation is tremendously supportive of your recovery and has extended help in times of crisis.
+4

## Spiritual

Your religious/spiritual belief system and associated social circle have deteriorated beyond recognition because the addiction has ravaged your values. You are no longer connected to this protective factor that has helped you abstain in the past.
-4

## Spiritual

Your journey throughout recovery has helped you develop a set of beliefs, principles, or values that give meaning or purpose to your life. You have developed faith in something beyond yourself (e.g., religious faith, service to others, meditation, etc.).
+3

## Spiritual

You try to get reacquainted with your spiritual circle of support, but face rejection due to hurtful actions done onto others in the past. The rejection triggers a relapse.
-3

## Spiritual

You attended a weekend retreat with your spiritual/religious community, which has strengthened your long-term optimism about living a drug-free lifestyle.
+2

## Spiritual

You hear wind of people gossiping in your spiritual/religious social circle about speculations of your demise regarding addiction. This loss of perceived support is a major trigger, but you resist the urge to use.
-2

## Spiritual

Your new found spiritual practice/religiosity has been a major catalyst that fosters empowerment and devout motivation to stay committed to recovery.
+1

## Spiritual

You consider yourself as an atheist or agnostic, so religious aspects of the Alcoholics Anonymous/Narcotics Anonymous program do not seem to be a good fit.
-1

BACK

CELEBRATE

DEATH

CELEBRATE

DEATH

CELEBRATE

DEATH

CELEBRATE

DEATH

## Death

You were involved in a bad drug deal and ended up getting shot and murdered.
GAME OVER ☹

## Celebrate

You found a partner who is supportive of your recovery and you are engaged to marry.
+4

## Death

While attempting to find drugs for the next fix, you find yourself in the wrong place at the wrong time and are killed by a stray bullet.
GAME OVER ☹

## Celebrate

You are able to afford your first vacation ever and have a great time simply being yourself.
+3

## Death

Your dealer gave you a bad batch of drugs heavily laced with other toxic substances and your body could not handle it, so you perish.
GAME OVER ☹

## Celebrate

You have complied with the terms of your probation and no longer have legal involvement with the justice system.
+2

## Death

Stressors of daily life in recovery became too stressful, so you relapse. Narcan was not available. The amount you previously used was significantly more potent and you overdose and die.
GAME OVER ☹

## Celebrate

Your recovery efforts have been met with such success, you have been asked to be a mentor and sponsor for others who are struggling with addiction.
+1

BACK

ANNIVERSARY

PRISON/JAIL

ANNIVERSARY

PRISON/JAIL

ANNIVERSARY

PRISON/JAIL

ANNIVERSARY

PRISON/JAIL

## Prison/Jail

You got caught with an illegal firearm while trying to buy drugs and will spend four years in jail.
SKIP FOUR TURNS ☹

## Anniversary

You have been clean for ONE year!
+4

## Prison/Jail

You are charged with a three-year sentence for endangering children while using drugs in the same household.
SKIP THREE TURNS ☹

## Anniversary

You have been clean for SIX months!
+3

## Prison/Jail

Money is tight, so you face charges and prison time for intent to distribute.
SKIP TWO TURNS ☹

## Anniversary

You have been clean for THREE months!
+2

## Prison/Jail

You are charged with multiple felonies (i.e., possession, paraphernalia, etc.) while on probation and charged with more prison time.
SKIP ONE TURN ☹

## Anniversary

You have been clean for ONE month!
+1

BACK

# CHAPTER 57

## Don't Judge a Book by Its Cover

*Matthew R. Shupp*

### Course Recommendations

| SOCIAL JUSTICE AND ADVOCACY PRINCIPLES | CORE CACREP STANDARDS | COUNSELING SPECIALIZATION |
|---|---|---|
| ☑ Social Constructs of Oppression and Privilege<br>☑ Intersections of Oppression | ☑ Career Development<br>☑ Group Work<br>☑ Helping Relationships<br>☑ Social and Cultural Diversity | ☑ Clinical Mental Health Counseling<br>☑ School Counseling<br>☑ Student Affairs and College Counseling |

## TOPIC

As the metaphoric title suggests, this activity examines the underpinnings of participants' explicit bias. With a focus on risk taking and personal disclosure, participants will examine the underpinnings of how oppression and privilege have been socially constructed in their lives. By exploring the danger of prejudging the worth or value of someone by outward appearance alone, participants will build strategies to combat bias in their day-to-day interactions.

## LEARNING OBJECTIVES

1. Participants will examine the underpinnings of explicit and implicit bias.
2. Participants will explore their multiple intersecting identities and examine their impact on their worldview.
3. Through self-disclosure, this activity will illuminate the importance of breaking through assumptions in order to examine the complexity of individuals that transcend assumptions and stereotypes.
4. This activity will provide an introduction to deeper discussions on power, privilege, and systematic oppression.

## TARGET POPULATION

This activity is ideal for graduate students in a CACREP-accredited Counseling and Student Affairs preparation program, specifically targeting courses on helping skills, personal growth, and multicultural development. Likewise, this activity is best suited for groups that are in the Performing stage of group development. Conducting this activity in earlier stages may limit its impact due to group skepticism and lack of established trust.

# GROUP SIZE

The ideal group size is 10–12 students. However, the activity can accommodate up to 20 students.

# TIME REQUIRED

The time required is approximately 30–45 minutes. However, an increased group size may increase the time commitment, dependent upon the amount of small group sharing that takes place.

# SETTING

The ideal setting for this activity is a classroom with movable furniture. Facilitators must protect confidentiality and privacy. Therefore, facilitators must be mindful of moveable walls or other space restrictions that may limit confidentiality and privacy and take steps to rectify any concerns that may arise.

# MATERIALS NEEDED

The only materials required are paper and writing utensils, which are typically provided by the participants.

# INSTRUCTIONS FOR CONDUCTING ACTIVITY

The facilitator of the activity should instruct participants to pull out a blank sheet of paper and a writing utensil. At the conclusion of this activity, three separate columns will be created, so it is imperative that participants allow room to readily identify each column.

The following disclaimer should also be shared: "This activity asks you to identify pieces of your identity. As such, you are asked to take a risk and, quite possibly, share intimate and personal aspects of your identity that others may not be aware of or are not readily identifiable to the outside observer. Please lean into this discomfort. If you feel triggered in any way at any particular point during the exercise, please be sure to let me know. This activity is challenging by choice, yet I hope that we will all create a brave space where all of you are willing to take this journey together."

The first prompt is as such: "I want you to list out all of the identities that you believe you belong to or that you find fit. For example, I might identify as male, a professor, a sibling, a son, and an athlete. However, your identities may also run deeper than that, and you may identify as a lover of theater, or an enthusiast of fine wine, or a fan of the original *Star Wars* trilogy, etc. Think critically of all of the pieces that make you uniquely you in this particular time and space. As you think through these identifiers, jot down the word or phrase on your sheet of paper."

The second prompt is as such: "Next, think back on those times when others thrust identities or labels upon you that were meant to hurt or tear you down, those things said where you felt harmed, excluded, or made fun of. Take a moment and create a second list with these negative identifiers. Then, consider the setting or circumstance associated with being marginalized or when the injustice was committed against you. Be sure to make note of these events in this column, as well."

The final prompt is as such: "Finally, think back on those times when others made statements about you that were affirming, statements that built you up and filled your heart with hope. What was said? Take a moment and create a third and final list with these positive affirmations."

Ask students to sit for a moment and personally reflect on the three columns. Then, break students up into groups of three to four. Group size should be limited to this number in order to provide adequate time for each member to share individual lists with the other group members. After 15–20 minutes, ask students to return to the full group. Trigger warning: adherence to group norms is essential given the level of risk involved. Safety is required in order for students to engage in sharing vulnerable pieces of their lived experience.

## DISCUSSION

Once participants return from their small group, conduct a debriefing session. Begin by asking the participants the following questions:

1.  What was it like to see your lists on paper? How did it make you feel?
2.  In your small group discussions, what did you share? Likewise, what did you hear?
3.  What assumptions were made about you (when referencing your second list)? How did you feel when these assumptions became others' primary identifier of you?
4.  What was it like to share your list of validating characteristics? Why was this important to share?
5.  What was it like to self-identify and see the list of your multiple intersecting identities? What might this suggest about you? About others?
6.  From participating in this activity, what new insights have you gained about yourself and others, specifically as they relate to both explicit and implicit bias?
7.  How might individuals' intersecting identities impact their experience and understanding of power, privilege, and systematic oppression?
8.  How might this activity help widen your worldview and the lens through which you view others and the world around you?
9.  What insights have you gained related to the importance of advocating for social justice and inclusion?
10. What are two to three potential action steps you can take to create socially just experiences for others?

## BIBLIOGRAPHY

Pope, R. L., Reynolds, A. L., & Mueller, J. A. (2004). *Multicultural competence in student affairs*. San Francisco: Jossey-Bass.

Pope, R. L., Reynolds, A. L., & Mueller, J. A. (2014). *Creating multicultural change on campus*. San Francisco, CA: Jossey-Bass.

## SUGGESTED BACKGROUND READING

Arminio, J. (2010). Waking up White: What it means to accept your legacy, for better and worse. In M. Adams, W. J. Blumenfeld, C. Castaneda, H. W. Hackman, M. L. Peters, & X. Zuniga (Eds.), *Readings for diversity and social justice* (2nd ed., pp. 125–126). New York: Routledge. (Original work published in 2000).

Arminio, J., Torres, V., & Pope, R. L. (Eds.). (2012). *Why aren't we there yet? Taking personal responsibility for creating an inclusive campus*. Sterling, VA: Stylus.

McIntosh, P. (1989, July/August). White privilege: Unpacking the invisible knapsack. *Peace and Freedom Magazine*, 10–12. Women's International League for Peace and Freedom, Philadelphia, PA.

Shupp, M. (2015, Fall). Becoming a better ally: Reflections from ACPA 2015. *ACPA-College Student Educators International Developments*, *13*(3). Retrieved from www.myacpa.org/developments

**HANDOUT**

# Handout 57.1: Don't Judge a Book by Its Cover Worksheet

| Identities | Negative Labels/Associated Event(s) | Positive Affirmations |
|---|---|---|
|  |  |  |
|  |  |  |
|  |  |  |
|  |  |  |
|  |  |  |
|  |  |  |
|  |  |  |
|  |  |  |
|  |  |  |

New insights gained:

Action plan for creating a more inclusive and welcoming environment for others:

# CHAPTER 58

# Mindful Counseling Advocacy Through Active Campaigning

## *Melissa Odegard-Koester*

### Course Recommendations

| SOCIAL JUSTICE AND ADVOCACY PRINCIPLES | CORE CACREP STANDARDS | COUNSELING SPECIALIZATION |
|---|---|---|
| ☑ Strategies for Change | ☑ Professional Counseling Orientation and Ethical Practices | ☑ Clinical Mental Health Counseling |

## TOPIC

Students will be apprised of current issues that affect clinical mental health counselors and their clients that require advocacy on the professional level. Through this activity, students explore current active campaigns located on the Government Affairs tab at www.counseling.org, familiarize themselves with the current issues, and construct a response they send to their representative and/or senator.

## LEARNING OBJECTIVES

1. Demonstrate knowledge of legislation and government policy relevant to clinical mental health counseling (CACREP, 2016).
2. Identify systemic factors that act as barriers to clients' development and/or access to services (Lewis, Arnold, House, & Toporek, 2003).
3. Demonstrate the ability to influence public policy through constructing a letter to your senator and/or representative that indicates knowledge of the concern and specific recommendations to address the concern.

## TARGET POPULATION

Mental health counseling students working on addressing macro-level advocacy for the profession and their clients

## GROUP SIZE

Flexible, but typically 10–15 counseling students

# TIME REQUIRED

The primary focus of the activity is to get students to do some investigating of current issues, review the current literature to assist them in their recommendations, and respond to their representative/senator. Ideally students would do this individually, but it could be adapted to facilitate in a group setting as well. If done individually, it will take approximately 5 hours (to account for research and literature review reading). If done as a group or an in-class activity, it would need to be adapted so students review research/ literature ahead of time in order to contribute to the discussion and construction of a response to their senator/representative.

# SETTING

The current setting in which this activity is utilized is a Mental Health Systems and Prevention course, which focuses on the professional role of the clinical mental health counselor. Students enrolled in the mental health counseling program are required to take this course following their completion of their Mental Health Counseling Foundations course. The primary focus of this activity meets the CACREP (2016) standards that demonstrate the application components of the clinical mental health specialty (CACREP 2016, Section 5.c.2i & Section 5.c.3.e.). However, this activity could be altered and used for school counselors as well, considering the professional role of school counselor is to advocate for their students on the micro and macro levels.

# MATERIALS NEEDED

The instructor shares the additional readings (referenced later in the chapter) with students in the course and prompts students to read and review prior to completing the activity. The instructor then shares a handout that highlights the instructions for completing the activity and provides a time frame for students to complete the activity. The students will need access to the web, a laptop or mobile device, and approximately 5 hours to complete the activity (includes reading, reviewing current issues, and constructing the response to their representative/senator). There are no foreseen precautions when using these materials.

# INSTRUCTIONS FOR CONDUCTING ACTIVITY

Following your review of the suggested readings for the class, please go to www.counseling.org and click on the Government Affairs tab. Next, review the various drop-down links (e.g., Overview, Documents and Resources, Recent Updates, etc.) Then click the Take Action link and click in the Actions box to review a list of the active issues. Upon your review, select the issue that you believe to be most concerning, and reflect upon what you believe you can do to address the concern. Be sure to consider any additional resources/ citations to support your concerns.

Following your thorough review of the literature and the suggested readings for this activity, you will be constructing a letter to your current district representative or state senator. You will construct a letter, no more than two pages, that highlights your concern and how you hope your representative/senator will consider/address this concern.

You will be graded on the following:

1. Accuracy and your ability to be succinct in your letter.
2. Creative suggestions as to why this particular issue should be of concern for the representative/senator (this will require background research on your representative/senator).

3. Citations support for your concern and your recommendations to address the concern.
4. Indication that you actually emailed your letter (usually you receive some type of generalized confirmation email upon sending your letter). You may copy and paste the email to the bottom of your letter when uploading or take a screen shot and submit.

# DISCUSSION

Following the completion and grading of the activity (I like to provide specific and constructive feedback on their letters first), the following questions will be discussed in class:

1. What were some common themes you noticed as you reviewed the suggested readings and additional supportive literature for this activity?
2. What did you become aware of as you researched the background of your representative/senator?
3. How did you determine which issue was most concerning and took priority in your response to your representative/senator?
4. What citations supported your recommendations for your concern?
5. In what ways is this activity reflective of the importance mental health counselors have in advocating for the profession? Clients?
6. As a result of the activity, how has your knowledge and awareness of legislation and government policy relevant to clinical mental health counseling shifted? Your commitment to addressing these concerns?

# BIBLIOGRAPHY

Council for Accreditation of Counseling and Related Educational Programs. (2016). *CACREP accreditation manual: 2009 standards*. Alexandria, VA: American Counseling Association.

Durfee, A., & Rosenberg, K. (2009). Teaching sensitive issues: Feminist pedagogy and the practice of advocacy-based counseling. *Feminist Teacher, 19*(2), 103–121. doi:10.1353/ftr.0.0047

Lewis, J., Arnold, M., House, R., & Toporek, R. (2003). *Advocacy competency domains*. Alexandria, VA: American Counseling Association.

Talleyrand, R., Chi-Ying Chung, R., & Bemak, F. (2006). Incorporating social justice in counselor training programs. In R. Toporek, L. Gerstein, N. Fouad, G. Roysircar, & T. Israel (Eds.), *Handbook for social justice in counseling psychology: Leadership, vision and action* (pp. 44–58). Thousand Oaks, CA: Sage Publications.

# SUGGESTED BACKGROUND READING

Kiselica, M., & Robison, M. (2001). Bringing advocacy to life: The history, issues, and human dramas of social justice work in counseling. *Journal of Counseling & Development, 79*, 387–397.

Lewis, J., Arnold, M., House, R., & Toporek, R. (2003). *Advocacy competency domains*. Alexandria, VA: American Counseling Association.

Office of Public Policy and Legislation. (2011a). *Effective advocacy with members of congress*. Alexandria, VA: American Counseling Association.

Office of Public Policy and Legislation. (2011b). *The effectiveness of need for professional counseling services*. Alexandria, VA: American Counseling Association.

Office of Public Policy and Legislation. (2011c). *Federal information resources for professional counselors*. Alexandria, VA: American Counseling Association.

# CHAPTER 59

# Guided Imagery on Career-Related Oppression of Clients of Color and Other Marginalized Groups

*Jenny L. Cureton, Victoria Giegerich, and Jennifer L. Murdock Bishop*

## Course Recommendations

| SOCIAL JUSTICE AND ADVOCACY PRINCIPLES | CORE CACREP STANDARDS | COUNSELING SPECIALIZATION |
|---|---|---|
| ☑ Social Constructs of Oppression and Privilege<br>☑ Intersections of Oppression | ☑ Career Development<br>☑ Social and Cultural Diversity | ☑ Career Counseling<br>☑ Clinical Mental Health Counseling<br>☑ School Counseling<br>☑ Student Affairs and College Counseling |

## TOPIC

Guided imagery, sometimes called visualization, can provide counseling professionals with a unique opportunity to experience psychological and physical responses to a potential situation. A guided imagery script that highlights career challenges of marginalized populations prompts participants to view career development needs in ways they may not have before. Guided imagery guidelines are provided to tailor activities to unique work settings and populations.

## LEARNING OBJECTIVES

The goal of the guided imagery activity is to build empathy and insight for career challenges experienced by marginalized populations. The learning objectives are:

1. To increase perspective taking via responses to the activity
2. To address societal concerns and career issues of marginalized populations
3. To elucidate barriers and career resiliency needs during the career/job counseling process with members of a marginalized population

# TARGET POPULATION

This activity is suited for counseling professionals and counselors-in-training of all specialties who address client career concerns. It is also applicable for use in group settings.

# GROUP SIZE

The activity can be conducted with a small or large group of participants, typically ranging from 3–20 participants in order to encourage group processing. It may also be conducted in counseling supervision and related sessions.

# TIME REQUIRED

Introduction and guided imagery: 15 minutes
Process: 15+ minutes
Total: 30+ minutes
On average 15–20 minutes are required to complete the guided imagery script independent of group size. It is important to prepare participants for the activity by providing an introduction to the activity that lasts approximately 5 minutes. Proceeding the activity, the facilitator may take 15 minutes or longer to process the experiences of participants.

# SETTING

The activity should take place in a quiet room free of distractions. Chairs that accommodate all participants should not be restrictive to size or height.

# MATERIALS NEEDED

No additional materials are required beyond the guided imagery script: *Guided Imagery Script: A Job Search Where the Institution Is Racist.*

# INSTRUCTIONS FOR CONDUCTING ACTIVITY

1. Alert your facilitation partner when you are ready to begin and close the door.
2. Ask participants to silence phones and other devices.
3. Read the script in the handout, which begins with a brief description of the activity, alternatives for handling any discomfort, and an invitation for participants to find a comfortable sitting position.
4. Debrief the activity using the discussion prompts.

# DISCUSSION

Suggested questions appear as follows. Facilitators are encouraged to connect participants' responses to career theories and current barriers to employment for clients of color and other populations.

1. What feelings or thoughts did you experience during the guided imagery? What did you notice about your reactions?
2. What was it like when the interview was occurring? What did you want to do?
3. As the person being interviewed in the guided imagery, what did you need most at that time?
4. What thoughts, feelings, or needs did you have when you were not granted the position and returned to work?
5. What was it like for you nearing the end of the imagery: how did you feel? What did you think? What did you want to do? What did you need most?
6. Reflecting on this experience, what meaning does it hold for your work as a counselor?
7. How is power used in the imagery?
8. In what ways was power related to privilege and oppression?
9. If the job seeker in the imagery was your client, how would you demonstrate cross-cultural communication skills to effectively interact with them about this incident?
10. What can a counselor do to address these career-related inequities and discriminatory practices?
11. What gaps do you need to address in your attitudes and beliefs, knowledge, skills, and actions in order to intervene with and for clients on multiple levels? What plan do you have to address them?

# BIBLIOGRAPHY

Anderson, S. K., Peila-Shuster, J. J., & Aragon, A. (2012). Cross cultural career counseling: Ethical issues to consider. *Career Planning and Adult Development Journal, 28*(1), 127–139.

Capodilupo, C. M., & Sue, D. W. (2013). Microaggressions in counseling and psychotherapy. In D. W. Sue & D. Sue (Eds.), *Counseling the culturally diverse: Theory and practice* (pp. 147–174). Hoboken, NJ: John Wiley & Sons, Inc.

Sue, D. W., Lin, A. I., Torino, G. C., Capodilupo, C. M., & Rivera, D. P. (2009). Racial microaggressions and difficult dialogues on race in the classroom. *Cultural Diversity and Ethnic Minority Psychology, 15*(2), 183–190. doi:10.1037/a0014191

# SUGGESTED BACKGROUND READING

Byars-Winston, A. M., & Fouad, N. A. (2006). Metacognition and multicultural competence: Expanding the culturally appropriate career counseling model. *The Career Development Quarterly, 54*(3), 187–201. doi:10.1002/j.2161-0045.2006.tb00151.x

Martz, E. (2001). Expressing counselor empathy through the use of possible selves. *Journal of Employment Counseling, 38*(3), 128–133. doi:10.1002/j.2161-1920.2001.tb00494.x

Nadal, K. L., Griffin, K. E., Wong, Y., & Hamit, S. (2014). The impact of racial microaggressions on mental health: Counseling implications for clients of color. *Journal of Counseling & Development, 92*(1), 57–66. doi:10.1002/j.1556-6676.2014.00130.x

# HANDOUT

## HANDOUT 59.1: GUIDED IMAGERY SCRIPT: A JOB SEARCH WHERE THE INSTITUTION IS RACIST

As many research projects, news reports, and personal accounts have shown, significant barriers remain throughout the job search process for members of oppressed and underrepresented groups. Guided imagery, sometimes called visualization, can provide a unique opportunity to experience psychological and physical responses to a set of potential situations. This allows us to view the needs of a population in ways we might not have done before. This exercise is designed to help people who might not face those barriers to imagine, in some small way, what it may be like for someone who does. For the purpose of this particular imagery, we will mainly focus on job-related oppression based on race and ethnicity. The exercise is not intended to be offensive to any party. If you are not a member of this or another oppressed group, this may allow you to imagine life as someone who is, if even for a short moment. If you are, you are still invited to participate in this exercise. We hope this will help others begin to understand what it may be like to live a while in your shoes.

In a moment, I will ask you to close your eyes. If you are not comfortable doing so, you may decide to participate by simply focusing your eyes on something close by. As with other discussions in graduate counseling courses, it is possible that what I describe may bring discomfort, or stronger feelings. If that happens, I encourage you to simply open your eyes to give yourself a break from the imagery. If, at any time, you decide, however, that you need to stop participating altogether, you can do so. And if you need to step out, my partner for the imagery will be available to speak with you, or to simply alert you when the imagery is over. I will lead a discussion following the activity for any who wish to share. It is very important that you do not talk, whisper, laugh, or make any comments during this guided exercise. If, at any time, you feel uncomfortable, and want to stop, you may. But if you are disruptive (by laughing, making inappropriate comments, or talking in any way), I will signal for you to leave the classroom.

And now we will begin the guided imagery. Get into a position in your seat that is as comfortable as possible. Uncross your legs if you'd like and close your eyes. Find a way of sitting that feels most comfortable. The imagery will last about 15–20 minutes. I will be clear when the imagery is over by cuing you to open your eyes.

For the first minute or two, just concentrate on your breathing. Pay attention to your breath going in and your breath going out. If you notice yourself becoming distracted, gently guide your thoughts back to the image set before you. There is no judgment. Only here and now. And this is a time only for you, when you can let yourself rest for this short period of time. Try to release all your preconceived notions about how the world is, how it works, and who is in it. We are going to go to a different place today, so allow yourself to experience it completely. Be open to what we are going to experience, and try to see things with new eyes and hear things with new ears. Allow yourself to truly be in the place I will describe. Take a deep breath in and out.

And now we are going to another place. In this place, you are the same, exact person you are now: with the same race and ethnicity, same values, likes and dislikes, dreams, achievements. But something is very different. In your mind's eye, imagine a day very much like today. You are sitting in a (workplace conference room/college classroom/session room at a professional conference). The session is just wrapping up, and you begin heading to a Career Fair for a scheduled interview. You have been searching for a new job for quite a while now, and you are very excited about the opportunity to interview.

You arrive at the fair. As you begin walking down the aisle of booths, you tug at the bottom of your suit jacket, straightening it, and take a deep breath to calm your nerves. You see the Job Interview Booth, set up with a small waiting area outside the draperies used to separate a few temporary interview spaces. As you approach the booth, an attendant greets you and asks you to wait while she alerts the interviewer. The attendant returns, glances up and down at what you are wearing, and says enthusiastically, "Wow, you sure look nice for your interview!" You quietly say, "Thanks." After several minutes, the interviewer comes from behind the draperies with his last interviewee, which he pats on the back as he comments, "I will definitely be in touch with you." As the interviewee turns to leave, you notice that not one of these people is from your racial group. Before you have a chance to consider it further, the interviewer leans down to say something under his breath to the attendant. She giggles. He quickly approaches you and shakes your hand hard. He introduces himself, but mispronounces your name. You correct him, and he repeats it. Wrong again. You shrug and say, "Yes, that's fine." The two of you step behind the draperies, where you sit down in simple chairs. The interviewer quickly scans your resume and application while you wait. You remember tweaking your resume for this job, wrestling with which name you should use. No matter how simply it is spelled, it seems most people have problems saying it. This time you'd proudly decided not to use a nickname. As you wait for his first question, you bite your bottom lip, wondering if you made a mistake.

After a few seconds, the interviewer looks up and says, somewhat loudly, "Well you sure do have an impressive resume! Did you use a resume service or did you make this yourself?" You're surprised by the question, but answer simply that you did it yourself. "Hmph!" he says. And the interview begins. "Let's start with me just getting to know you a little, okay? Tell me, are you from here? Or did your family move here?" You are unsure what the point of the question is, but you really want this job so you respond, "Yes, I'm from here." The interviewer continues to ask you questions—some seem to be relevant to the job itself, others you don't find as clear. He asks you about your weaknesses, your attendance at previous jobs, why you would want to work for a company like theirs, and so on. Several times, you are interrupted or stopped short of finishing your answer.

At one point, he looks down at your application again and says, "So, you don't have any criminal background to put on here? And you're legal and everything?" You are almost too shocked to respond at this point. You clearly state, "No, no I don't. And yes, I'm legal," though you're not even sure he's listening. Finally, he stands up and escorts you out of the Job Interview Booth. You walk away, full of feelings and numb all at the same time.

The next day, having returned home from the conference, you are heading out the door for (work/school), when your phone beeps with a new email. It's from the interviewer! You read it quickly: "Thanks again for attending the Career Fair job interview today. It was nice talking to you. Unfortunately, we have decided on another candidate for the position. It is very important to us that our new hires fit well into our company culture. And the person we selected was able to clearly demonstrate a capacity to contribute to the direction we want for the company. Best of luck with your job search. And again, good job on that resume." As you get in your car and start your commute, you remember another time when you felt this way. It was a long time ago. You were in high school, and had asked to talk to your counselor for advice about applying for college. You can still see his face. It was a different color from yours, just like most of the teachers. Staring you straight in the eyes, he said, "I'm not sure you're quite cut out for that yet, are you? I mean most people like you can find a good job after graduation and that'd probably be better anyway. Let's just focus on getting to graduation, okay? That's a hard enough goal as it is!"

You continue your drive to (work/school), mostly on auto-pilot, still tired from the events of the conference. As you walk in the front door and head toward your (office/classroom), some people politely greet you; others barely look up. When you arrive at your desk, you are surprised to find a note! "Welcome back!" it says in typed black letters, but scrawled in red pen underneath is a racial slur. Like a slap in the face, you tell yourself for the millionth time: I have GOT to get (a new job/finish this degree or find a new university).

Take a moment to consider this. Be aware of your thoughts, your feelings, your questions. Really get in touch with how it feels to be in the other person's shoes. Sit quietly and reflect for a little while. In a moment, I'll ask you to open your eyes. Now begin to become aware of what is around you. Feel the floor under your feet, and the seat underneath you. Wiggle your fingers a bit. Please continue to be respectful of those around you. If you haven't already done so, please open your eyes.

# CHAPTER 60

# Uncovering Racial Battle Fatigue
## Understanding the Impact of Everyday Racism

*Monica Boyd-Layne and Kesha Burch*

**Course Recommendations**

| SOCIAL JUSTICE AND ADVOCACY PRINCIPLES | CORE CACREP STANDARDS | COUNSELING SPECIALIZATION |
|---|---|---|
| ☑ Social Constructs of Oppression and Privilege | ☑ Helping Relationships<br>☑ Professional Counseling Orientation and Ethical Practice<br>☑ Social and Cultural Diversity | ☑ Clinical Mental Health Counseling<br>☑ |

## TOPIC

The vignettes contained in this activity demonstrate the impact that everyday racism can have on African American clients in the counseling population. The real-life scenarios and compatible audio/visual links allow participants to simulate the experiential reality of counseling individuals with racial battle fatigue (RBF) and consider appropriate assessment and intervention strategies that are critical to multicultural counseling.

## LEARNING OBJECTIVES

1. Participants will learn to identify psychological stress associated with racism and racialized circumstances, including oppression, microaggression, and trauma at the interpersonal, institutional, and community levels.
2. Participants will exercise critical thinking about interventions with race based psychological stress from the perspective of a counselor, a supervisor, and a counselor educator.
3. Participants will consider the appropriate professional roles and responses that counselors might employ to address social justice issues through the discussion and debrief portion of this activity.

## TARGET POPULATION

The activity stimulates critical thinking from the perspective of a counselor, a supervisor, and a counselor educator. This makes the experiential exercises useful for master's-level clinical mental health counseling students and doctoral-level counselor education students. The discussion questions are designated with an (M) for items most appropriate for master's-level participants, or a (D), which are most appropriate for doctoral-level students.

## GROUP SIZE

The learning from this exercise comes from thoughtful reflection on the questions provided and the subsequent discussion. The activity is appropriate for small groups or large groups of up to 30 participants, and can be adapted for individual or triadic supervision.

## TIME REQUIRED

The suggested time to facilitate this activity using one vignette is 60 minutes. You may choose to facilitate this activity running multiple vignettes concurrently. In this case, please allow 15–20 minutes for each additional vignette. This activity is designed for use with those who have a working knowledge of the concepts of racism, oppression, microaggression, microassault, microinsult, microinvalidation, and racial battle fatigue (see Sue, 2013). If students have not been introduced to these concepts, a list of terms with definitions may be used to familiarize them with ideas that are important to the activity. Please allow additional time to introduce the terms as needed.

## SETTING

This activity can be used in a variety of educational and training settings. It is best suited for master's-level or doctoral-level classroom use for students in clinical mental health counseling, counselor education, or related disciplines. Clinical supervisors may also find this activity useful in either group, triadic, or individual supervision. Facilitators are encouraged to select discussion questions that are most appropriate for their setting or audience.

## MATERIALS NEEDED

The materials needed include an Internet connected device to view video links and a projector to display video clip(s) to a large group, if desired. Participants should have paper and pens available to record notes and responses from small group or large group discussion.

## INSTRUCTIONS FOR CONDUCTING ACTIVITY

The videos that accompany the vignettes depict current events. The subject matter and content of the videos may be uncomfortable to some individuals, because they address racism, violence, and systemic oppression. While the videos show real individuals, the associated vignettes are fictional and do not represent actual persons. Video links are included to simulate the scenarios described in the vignettes.

1. Prior to the activity, make sure students have knowledge of the following terminology, racism, oppression, microaggression, microassault, microinsult, microinvalidation, and racial battle fatigue (see suggested references). Participants should be encouraged to utilize these terms when discussing the video.
2. Decide which of the accompanying vignettes will be used for the activity. Photocopy enough vignettes and discussion questions for each participant.

3. Prepare the video clip and projector, if desired.
4. Review the vignette/video in a large group format. Break large groups of eight or more into smaller groups of three to five participants for small group discussions.
5. Ask participants to consider the discussion questions. Make sure one participant is assigned the recorder for each small group.
6. Have the participants return to the large group to debrief and discuss their responses to the questions.

## DISCUSSION

A core set of queries follows each vignette. The discussion questions address issues of oppression, social justice, and advocacy within the counseling relationship. The exercise guides participants toward perspective taking and supports the integration of basic counseling skills for work with multicultural populations. Each vignette contains scenarios for clients, counselors, and counselor educators.

## BIBLIOGRAPHY

Gladstein, G. A., & Feldstein, J. C. (1983). Using film to increase counselor empathic experiences. *Counselor Education and Supervision, 23*, 125–131.

Guiffrida, D. A., & Douthit, K. Z. (2010). The Black student experience at predominantly White colleges: Implications for school and college counselors. *Journal of Counseling and Development, 88*(3), 311–318.

Sue, D. W., & Sue, D. (2013). *Counseling the culturally diverse: Theory & practice* (6th ed.). New York, NY: John Wiley.

Villalba, J. A., & Redmond, R. E. (2008). Crash: Using a popular film as an experiential learning activity in a multicultural counseling course. *Counselor Education and Supervision, 47*, 264–276.

## SUGGESTED BACKGROUND READING

Hardiman, R., Jackson, B., & Griffin, P. (2007). Conceptual foundations for social justice education. In M. Adams, L. A. Bell, & P. Griffin (Eds.), *Readings for Diversity and Social Justice* (2nd ed.). New York: Routledge.

Ratts, M. J., Singh, A. A., Nassar-McMillan, S., Butler, S. K., & McCullough, J. R. (2016). Multicultural and social justice counseling competencies: Guidelines for the counseling profession. *Journal of Multicultural Counseling and Development, 44*(1), 28–48.

Smith, W. A., Hung, M., & Franklin, J. D. (2011). Racial battle fatigue and the education of black men: Racial microaggressions, societal problems, and environmental stress. *Journal of Negro Education, 80*(1), 63–82.

Smith, W. A., Hung, M., & Franklin, J. D. (2012). Between hope and racial battle fatigue: African American men and race-related stress. *The Journal of Black Masculinity, 2*(1), 35–58.

Sue, D. W., Capodilupo, C. M., Torino, G. C., Bucceri, J. M., Holder, A. M. B., Nadal, K. L., & Esquilin, M. (2007). Racial microaggressions in everyday life: Implications for clinical practice. *American Psychologist, 62*(4), 271–286.

## HANDOUT

# Handout 60.1: A Case of Complicated Grief

## VIGNETTE 1: *A CASE OF COMPLICATED GRIEF*

Sam is a 20-year-old African American cisgender male who lives in Milwaukee, Wisconsin. He has recently lost his brother in an officer involved shooting with the Milwaukee Police Department. A video of Sam went viral where he expresses his emotion about the death of his brother and the violence that besieges his community.

The local funeral home director who handled the slain brother's services referred Sam to a satellite office of a community mental health center that is located in The Boys and Girls Club in Sam's neighborhood. Sam agrees to see a counselor because his family and his girlfriend have noticed that he has been withdrawn and not himself since his brother's death.

Sam meets with Mark, a 26-year-old cisgender male counselor intern. Mark is a master's-level student at Milwaukee State University's clinical mental health counseling program. Mark is also African American. Mark expects to work with Sam on grief issues, but discovers that Sam's depressed mood and hopelessness are as much about his relationship to community violence and response to the same issues that have galvanized the Black Lives Matter movement as they are to the death of his brother. Mark works with Sam, and he begins to question if he is allowed to address race and social justice issues in the counseling relationship. Mark decides to seek supervision from the assigned doctoral-level student supervisor from his counseling program.

Justin, Mark's supervisor, is a 35-year-old white cisgender male. Justin is a third-year doctoral student at Milwaukee State University who has a specialty in trauma and grief. In addition to supervising master's-level interns, Justin also co-teaches the counseling seminar class with Dr. Reynolds. Dr. Reynolds is an associate professor of Clinical Mental Health Counseling. She is a 46-year-old white cisgender woman, considered an ally among faculty and students of color at Milwaukee State University.

> Suggested video: Brother of Black Man Who Was Shot by Police in Milwaukee WI www.youtube.com/
> watch?v=4bWnS43fZqI
> © Boyd-Layne, M. & Burch, K.S.

## QUESTIONS FOR DISCUSSION OF VIGNETTE 1: *A CASE OF COMPLICATED GRIEF*

1.  What do you think Sam the client might be experiencing? (M, D)
2.  What interpersonal factors between the counselor Mark and the client Sam might be relevant to discuss? Why is this important? (M)
3.  Is it likely that Sam and his counselor Mark have had similar experiences? If so, in what ways might that affect the counselor relationship? (M, D)
4.  Is it appropriate for Mark to discuss race and social justice issues while counseling Sam? Why or why not? If you were Mark's supervisor Justin how would you address this concern? (M, D)
5.  How might Mark assist Sam in developing self-advocacy as a tool to address the issues of race and racially motivated violence in the community? (M, D)
6.  What interpersonal factors between Mark the counselor and Justin the supervisor might be relevant to discuss? Why is this important? (M, D)

7.  How might it be helpful for Justin to identify intrapersonal bias related to the social identity of Mark and/or Sam? (M, D)
8.  What type of assignments could Dr. Reynolds include in the seminar class that might assist students to build competency in multicultural social justice? (D)
9.  How would you explain to your students/supervisee the counselor's role in addressing social justice issues both inside and outside of the classroom? (M)
10. What opportunities for advocacy might exist in this scenario? (M, D)
11. Discuss how trauma is often overlooked and sometimes pathologized in African American clients. (M, D)

M = questions best suited for master's-level instruction
D = questions best suited for doctoral-level instruction
© Boyd-Layne, M. & Burch, K.S.

# Handout 60.2: A Case of Mistaken Identity

## VIGNETTE 2: *A CASE OF MISTAKEN "IDENTITY"*

Steve is a 20-year-old African American cisgender male undergraduate student at a predominately white public university in the Midwest. Steve is a pre-med student, and he is stressed with his science courses. Steve's organic chemistry professor suggested he utilize the university counseling center to help with stress management. Steve declined to go to the counseling center because he did not want to take time away from his studies.

Every week Steve spends many hours in the university library. Often, he is there until closing. One evening as Steve entered the library dressed in a hoodie he was stopped by a campus security guard, who accused him of trespassing. Steve did not have his student ID on him, and the security guard denied him access to the library, stating that he "did not look like a student" at the university. This incident caused Steve to feel anger, humiliation, and embarrassment. He went home to sleep it off. The next morning, he decided this was an unfortunate, but isolated incident.

One week later, Steve stopped by the student union and overheard a group of Black students discussing incidents of racism and racial harassment on campus that are similar to his experience. He struck up a conversation with one of the students, who invited Steve to get involved in student demonstrations that will protest the treatment of Black students on campus and raise awareness about Black Lives Matter. Steve declined the invitation to participate in the protest based on his strenuous study schedule, but he was unable to put what he overheard out of his mind.

On the following Saturday, Steve was headed to the library, and he observed a student protest. As he approached the door of the library he experienced the symptoms of a panic attack, which included inability to catch his breath, rapid heartbeat, sweaty palms, and feeling faint. Steve took a seat in the library and decided he would visit the counseling center on Monday.

Mark is a 26-year-old African American cisgender male counseling intern who was assigned to be Steve's counselor. Mark attends a master's-level counseling program in clinical mental health counseling at a neighboring university that is also predominately white. Mark reads Steve's intake folder and is very interested in using CBT to address Steve's symptoms of panic disorder. However, after the fourth session Mark seeks supervision around Steve's increasing focus on racism and belief that the topic of racism should be included as part of the sessions.

Justin, Mark's supervisor, is a 35-year-old white cisgender male. Justin is a third-year doctoral student with a specialty in CBT. In addition to supervising master's-level interns, Justin also co-teaches the counseling seminar class with Dr. Reynolds. Dr. Reynolds is an associate professor of Clinical Mental Health Counseling. She is a 46-year-old white cisgender woman, considered an ally among faculty and students of color.

Suggested video: University of Missouri Student Homecoming Parade Demonstration https://youtu.be/ u6zwnmlzZSQ

## QUESTIONS FOR DISCUSSION OF VIGNETTE 2: *A CASE OF MISTAKEN "IDENTITY"*

1.  What do you think Steve the client might be experiencing? (M, D)
2.  What interpersonal factors between the counselor Mark and the client Steve might be relevant to discuss? Why is this important? (M)
3.  Is it likely that Steve and his counselor Mark have had similar experiences? If so, in what ways might that affect the counselor relationship? (M, D)
4.  Is it appropriate for Mark to discuss race and social justice issues while counseling Steve? Why or why not? If you were Mark's supervisor Justin how would you address this concern? (M, D)
5.  What interpersonal factors between Mark the counselor and Justin the supervisor might be relevant to discuss? Why is this important? (M, D)
6.  How might it be helpful for Justin to identify intrapersonal bias related to the social identity of Mark and/or Steve? (M, D)
7.  What type of assignments could Dr. Reynolds include in the seminar class that might assist students to build competency in multicultural social justice? (D)
8.  How would you explain to your students/supervisee the counselor's role in addressing social justice issues both inside and outside of the classroom? (M)
9.  How might Dr. Reynolds use her position as a faculty member to address the negative experiences students of color have been having on campus? (D)
10.  What opportunities for advocacy might exist in this scenario? (M, D)
11.  Discuss how trauma is often overlooked and sometimes pathologized in African American clients. (M, D)

M = questions best suited for master's-level instruction
D = questions best suited for doctoral-level instruction

# Handout 60.3: A Case of Vicarious Trauma

## VIGNETTE 3: *A CASE OF VICARIOUS TRAUMA*

Raynell is a 25-year-old African American cisgender male who works as a management trainee at Enterprise Rent-a-Car. He holds an associate's degree in business from a community college. He has several close childhood friends who are active within the Black Lives Matter movement, and they keep him updated through social media.

Raynell has had several conversations about the insidiousness of racism and microaggression with his friends. He begins to take notice of incidents that disturb him at his job. For example, a coworker recently told him that she did not "consider him to be Black," because he was "so articulate." On another occasion while having a conversation about possible racist behavior by a customer, Raynell's colleague exclaimed, "I am so over people making everything about race." Raynell's anger finally reached a boiling point, causing an argument when his coworker suggested that affirmative action instead of his qualification was the reason for him being included in the training program. The manager witnessed the argument between Raynell and his coworker, and Raynell was directed to seek counseling for anger management with no consequence given to the white coworker.

Raynell meets with his counselor Mark, a 26-year-old African American cisgender male counselor trainee. Mark attends a master's-level counseling program in clinical mental health counseling at a local university. Raynell is relieved to see Mark, and says during the first session that he knows Mark will understand him.

Justin, Mark's supervisor, is a 35-year-old white cisgender male. Justin is a third-year doctoral student. In addition to supervising master's-level interns, Justin also co-teaches the counseling seminar class with Dr. Reynolds. Dr. Reynolds is an associate professor of Clinical Mental Health Counseling. She is a 46-year-old white cisgender woman, considered an ally among faculty and students of color.

Suggested video: BBC News—Anger After Videos Emerge of Two Fatal Shootings of Black Men by Police https://youtu.be/jR7HqAXdRzc

# QUESTIONS FOR DISCUSSION OF VIGNETTE 3:
## *A CASE OF VICARIOUS TRAUMA*

1.  What do you think Raynell the client might be experiencing? (M, D)
2.  What interpersonal factors between the counselor Mark and the client Raynell might be relevant to discuss? Why is this important? (M)
3.  Is it likely that Raynell and his counselor Mark have had similar experiences? If so, in what ways might that affect the counselor relationship? (M, D)
4.  Is it appropriate for Mark to discuss race and social justice issues while counseling Raynell? Why or why not? If you were Mark's supervisor Justin how would you address this concern? (M, D)
5.  What are the multicultural implications of career counseling that counseling supervisors need to consider? (D)
6.  What interpersonal factors between Mark the counselor and Justin the supervisor might be relevant to discuss? Why is this important? (M, D)
7.  How might it be helpful for Justin to identify intrapersonal bias related to the social identity of Mark and/or Raynell? (M, D)
8.  What type of assignments could Dr. Reynolds include in the seminar class that might assist students to build competency in multicultural social justice? (D)
9.  How would you explain to your students/supervisee the counselor's role in addressing social justice issues both inside and outside of the classroom? (M)
10. What opportunities for advocacy might exist in this scenario? (M, D)
11. Discuss how trauma is often overlooked and sometimes pathologized in African American clients. (M, D)

M = questions best suited for master's-level instruction
D = questions best suited for doctoral-level instruction

# CHAPTER 61

# Using the World Café Method to Understand Counseling Underserved and Homeless Families

*Ana Estrada, Tabitha Tabbert, Rebecca Byler, Lauren Levy, and Wendell J. Callahan*

## Course Recommendations

| SOCIAL JUSTICE AND ADVOCACY PRINCIPLES | CORE CACREP STANDARDS | COUNSELING SPECIALIZATION |
|---|---|---|
| ☑ Social Constructs of Oppression and Privilege<br>☑ Intersections of Oppression<br>☑ Strategies for Change | ☑ Group Work<br>☑ Helping Relationships<br>☑ Social and Cultural Diversity | ☑ Clinical Mental Health Counseling<br>☑ Marriage, Couple, and Family Counseling<br>☑ School Counseling<br>☑ Student Affairs and College Counseling |

## TOPIC

Applying the World Café Method to increase students' awareness and knowledge in counseling underserved populations

## LEARNING OBJECTIVES

Students will:

1. Understand and experience the World Café Method as an effective conversational process that promotes collaborative group learning.
2. Apply the World Café Method to identify the needs of underserved and homeless families.
3. Learn about possible counseling strategies generated by other students in working with underserved and homeless populations.
4. Document their understanding of ways to engage, promote social and economic justice, and provide innovative approaches and counseling strategies to underserved and homeless populations.
5. Participate in a constructive dialogue with the larger group and facilitators of the World Café Method.

# TARGET POPULATION

This activity can be used in a variety of beginning and advanced counseling courses. With regard to counseling underserved and homeless families, this activity can be applied in a Marriage, Couple, and Family Counseling course.

# GROUP SIZE

This activity is ideal for a group size of 20 students, who can join four small groups to begin the process.

# TIME REQUIRED

It is recommended to complete this exercise within an hour to allow for all four rotations and small and large group discussions. Larger groups might need more time for the group discussions. Time required for this activity depends on the group size and the purpose (e.g., questions or discussion points) of the World Café.

# SETTING

This activity can take place in a room large enough for small group rotations such as classrooms and conference rooms.

# MATERIALS NEEDED

Each table should be equipped with markers and poster paper to document group ideas. To help create a café-like atmosphere, markers can be colorful, tables decorated with a vase of flowers, soft music in the background, and coffee and tea can be available.

# INSTRUCTIONS FOR CONDUCTING ACTIVITY

1. Introducing the process:
   a. Begin the World Café by explaining the purpose of the activity, which in this example is to understand how to identify, engage, and generate ideas from the literature and our own experience for counseling underserved and homeless families.
   b. Invite the students to break into small groups at separate tables, and ask each table of students to pick a host. The host will stay at the table while the other students rotate from one table to another.
   c. Inform the students about how much time (e.g., 10 minutes) each table will have to converse before rotating. Notify students that a large group reflection will take place after the small group rotations.
   d. While explaining the process, instructors should strive to create an inviting and comfortable space for their students.
2. Important topics
   In order to focus the small group discussion, the poster sized paper at each table will pose a question to the small groups such as:
   - "What can we learn from the literature about vulnerable and homeless families?"
   - "What ways can be utilized to identify, engage, and motivate vulnerable and homeless families?"

- "What strategies could be used to promote social and economic justice for vulnerable and homeless families?"
- "What innovative approaches and counseling strategies could be utilized with underserved and homeless families?"

3. Small group rotations

   At the end of the first, second, and third conversations, the instructor will ask for a student to remain at the table while the other small group students rotate to the next table and question. The student will summarize the previous discussion and then allow the group to add to the conversation, highlighting areas they agree with and generating new ideas or strategies. Inviting a student to remain at the table and summarize the previous discussion will be repeated after the second and third rounds. It is ideal for different students to remain at the table to capture, summarize, and relay ideas to the entering group of students. This procedure often provides more stimulation and engagement among students.

4. Large group reflection

   After all of the students rotate through each table, each small group will share their main "takeaways," followed by a large group discussion. During the large group reflection, students can share any insights that emerged at any of the tables with the large group.

## DISCUSSION

1. What was your experience of the World Café Method today?
   a. What did you like about this method?
   b. What would you improve or change about this method?
   c. Were you able to effectively share your thoughts about the topics at each table?

## BIBLIOGRAPHY

Stefaniak, J. E., Mi, M., & Afonso, N. (2015). Triangulating perspectives: A needs assessment to develop an outreach program for vulnerable and underserved populations. *Performance Improvement Quarterly*, 28(1), 49–68. doi:10.1002/piq.21186

Steier, F., Mesquita da Silva, F., & Brown, J. (2015). *The world café in action research settings*. Thousand Oaks, CA: Sage Publications.

## SUGGESTED BACKGROUND READING

The World Café Community Foundation. Retrieved from www.theworldcafe.com/

# CHAPTER 62

## Becoming a Reflective Researcher and Social Advocate

*Tiffany J. Peets*

### Course Recommendations

| SOCIAL JUSTICE AND ADVOCACY PRINCIPLES | CORE CACREP STANDARDS | COUNSELING SPECIALIZATION |
|---|---|---|
| ☑ What Is Social Justice and Advocacy? | ☑ Research and Program Evaluation | ☑ Clinical Mental Health Counseling <br> ☑ School Counseling <br> ☑ Student Affairs and College Counseling |

## TOPIC

By utilizing weekly reflective prompts to develop a research journal, counseling graduate students will increase their awareness regarding research issues, social justice, and advocacy.

## LEARNING OBJECTIVES

1. Students will review and assess professional counseling literature for incorporation (or lack thereof) of participants and practices that would benefit or neglect the voices and issues of the underserved/underrepresented.
2. Students will increase their awareness of the issues and limitations in the current counseling research body regarding underserved, underrepresented, and minorities.
3. Students will increase their overall understanding of the role of research in social justice and advocacy.
4. Students will reflect on utilizing research for the purpose of social justice and advocacy.

## TARGET POPULATION

Students in first or second semester in a graduate program for mental health counseling

## GROUP SIZE

24–25 students (divided into groups of four or five students)

# TIME REQUIRED

2–3 hours total of individual reflective journaling throughout six to eight weeks. 20 minutes of small group/roundtable discussion each week during class meeting times.

# SETTING

University library and typical classroom

# MATERIALS NEEDED

- Small notebook and pencil
- Access to computer for research purposes

# INSTRUCTIONS FOR CONDUCTING ACTIVITY

Often upon entering a Counseling graduate program, students may hear the words "social justice" and "advocacy." However, one might question whether or not new graduate students feel that those words can translate these notions into tangible action. Students may ask, "What truly is social justice and how does one advocate for clients or underserved populations?" As a counselor educator that teaches Research in Counseling (an initial required graduate core course), I often have students share their perception that a research course is that of only statistical concepts and understanding professional literature. However, this course can present as an optimal time to activate social justice and advocacy thinking. Indeed, an instructor can easily integrate discussion/assignments that empower students to translate research into tangible advocacy and social justice. This "typical" literature review assignment presents as the ideal opportunity to inspire social justice and advocacy thinking to set a foundation for the students as they move through the graduate counseling curriculum.

### Directions

1. Students will be introduced to the literature review assignment, how to complete a search for professional articles and resources, as well as the overall expectations of writing a graduate-level research paper. Students may choose a topic that is personally interesting, as well as relevant and meaningful to his or her professional development as a school or mental health counselor. Students are advised that a literature review is more than a gathering of previous research on a topic, but also an opportunity to demonstrate one's ability to critically read the literature, identify major points, and synthesize the information into a coherent and thorough manuscript that summarizes what is known about a topic, what are the strengths or weaknesses in the literature/research, and what questions remain. This assignment will be due in eight weeks. A topic and initial search of literature must be completed within the next two weeks.
2. During that same class meeting (with a notebook and journal in hand), students will be given a preliminary prompt for their research journal, "How can research be used to generate and facilitate advocacy?" Students will utilize 10–20 minutes to write during class time. This reflection will NOT be shared with the class or small groups at this time.
3. Students will be advised to bring their journal to class each week for the next six weeks to receive the weekly reflective prompt. Each response will be one handwritten page within the journal. The student is given the upcoming week to complete his or her reflection.

4. Each class meeting moving forward, the students will be divided into groups of four or five members. The small group members will be allowed approximately 20 minutes to dialogue and share recent reflections with one another.

5. Upon the completion of the six weeks, instructor will facilitate a whole class/large group discussion reflecting on the overall journaling experience and lessons learned.

6. Optional cumulative assignment: instructor may include an additional assignment in which the student must augment or conclude their literature review with an Advocacy Action Plan for the clients/students of their specific interest. The action plan must provide related objectives; measurable and specific goals paralleling the timeline of three months, six months, one year, and two years; identified roadblocks; and accessible allies, activators, and resources. The action plan will conclude with a written overall/driving mission or outcome impact statement.

## DISCUSSION

Prompt 1: did you choose a topic of interest that specifically involves or focuses on addressing issues of or further understanding underserved, minority, or marginalized individuals or groups? Why or why not?

Prompt 2: within your topic of choice and the research articles you've reviewed thus far, were marginalized, underserved, or minority populations included in the studies? Were the researchers thoughtful about including diverse individuals as actual research participants? If not, did they address this in the limitations?

Prompt 3: with your topic in mind, were the assessments/instruments being used for data collection reliable and valid for minority and other underrepresented populations? Were the researchers using methods that were mindful about the barriers that may impact minority and other underrepresented groups? If not, what barriers need to be addressed to facilitate more minorities or underserved being involved in this topic/specific research?

Prompt 4: with your topic in mind, how could you utilize this information and your specific research to advocate for the underrepresented? How would you like to evolve or improve the current body of research to be a voice for or better represent the issues of the underserved?

Prompt 5: as you develop as a professional counselor, how do you envision yourself using and/or contributing research to the benefit of your "unheard," underrepresented, or minority students/clients and the overall counseling profession? Have other topics of interest emerged?

Prompt 6: review and reflect on your preliminary entry; how can research be used to generate and facilitate advocacy? Have you expanded your awareness? What was the most important or surprising thing you've discovered?

## BIBLIOGRAPHY

Arthur, N., & Lalande, V. (2008). Diversity and social justice implications for outcome approaches to evaluation. *International Journal for the Advancement of Counseling, 31*(1), 1–16.

Salkind, N. J. (2011). *"Ethical and multicultural issues in research" exploring research* (8th ed.). Upper Saddle River, NJ: Pearson. (course textbook).

# CHAPTER 63

# Career Counseling and Advocacy for Diverse Populations

*Amber Hughes*

## Course Recommendations

| SOCIAL JUSTICE AND ADVOCACY PRINCIPLES | CORE CACREP STANDARDS | COUNSELING SPECIALIZATION |
|---|---|---|
| ☑ Social Constructs of Oppression and Privilege<br>☑ Intersections of Oppression | ☑ Career Development | ☑ Career Counseling<br>☑ Clinical Mental Health Counseling<br>☑ School Counseling<br>☑ Student Affairs and College Counseling |

## TOPIC

Diverse populations have specific career considerations. This activity will give career counseling students an opportunity to research a specific population's career issues and share their findings with classmates.

## LEARNING OBJECTIVES

1. Students will apply their knowledge of career counseling with diverse populations to the case study.
2. Students will investigate current work-related laws and issues impacting the populations represented by their case study.
3. Students will develop a plan for counseling, educating, and advocating for the client in their case study.

## TARGET POPULATION

Graduate students in a career counseling course

## GROUP SIZE

10–30

## TIME REQUIRED

60–90 minutes

## SETTING

This activity can be conducted in any classroom setting. Students will need access to computers to research their case study. A projector may be used for the presentation of findings, though this is not required.

## MATERIALS NEEDED

Computers with Internet access—one per group should be sufficient. Electronic or paper copies of case studies.

## INSTRUCTIONS FOR CONDUCTING ACTIVITY

1. Have students break into small groups (size dependent on the number of students and the number of computers and case studies available).
2. Give each group one case study to use for the activity.
3. Students should read the case study and create a PowerPoint or document to share in an informal presentation to the large group. Their presentation should contain the following:
   a. Cultural considerations for career counseling with this client.
   b. What work and career-related issues are specific to this client's culture?
   c. Are there any relevant laws or rights this individual should know related to career?
   d. How might a career counselor approach career counseling with this client?
   e. Include one question for discussion with your classmates.
4. Once students have responded to each question, bring the groups together into the large group to share the results of their research and discussion.

## DISCUSSION

1. Each group is asked to develop a discussion question based on their case study and findings. Following each group presentation, assist the group members in facilitating a discussion about their case.
2. After all presentations are completed, discuss the activity and topic with the class.
3. What did you learn from this activity?
4. Was there anything that surprised you about your research or your classmates' research on diverse groups and career?
5. Is there anything you find confusing about this information?
6. Do you have any other questions or comments?

## BIBLIOGRAPHY

Busacca, L. A., & Rehfuss, M. C. (Eds.). (2017). *Postmodern career counseling: A handbook of culture, context, and cases.* Hoboken, NJ: John Wiley & Sons.
Duffy, R. D., Blustein, D. L., Diemer, M. A., & Autin, K. L. (2016). The psychology of working theory. *Journal of Counseling Psychology, 63*(2), 127. doi:10.1037/cou0000140
Savickas, M. L. (2011). *Career counseling.* Washington, DC: American Psychological Association.

## SUGGESTED BACKGROUND READING

Chapter or chapters from a career counseling textbook discussing career counseling with diverse populations.

## HANDOUT

# Handout 63.1: Case Studies for Diversity in Career Activity

## CASE 1

Joseph is a 32-year-old gay man living in Mobile, Alabama. He is a mechanical engineer with a degree from Purdue University. Joseph has worked for nearly ten years at a manufacturing company. He would like to advance in his field, but is unsure of how to do so.

Read the case study and create a PowerPoint or document to share in an informal presentation to the large group. Your presentation should contain the following:

a. Cultural considerations for career counseling with this client.
b. What work and career-related issues are specific to this client's culture?
c. Are there any relevant laws or rights this individual should know related to career?
d. How might a career counselor approach career counseling with this client?
e. Include one question for discussion with your classmates.

## CASE 2

Deron is 24 years old and African American. He graduated from high school and joined the National Guard. His unit was deployed three times in the past five years. Deron works construction as a day laborer making $10 an hour. He still lives with his parents because he can't afford a place of his own. Deron wants more out of life, but doesn't know what or how to get it.

Read the case study and create a PowerPoint or document to share in an informal presentation to the large group. Your presentation should contain the following:

a. Cultural considerations for career counseling with this client.
b. What work and career-related issues are specific to this client's culture?
c. Are there any relevant laws or rights this individual should know related to career?
d. How might a career counselor approach career counseling with this client?
e. Include one question for discussion with your classmates.

## CASE 3

Rabia is a 20-year-old woman from Afghanistan. She immigrated to the U.S. with her parents when she was 15. She lives in rural southwest Virginia. Rabia graduated from high school and is attending the local community college. She struggles with her studies because English is her second language, and she's only been speaking it for five years. Rabia is considering dropping out of school, but is worried she won't be able to find a job without a degree.

Read the case study and create a PowerPoint or document to share in an informal presentation to the large group. Your presentation should contain the following:

a. Cultural considerations for career counseling with this client.

b.  What work and career-related issues are specific to this client's culture?
c.  Are there any relevant laws or rights this individual should know related to career?
d.  How might a career counselor approach career counseling with this client?
e.  Include one question for discussion with your classmates.

# CASE 4

Richard is a 45-year-old deaf man. He has been working as an accountant for his family's firm since he graduated from college 20 years ago. Richard recently met a woman he would like to marry. Unfortunately, she lives several hours from him and cannot move as she has kids in high school. Richard is fine with moving to her area, but is concerned about finding a job. He has never had to apply for jobs, interview, and discuss his disability with employers before since he has always worked with family.

Read the case study and create a PowerPoint or document to share in an informal presentation to the large group. Your presentation should contain the following:

a.  Cultural considerations for career counseling with this client.
b.  What work and career-related issues are specific to this client's culture?
c.  Are there any relevant laws or rights this individual should know related to career?
d.  How might a career counselor approach career counseling with this client?
e.  Include one question for discussion with your classmates.

# CASE 5

Susan is a 35-year-old account executive for a large marketing company. She is extremely successful in her career, having been recently promoted. Susan is also pregnant with her second child. She works 50+ hours per week and hates her job. She wants to change careers for something that would require her to work less and that would be less stressful. However, she is afraid of making a drastic change in her career at this point.

Read the case study and create a PowerPoint or document to share in an informal presentation to the large group. Your presentation should contain the following:

a.  Cultural considerations for career counseling with this client.
b.  What work and career-related issues are specific to this client's culture?
c.  Are there any relevant laws or rights this individual should know related to career?
d.  How might a career counselor approach career counseling with this client?
e.  Include one question for discussion with your classmates.

# CHAPTER 64

## Enhancing the Development of Counselors-in-Training
### The Use of Experiential Activities to Cultivate Multicultural Social Justice Counseling Competencies in Group Supervision

*Jennifer E. Beebe and Kristine M. Augustyniak*

### Course Recommendations

| SOCIAL JUSTICE AND ADVOCACY PRINCIPLES | CORE CACREP STANDARDS | COUNSELING SPECIALIZATION |
|---|---|---|
| ☑ What Is Social Justice and Advocacy? | ☑ Group Work<br>☑ Helping Relationships<br>☑ Social and Cultural Diversity | ☑ Addiction Counseling<br>☑ Clinical Mental Health Counseling<br>☑ Marriage, Couple, and Family Counseling<br>☑ School Counseling<br>☑ Student Affairs and College Counseling |

## TOPIC

The purpose of this experiential activity is to facilitate the self-awareness of counselors-in-training regarding their attitudes, beliefs, assumptions, biases, and self-awareness related to their role as developing clinicians. This activity will help students examine their worldviews and identify areas of growth and strength.

## LEARNING OBJECTIVES

1. Supervisees/students will examine the developmental domains identified in the multicultural and social justice counseling competencies (MSJCC) (Ratts, Singh, Nassar-McMillian, Butler, & Rafferty, 2016). For instance, (a) counselor self-awareness, (b) client worldview, (c) the counseling relationship, (d) counseling advocacy and interventions (Ratts et al., 2016).
2. Supervisees/students will identify goals (e.g., attitudes, beliefs, knowledge, skills, and actions) for personal and professional development related to the MSJCC (Ratts et al., 2016).
3. Supervisees/students will identify areas of growth related to their clinical development (e.g., values, beliefs, biases).

4. Supervisees/students will have an increased understanding of how the intersections of their personal development and worldview can impact the counseling relationship.

## TARGET POPULATION

Graduate students or supervisees in a master's-level counseling program. This activity may be used in an introductory counseling class, social justice course, or practicum or internship.

## GROUP SIZE

10–12 students

## TIME REQUIRED

60–90 minutes

## SETTING

This activity can be conducted in a classroom setting; however, a smaller setting is ideal. For example, this activity can be utilized in group supervision in a seminar setting.

## MATERIALS NEEDED

The professor will instruct students to bring two to three (depending on class size) items to class that represent their worldview. A worldview is defined as perception of self, others, values, and the world (Young, 2013). Examples of items include a jar of spaghetti sauce, doctoral hood, and child's shoe.

## INSTRUCTIONS FOR CONDUCTING ACTIVITY

This activity has been adapted from an activity entitled Worldview Box by Young (2013).

### Activity Steps

1. Participants will display their items on a table. The professor will begin the activity in order to provide a model for the students. The professor will share the items. For example, possible items may be a doctoral hood, child's shoe, and jar of spaghetti sauce.
2. The individual to the left of the participant will interpret the possible meaning that each of the items has to the individual.
3. After the interpretation, the individual will share the actual meaning of the items with the group and how they reflect their worldview. The instructor may model this activity by providing a personal example. For example, I have selected my daughter's shoe to represent the importance of being a positive role model for my young daughters. The small shoe is a reminder to me that I am responsible to teach them healthy ways to live, love, and be in the world. I have the awesome challenge of teaching them how to navigate stressful situations, develop healthy coping strategies, appreciate the value of hard work, passion, and strength. The shoe reminds me of the power of vicarious learning and the important role that I have as a Mom. Thus, the actual meaning is the importance of being a Mom and the insight that my daughters will walk in my shoes.

4. Using the model demonstrated by the leader, students will take turns identifying the possible meanings and then sharing the actual meaning with the group. The order in which group members share their experiences is irrelevant.
5. Processing: after everyone has shared their items, we will process the values, beliefs, and assumptions/biases and how these impact the perception of people and events. In particular, we will discuss how these impact the counseling relationship.
6. Following the activity, the professor may prompt processing with questions such as:
   a. What was the experience like for you?
   b. What were some of the assumptions/biases or values that you made when you first examined the items brought in by your peers?
   c. How can we translate this experience to be useful for our role as counselors-in-training?
7. The professor will hand out the multicultural and social justice counseling competencies framework (Ratts et al., 2016). As a class students will examine the framework and review the following:
   a. Supervisees/students will examine the developmental domains identified in the MSJCC (Ratts et al., 2016). For instance, (a) counselor self-awareness, (b) client worldview, (c) the counseling relationship, (d) counseling advocacy and interventions (Ratts et al., 2016).
   b. Supervisees/students will identify goals (e.g., attitudes and beliefs, knowledge, skills, and actions) for personal and professional development related to the MSJCC (Ratts et al., 2016).
   c. Supervisees/students will have an increased understanding of how the intersections of their development and personal worldview can impact the counseling relationship.
8. The professor will encourage the synthesis of the activity by prompting with the following questions:
   a. What was the experience like for you?
   b. What were some of the assumptions/biases or values that you made when you first examined the items brought in by your peers?
   c. How do our identity and personal experiences impact our ability to connect with our clients?
   d. How do your personal experiences, diverse characteristics, and intersection of identities (e.g., gender, race/ethnicity, ability, etc.) impact your role as a professional counselor?
   e. How can we translate this experience to be useful for our role as counselors-in-training?

## DISCUSSION

As 21st century counselor educators, facilitating multicultural and social justice counseling competencies (MSJCC) among counselors-in-training is a critical component of training. As a result, we aim to cultivate opportunities for students to challenge their assumptions and evaluate their personal experiences and diverse characteristics and intersection of identities (e.g., gender, race/ethnicity, ability, etc.) (Ratts et al., 2016) as they relate to their development as professional counselors. The use of experiential activities during group supervision can be an effective strategy to foster multicultural and social justice competencies among counselors-in-training.

The purpose of this experiential activity is to examine counselors-in-training attitudes, beliefs, and self-awareness related to others' worldviews. This activity explored the counselor's self-awareness as it relates to their assumptions, values, and biases related to others' worldview. A counselor's worldview (perception of self, others, and the world) and values are important factors during the process of becoming a professional counselor. Supervisors would benefit from knowing the tenets of the MSJCC and should have an understanding of the conceptual framework (e.g., Ratts et al., 2016).

## BIBLIOGRAPHY

Ratts, M. J., Singh, A. A., Nassar-McMillan, S., Butler, K., & McCullough, J. R. (2016). Multicultural and social justice counseling competencies: Guidelines for the counseling profession. *Journal of Multicultural Counseling and Development, 44*, 28–48. doi:10.1002/jmcd.12305
Young, E. M. (2013). *Learning the art of helping: Building blocks and techniques* (5th ed.). NJ: Prentice Hall.

## SUGGESTED BACKGROUND READING

Ratts, M. J., Singh, A. A., Nassar-McMillan, S., Butler, K., & McCullough, J. R. (2016). Multicultural and social justice counseling competencies: Guidelines for the counseling profession. *Journal of Multicultural Counseling and Development, 44*, 28–48. doi:10.1002/jmcd.12305

Ratts, M. J., Toporek, R. L., & Lewis, J. A. (2010). *ACA advocacy competencies: A social justice framework for counselors.* Alexandria, VA: American Counseling Association.

Sue, D. W., Arrendondo, P., & McDavis, R. J. (1992). Multicultural counseling competencies and standards: A call to the profession. *Journal of Multicultural Counseling and Development, 20*, 64–88. doi:10.1002.j.2161-1912.1192.tb00564.x

# CHAPTER 65

# Refugee Scavenger Hunt

*Mary-Anne Joseph and DeAnna Henderson*

## Course Recommendations

| SOCIAL JUSTICE AND ADVOCACY PRINCIPLES | CORE CACREP STANDARDS | COUNSELING SPECIALIZATION |
|---|---|---|
| ☑ What Is Social Justice and Advocacy? <br> ☑ Intersections of Oppression <br> ☑ Strategies for Change | ☑ Human Growth and Development <br> ☑ Professional Counseling Orientation and Ethical Practice <br> ☑ Social and Cultural Diversity | ☑ Career Counseling <br> ☑ Clinical Mental Health Counseling <br> ☑ Marriage, Couple, and Family Counseling |

## TOPIC

This activity is intended to assist students in developing a working knowledge of community resources available to assist refugee clientele who are working to establish a new life in a new country.

## LEARNING OBJECTIVES

- To assist participants in learning about the challenges faced by refugees who are restarting their lives in a new country
- To assist participants in developing a working knowledge of community resources available to refugees
- To assist participants in learning how to develop an active plan of service to assist clientele who are a part of a refugee population

## TARGET POPULATION

This activity is suited for counseling students and/or counselor trainees.

## GROUP SIZE

This activity is well suited for groups of 8–12 participants.

## TIME REQUIRED

This activity takes approximately 45–60 minutes. The length of time needed to complete the activity may e impacted by the number of members in the group.

# SETTING

This activity should be completed in a computer lab where each student has access to a computer with Internet access. The activity can also be completed in a classroom setting if students have access to Internet resources.

# MATERIALS NEEDED

12–16 pens/pencils and sheets of paper for each participant in the group. 12–16 computers, one computer for each participant in the group. 12–16 note cards for hints (housing, employment, counseling, education). Three to four case scenarios of refugee clientele.

# INSTRUCTIONS FOR CONDUCTING ACTIVITY

1.  Break participants into small groups of three to four members.
2.  Provide each small group with a copy of a different case scenario.
3.  Provide each small group with one note card that contains a clue to aide them in locating the first resource to assist their client.
4.  Ask the participants to write the name of the resource and a brief description of the services provided by the resource on the back of the note card.
5.  Inform the small groups that they have 10 minutes to solve each clue.
6.  Once the resources and its description have been placed on the back of the note card, participants are to return the note card to the instructor for confirmation of accuracy prior to the 10-minute deadline.
7.  If the resource provided by the small group is accurate, the small group is to be provided with a second clue. This process is to be repeated until all clues have been solved by the small group. Small groups will earn 5 points for solving each clue with the use of one hint.
8.  If the resource is incorrect students are provided a second clue to aide in leading the small group in identifying the accurate resource. Participants may receive a maximum of three clues to assist them in identifying the appropriate community resource to assist their client. After the first clue the small group loses 2 points for every additional clue needed to identify the resource.
9.  Once all small groups have successfully completed the scavenger hunt the winning small group is to be presented with an academic prize to be selected by the instructor.

# DISCUSSION

*   Ask each small group to present its case scenario to the entire group.
*   After presenting its case scenario to the entire group, ask each small group to present its service plan/resources to the entire group.
*   Describe the process by which the participants will debrief the activity. Include helpful questions or prompts for the participants.

# BIBLIOGRAPHY

Bigot, A., Blok, L., Boelaert, M., Chartier, Y., Corijn, P., Davis, A., & Griekspoor, A. (1997). *Refugee health: An approach to emergency situation*. London: Macmillan.

Griffiths, D. J., Sigona, N., & Zetter, R. (2005). Refugee community organizations and dispersal: Networks, resources and social capital: Policy Press. *Journal of Ethnic & Migration Studies, 32*(5), 881–898. doi:10.1080/13691830600704529

Jacobsen, K. (1996). Factors influencing the policy responses of host governments to mass refugee influxes. *International Migration Review, 30*(3), 655–678.

# SUGGESTED BACKGROUND READING

Bigot, A., Blok, L., Boelaert, M., Chartier, Y., Corijn, P., Davis, A., & Griekspoor, A. (1997). *Refugee health: An approach to emergency situations*. London: MacMillan.

Griffiths, D. J., Sigona, N., & Zetter, R. (2005). Refugee community organizations and dispersal: Networks, resources and social capital: Policy Press. *Journal of Ethnic & Migration Studies, 32*(5), 881–898. doi:10.1080/13691830600704529

Jacobsen, K. (1996). Factors influencing the policy responses of host governments to mass refugee influxes. *International Migration Review, 30*(3), 655–678.

## HANDOUT

# Handout 65.1: Refugee Scavenger Hunt

## THE CASE OF SOMALI REFUGEES

A family of five Somali refugees is referred to your agency, and you receive the case. The family includes a father and a mother and three small children: a 3-year-old daughter, and two sons ages 6 and 8. The political unrest in Somalia led the Abdi family to flee and seek political asylum. Since arriving in America, the family has encountered several challenges. The father needs to find a job, learn English, and ensure his children are enrolled in school.

The family arrived in Columbus, Ohio, after a lengthy transition and does not have relatives nearby. The closet relatives are in Charlotte, North Carolina. Prior to fleeing, Mr. Abdi had a successful small business and is looking to find employment that is equal to or at a higher level. However, Mr. Abdi is having difficulty in finding employment. Many of the employers seem to be fearful of him and look at him strangely. He thought he overheard someone say he was a "terrorist." He is becoming frustrated with the lack of respect for his experience and has begun to drink in excess. He also frequently yells at his wife and children.

The family arrives to your agency seeking assistance with employment, food, housing, and education for the children. What public resources would you recommend for the Abdi family?

## THE CASE OF IRANIAN REFUGEES

Afari Darvish, a widow and mother of two, is fleeing Iran due to her collaboration with the American soldiers in educating females. Her husband has already been killed by Afghan soldiers due to his role in the education of females. Afari has two young daughters, and she feels strongly about them receiving an education. She has fled her home country and arrived in Los Angeles, California, with her two teenage daughters. Afari is self-taught and needs a job to support her two teenage daughters, who speak little English. The family arrives to your agency seeking assistance with employment, housing, and enrolling the teens into school. What public resources would you recommend for the Darvish family?

# CHAPTER 66

# Career Counseling
## Special Populations Group Presentation

*Katherine Nordell Fort*

## Course Recommendations

| SOCIAL JUSTICE AND ADVOCACY PRINCIPLES | CORE CACREP STANDARDS | COUNSELING SPECIALIZATION |
|---|---|---|
| ☑ Intersections of Oppression<br>☑ Strategies for Change | ☑ Career Development<br>☑ Social and Cultural Diversity | ☑ Career Counseling<br>☑ Clinical Mental Health Counseling<br>☑ Student Affairs and College Counseling |

## TOPIC

Students will form groups for a presentation focusing on a specific career-related issue/concern in relation to an underserved/underrepresented population of their choice. Groups will conduct 30–45 minute presentations and create a two-page handout detailing specific career issues, concerns, and challenges of this population and will provide local resources connected to that population.

## LEARNING OBJECTIVES

1. Describe how social, cultural, and political factors influence career decision-making processes (CACREP Professional Identity G.4.d & g; G.2. a, b, & f, G.5 a, b, & c; CACREP Clinical Mental Health Counseling D.5; E.1 & F.3; CACREP Career Counseling E.1, 2, 4, 5).
2. Identify interrelationships among and between work, family, and other life roles and factors including the role of diversity and gender in career development (CACREP Professional Identity G.4.d & g; G.2. a, b, & f, G.5 a, b, & c; CACREP Clinical Mental Health Counseling D.5; E.1 & F.3; CACREP Career Counseling E.1, 2, 4, 5).
3. Understand career counseling processes, techniques, and resources, including those applicable to specific populations (CACREP Professional Identity G.4.d & g; G.2. a, b, & f, G.5 a, b, & c; CACREP Clinical Mental Health Counseling D.5; E.1 & F.3; CACREP Career Counseling E.1, 2, 4, 5).

## TARGET POPULATION

ster's in Counseling students taking a Career Counseling course.

## GROUP SIZE

Two to four students per group

## TIME REQUIRED

Two weeks for research and preparation; 30–45 minutes per presentation

## SETTING

Career Counseling course

## MATERIALS NEEDED

Internet, PowerPoint, word processor

## INSTRUCTIONS FOR CONDUCTING ACTIVITY

1. Students will form groups of two to four members based on their interests in working with a specific underserved/underrepresented population.
2. Students should then focus on a specific career-related issue/concern in relation to this population.
3. Students should then conduct research on this career issue/concern connecting to academic journal articles, appropriate career counseling theories, and local and national resources and statistics.
4. Groups will conduct 30–45 minute presentations educating their peers on this particular issue and population.
5. Finally, groups should create a two-page handout detailing the specific career issue(s), concern(s), and challenge(s) in regard to this population and will provide local and national resources connected to that population.

## DISCUSSION

- What career issues are unique to specific underserved/underrepresented populations?
- What can counselors do to improve their work when approaching these issues with clients from this population?
- How is this population impacted by systems of power, privilege, and oppression within the education system? The job search process? The job market?
- What can counselors do to practice social justice advocacy in the context of helping those in this population with the career exploration process?
- What further education/awareness is needed to better serve this population?
- What future research could be conducted to better inform counselors of issues specific to this population?

## BIBLIOGRAPHY

Gysbers, N. C., Heppner, M. J., & Johnston, J. A. (2014). *Career counseling: Holism, diversity, & strengths* (4th ed.). Boston, MA: Allyn and Bacon.

Swanson, J., & Fouad, N. (2010). *Career theory and practice: Learning through case studies* (3rd ed.). Thousand Oaks, CA: Sage Publications.

# CHAPTER 67

# "I Am . . ." Character Strengths Mandala for Understanding Strengths and Making Change

*Ana Estrada, Lauren Levy, Tabitha Tabbert, Rebecca Byler, and Wendell J. Callahan*

## Course Recommendations

| SOCIAL JUSTICE AND ADVOCACY PRINCIPLES | CORE CACREP STANDARDS | COUNSELING SPECIALIZATION |
|---|---|---|
| ☑ Social Constructs of Oppression and Privilege<br>☑ Intersections of Oppression<br>☑ Strategies for Change | ☑ Group Work<br>☑ Helping Relationships<br>☑ Social and Cultural Diversity | ☑ Clinical Mental Health Counseling<br>☑ Marriage, Couple, and Family Counseling<br>☑ School Counseling<br>☑ Student Affairs and College Counseling |

## TOPIC

The "I am . . ." Character Strengths Mandala is an activity that helps students become conversant in their strengths and explore ways to utilize these strengths to assist with social justice issues (e.g., poverty, racism, sexism). This activity can also be utilized with counseling clients to help them focus on their own strengths and promote a positive sense of self.

## LEARNING OBJECTIVES

1. Increase students' awareness of their character strengths.
2. Facilitate conversation among students about ways to utilize their strengths to advocate for others and assist with social justice issues.
3. Encourage students to think critically about ways to apply their strengths to advocate for a specific social justice issue.
4. Allow students to understand and experience an intervention that can be utilized when working in a counseling setting to reveal strengths and promote a positive sense of self for marginalized clients.

## TARGET POPULATION

This activity is appropriate for students in any beginning or advanced counseling course (e.g., school, addictions, marriage, and family counseling) with a social justice element.

## GROUP SIZE

It is recommended that this activity be carried out in a class with no more than 30 students to enhance the depth of the discussion following the activity.

## TIME REQUIRED

At least 60 minutes should be allotted to complete this activity and its corresponding discussion.

## SETTING

This activity can take place in any classroom setting.

## MATERIALS NEEDED

- One "I am . . ." Mandala template per participant
- One Character Strengths Menu per participant
  - Adaptation: the words listed in the Character Strengths Menu can be adjusted depending on the demographics of the participating students and the focus of the counseling class in which the activity is carried out.
- Table(s) or another hard surface
- Chairs for students to sit on while they work
- At least one writing utensil for each participant (pencil, pen, or other)
- Optional: craft supplies/additional writing utensils (markers, crayons, colored pencils) to decorate mandalas

## INSTRUCTIONS FOR CONDUCTING ACTIVITY

1. Ask students to reflect on current social justice issues and select a single issue they are passionate about. You may consider providing students with examples relevant to the focus of the class (5 minutes).
2. Hand out "I am . . ." Mandala and Character Strengths Menu to students (2 minutes).
3. Explain to students that this activity can be utilized in a therapeutic setting when working with clients from marginalized groups to promote a positive sense of self and focus the client on their strengths (5 minutes).
   - Adaptation: depending on the focus of your class, you may consider explaining how this could benefit marginalized clients within the context of the course material. (e.g., in an addictions course, you may consider explaining how this could benefit marginalized clients struggling with substance abuse).
4. Ask students to identify character strengths from the Character Strengths Menu that represent them (10 minutes).

5. Ask students to fill in each wedge of the "I am . . ." Mandala template with the character strengths they selected (5 minutes).
6. Optional: provide time for students to decorate the empty space surrounding the mandala as they wish. You may prompt them to decorate the space in a way that illustrates their identity or their social justice interests (additional 10–15 minutes).
7. Ask students to write down ways they can utilize their character strengths to assist with the social justice issue they selected at the beginning of the activity (10 minutes).
8. Provide students time to share about their mandalas either in pairs, in small groups, or as a whole depending on the class size, setting, and student demographics. When students share, they should say, "I am . . ." before each character strength they selected. Larger class sizes should be broken into smaller groups or pairs to share during this portion of the activity (10–15 minutes).
9. Lead a debrief with the entire class using the suggested prompts or an adaptation of the following suggested prompts. Adaptations can be made to fit the specific focus of your course (15–20 minutes).

## DISCUSSION

Students should debrief this activity as a whole. Helpful prompts to the group may include:

1. What was it like for you to identify personal strengths for yourself during this activity?
2. What did you like or dislike about this activity?
   a. Do you see yourself using this activity with your clients in the future?
   b. If so, in what scenarios?
   c. If necessary, how could you adapt this activity when working with different clients?
3. How could you utilize your character strengths to advocate for others, including marginalized clients?
4. How could you utilize the strengths you identified in this exercise to take action on the social justice issue you selected at the beginning of this activity?
5. What is one item from the list you created that you can do this week to assist with the social justice issue you selected?

## BIBLIOGRAPHY

Estrada, A. U. (2013). *Character strengths menu*. Unpublished manuscript. University of San Diego.
Estrada, A. U., Abercrombie, J., Lippman, C., & Martinez, M. (2016, July). *Positive psychological interventions with immigrant youth*. Workshop presented at the annual meeting of the American Mental Health Counselors Association (AMHCA), New Orleans, LA.
Lopez, S. J., Teramoto-Pedrotti, J., & Snyder, C. R. (Eds.). (2015). *Positive psychology: The scientific and practical explorations of human strengths* (3rd ed.). Thousand Oaks, CA: Sage Publications.
Lyubormirsky, S. (2007). *The how of happiness: A new approach to getting the life you want*. New York: Penguin Books.
[Untitled illustration of an "I am" Mandala]. Retrieved September 14, 2017 from www.pinterest.com/pin/101612535316158894/

**HANDOUT**

# Handout 67.1: "I Am . . ." Mandala

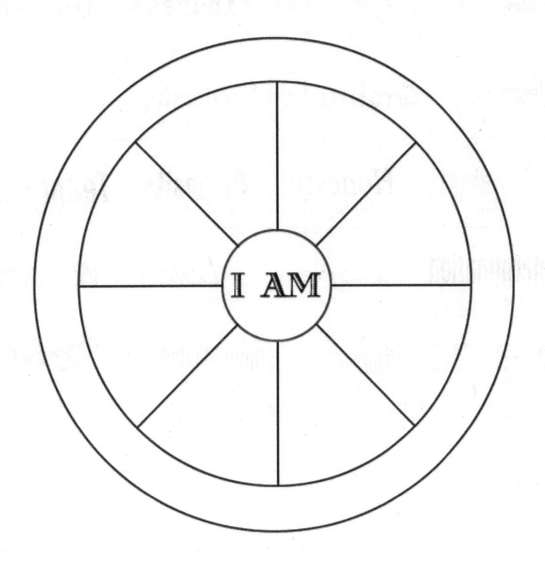

# Handout 67.2: Character Strengths Menu

| *Appreciation for Beauty*<br>~awe, wonder | Forgiveness<br>~mercy, giving another chance | **Kindness**<br>~nice, generous | SELF-CONTROL<br>~cautious, modest, disciplined |
|---|---|---|---|
| Bravery<br>~courage | Gratitude<br>~thankful, considerate | Leadership<br>~group representative | Social Intelligence<br>~social skills |
| Creativity<br>~originality | Honesty<br>~true with self and others | Curiosity<br>~love to learn and discover | Teamwork<br>~loyalty, citizenship |
| Determination<br>~hard working | Hope<br>~optimism | Love<br>~caring for those who care for you | Wisdom<br>~sense, insight |
| FAIRNESS<br>~justice, equality | Humor<br>~playful | Open Mindedness<br>~seeling all sides of an issue | Zest<br>~excitement, energy |

# CHAPTER 68

# Peer to Peer Ecological Systems Diagrams

*James H. Castillo*

## Course Recommendations

| SOCIAL JUSTICE AND ADVOCACY PRINCIPLES | CORE CACREP STANDARDS | COUNSELING SPECIALIZATION |
|---|---|---|
| ☑ What Is Social Justice and Advocacy? <br> ☑ Social Constructs of Oppression and Privilege | ☑ Group Work <br> ☑ Helping Relationships <br> ☑ Human Growth and Development <br> ☑ Social and Cultural Diversity | ☑ Addiction Counseling <br> ☑ Clinical Mental Health Counseling <br> ☑ Marriage, Couple, and Family Counseling <br> ☑ School Counseling <br> ☑ Student Affairs and College Counseling |

## TOPIC

Using ecological theory to cultivate trainee and client awareness of environmental influencers of individual development

## LEARNING OBJECTIVES

1. Understand Bronfenbrenner's (1979) Ecological Systems Theory. Ecological systems describe a set of nested structures where the developing person interacts within their environment. The systems are organized in four circles within each other. From the innermost to outermost, the systems are the microsystem, mesosystem, exosystem, and macrosystem. Bronfenbrenner described the microsystem as the relationships and connections made between an individual and persons or objects in their present setting (e.g., family members, friends, workplace, school, etc.). The mesosystem is the interconnectedness of microsystems or the ways in which situations interrelate (e.g., how an individual's family and school community communicate). The exosystem involves one or more settings that an individual is not directly involved with, but does impact the individual (e.g., mass media, social service system, educational systems, etc.). The macrosystem is described as the generalized patterns or overarching patterns of ideology and/or culture within a given society (e.g., democracy, white privilege, systematic oppression, etc.).
2. Identify two areas within each ecological system (i.e., microsystem, mesosystem, exosystem, and macrosystem) that have positively and negatively impacted their engagement in society. For example, an individual may share, within their microsystem, the relationships with their peers at graduate school.

However, their relationships with immediate family members are less supportive and bring about anxiety, which is an example of a negative influence.
3. Be able to utilize this activity with individuals in counseling settings to empower and heighten awareness of ecological systems and acknowledge/validate the lived experiences of others.

## TARGET POPULATION

Counselors and supervisors-in-training at the master's or doctoral level

## GROUP SIZE

This activity may be utilized in groups of all sizes. A counselor or supervisor may utilize this activity individually or in a dyad. A counselor educator may utilize this activity in a class by having students complete and share with a partner. Additionally, this activity may be completed as an individual assignment, then brought to a class or group to share with peers.

## TIME REQUIRED

Time will vary depending on the number of students that need to present; however, with 15 students this activity may be completed in 45 minutes.

## SETTING

This activity may be completed in a classroom, conference room, or equivalent space that offers counselors and/or supervisors-in-training appropriate space to draw. This activity may also be completed online by having students create the document electronically and engage in a discussion using a discussion board feature on a learning management system.

## MATERIALS NEEDED

Each student will need:

1. A blank white sheet of 8 ½" × 11" computer paper
2. Colored pencils/markers

## INSTRUCTIONS FOR CONDUCTING ACTIVITY

1. At the start of the activity, the instructor will ensure that all individuals have paper and access to colored pencils/markers.
2. To begin, the instructor will say, "Today we are going to further our understanding and utilization of ecological systems in counseling and/or supervisory settings. First, take 2–3 minutes to create your own ecological systems map. Be sure to include all systems (i.e., microsystem, mesosystem, exosystem, macrosystem)."

3. After 2 minutes the instructor continues, "Now that you have your ecological systems outlined, identify at least two components within each system that have impacted your engagement in society. Be sure to identify components within each system that represent positive and negative impacts."
4. The instructor will continue, for example, by stating, "Within the microsystem, you might list your graduate school cohort and your immediate family if these systems influence how you engage in society day to day. Perhaps you are very close to your graduate cohort as you spend many hours studying and connecting on the stress of graduate life! You feel your cohort is supportive and you wouldn't be able to finish this program without them! At the same time, your immediate family relationship is more strained because you have a volatile relationship with an older sibling. This relationship, on the other hand, creates a lot of stress in your life, and some days it is really overwhelming. At the macrosystem level, you might highlight the freedom to vote and democracy as positive cultural ideologies in this country. But at the same time, you recognize a social injustice. As a member of a marginalized group, you highlight systemic oppression as creating greater challenges for individuals to access quality education, medical care, and employment with livable wages when compared to members of privileged groups."
5. "Take 10 minutes to work your way around each of the ecological systems to identify positive and negative influences within each system specific to your life."
6. After 10 minutes, "Now, turn to a partner and exchange maps. Take 2 minutes to attend to the influences your peer has identified."
7. After 2 minutes, "Now that you have reviewed the system of a peer, share with one another similarities and differences. Acknowledge and validate their experiences as they may be different from your own. From a social justice perspective, how do you and your partner make meaning from your ecological similarities and differences?"
8. "Take 10 minutes to engage in this reflective and collaborative discussion."
9. Following the 10 minutes the instructor shifts to formal discussion and processing.

## DISCUSSION

1. "Let's come back to a larger group now that you've all had an opportunity to reflect on your own ecological system and that of a peer. Let's go around and hear from each pair about their experiences."
2. To a student: "What was most salient to you from reading the map of _____? What common areas, if any, were there between your maps? What areas were different? What was most meaningful to each of you in this experience? What meaning or understanding did you make of your maps and the experiences each of you have had? How has your knowledge about societal issues, beliefs, values, and worldviews been shaped by the events and/or relationships within your ecological systems? Within your partners' systems? How does understanding your ecological system prepare you to be a social justice advocate for your client? In areas where you and a peer had different experiences, how did you come to understand their experiences?"
3. Additional questions to connect the activity with social justice advocacy and counseling: "As counselors and advocates, how might this activity assist us in our work with clients/supervisees?" "In what ways could the experiences and relationships as outlined in your ecological system impact your counseling relationships?"

## BIBLIOGRAPHY

Bronfenbrenner, U. (1979). *The ecology of human development: Experiments by nature and design.* Cambridge: Harvard University Press.
Murphy, J. W., Pardeck, J. T., & Callaghan, K. A. (1988). The ecological model, holism, and socially sensitive counseling. *International Journal of Adolescence and Youth, 1*(2), 173–184. doi:10.1080/02673843.1988.9747634
Neville, H. A., & Mobley, M. (2001). Social identities in contexts: An ecological model of multicultural counseling psychology processes. *The Counseling Psychologist, 29*(4), 471–486. doi:10.1177/0011000001294001

# CHAPTER 69

# The Use of Role Playing to Promote Self-Advocacy With Parents Faced With Homelessness

*Ana Estrada, Rebecca Byler, Lauren Levy, Tabitha Tabbert, and Wendell J. Callahan*

## Course Recommendations

| SOCIAL JUSTICE AND ADVOCACY PRINCIPLES | CORE CACREP STANDARDS | COUNSELING SPECIALIZATION |
|---|---|---|
| ☑ Social Constructs of Oppression and Privilege<br>☑ Intersections of Oppression<br>☑ Strategies for Change | ☑ Group Work<br>☑ Helping Relationships<br>☑ Social and Cultural Diversity | ☑ Clinical Mental Health Counseling<br>☑ Marriage, Couple, and Family Counseling<br>☑ School Counseling<br>☑ Student Affairs and College Counseling |

## TOPIC

Building the capacity of parents who are homeless to advocate for family resources

## LEARNING OBJECTIVES

Students will:

1. Engage more effectively in self-advocacy.
2. Develop a stronger sense of the strengths and contributions they bring to a negotiation process.
3. Generate and consider several existing resources or solutions to address a problematic situation.
4. Increase their ability to define a specific and realistic request for resources or for change in a situation.
5. Value themselves throughout the negotiating process.

## TARGET POPULATION

This activity is specifically developed to assist students in developing their counseling skills in advocating for vulnerable and marginalized populations. It can be used in a variety of beginning and advanced counseling courses, as well as being applied in a Marriage, Couple, and Family Counseling course.

# GROUP SIZE

This activity is ideal for a group size of 20 students who can join into two groups of ten. Within the groups, two individuals will roleplay the scenario, while the other students observe. The students will then discuss and reflect on what they noticed. This activity can also be a space for small group reflection, with four groups of five, or for large group discussion, with the rest of the class as observers. Group size is up to the discretion of the instructor.

# TIME REQUIRED

Time needed for this activity depends on the size of the group. Each roleplay can take up to 10 minutes, which includes the time for reflection.

# SETTING

This activity can take place in a room large enough to accommodate 20 students such as classrooms and conference rooms.

# MATERIALS NEEDED

The instructor will prepare scenarios for the group to roleplay and problem solve based on members' input. Examples in this group can involve new and uncomfortable scenarios such as feelings of oppression, racism, groups that are stigmatized, an individual struggling to acculturate to the environment, and an individual in a low SES group.

# INSTRUCTIONS FOR CONDUCTING ACTIVITY

1. **Introduce the Process to Participants:** outline the following steps.
2. **Query the Group for Scenarios:** it is important to ask the group to generate three to four scenarios they (might) encounter and for which they would benefit from learning more about ways to negotiate and advocate for themselves and their families.
3. **Observe First Roleplay:** during the meeting, group members are instructed to observe group facilitators roleplay a difficult scenario that requires self-advocacy.
4. **Feedback on First Roleplay:** after the group members have observed the roleplay they will provide feedback including their reactions to the roleplay and suggestions for alternative ways of responding to the situation.
5. **Engage as Actors in Second Roleplay:** a second roleplay will be conducted with group members taking the lead roles with a facilitator. The second roleplay will also focus on confronting and negotiating an uncomfortable situation in a calm and clear manner. This roleplay will be followed by a similar debrief as in step 3.

# DISCUSSION

Group members will come together and reflect on the following questions from their role/perspective as an observer or actor in the roleplay:

- What did you observe in the roleplays?
- What did you *like* about how the actors advocated for themselves or their families?
- What would you do differently?
- What other solutions do you suggest?
- Are these strategies you might apply in a similar situation?

# BIBLIOGRAPHY

Doron, I. (2007). Court of ethics: Teaching ethics and ageing by means of role-playing. *Educational Gerontology*, *33*(9), 737–758. doi:10.1080/03601270701364479

Krain, M., & Shadle, C. J. (2006). Starving for knowledge: An active learning approach to teaching about world hunger. *International Studies Perspectives*, *7*(1), 51–66. doi:10.1111/j.1528-3577.2006.00230.x

# CHAPTER 70

## Thought Bubble Biases

*Sara Haas and Eric Dafoe*

### Course Recommendations

| SOCIAL JUSTICE AND ADVOCACY PRINCIPLES | CORE CACREP STANDARDS | COUNSELING SPECIALIZATION |
|---|---|---|
| ☑ Social Constructs of Oppression and Privilege<br>☑ Intersections of Oppression<br>☑ Strategies for Change | ☑ Group Work<br>☑ Helping Relationships<br>☑ Social and Cultural Diversity | ☑ Clinical Mental Health Counseling<br>☑ Marriage, Couple, and Family Counseling<br>☑ School Counseling<br>☑ Student Affairs and College Counseling |

## TOPIC

The primary focus of the activity is to raise awareness on how cross-cultural biases and preconceived views impair counselors' effectiveness with clients.

## LEARNING OBJECTIVES

- Counselors-in-training will understand the impact their biases have on the client-counselor relationship.
- Counselor-in-training will explore ways to advocate for their clients.
- Counselors-in-training will be able to utilize this activity with other professionals such as school teachers.

## TARGET POPULATION

The target population is school counselors-in-training, but the activity could be utilized for any counselors-in-training.

## GROUP SIZE

Should have at least ten participants, but the activity was created for a class size of 15 to 25 students.

## TIME REQUIRED

Activity typically takes 45 minutes, which includes time for discussion following the activity.

## SETTING

The classroom should have a well-established sense of emotional safety prior to beginning this activity. The authors recommend using this activity mid-semester. This activity should take place in a room with a door to support a higher level of vulnerability. Because the activity is designed for counselors-in-training, the picture in the handout will need a wall or other surface on which to adhere it for classroom display.

## MATERIALS NEEDED

• One thought bubble per participant (two per each participant if there are less than 20 participants)
• Markers for each participant to write with
• Scissors for each participant to cut out thought bubbles
• Tape to secure the thought bubbles
• A printed picture of a child for the wall, preferably on paper 11" × 17" or larger. If the activity is utilized in a counseling class not focused on children, the picture may be switched with an adult picture.

## INSTRUCTIONS FOR CONDUCTING ACTIVITY

1. Prior to the activity, print out a picture of a child from a diverse background on 11" × 17" paper.
2. Tape the picture on the front wall of the classroom.
3. Begin a class discussion related to the internal thoughts that occur when we see someone who appears the same or different from the participant.
4. Ask each student to write one personal or societal reaction related to a cultural bias in the provided thought bubble she or he had when looking at the picture.
5. Once the students have written in the thought bubble, ask them to cut out the bubble.
6. Ask them to tape the thought bubble on top of the child in a space not occupied by another bubble.
7. Once the child is almost fully covered with thought bubbles, the discussion begins.

## DISCUSSION

Begin the discussion by asking about the activity and using the following discussion questions if appropriate: how much of the picture of the child is hidden by thought bubbles? Are you able to see the person of the child when she/he/they are concealed by biases? How do cultural biases affect the child's experience of school? How do the internal thoughts we have negatively influence our views of this child? What is the effect of these thought bubble biases on how we might support or provide interventions for this student? How might a teacher's biases affect the way we work with a student like in the picture? How do these biases influence students before they even step foot into a school? How might oppressive acts endured by the family have an impact on the student? What are some forms of advocacy to explore to combat these oppressive acts?

Once the instructor has connected the discussion around the image of the child, the discussion then focuses on the counselor-in-training's own biases and/or oppressive experiences. Offer the following questions if appropriate: as a school-aged child, what was the impact of others' biases on you? Did you behave or act differently because of these biases? How do cultural biases you experienced as a child have an effect on you as an adult? Consider your impact on others: what thought bubble biases have you had in the past month? Now that you have a burgeoning awareness around this, how can you change your own thought bubble biases? In what ways can you assist others in changing their thought bubble biases?

# BIBLIOGRAPHY

Boysen, G. A. (2010). Integrating implicit bias into counselor education. *Counselor Education and Supervision, 49*(4), 210–227.

Chung, R., & Bernak, F. (2002). The relationship of culture and empathy in cross-cultural counseling. *Journal of Counseling and Development, 80*(2), 154–159.

# SUGGESTED BACKGROUND READING

Anderson, K. L. (2010). *Culturally considerate school counseling: Helping without bias.* Thousand Oaks, CA: Corwin Press.

Sue, D. W., & Sue, D. (2013). *Counseling the culturally diverse: Theory and practice* (5th ed.). Hoboken, NJ: John Wiley.

# HANDOUT

## Handout 70.1: Thought Bubbles

# CHAPTER 71

## Other Side of the Tracks

*Andy Felton*

### Course Recommendations

| SOCIAL JUSTICE AND ADVOCACY PRINCIPLES | CORE CACREP STANDARDS | COUNSELING SPECIALIZATION |
|---|---|---|
| ☑ What Is Social Justice and Advocacy?<br>☑ Social Constructs of Oppression and Privilege<br>☑ Intersections of Oppression | ☑ Group Work<br>☑ Helping Relationships<br>☑ Human Growth and Development<br>☑ Professional Counseling Orientation and Ethical Practice<br>☑ Social and Cultural Diversity | ☑ Clinical Mental Health Counseling<br>☑ Marriage, Couple, and Family Counseling<br>☑ School Counseling<br>☑ Student Affairs and College Counseling |

## TOPIC

The point of this program is to create an environment where participants examine their feelings and gain some exposure associated with being in the minority or majority group while examining categories of diversity.

## LEARNING OBJECTIVES

1. To increase participants' awareness of their own personal biases and prejudices
2. To increase understanding about oppression and experiences of those being oppressed
3. To explore methods of working with individuals facing forms of oppression and work toward social justice

## TARGET POPULATION

Counselors-in-training and established helping professionals working with others

## GROUP SIZE

10–30 people

# TIME REQUIRED

60–90 minutes, depending on size of group and number of words you choose to use for the activity

# SETTING

This activity can be conducted in a classroom/conference room. You will want enough space for everyone to be able to stand in a single file line as well as circle up in a group for debriefing/processing.

# MATERIALS NEEDED

For this activity, you will need four pieces of colored paper (e.g., one red, one yellow, one orange, and one pink sheet). However many participants you have, you will need slips (one-quarter the standard sheet size) of paper that correspond with the four big sheets you are using (e.g., if you have 15 participants, you will need 15 red, 15 yellow, 15 orange, and 15 pink slips). Each participant will need a writing utensil and a surface (wall or table) to write on at each station. Scotch or painting tape that can be put on the floor and wall is also needed.

# INSTRUCTIONS FOR CONDUCTING ACTIVITY

1. Place two pieces of tape, at least 3 feet in length, to make "tracks" parallel to one another on the floor about 1 or 2 feet apart.
2. On each full sheet of paper list four demographics (can do more if you like; e.g., red sheet: heterosexual, Christian, African American, person with a physical disability; yellow sheet: homosexual*, Muslim, Caucasian, person with a mental disability; etc.). These will be your different stations.
3. Arrange (tape to wall or place on table) the stations around the room and have the matching colored slips available at each station. Be sure to have the full sheets with demographic words covered so participants cannot read what is on the paper until instructed to do so.
4. As participants enter the room tell them to set their belongings down and assign them a color to begin so approximately one-quarter of the participants will begin at each station. Be sure to tell them not to look at the sheet until you tell them to begin.
5. Instruct the participants to pick up a writing utensil and the corresponding slip of paper.
6. Inform participants that there are four words (or however many you wrote) at each station. They will be expected to write the first three words that come to mind for each word on the list, so they should have a total of 12 words on their slip of paper.
7. On your signal, participants will be given 60 seconds to write anonymously three adjectives for each word on the list (again a total of 12 adjectives). Remind them that it is supposed to be the first adjectives that come to mind.
8. After the 60 seconds are complete, individuals will place their responses face down in a pile and rotate clockwise to the next station.
9. Participants will repeat steps 7 and 8 until each group has gone to each station.
10. After each group has made the full rotation, the facilitator will instruct everyone to line up in a single file on one piece of tape, on one "track." Everyone will be facing the other piece of tape, "track," on the floor. The facilitator will collect all responses from around the room. Be sure to keep all slips organized by matching colors.

* Editor note: the term "homosexual" was intentionally used by the author for purposes related to this activity. If you are concerned to use this term for this activity, an option is to use more inclusive terminology including, but not limited to, lesbian, gay, bisexual, transgender, queer, intersexual, asexual, pansexual, polygamous, and kinky.

11. Explain to the group that they are currently on one side of the tracks. Inform them that you will begin to read the lists and if there is a time they identify with the word on the list, they should step to the "other side of the tracks," turn around, and face the other line. Encourage participants to maintain eye contact with those on the other side of the track.

12. Carefully word your instructions as follows: If you IDENTIFY with *only one demographic you listed on the original list*, please step to the other side of the tracks. For example: "If you identify with heterosexual, please step to the other side of the tracks." The phrase "identify with" is very important. If they ask you to define it, don't. Tell them it is their own interpretation.

13. Read the responses the participants provided for that specific word (e.g., read the responses given for "heterosexual"). Be sure to remind participants to try to maintain eye contact with someone across from them.

14. After reading all responses given for the one demographic, tell the members to "get back on track" so everyone will return to their initial starting point (e.g., once you read the entire list created for "heterosexual" you can then tell participants to get back on track).

15. Repeat steps 12–14 until you have completed each demographic and the responses for each demographic. Then have everyone circle up to debrief the activity.

# DISCUSSION

1. Have participants circle up in the room to engage in an open discussion.
2. Ask members about what they experienced throughout the activity.
   a. What was it like to be on one side of the tracks over the other?
   b. How might being on one side or another relate to social justice? Being marginalized? Being in the majority?
3. How was it maintaining eye contact throughout the activity?
   a. If there was a time it was difficult to maintain eye contact, how come?
   b. How might this relate to being in the minority? In the majority?
4. What surprised you about the words you heard?
   a. What did you experience when hearing the words read?
   b. How did you want to respond to some of the words you heard?
5. Were you surprised by the words you wrote down?
   a. What surprised you about them?
   b. What did you experience when writing your responses down?
   c. What do you think influences the responses we write down?
6. What was your definition of "identify" (personal/relating to/understanding all different)?
7. Was there a time you did identify with the label but did not go across to the other track? Talk about that.
8. What was most challenging about this activity?
9. Were there ever moments you felt the need to explain or justify yourself? What was going on for you then?
10. How does this exercise apply to the real world?
11. How can this experience translate to your future work (or current work) as a counselor?
12. How can you continue to explore and change the current lens you have on the world?

# BIBLIOGRAPHY

Arredondo, P. (1999). Multicultural counseling competencies as tools to address oppression and racism. *Journal of Counseling & Development, 77*(1), 102–108. doi:10.1002/j.1556-6676.1999.tb02427.x

Arthur, N., & Achenbach, K. (2002). Developing multicultural counseling competencies through experiential learning. *Counselor Education & Supervision, 42*(1), 2–14. doi:10.1002/j.1556-6978.2002.tb01299.x

Peer Diversity Educators. (2006). *The wrong side of the tracks.* University of Wisconsin-Eau Claire.

Sue, D. W., Arredondo, P., & McDavis, R. J. (1992). Multicultural counseling competencies and standards: A call to the profession. *Journal of Counseling & Development, 70*(4), 477–486. doi:10.1002/j.2161-1912.1992.tb00563.x

## SUGGESTED BACKGROUND READING

Arredondo, P. (1999). Multicultural counseling competencies as tools to address oppression and racism. *Journal of Counseling & Development, 77*(1), 102–108. doi:10.1002/j.1556-6676.1999.tb02427.x

Sue, D. W., Arredondo, P., & McDavis, R. J. (1992). Multicultural counseling competencies and standards: A call to the profession. *Journal of Counseling & Development, 70*(4), 477–486. doi:10.1002/j.2161-1912.1992.tb00563.x

# CHAPTER 72

# Advocating for Jessica

## Zeynep Yilmaz

## Course Recommendations

| SOCIAL JUSTICE AND ADVOCACY PRINCIPLES | CORE CACREP STANDARDS | COUNSELING SPECIALIZATION |
|---|---|---|
| ☑ What Is Social Justice and Advocacy?<br>☑ Social Constructs of Oppression and Privilege | ☑ Group Work<br>☑ Helping Skills<br>☑ Social and Cultural Diversity | ☑ Clinical Mental Health Counseling<br>☑ School Counseling<br>☑ Student Affairs and College Counseling |

## TOPIC

The purpose of this experiential group activity is to practice implementing different levels of counseling and advocacy interventions that were listed in the 2015 American Counseling Association multicultural and social justice counseling competencies. The created activity is designed to help counseling students to understand how the advocacy competencies play an important role in the counseling setting as well as improve their advocacy skills. When creating the group activity, the author was influenced by the Toporek, Lewis, and Crethar (2009) article.

## LEARNING OBJECTIVES

At the end of this experiential group activity, participants will be able to:

1. Implement different levels of counseling and advocacy interventions for their future or current clients.
2. Improve their advocacy competencies.
3. Understand the importance of having such competencies to better assist their clients in counseling.

## TARGET POPULATION

Students who are in different graduate counseling programs and counselors who work in different settings

## GROUP SIZE

Three to five people for each group. At least six people are required to do the activity.

# TIME REQUIRED

30–40 minutes, depending on how many participants are present

# SETTING

The designed activity can be done in a variety of settings such as a classroom or a regular room with removable chairs. The ideal location needs to have removable chairs for grouping students or counselors.

# MATERIALS NEEDED

- Handouts
- Paper
- Pencil

# INSTRUCTIONS FOR CONDUCTING ACTIVITY

Activity notes:

1. If you can, require the following articles to be read by participants prior to the activity.
   Toporek, R. L., Lewis, J. A., & Crethar, H. C. (2009). Promoting systemic change through the ACA advocacy competencies. *Journal of Counseling & Development, 87*(3), 260–268.
   Ratts, M. J., Singh, A. A., Nassar-McMillan, S., Butler, S. K., McCullough, J. R., & Hipolito-Delgado, C. (2015). *Multicultural and social justice counseling competencies*. Retrieved from www.counseling. org/docs/default-source/competencies/multicultural-and-social-justice-counseling-competencies. pdf?sfvrsn=20
2. Please indicate that participation in this activity is totally optional.
3. Please do not require anybody to participate in the activity.

Please follow the following steps in order to conduct this activity with the participants:

Step 1: divide your participants into small groups, making sure each group has approximately the same number of participants. Depending on the number of participants, you can group your participants into three to six small groups. Tell groups that each group needs to choose a person to report their written responses.

Step 2: after grouping your participants, assign two of the six different levels of counseling and advocacy interventions that were listed in the 2015 American Counseling Association multicultural and social justice counseling competencies to each group.

Step 3: if you have three groups, assign the first two for the first group, numbers three and four for the second group, and the last two for the last group. For example, the first group can have the intrapersonal and interpersonal; the second group can have institutional and community; and the third group can have public policy and international/global levels. If you have six groups, you can assign only one level of counseling and advocacy intervention to each group.

Step 4: pass the first handout to each participant.

Step 5: allow 10–12 minutes for your participants to read the first handout. Directions are included on the handout.

Step 6: pass out the second handout, titled "Case Presentation for Advocating for Jessica." Directions are included on the handout.

Step 7: give 6–8 minutes for groups to write responses.

Step 8: bring the participants back into the larger group and facilitate the discussion for the last 10 minutes.

Step 9: each group's reporter will then present their recommendations for implementing counseling and advocacy interventions for Jessica along with their choices for acting "with" Jessica versus "on behalf of" her.

# DISCUSSION

The following process is to be used for the discussion:

1.  Ask other groups if they have any other counseling and advocacy interventions for the specific level of intervention that is being discussed.
2.  Ask each group why they chose acting "with" Jessica instead of "on behalf of" her for each specific implemented intervention. Also, ask the other groups whether they would have made similar choices along with the reason for this.
3.  Ask your participants what level of intervention that they would feel most comfortable with.
4.  If they respond, ask why one level of counseling and advocacy intervention is easier to apply than others.
5.  Do not forget to allow participants to ask any questions that they may have.

# BIBLIOGRAPHY

Ratts, M. J., Singh, A. A., Nassar-McMillan, S., Butler, S. K., McCullough, J. R., & Hipolito-Delgado, C. (2015). *Multicultural and social justice counseling competencies*. Retrieved from www.counseling.org/docs/default-source/competencies/multicultural-and-social-justice-counseling-competencies.pdf?sfvrsn=20

Toporek, R. L., Lewis, J. A., & Crethar, H. C. (2009). Promoting systemic change through the ACA advocacy competencies. *Journal of Counseling & Development*, 87(3), 260–268.

# SUGGESTED BACKGROUND READING

Ratts, M. J., Singh, A. A., Nassar-McMillan, S., Butler, S. K., & McCullough, J. R. (2016). Multicultural and social justice counseling competencies: Guidelines for the counseling profession. *Journal of Multicultural Counseling & Development*, 44(1), 28–48. doi:10.1002/jmcd.12035

# HANDOUT

# Handout 72.1: Counseling and Advocacy Interventions

## DIRECTIONS

This handout includes the six different levels of counseling and advocacy interventions that were listed in the American Counseling Association (ACA) multicultural and social justice counseling competencies. The six different levels of counseling and advocacy competencies are: intrapersonal, interpersonal, institutional, community, public policy, and international/global. Please read the full version of multicultural and social justice counseling competencies at the following link: www.counseling.org/knowledge-center/competencies in order to fully understand the different levels of counseling and advocacy interventions. You will be allowed 10 minutes to read this handout. If you need additional time, please let your instructor know. Please review more in depth two of the levels that were specifically assigned to your group.

Modified from Ratts, M. J., Singh, A. A., Nassar-McMillan, S., Butler, S. K., McCullough, J. R., & Hipolito-Delgado, C. (2015). *Multicultural and social justice counseling competencies*. Retrieved from www.counseling.org/docs/default-source/competencies/multicultural-and-social-justice-counseling-competencies.pdf?sfvrsn=20

## IV. COUNSELING AND ADVOCACY INTERVENTIONS

"Privileged and marginalized counselors intervene with, and on behalf, of clients at the intrapersonal, interpersonal, institutional, community, public policy, and international/global levels."

a. "Intrapersonal: The individual characteristics of a person such as knowledge, attitudes, behavior, self-concept, skills, and developmental history.
   Intrapersonal Interventions: Privileged and marginalized counselors address the intrapersonal processes that impact privileged and marginalized clients."

(p. 11)

b. "Interpersonal: The interpersonal processes and/or groups that provide individuals with identity and support (i.e. family, friends, and peers).
   Interpersonal Interventions: Privileged and marginalized counselors address the interpersonal processes that affect privileged and marginalized clients."

(p. 12)

c. "Institutional: Represents the social institutions in society such as schools, churches, community organizations.
   Institutional Interventions: Privileged and marginalized counselors address inequities at the institutional level."

(p. 12)

d. "Community: The community as a whole represents the spoken and unspoken norms, values, and regulations that are embedded in society. The norms, values, and regulations of a community may either be empowering or oppressive to human growth and development.

Community Interventions: Privileged and marginalized address community norms, values, and regulations that impede on the development of individuals, groups, and communities."

(p. 13)

e. "Public Policy: Public policy reflects the local, state, and federal laws and policies that regulate or influence client human growth and development.
Public Policy Interventions: Privileged and marginalized counselors address public policy issues that impede on client development with, and on behalf of clients."

(p. 13)

f. "International and Global Affairs: International and global concerns reflect the events, affairs, and policies that influence psychological health and well-being.
International and Global Affairs Interventions: Privileged and marginalized counselors address international and global events, affairs and polices that impede on client development with, and on behalf of, clients."

(p. 14)

# Handout 72.2: Case Presentation for Advocating for Jessica

## THE CASE OF JESSICA

## Directions

To bring further clarity about how the advocacy competencies play an important role in counseling, please first read the following presented case carefully. Using the two different levels of counseling and advocacy interventions that were assigned to your group, please implement at least three counseling and advocacy interventions for the case. For the counseling and advocacy interventions that you implement with your group members, please indicate whether you will be acting "with" Jessica or acting "on behalf of" her. Please write your responses on the paper that your instructor passed out.

## Case

You work at a community mental health agency as a counselor. One of your clients whose name is Jessica has been referred to you by her school counselor because her mother was very concerned about Jessica's severe depression and anxiety that she was having after her spinal cord injury due to a car accident. You have been seeing Jessica for four sessions, and it seems that you have started building a good relationship with her.

Jessica is a 15-year-old Hispanic female who was born and raised in the United States. Her family came to the United States approximately 30 years ago. She has two older brothers and two younger sisters. Last summer, Jessica was involved in a car accident with her father that resulted in her having a spinal cord injury. Jessica is still able to use her upper limbs after the accident; however, her spinal cord injury requires her to use a wheelchair. After her injury, Jessica became very depressed, and her grades went down. Jessica goes to a private high school that is affiliated with a Catholic church. She has been receiving a full scholarship to attend the private school for the last three years. The building in which she attends school is not considered accessible for students with disabilities, as it does not have power-assist doors on the restrooms or elevators. The school does not have any student with a major physical disability except Jessica, and accessibility for Jessica was not an issue before she acquired her disability. Right now, Jessica's mother comes to school a few times each day to accompany her to the restroom. This requires a lot of time and energy for her mother. Jessica is also unable to attend many extracurricular activities due to the lack of somebody accompanying her. Her mother and father have begun to have a lot of fights at home during the last few months. In addition, her father was fired by his employer after he had a fight with a customer two months ago.

In the last counseling session Jessica shared the following concerns with you. "I feel like I'm a burden for everybody in the family. I think my family does not like me anymore because of my disability. I'm not as successful as I used to be and I feel depressed. My grades are very low and I do not want to study. Why should I bother to be a successful student? I cannot even go to the restroom by myself, so how can I would get a job? You know, my school is not accessible, and I cannot complain about this because my mother told me to not talk to school administrators. She said that if I talk to them about the restroom doors and the elevator, the school would no longer give me a scholarship. I do not want to go to another school because I really like my friends there. I hate my dad. You know, he almost killed me, and I have a disability just because of him. I rarely talk to him. He always yells at us at home, and he never helps my mother do anything. I do not even know why he still lives with us. It is so bad for my mother as she still loves him, but I do not understand how she could." Jessica started crying and said, "My life became a mess after this accident!" She added, "Last night, I heard my parents talking about getting divorced in Spanish. I guess they forgot that I can speak it." Jessica also talked about feeling very anxious around her parents and her teachers. She said that she does not want to go out anymore with her friends. Lastly, Jessica talked about the summer trip where she will go with her church choir to Mexico. "You know, this trip was always my dream, but I'm sure I won't be able to go because there won't be anybody who could help me. I also have no idea whether the places we will be visiting are accessible or not. I do not want to be a problem in the group."

Note: be aware that Title III of the Americans With Disabilities Act does not cover religious institutions; thus, private schools that are directly operated by religious institutions are not covered by the ADA. In other words, schools that are under this category do not have to be accessible for students with disabilities.

# CHAPTER 73

## Filling in the Gaps
### Group Theory and Multicultural Applications

*Kristopher Hall*

| Course Recommendations | | |
|---|---|---|
| **SOCIAL JUSTICE AND ADVOCACY PRINCIPLES** | **CORE CACREP STANDARDS** | **COUNSELING SPECIALIZATION** |
| ☑ Strategies for Change | ☑ Group Work<br>☑ Theories | ☑ Clinical Mental Health Counseling<br>☑ School Counseling |

## TOPIC

The focus of this activity is to have students understand how to integrate real-world needs of the populations they will serve with group theory.

## LEARNING OBJECTIVES

1. Demonstrate an understanding of group theory.
2. Assess how group theory needs to be applied to work with diverse populations.

## TARGET POPULATION

Students taking group counseling classes, preferably after completing their multicultural counseling course

## GROUP SIZE

This is an activity that can be completed in groups of four or fewer.

## TIME REQUIRED

This assignment should be given at the beginning of the semester, with weekly presentations to process the information. The presentations should take between 30 and 45 minutes.

# SETTING

Plan to conduct this activity in a classroom that allows students to make smaller groups.

# MATERIALS NEEDED

The presentations may include any mode preferred by the instructor including PowerPoint, Prezi, or Keynote. The students may also include any media necessary to share the knowledge effectively.

# INSTRUCTIONS FOR CONDUCTING ACTIVITY

At the beginning of the class, the instructor should divide the class into groups based on the theories they will be covering during the semester. The instructor should then have the class answer the following prompts within their groups:

1. OVERVIEW OF THEORY
   Provide enough background information so that the class has a good general understanding of the theory you are presenting. It is better to proceed as if your audience has no prior knowledge of the topic. Include such information as:
   a. Brief history of the theorist/s
   b. Key concepts/tenets of the theory
   c. Definitions of key terms
   d. Who is reflected primarily in the creation of the theory
2. APPLICATION OF THEORY
   a. What does the theory say specifically about how to conduct group counseling?
   b. With what populations and issues is this theory most useful?
   c. How would this theory need to be adapted to work with marginalized populations?
   d. What resources would be necessary to conduct groups in schools/community using this theory?
3. THE GROUP THERAPEUTIC PROCESS
   a. How do the unique techniques of this theory apply to how groups are run?
   b. How does the theory apply to EACH STAGE of group development?
   c. What techniques are unique to the theory?
   d. Case examples addressing multiple populations (this should include links to case studies or refereed journal articles that have used this theory).
4. ADVOCACY AND ADVANCEMENT
   a. Which cultural groups do you feel this theory would work best with?
   b. How would you facilitate a group using this theory while addressing multiple populations?
   c. How might diverse populations be damaged by the use of this theory?
   d. If this theory is being practiced ineffectively at your site, how would you advocate for change?

The following presentation should answer each of these questions in some form. Students are able to use whatever means of presentation they would like to ensure that the class stays interested and focused.

# DISCUSSION

The instructor should probe the students after completing the presentation. This should include questions regarding how populations were not represented during the creation of the theory and how this impacts application. Additionally, there should be discussion around what may or may not make this theory applicable across populations and how to adapt that theory if it is not.

## BIBLIOGRAPHY

Chang, C. Y., Crethar, H. C., & Ratts, M. J. (2010). Social justice: A national imperative for counselor education and supervision. *Counselor Education and Supervision, 50*(2), 82–87.

Decker, K. M., Manis, A. A., & Paylo, M. J. (2016). Infusing social justice advocacy into counselor education: Strategies and recommendations. *Journal of Counselor Preparation and Supervision, 8*(3).

# CHAPTER 74

## Privilege in a Hat

*Margaret Lamar*

### Course Recommendations

| SOCIAL JUSTICE AND ADVOCACY PRINCIPLES | CORE CACREP STANDARDS | COUNSELING SPECIALIZATION |
|---|---|---|
| ☑ What Is Social Justice & Advocacy?<br>☑ Social Construct of Oppression and Privilege | ☑ Helping Relationships<br>☑ Professional Counseling Orientation and Ethical Practice<br>☑ Social and Cultural Diversity | ☑ Clinical Mental Health Counseling<br>☑ Couple, Marriage, and Family Counseling<br>☑ School Counseling<br>☑ Student Affairs and College Counseling |

## TOPIC

This activity is designed to teach students about power and privilege as experienced by themselves and others.

## LEARNING OBJECTIVES

1. Students will identify their own privileges and understand the impact of those privileges on others.
2. Students will increase their understanding of the lack of access to privilege experienced by others.
3. Students will understand how their clients may experience privilege, or lack of privilege, in their own lives and in the counseling process.
4. Students will strengthen their ability to engage in respectful dialogue with colleagues around the topic of power and privilege.

## TARGET POPULATION

This activity is suited for master's counseling students in any specialization.

## GROUP SIZE

This activity can be adapted to work for 6–25 participants.

# TIME REQUIRED

Allow at least 30 minutes for this activity. If the group is larger, you may want to plan on at least 45 minutes to give more students the opportunity to share their thoughts.

# SETTING

Plan to conduct this activity in a classroom or other space that offers privacy so students feel safe to discuss the content of the activity, which may be more sensitive in nature.

# MATERIALS NEEDED

Each student will need one or two slips of paper and a writing instrument. The number of papers given to each student may be altered, depending on the size of the group and how much time is available to complete the activity.

# INSTRUCTIONS FOR CONDUCTING ACTIVITY

1. Introduce the activity by using the following script: "Today we are going to discuss the privileges that we, and our clients, may or may not hold. I want you to write down one to two privileges. These can be privileges you have access to or ones that you do not. We will all read them aloud and discuss them. Our discussion today may be challenging and will, hopefully, give us an opportunity to reflect on ourselves and our work with others."
2. Begin passing out one or two slips of paper to each student.
3. Ask students to write down a privilege on each slip of paper. Inform students that these privileges may be ones that the individual student has access to or ones to which they do not. Depending on your group of students, you may provide examples (e.g., I can go for a run at night without fearing for my safety; I see people who look like me on television and in movies; I can walk down the street holding my partner's hand without fear of judgment; etc.). Tell students these privileges will be read aloud anonymously.
4. Collect the slips of paper and put them in a hat or bowl.
5. Before reading the privileges, remind students of any community agreements or rules for the class, especially those that relate to communicating with respect, listening without judgment, and being open to learning from the experience of others.
6. Choose a slip of paper from the hat and read the privilege aloud. Ask students for their reactions to that privilege. Depending on the development of your student group, you may give more specific prompts, such as "can anyone talk about their relationship with that privilege, either having access to it or not?" or, "what is the first thing that pops into your mind when you hear this privilege?" Using group facilitation skills, encourage students to respond respectfully to each other and process points of connection or tension.
7. Pass the hat around the group, allowing students to choose a slip of paper and read it aloud. Continue to facilitate the discussion between students' experiences and the privileges being read aloud. Connect student responses, highlight shared experiences, and normalize the experiences of students where appropriate.
8. Depending on the size of the group, you may read all the slips of paper, or you may choose to end the activity in order to provide time for debriefing. Before moving to discussing the activity, if all the slips of paper were not read, ask if any student wrote a privilege they were hoping to discuss. Make sure students know they will lose anonymity in sharing the privilege they wrote down. Once you have completed this, move to debrief the activity.

# DISCUSSION

Approximately 10 minutes before the end of your allotted time or when all the slips of paper have been read, ask students to share their thoughts about this activity. You may specifically ask:

- What thoughts, feelings, or ideas came up for you during this discussion?
- What reactions did you have to this activity?
- What did you learn about yourself or others during this activity?

Finally, ask students to make connections between the privileges discussed and their work with clients. For example,

- How can you use your knowledge of these privileges in your work with clients?
- How might the lack of access to privilege influence how your client experiences your counseling agency or process?
- How might your own privilege impact your work with clients?

At this point, you may also focus the discussion on the specific client populations with which your students are planning to work. For school counselors or college/university counselors, you could ask students to discuss how their clients might experience those privileges on campus. For clinical mental health or marriage/family counselors, students can consider how these privileges impact their clients' relationships or how clients experience them when navigating their counseling agency.

# BIBLIOGRAPHY

Ancis, J. R., & Szymanski, D. M. (2001). Awareness of white privilege among white counseling trainees. *The Counseling Psychologist, 29*(4), 548–569.

Hays, D. G., Dean, J. K., & Chang, C. Y. (2007). Addressing privilege and oppression in counselor training and practice: A qualitative analysis. *Journal of Counseling & Development, 85*, 317–324.

Watt, S. K., Curtis, G. C., Drummond, J., Kellogg, A. H., Lozano, A., Nicoli, G. T., & Rosas, M. (2009). Privileged identity exploration: Examining counselor trainees' reactions to difficult dialogues. *Counselor Education and Supervision, 49*, 86–105.

# SUGGESTED BACKGROUND READING

Sue, D. W., Lin, A. I., Torino, G. C., Capodilupo, C. M., & Rivera, D. P. (2009). Racial microaggressions and difficult dialogues on race in the classroom. *Cultural Diversity and Ethnic Minority Psychology, 15*(2), 183–190.

Watt, S. K. (2007). Difficult dialogues, privilege and social justice: Uses of the privileged identity exploration (PIE) model in student affairs practice. *The College Student Affairs Journal, 26*(2), 114–126.

# CHAPTER 75

# Historical Experience of Addiction
## Effect of Biased Treatment Toward Diverse Populations

*Jeanna R. Knight and Dixie Meyer*

## Course Recommendations

| SOCIAL JUSTICE AND ADVOCACY PRINCIPLES | CORE CACREP STANDARDS | COUNSELING SPECIALIZATION |
|---|---|---|
| ☑ What Is Social Justice & Advocacy?<br>☑ Social Construct of Oppression and Privilege | ☑ Helping Relationships<br>☑ Social and Cultural Diversity | ☑ Addiction Counseling<br>☑ Clinical Mental Health Counseling<br>☑ Couple, Marriage, and Family Counseling<br>☑ Student Affairs and College Counseling |

## TOPIC

This activity provides an opportunity to research addictions across time periods. The goal of the activity is to observe how perceptions, oppressions, and biases toward people of various groups influence available treatment. After the activity, the class will discuss how service providers approached each client, addressed presenting problems, and attempted to treat psychological and emotional needs of clients.

## LEARNING OBJECTIVES

The objectives of the activity are to:

1. Increase awareness of and education on addiction treatment toward diverse populations.
2. Evaluate how a client's ethnicity and/or socioeconomic status influence how mental health professionals approach client treatment.
3. Increase awareness of personal and general biases toward various demographic groups (e.g., ethnicity, socioeconomic status, or personal history).
4. Explore and discuss how professionals can use a sensitive approach to treat addictions.

## TARGET POPULATION

The activity can be utilized with undergraduate or graduate students.

# GROUP SIZE

This activity can be adapted to work for 6–25 participants.

# TIME REQUIRED

This activity will take approximately four weeks to complete. Each student should choose one target population to match to one specific time period. Students may consider some of the following groups as examples of groups that are affected by biases:

- African Americans
- Caucasians
- Ex-offenders
- LGBTQ persons
- Low-income families
- War veterans

Students will need a minimum of two weeks to conduct research on their history of addiction treatment approaches for people within the selected population and time period. No two students should research the same group during the same time period. Students will need two weeks to prepare a presentation that will creatively convey what they learned. More time may be needed depending on the class size. Students will present their research in class. Presentations should last 15–30 minutes. Following each presentation, 5 minutes should be allotted for questions.

# SETTING

Students should conduct research outside of class to present in class via one of the following manners:

- A PowerPoint presentation
- A speech (or other oral presentation) from the perspective of a member of the target population or a treatment provider during the selected time period
- An enactment that demonstrates biases and treatment approaches for their selected population and time period

# MATERIALS NEEDED

- Index or note cards.
- Students may choose to utilize materials that enhance their presentation.

# INSTRUCTIONS FOR CONDUCTING ACTIVITY

The instructor should write each target population and each time period on individual index or note cards. Target populations and time periods should be separated into two piles of cards. Students should pick one card from each pile to determine which population and time period they are assigned. Each pile of cards should be shuffled, and students should continue to pick from each pile until all students have a population and time period. No two students should have the same population and time period.

The research: students may conduct research via journal articles, reliable Internet sources, books, or personal interviews.

The presentation: students will give a 15–30 minute presentation. Presentations should present background information of the population group within the context of the social and political climate of the selected time period. Cultural perceptions and education around addiction should be explained during the presentation. The combination of social, political, economic, and medical biases in light of the group's personal cultural values and beliefs should be described.

## DISCUSSION

Following the activity, the instructor should engage students in a meaningful dialogue to encourage cultural competency around the issue of addiction treatment for diverse populations. Conversation should be guided toward discussion of ways to better serve diverse groups. Some helpful questions to propose to students may include: what are your initial reactions about the client's experience of living with addiction during the given time period? What questions would you ask the client about his/her/their experiences with addiction? In what ways is the client empowered? Did you become aware of any personal biases or potential blind spots during this activity? If the client's physical appearance, social status, or financial ability were different, do you think the client's needs would have been addressed differently? What resources or referrals would you offer after speaking with the client during the presented time period? How would you approach finding resources and treatment for this population now?

## BIBLIOGRAPHY

Acevedo, A., Garnick, D. W., Dunigan, R., Horgan, C. M., Ritter, G. A., Lee, M. T., . . . Wright, D. (2015). Performance measures and racial/ethnic disparities in the treatment of substance use disorders. *Journal of Studies on Alcohol and Drugs, 76*(1), 57–67.

Harnish, A., Corrigan, P., Byrne, P., Debra, A., Rodrigues, S., & Smelson, D. (2016). Substance use and mental health stigma in veterans with co-occurring disorders. *Journal of Dual Diagnosis, 12*(3–4), 238–243.

Hicks, D. (2000). The importance of specialized treatment programs for lesbians and gay patients. *Journal of Gay & Lesbian Psychotherapy, 3*(3–4), 81–94.

Punukollu, B., Chowdary, Z. A., & Felton, G. (2010). Addiction in ethnic minorities. In R. Bhattacharya, S. Cross, & D. Bhugra (Eds.), *Clinical topics in cultural psychiatry* (pp. 182–195). xix, 424 pp. London, UK: Royal College of Psychiatrists.

Taliaferro, J. D., Lutz, B., Moore, A. K., & Scipien, K. (2014). Increasing cultural awareness and sensitivity: Effective substance treatment in the adult lesbian population. *Journal of Human Behavior in the Social Environment, 24*(5), 582–588.

## SUGGESTED BACKGROUND READING

White, W. L. (2014). *Slaying the dragon: The history of addiction treatment and recovery in America* (2nd ed.). Bloomington, IL. Chestnut Health Systems.

# CHAPTER 76

# Letting Go
## Reflecting on the Impacts of Power, Privilege, and Identity

*Kristin Vincenzes and Meredith Drew*

## Course Recommendations

| SOCIAL JUSTICE AND ADVOCACY PRINCIPLES | CORE CACREP STANDARDS | COUNSELING SPECIALIZATION |
| --- | --- | --- |
| ☑ Social Constructs of Oppression and Privilege | ☑ Group Work<br>☑ Helping Relationships<br>☑ Professional Counseling Orientation and Ethical Practice<br>☑ Social and Cultural Diversity | ☑ Addiction Counseling<br>☑ Career Counseling<br>☑ Clinical Mental Health Counseling<br>☑ Marriage, Couple, and Family Counseling<br>☑ School Counseling<br>☑ Student Affairs and College Counseling |

## TOPIC

The primary focus of this activity is to help students/supervisees reflect on how one's own heritage, attitudes, beliefs, understandings, and/or acculturative experiences (to include experiences with discrimination and/or oppression) may impact their worldview (CACREP, 2016) as well as impact their work with diverse clients.

## LEARNING OBJECTIVES

1.  Students will reflect on their life journey and identify the impact of heritage, attitudes, beliefs, understandings, and acculturative experiences (to include possible experiences with discrimination and/or oppression) on their own worldview.
2.  Students will identify one attitude, belief, or acculturative experience (including an experience with discrimination or oppression) that may create a barrier to providing quality counseling to diverse clients. Students may choose to reflect on their cultural identity and how this may have impacted their experience with power and privilege.
3.  Students will share this potential barrier with their peers as well as create a goal for helping them to let go of it so that it does not impact their work with clients who may have different attitudes, beliefs, understandings, or acculturative experiences.

## TARGET POPULATION

This activity is used with graduate-level students who are participating in a process group as part of their group counseling course, or it may be used with students in a multicultural counseling course, practicum, and/or internship. It may also be used with supervisees who are working toward their professional counseling license.

## GROUP SIZE

Two to eight is the preferred group number. Due to the sensitivity of people's individual experiences, beliefs, attitudes, and worldview, it is recommended to have a smaller number of students in the group.

## TIME REQUIRED

Depending on the amount of group members, this activity will take approximately 45 minutes. It can be increased or decreased based on time restrictions.

## SETTING

This activity was designed for face-to-face implementation in a classroom setting and then moving outside to let balloons go. If students cannot go outside to let the balloons go, a safety pin may be used as an alternative option. In addition, online counseling programs that have the capability of virtual classrooms can easily modify this activity. The group leader notifies the students prior to the next virtual class to bring a marker and paper to group. During the virtual class, the group leader/supervisor will follow the same directions as follows, but instead of using a balloon, students will use paper. While the students cannot let the balloon go, they are informed that they can choose how they want to let go of their negative issue or concern. Options may include throwing it away, shredding it, or putting it in an envelope, sealing it, and asking a trusted adult to hold onto it but not open it.

## MATERIALS NEEDED

Each group member needs a helium filled balloon with string attached and a marker. Group leaders will need to bring these materials to group/supervision. Another alternative is to ask the students to bring their own balloon, marker, and safety pin to group. The activity is done in the same manner, but at the end of the group each student is asked to pop their balloon.

## INSTRUCTIONS FOR CONDUCTING ACTIVITY

Introduction to the activity:

As the group leader, it is helpful to the group members to also participate and act as a model during the activity. When preparing group members to participate in this activity, it is first important to ask them to reflect on their life journey thus far. Then ask the group members to think about their own heritage, attitudes, beliefs, understandings, and acculturative experiences and how these things may impact the counseling they provide to diverse clients. In order to ensure that we do not push our own values, beliefs, and experiences onto our clients, we must first recognize how they may impact our worldview as well as the work we will provide to our clients.

**Step-by-Step Directions**

1. Allow each group member to choose a helium inflated balloon and a marker.
2. Instruct members to take some time to reflect on how their lives have been impacted by heritage, attitudes, beliefs, understandings, acculturative experiences, discrimination, and/or oppression.
3. Ask each member to pick one area that they feel they need to "let go" in order to effectively work with clients of diverse cultures and experiences. After they identify their potential barrier, ask them to write or draw on one side of the balloon what they want to let go.
4. After 5–10 minutes of reflecting and writing, instruct group members to think about how they would replace that potential barrier in their life.
5. On the other side of the balloon, ask members to write/draw how they would like to replace their potential barrier, or they may write/draw a goal that will help them to let go of the potential barrier.
6. After group members are finished, each individual is encouraged to share with the group what they want to let go. Then each member is encouraged to share with the group how they plan to replace that potential barrier so that it does not negatively impact their work with clients.
7. After they share, they let the balloon go.
8. Members watch each balloon take off.
9. After each member releases their balloon, the group reflects on the experience of watching their message fly into the air.
10. As they reflect on what is leaving, group members discuss how they will incorporate their positive message/plan into their life.

# DISCUSSION

For some group members, this activity can be cathartic and really meaningful because they are able to watch the balloon leave. In the meantime, it allows each member to reflect on what they would want or need to help move past the potential barrier. For those who may not feel relief by watching the balloon fly away, the discussion of the process becomes instrumental as they discuss how their own attitudes, beliefs, or acculturative experiences (to include an experience with discrimination or oppression) may impact their roles as counselors. The discussion on this activity will also benefit the students/supervisees not only by helping them to be more reflective, but also by helping them to create goals for themselves. As you close the activity, they leave with the visual of letting go. Group leaders may choose to provide the students with a rock and ask the students to write one word on it to help remind themselves of the activity. This object provides the students with a tangible memory of what they are letting go of and the how they will move forward. Some ideas for discussion prompts include:

- Why is it important for clinicians to be self-aware and acknowledge their own experiences with cultural identity, power, and privilege?
- How did it feel to acknowledge and write down your own experiences with cultural identity and/or social injustice(s)?
- How might watching your social injustice(s) be released and fly away impact you as an individual and/or clinician?
- How can your own awareness/experiences propel you to advocate for the needs of others?
- How do you think this experience can impact the work you do with culturally diverse clients who have experienced oppression and need advocacy?
- How did it feel to discuss the experiences that you identified? Was it difficult to acknowledge privilege that you may have? Was it difficult to acknowledge discrimination or oppression that you may have experienced?
- What roadblocks did you encounter when doing this activity? How did you overcome them?

# BIBLIOGRAPHY

American Counseling Association. (2014). *ACA code of ethics and standards of practice*. Retrieved from www.counseling. org/Resources/aca-code-of-ethics.pdf

Ametrano, I. (2014). Teaching ethical decision making: Helping students reconcile personal and professional values. *Journal of Counseling & Development, 92*(2), 154–161. doi:10.1002/j.1556-6676.2014.00143.x

Council for Accreditation of Counseling and Related Educational Programs [CACREP]. (2016). *2016 standards for accreditation*. Alexandria, VA: Author.

Jacobs, E., Masson, R. L., Iarvill, R., & Schimmel, C. (2012). *Group counseling strategies & skills* (7th ed.). Belmont, CA: Brooks/Cole.

Samid, L. L., & Stockton, R. (2002). Letting go of grief. *The Journal for Specialists in Group Work, 27*(2), 192–204. doi:10.1080/742848691

Wilson, C. J., Barnes-Holmes, Y., & Barnes-Holmes, D. (2014). How exactly do I "let go"? The potential of using ACT to overcome the relaxation paradox. *SAGE Open*, 1–8. Retrieved from www.sgo.sagepub.com. doi:10.1177/ 2158244014526722

# SUGGESTED BACKGROUND READING

Crethar, H. C., & Winterowd, C. L. (2012). Values and social justice in counseling. *Counseling & Values, 57*(1), 3–9. doi:10.1002/j.2161-007X.2012.00001.x

Francis, P. C., & Dugger, S. M. (2014). Professionalism, ethics, and value-based conflicts in counseling: An introduction to the special section. *Journal of Counseling & Development, 92*(2), 131–134. doi:10.1002/j.1556-6676.2014.00138.x

Kocet, M. M., & Herlihy, B. J. (2014). Addressing value-based conflicts within the counseling relationship: A decision-making model. *Journal of Counseling & Development, 92*(2), 180–186. doi:10.1002/j.1556-6676.2014.00146.x

# CHAPTER 77

# Live Discussion Board to Foster Dialogue in White Racial Identity Development

*James H. Castillo*

## Course Recommendations

| SOCIAL JUSTICE AND ADVOCACY PRINCIPLES | CORE CACREP STANDARDS | COUNSELING SPECIALIZATION |
|---|---|---|
| ☑ Social Constructs of Oppression and Privilege<br>☑ Intersections of Oppression | ☑ Helping Relationships<br>☑ Social and Cultural Diversity | ☑ Addiction Counseling<br>☑ Career Counseling<br>☑ Clinical Mental Health Counseling<br>☑ Marriage, Couple, and Family Counseling<br>☑ School Counseling<br>☑ Student Affairs and College Counseling |

## TOPIC

Teaching skills in critical self-reflection, acknowledgement, and validation of another's lived experiences and recognition of power and privilege through engagement in structured professional dialogue on challenging topics. Enhancing the self-awareness of counselors and supervisors-in-training, who represent all groups (privileged and marginalized), through critical reflection on white racial identity development.

## LEARNING OBJECTIVES

1. Read and respond to peers in a silent structured dialogue surrounding white racial identity development and privilege.
2. All students, regardless of group membership, will critically reflect on their own personal experiences related to whiteness and privilege.
3. Demonstrate an ability to acknowledge, validate, and critically explore the experiences of their peers by creating a safe and supportive environment.

## TARGET POPULATION

Counselors and supervisors-in-training at the master's or doctoral level

# GROUP SIZE

For this activity, 10–25 students is preferred. Due to the nature of this activity, larger classes offer greater opportunities for diverse perspectives to be shared.

# TIME REQUIRED

30–45 minutes. As the number of students engaging in the activity increases beyond 15, please allocate an additional 3–5 minutes per student to ensure enough time is available for process questions at the conclusion of the activity. If this activity is facilitated online, discussions may occur throughout the week.

# SETTING

This activity may be completed in a classroom, conference room, or equivalent space that offers counselors and supervisors-in-training appropriate space to write. Thus, there is flexibility as to where the activity may occur. This activity may also be adapted for online usage via a learning management platform (e.g., Blackboard or Canvas) by enabling the discussion board feature on the platform. The instructor may enable the anonymous feature to recreate the experience created in the in-class experience. Students may then post their questions to the discussion board and engage in the structured discussion with their peers.

# MATERIALS NEEDED

Each student will need one piece of standard 8 ½" × 11" lined paper and a writing utensil. Writing utensils need to be of the same type to ensure anonymity during the activity. Similarly, all paper used needs to be of the same type to ensure anonymity. Therefore, the facilitator must provide the paper and utensils at the start of the activity.

   This activity scaffolds the development of engaging in difficult conversations and trains students to reflect on and validate experiences pertaining to privilege and power of a peer who may have different experiences from their own. The use of materials in class or the enabling of features in the online format that provide anonymity in class for this exercise provides students with a structured and supervised experience.

# INSTRUCTIONS FOR CONDUCTING ACTIVITY

1. Instructor may follow this script when facilitating this activity: "We'll be continuing our growing understanding and awareness of white racial identity development and privilege as discussed in the Sue and Sue (2016) reading this week."
2. "Today we'll be engaging in a silent and live discussion board whereby as a learning community we'll be able to reflect on our own experiences surrounding whiteness and privilege in our current society, gain awareness and an understanding of the individual experiences of our peers, and engage in an open and structured conversation."
3. "This will also be an opportunity to learn your positionality and how you came to learn and be aware of issues surrounding whiteness and privilege."
4. "No matter our setting of practice, as counselors it is important for us to be aware of our personal biases and positionalities toward groups whom we do not self-identify with or toward those with whom we've been identified as a member of society, in order to engage in a nonjudgmental alliance with the individuals we work with."

5.  "The purpose of this activity is to begin developing the skillset of acknowledging your own narrative lens, acknowledging and validating that of a peer who may or may not share the same position, and acknowledging your assumptions and worldviews regarding race and power. This activity also serves to push your self-awareness of your own privilege and/or marginalization in society by engaging in a professional, nonjudgmental discussion whereby curiosity and reflexivity can occur with your peers."

6.  "I am going to pass around paper and pens. Please take one sheet of paper and one pen. You are going to be asked to respond to a statement then engage in a series of written dialogues with your peers; therefore, to provide structure, and a safe environment to practice engaging in such critical discourse, the paper and pens will provide everyone with the same tools to assist us in maintaining anonymity."

7.  The instructor places the following prompt on the board/PowerPoint slide for all to see, "What does it mean to be white?"

8.  The instructor continues, "Please take a moment to collect your thoughts surrounding this statement. In a moment, you'll be asked to silently write your thoughts and reflections about this statement. You'll be given 4 minutes to do so, starting now."

9.  "OK, you may begin writing. You have 4 minutes."

10. With 1 minute remaining the instructor says, "One more minute, please begin finishing up your thoughts."

11. After 4 minutes, "Please turn your papers over and pass them forward (or toward the direction of the instructor)." Instructor collects all of the papers, shuffles them. Prior to redistributing the papers the instructor says, "I will be passing back the papers. There is a chance that you may receive your own. If you do, do not say anything, wait for my next instructions."

12. Instructor redistributes the papers, then says, "Please close your eyes." Wait to make sure all have closed their eyes, then continue, "If you received your own reflection please raise your hand." Instructor waits. If individuals have received their own the instructor then collects those reflections and redistributes them and then says, "Please open your eyes."

13. Instructor to the class, "Now, you will have 4 minutes to read the reflection in front of you and respond. I ask that your response be structured in this way. First, acknowledge and validate the perspective/experience/reflection of your peer, then provide a response that furthers the conversation. You may agree, be critical, etc."

14. After providing the instructions, instructor says, "You may begin." At 1 minute left the instructor prompts about the remaining time.

15. The instructor then repeats steps 11–14 for as many cycles as desired and that time allows. Please note that as cycles increase, it may become increasingly difficult to ensure that all individuals reflect and respond to a dialogue they haven't already engaged in. However, as cycles increase (e.g., after four), individuals may reflect on a dialogue they've already contributed to as long as they were not the last respondent to the conversation.

16. In the event that more than four cycles occur, the instructor may say, "We will be doing another cycle; at this point, it is OK to receive a conversation you have already engaged in. At this point, when you close our eyes, only raise your hand if you were the last respondent on the new dialogue in front of you."

17. After the class has completed the desired number of cycles the instructor once again collects all of the papers.

## DISCUSSION

1.  The instructor then says, "I am going to redistribute these dialogues. It does not matter if you receive a conversation that you participated in, so please do not acknowledge that."

2.  Instructor passes papers out, then says, "We are going to read these dialogues out loud. I ask that you read the conversation verbatim to the best of your ability. Then at the conclusion, provide a synthesis and identify themes you recognize."

3. "Thanks for sharing that, (student); what meaning do you make of this conversation?" "How would you summarize this conversation?" "How has this experience prepared you to explore issues related to power, privilege, and/or marginalization with clients/supervisees?" "How has this activity impacted your openness to learn about advantages and disadvantages experienced by members of privileged and marginalized groups?" "In what ways has your self-awareness of beliefs and biases toward privileged and/or marginalized groups changed?"

4. Instructor elicits engagement from all individuals. If individuals choose not to read out loud ask for another peer to read out loud for them. As all individuals have already participated via writing, sharing the conversations orally is optional though encouraged.

5. Instructors may adapt this step and ask that a different student provide a synthesis/identification of themes following the oral reading of the conversation. This develops listening, critical thinking, reflecting, and summarizing skills in trainees.

6. Individuals may repeat this exercise with numerous topics in the field of counseling and supervision to facilitate discussion among trainees.

# BIBLIOGRAPHY

Hays, D. G., & Chang, C. Y. (2003). White privilege, oppression, and racial identity development: Implications for supervision. *Counselor Education and Supervision, 43*(2), 134–145. doi:10.1002/j.1556-6978.2003.tb01837.x

Sue, D. W., & Sue, D. (2016). *Counseling the culturally diverse* (7th ed.). Hoboken, NJ: Wiley.

# CHAPTER 78

## Connecting With Others
### Countering Social Bias With a Compassion-Based Practice

*Reginald W. Holt*

### Course Recommendations

| SOCIAL JUSTICE AND ADVOCACY PRINCIPLES | CORE CACREP STANDARDS | COUNSELING SPECIALIZATION |
|---|---|---|
| ☑ Social Constructs of Oppression and Privilege<br>☑ Strategies for Change | ☑ Group Work<br>☑ Helping Relationships<br>☑ Professional Counseling Orientation and Ethical Practice<br>☑ Social and Cultural Diversity | ☑ Clinical Mental Health Counseling<br>☑ School Counseling<br>☑ Student Affairs and College Counseling |

## TOPIC

This contemplative exercise is designed to enhance awareness of personal attitudes, biases, and/or prejudices regarding individuals whom we perceive to differ from ourselves in terms of race, culture, age, ability status, social class, religion, gender, affectional orientation, etc. By becoming self-aware of how our judgments may contribute to the marginalization and oppression of others (whether subtly or blatantly), counselors-in-training may then challenge themselves to view others less through a lens of differences and more through a lens of similarities. This compassion-based insight will allow students to recognize that despite self-perceived differences, we all share a common desire to experience true happiness and be free from pain and suffering. Moreover, counselors-in-training are encouraged to intentionally send wishes of loving-kindness to others. When these exercises are consistently and successfully practiced, the ability to see the connection between all beings is deepened, the seeds of good will are sown, and a fundamental step toward compassion-based advocacy work is paved.

## LEARNING OBJECTIVES

1. Increase the ability of counselors-in-training to recognize their automatic reactions (i.e., thoughts, emotions, physical sensations, beliefs, attitudes, prejudices, perceptions) when contemplating diverse populations.
2. Improve ability to withhold judgment, reduce social bias, and suspend negative reactivity toward others who are perceived to be different.
3. Improve effectiveness in working with members of at-risk populations who experience marginalization, oppression, and discrimination.

4. Improve ability to connect with others through mindfulness- and compassion-based practices.
5. Minimize attitudinal barriers and social biases that may interfere with effective social justice and advocacy work.

# TARGET POPULATION

Counselors-in-training. Master's- and doctoral-level graduate students. Advanced students in counselor education.

# GROUP SIZE

2–10+: may be facilitated by supervisor in an individual meeting with a counselor-in-training or by a counselor educator in a classroom setting with graduate students

# TIME REQUIRED

45–60 minutes

# SETTING

Counselor education classroom. Counselor-in-training supervision setting.

# MATERIALS NEEDED

- Chairs
- Bell
- Whiteboard/markers (or chalkboard/chalk)

# INSTRUCTIONS FOR CONDUCTING ACTIVITY

1. Read the following script to the group: "Take a moment to find a comfortable position in your chair. Attempt to maintain a posture that supports this exercise by sitting in an upright position that is dignified and attentive, yet relaxed. Legs should be uncrossed, with both feet placed on the floor. If you are comfortable closing your eyes, please do so; otherwise, you may leave them slightly open while maintaining a soft downward gaze a few feet in front of you."
2. This exercise will begin with ringing a bell three times. Tell the group, "With each ring, slowly and deliberately breathe in and breathe out while allowing yourself to settle in and let go. Not attempting to change or alter anything in any way, simply notice the natural movements of your breath. If your mind begins to wander, and it will because that is its tendency, acknowledge that your mind has wandered and then return your focus to the breath. Anchor your attention on each in-breath and on each outbreath. It may be helpful to notice the rising and falling of the abdomen with each cycle of the breath. Continue this practice on your own for a few moments."
3. "Now that you have settled in by gathering your attention on your breath, shift your focus and allow yourself to imagine the following scenario. And while you are imagining this scene, notice any automatic reactions that you may experience. They may be in the form of thoughts, feelings, or physical

sensations, or they may be observed as specific beliefs, attitudes, or perceptions. More than likely, you will experience a combination of these reactions. Whatever occurs, simply notice them as they occur without judgment. See if you can make space for your reactions as they appear and eventually fade away."

4. "When you are ready, imagine you are in a public setting where there are many people. It doesn't matter what setting in which you picture yourself. You may be walking across campus, through a store, or on a city sidewalk. Perhaps you are in an unfamiliar neighborhood that is far from your home. Take a few moments to notice what is around you. Is the environment noisy or quiet? Is it crowded, or are there only a few people in the area? If you are outside, how is the weather? Take a few moments to picture the situation and notice all the sights and sounds around you."

5. "Now imagine there is someone you do not know who is walking in your direction. As the individual gets closer, you notice there is something very different about this person that markedly contrasts with whom you are. Maybe it is the color of the person's skin or perhaps their hairstyle. How do these differ from yours? Maybe it's the person's style of dress? What image does this evoke in your mind? Maybe they are wearing an article of clothing or a piece of jewelry that is associated with a particular religion. How do they appear to differ from your own religious upbringing? Perhaps there are two same sex persons holding hands while pushing an infant in a stroller. It's quite possible that the person is not considered "able bodied" because they are walking with a cane or using a wheelchair for mobility. In this moment notice what is going through your mind—what are your automatic reactions? Try to make space for any thought, feeling, or image that appears. Are you making any initial judgments based upon the way the person speaks, acts, or looks? Whatever is happening, allow and recognize it."

6. "Now imagine that as the person gets closer to you, several other similar people join this individual. This particular group appears to be opposite to those with whom you are typically familiar. They are not anything like the people you have interacted with throughout your life. They differ from your family, friends, and coworkers. Perhaps they are talking loudly, with an accent, or in a different language. Maybe their clothing is distinctive and unusual. Whatever you see, notice what is happening in your mind now? What is arising? Are there any sensations that you feel in your body? If yes, where do they reside . . . what are they saying? Notice if you have an impulse to react in any specific way. Whatever is happening, see if you can create a holding space to purposely observe your reactions without pushing them away?"

7. "This group continues to approach you; they are getting very close now. As they near your physical proximity, notice any thoughts that may be going through your mind. What is happening right now in this moment . . . and in this moment . . . and in this moment? Are you experiencing any feelings? What about physical sensations? Are there any judgments and biases? Did a stereotype of this group form in your mind? If so, what was it? Are you being critical or opinionated? Can you notice whatever is occurring without judging yourself? Can you observe your reactions and consider how they may interfere with advocating for others? Are you able to acknowledge these while maintaining a sense of compassion?"

8. "Now imagine that this group stops directly in front of you. Allow yourself to shift from being aware of how they differ from you to becoming aware that they, too, are fellow human beings who share many similarities. While considering these individuals who are in your presence, silently repeat the following phrases:

*These individuals have a body . . . just like me. At times, they experience illness and physical pain . . . just like me. These individuals also have a mind . . . just like me. And they have feelings . . . just like me. At times, they struggle with life's challenges . . . just like me. At times, they experience fear and anxiety . . . just like me. This group has also faced limitations . . . just like me. At some point in their lives they felt sad, isolated, and lonely . . . just like me. At other times, they felt angry and frustrated . . . just like me. These individuals have been hurt, abandoned, and rejected . . . just like me. At other times, they have experienced loss and deep grief . . . just like me. And there have been occasions when their emotional pain turned into suffering . . . just like me.*

*And just like me, they want to be healthy. And just like me, they want to be accepted. And just like me, they want to be supported. And just like me, they want to be given opportunities. And just like me, they want to feel safe. And just like me, they want to experience peace and happiness. And just like me, they want to be connected with others. And just like me, they want to be loved. And just like me, they want to be free from pain and suffering. And just like me, they want to be liberated from all sources of oppression.*

Now that you have considered the similarities you share with this group, allow yourself to notice what you are currently feeling while breathing in and breathing out. See if you can connect at an even deeper level with their pain and suffering. Are you able to take this on? See if you can help transform their suffering by wishing them to be free from all sources of pain. Further this practice by extending loving-kindness and sending well wishes to them. Do this while gently placing both hands on your heart and feeling their warmth:

*May those who are afraid find safety.*
*May those who are helpless find strength.*
*May those who are hopeless find encouragement.*
*May those who are in pain find comfort.*
*May those who are overlooked find belonging.*
*May those who are at war find peace.*
*May those who are suffering find relief.*
*May those who are challenged find resources.*
*May those who are oppressed find opportunities.*
*May those who are alone find support.*
*I wish all these things for all fellow human beings everywhere because they are just . . . like . . . me."*

9. "Now, while allowing this scenario to fade away into the background, take a few moments to non-judgmentally notice any thought, emotion, belief, attitude, or physical sensation that you may be experiencing. Just briefly scan through your mind and body without getting caught up in anything. Once you have done this, gently return your attention to your breath and slowly and deliberately complete a cycle of three breaths."

10. "As this exercise comes to a close, acknowledge the time you dedicated to the practice of connecting with others while helping to transform their suffering. Now, at the sound of the bell, gradually open your eyes and bring your awareness back to the room and those around you."

Mindfulness activity adapted from Bowen, Chawla, and Marlatt (2011), Teasdale, Williams, and Segal (2014), and Barbezat and Bush (2014).

## DISCUSSION

After the meditation concludes, the counselor educator (or supervisor) should process this exercise with the group. The following questions may be used as prompts to stimulate a discussion between group members. The facilitator may list various answers on the whiteboard to look for commonalities and differences in reactions and responses. The facilitator should emphasize that accepting ourselves and others, as well as cultivating compassion for ourselves and others, are typically the first steps that must be taken before true social justice advocacy work can occur.

1. What automatic reactions occurred during this exercise? Consider any thoughts, emotions, physical sensations, beliefs, attitudes, prejudices, and perceptions.
2. How did it feel to adopt a nonjudgmental stance while examining the automatic reactions that occurred during the scenario?
3. How does developing awareness and acceptance of our own automatic reactions contribute to becoming a more effective advocate for others who are marginalized and oppressed?
4. If counselors remain unaware and unaccepting of their personally held beliefs and biases, how might this affect their ability to successfully advocate for others? Consider the impact on levels such as . . .

a. Therapeutic relationships
b. Smaller groups and communities
c. Larger systems and institutions

5. What did you experience when you shifted from noticing the differences between you and this group to intentionally relating their pain and suffering with your own?

6. What was it like when you purposely wished others to be free from pain and suffering?

7. How do you imagine the compassion-based activity helps to minimize attitudinal barriers that interfere with effective social justice and advocacy work?

8. What additional steps are you willing to take that will cultivate compassion for yourself and others?

9. How might these additional steps also involve efforts to alleviate the suffering of others (include specific examples of compassion in action and advocacy work)?

# BIBLIOGRAPHY

Barbezat, D. P., & Bush, M. (2014). *Contemplative practices in higher education: Powerful methods to transform teaching and learning.* San Francisco, CA: Jossey-Bass.

Bowen, S., Chawla, N., & Marlatt, G. A. (2011). *Mindfulness-based relapse prevention for addictive behaviors: A clinician's guide.* New York: The Guilford Press.

Ivers, N. N., Johnson, D. A., Clarke, P. B., Newsome, D. W., & Berry, R. A. (2016). The relationship between mindfulness and multicultural competence. *Journal of Counseling and Development, 94,* 72–82.

Luke, A., & Gibson, B. (2015). Mindfulness meditation reduces implicit age and race bias: The role of reduced automaticity of responding. *Social Psychological and Personality Science, 6,* 284–291.

Luke, A., & Gibson, B. (2016). Brief mindfulness meditation reduces discrimination. *Psychology of Consciousness: Theory, Research, and Practice, 3,* 34–44.

Parks, S., Birtel, M. D., & Crisp, R. J. (2014). Evidence that a brief meditation exercise can reduce prejudice toward homeless people. *Social Psychology, 45,* 458–465.

Teasdale, J., Williams, M., & Segal, Z. (2014). *The mindful way workbook: An 8-week program to free yourself from depression and emotional distress.* New York: The Guilford Press.

# SUGGESTED BACKGROUND READING

Dass, R., & Bush, M. (1992). *Compassion in action: Setting out on the path of service.* New York: Bell Tower.

Germer, C., Siegel, R., & Fulton, P. (2013). *Mindfulness and psychotherapy* (2nd ed.). New York: The Guilford Press.

Masuda, A. (Ed.). (2014). *Mindfulness and acceptance in multicultural competency: A contextual approach to sociocultural diversity in theory and practice.* Oakland, CA: New Harbinger Publications.

# CHAPTER 79

## Career Discrimination Interview

*Marisa White*

### Course Recommendations

| SOCIAL JUSTICE AND ADVOCACY PRINCIPLES | CORE CACREP STANDARDS | COUNSELING SPECIALIZATION |
|---|---|---|
| ☑ Social Constructs of Oppression and Privilege<br>☑ Intersections of Oppression | ☑ Career Development<br>☑ Social and Cultural Diversity | ☑ Career Counseling |

## TOPIC

The focus of this activity is to help students understand how specific cultures experience career challenges. Students will identify the barriers, experiences, and advocacy solutions that could be implemented to help overcome the obstacles.

## LEARNING OBJECTIVES

The student will:

1. Summarize the history of career oppression or discrimination for one culture (people with disabilities, African Americans, women, etc.).
2. Interview a person about career obstacles that relate to cultural oppression.
3. Distinguish advocacy techniques that can be used to overcome identified discrimination or oppression in a career setting.
4. Design an advocacy plan that they could use in teaching a client about self-advocacy.

## TARGET POPULATION

Students in a counselor education program career course or multicultural course

## GROUP SIZE

Any size

# TIME REQUIRED

This assignment could be done in stages or as a final project for a class. The student will interview a person who has experienced career oppression related to their cultural identity. The student could present the information as a case study to the class or could write about the experience in a paper. The interview will last 30 minutes.

# SETTING

The student will conduct an interview outside of the classroom. Interviews are to be conducted in a private and safe location. A classroom setting would be appropriate for presenting the historical information and advocacy plan.

# MATERIALS NEEDED

- A paper and pen/pencil will be needed for the interview.
- A computer will be needed to type up the assignment.
- PowerPoint will be needed to create a presentation.

# INSTRUCTIONS FOR CONDUCTING ACTIVITY

1. In week one, the student will research the history of career discrimination experienced by one cultural group (ableism, racism, sexism, heterosexism, sizeism, classism, etc.). Students can complete a three-page paper identifying at least five historical events that impacted the careers of the identified population.
   a. Think about the access to career resources for your population as a social justice issue (Busacca & Rehfuss, 2016).
2. In week two, the student will identify a person to interview who has experienced career discrimination.
   a. The student will interview a person about career obstacles that relate to cultural oppression. The interview should last approximately 30 minutes. The interview can only be recorded with written permission of the interviewee. Interview questions might include:
      - Do you feel like cultural characteristics have prevented you from advancing in your career or job?
      - Can you tell me about the first time you experienced discrimination in the workplace?
      - What was the most impactful discrimination that you have experienced in the workplace?
      - Have you ever advocated for yourself in a work setting (filed a grievance/complaint, talked to a boss about the discrimination, etc.)? Please explain why or why not.
      - What do you see as barriers to overcoming workplace discrimination?
      - Do you feel empowered to change the workplace discrimination? Please explain.
3. In week three, the student will distinguish advocacy techniques that can be used to overcome identified discrimination or oppression in a career setting. The student will then design an advocacy plan that they could use to empower the client/interviewee or teach the client about self-advocacy.
   a. Remember that the plan should be client specific. Please consider the time, energy, cost resources, allies needed, etc.
4. The student will present a PowerPoint presentation. All of the following topics must be included. The student may have more than ten slides, but should remember to be clear and concise.
   a. Slide 1—title
   b. Slide 2—introduction to topic

c. Slides 3–4—overview of history
d. Slides 5–6—summary of interview/case
e. Slides 7–8—advocacy plan
f. Slide 9—conclusion
g. Slide 10—references

# DISCUSSION

Discussion about career discrimination can occur in several ways. Having a guest speaker to discuss how they feel their cultural identity has impacted their career experiences helps the students see how discrimination impacts clients. Sharing the instructor's experiences with workplace discrimination also helps students identify how culture impacts career experiences. These examples can help the student associate self-advocacy as vital in the development of social cognitive career theory (Sharf, 2016). Moreover, real-life examples of career discrimination can help students conceptualize how social justice and advocacy competencies can be part of the career counseling process (Busacca & Rehfuss, 2016). It is also good to explain to the students that this assignment will address cultural dynamics, career approaches, and social justice advocacy strategies. In addition, the students will use basic counseling skills when conducting the interview.

# BIBLIOGRAPHY

Busacca, L. A., & Rehfuss, M. C. (Eds.). (2016). *Postmodern career counseling: A handbook of culture, context, and case.* Alexandria, VA: American Counseling Association.
Sharf, R. S. (2016). *Applying career development theory to counseling* (6th ed.). Belmont, CA: Brooks/Cole.

# SUGGESTED BACKGROUND READING

Some of these readings are outside of the career counseling literature, and some are dated, as it is important for students to see the history of these trends and how career discrimination impacts all disciplines.

Ali, S. R., Yamada, T., & Mahmood, A. (2015). Relationships of the practice of hijab, workplace discrimination, social class, job stress, and job satisfaction among Muslim American women. *Journal of Employment Counseling, 52*(4), 146–157.
Baert, S. (2016). Wage subsidies and hiring chances for the disabled: Some causal evidence. *European Journal of Health Economics, 17,* 71–86.
Bayl-Smith, P. H., & Griffin, B. (2014). Age discrimination in the workplace: Identifying as a late-career worker and its relationship with engagement and intended retirement age. *Journal of Applied Social Psychology, 44*(9), 588–599.
Chung, Y. B. (2001). Work discrimination and coping strategies: Conceptual frameworks for counseling lesbian, gay, and bisexual clients. *The Career Development Quarterly, 50,* 82–95. doi:10.1002/j.2161-0045.2001.tb00887.x
Dispenza, F., Brown, C., & Chastain, T. E. (2015). Minority stress across the career-lifespan trajectory. *Journal of Career Development, 43*(2), 103–115.
Herek, G. M. (2007). Confronting sexual stigma and prejudice: Theory and practice. *Journal of Social Issues, 63,* 905–925. doi:10.1111/j.1540-4560.2007.00544.x
Howard, K. A. S., Carlstrom, A. H., Katz, A. D., Chew, A. Y., Ray, G. C., Laine, L., & Caulum, D. (2010). Career aspirations of youth: Untangling race/ethnicity, SES, and gender. *Journal of Vocational Behavior, 79,* 98–109.
Lee, D. L., Rosen, D., & Burns, V. (2013). Over a half-century encapsulated: A multicultural content analysis of the Journal of Counseling Psychology, 1954–2009. *Journal of Counseling Psychology, 60*(1), 154–161.
Lewis, J. A., Lewis, M. D., Daniels, J. J., & D'Andrea, M. J. (2011). *Community counseling: A multicultural-social justice perspective* (4th ed.). Belmont, CA: Brooks/Cole.
Noonen, M. C., Corcoran, M. E., & Courant, P. (2005). Pay differences among the highly trained: Cohort differences in the sex gap in lawyers' earnings. *Social Forces, 84*(2), 853–872.
Rodgers, J., & Rubery, J. (2003). The minimum wage as a tool to combat discrimination and promote equality. *International Labour Review, 142*(4), 543–556. doi:10.1111/j.1564-913X.2003.tb00543.x

Sangganjanavanich, V. F., & Headley, J. A. (2013). Facilitating career development concerns of gender transitioning individuals: Professional standards and competencies. *The Career Development Quarterly, 61*(4), 354–366.

Schneider, M. S., & Dimito, A. (2010). Factors influencing the career and academic choices of lesbian, gay, bisexual, and transgender people. *Journal of Homosexuality, 57,* 1355–1369. doi:10.1080/00918369.2010.517080

Van-belle, J., Marks, S., Martin, R., & Chun, M. (2006). Voicing one's dreams: High school student with developmental disabilities learn about self-advocacy. *Teaching Exceptional Children, 38*(4), 40–46.

Doctorate-level students would include:

Glosoff, H. L., & Durham, J. C. (2010). Using supervision to prepare social justice counseling advocates. *Counselor Education and Supervision, 50*(2), 116–129.

# Author Index

# Social Justice and Advocacy Principles Index

## WHAT IS SOCIAL JUSTICE AND ADVOCACY?

## CYCLE OF SOCIALIZATION AND LIBERATION

# SOCIAL CONSTRUCTS OF OPPRESSION AND PRIVILEGE

# INTERSECTIONS OF OPPRESSION

# SOCIAL JUSTICE ADVOCACY: STRATEGIES FOR CHANGE

# Core CACREP Course Index

## ASSESSMENT AND TESTING

## CAREER DEVELOPMENT

## GROUP WORK

# HELPING RELATIONSHIPS

# HUMAN GROWTH AND DEVELOPMENT

# PROFESSIONAL COUNSELING ORIENTATION & ETHICS PRACTICE

# RESEARCH AND PROGRAM EVALUATION

# SOCIAL AND CULTURAL DIVERSITY

# THEORIES

# Counseling Specialization Index

## ADDICTION COUNSELING

## CAREER COUNSELING

# CLINICAL MENTAL HEALTH COUNSELING

# MARRIAGE, COUPLE, AND FAMILY COUNSELING

# SCHOOL COUNSELING

# STUDENT AFFAIRS AND COLLEGE COUNSELING